Reading the American West

Primary Sources in American History

Mitchel Roth

Sam Houston State University

An Imprint of Addison Wesley Longman, Inc.

New York • Reading, Massachusetts • Menlo Park, California • Harlow, England
Don Mills, Ontario • Sydney • Mexico City • Madrid • Amsterdam

For permission to use copyrighted material, grateful acknowledgement
is made to the copyright holders on pages 341 through 342, which are
hereby made part of this copyright page.

Reading the American West by Mitchel Roth.

Please visit our website at http://longman.awl.com

ISBN: 0-321-04409-6

2345678910-CRS-010099

Contents

Preface

There has never been a consensus among historians as to the exact geographical dimensions of the West. The term "West" itself can be a contradiction in terms. To Mexicans, the American West was the north. Chinese newcomers probably considered it the east. And French fur trappers must surely have appraised it as the south. Despite these contradictions, the concept of the West has never *not* existed in American history. When Columbus set foot on the island of San Salvador on October 12, 1492, he walked into a western wilderness a unique environment inhabited by different people and strange creatures. It was no different for Cabeza de Vaca as he came ashore on the south Texas coast, or for Captain John Smith in 1607 when he strolled into the woods near the mouth of the James River in what is today Virginia, or for Meriwether Lewis and William Clark in 1803 when President Thomas Jefferson sent them out to explore the Louisiana Purchase, or for southern empresarios in the 1820s trying to make a fortune in Texas, or for Oklahoma dirt farmers in 1935 escaping the Dust Bowl for greener pastures in California. Even after the continent had filled with people from the Atlantic to the Pacific, and the nineteenth century had given way to the twentieth, the West continued to exist in the American imagination, enlivening popular culture, setting the tone of political debate, and establishing the boundaries of discourse between men and women.

In terms of high culture, the West did not receive its real intellectual place in the sun until 1893, when historian Frederick Jackson Turner wrote his legendary essay "The Significance of the Frontier in American History." At a time when most intellectuals were still looking east-to New York and Boston and Philadelphia and London and Paris-for the origins of American civilization, Turner gazed in the opposite direction, arguing that the continuing existence of the frontier over the course of three centuries had shaped politics, culture, and society in the New World. Life on the western frontier had always put a premium on hard work, self-reliance, individual initiative, and the struggle to survive. Out of that struggle, not just out of the political philosophies of people like Thomas Hobbes or John Locke, emerged the makings of democracy.

According to Turner, the frontier had also given America a social safety valve, a way of avoiding the debilitating class struggles and revolutionary upheavals so endemic to European history. The abundance of land in the United States gave the society a way of venting its frustrations. Discontented people, Turner claimed, who felt they had reached dead ends in their lives, had something else to do besides throw caution to the wind and rebel. They could move west, where land and opportunity always existed, and take up new farms and new lives. They could, in essence, reinvent themselves by pulling up stakes and following the sun. The American environment institutionalized the "second chance," giving people the opportunity to start over.

From the early nineteenth century to the late twentieth century, American popular culture glorified the white men who had pioneered the trail west. Explorers, trappers, hunters, gunfighters, cowboys, and soldiers became the stuff of legend. Newspapers, magazines, dime novels, radio, films, and finally television made heroes out of the likes of Kit Carson, Jim Bridger, George Rogers Clark, Zebulon Pike, Buffalo Bill Cody, Wyatt Earp, Bat Masterson, Wild Bill Hickock, George Armstrong Custer, Daniel Boone, and Davy Crockett. Even men who simply personified or portrayed the West-like John Wayne or Clint Eastwood-became heroes in their own right.

Historians have long since debated the so-called Turner thesis. The measure of a historian's influence is the extent to which his or her colleagues take exception to conclusions. Turner has been the most influential historian in United States history because his thesis precipitated so much debate for so long. For generations, Frederick Jackson Turner defined the nature of historical inquiry and scholarly debate about the American past. In books, articles, and papers at scholarly meetings, as well as in graduate seminars and convention smokers, historians argued about the origins of American culture, the roots of democracy, and the reality of the safety valve.

But they did not argue about fundamental paradigms, about the morality of conquest, the rights of indigenous peoples, or the inherent rationale of Manifest Destiny. In essence, they did not question the virtue of Manifest Destiny—that the New World had been designed by nature for European conquest.

In recent years, however, a new generation of historians, transcending the paradigms of the Turner thesis, has embarked on a search for missing persons in the heroic West. Few women can be found in the traditional literature, except for absurd icons and predictable stereotypes. The only heroines of the so-called Old West were people like Annie Oakley or Calamity Jane, women who handled six-guns as well, or at least nearly as well, as any man. And the pioneer women in the novels of Zane Grey or Louis L'Amour, or the films of John Ford and John Wayne, are cardboard figures completely divorced from the real experiences of real women on the real frontier. Freshly scrubbed with elegant coiffures and manicured nails, they have the tiniest of waists bound up in laced corsets. Long-sleeved, high-collared, long dresses fresh from the dry cleaners cover their bodies. They look like they are ready to have tea with the queen, not to hack out a new life on the water-starved plains and dusty deserts of the West.

Nor have there been real people of color in the traditional histories of the frontier. The Indians who inhabit those pages are either noble red men or vicious savages; the Mexicans either hardbitten desperadoes or smiling incompetents; the Chinese either inscrutable laborers or mysterious entrepreneurs speaking pidgin English; and the African Americans little more than "step-n-fetch it" misfits.

The new historians are working to repopulate the frontier west, to put other people there besides white men. Women in the west were entrepreneurs, prostitutes, teachers, nurses, physicians, midwives, and civil servants, not just homemakers. And when they were homemakers, they often found themselves managing farms and large families by themselves while their husbands were on the road trying to work for desperately needed cash. Black people in the West were not just bus boys, stable boys and pullmen; they also worked as cowboys, farmers, miners, construction workers, teamsters, businessmen, and stevedores. Hispanics of the Southwest occupied every rung of the social ladder and performed every occupation and profession. And the Chinese did a great deal more than hammer spikes on the transcontinental railroads or run their own laundries. They created a business and professional infrastructure in the towns and cities of the West that allowed them to triumph in a racist society.

This collection of important documents in Western history has been assembled to fill an existing gap in which documents such as the Taylor Grazing Act of 1934, the Chinese Exclusion Act, the Treaty of Guadalupe Hidalgo, or the Mining Law of 1872 are often referred to but rarely reproduced for classroom use. In addition to the documents, students will hear the voices of freed slaves living on the frontier, a Chinese immigrant in Oakland, a Mexican American litigant denied housing because of his race, as well as inhabitants of the twentieth-century nuclear West. Each passage is accompanied by an introduction placing the document in its historical context.

Many of the readings and documents are rooted in the twentieth-century West, long after Frederick Jackson Turner declared the end of the American frontier. As historian Patricia Limerick has made clear in her 1987 groundbreaking book *The Legacy of Conquest: The Unbroken Past of the American West,* the process of settling the American West did not end in 1890, but continues into the twenty-first century.

Today we are just a few years away from the twenty-first century, and a long way away from the era of fur trappers, open cattle ranges, free homesteads, Indian wars, and exploration. But the past lives on. A 1995 Harris poll named John Wayne as America's favorite actor, even though he had been dead for sixteen years. In 1996, American Indian groups in New Mexico threatened to blockade interstate highways 10, 40, and 25 unless they were allowed to keep their gambling casinos open. A few months later, President Bill Clinton enraged western interest groups by declaring 1.8 million acres of Utah land a national monument, which permanently removed the region from economic development. The West is still with us.

I would like to acknowledge the contributions and assistance of several outside reviewers, including Ty Cashion at Texas A&M-Commerce, who offered many helpful suggestions and helped me, in places, navigate through the intricacies of the contemporary American West. I am also indebted to James Olson of Sam Houston State University for his support and inspiration during this project. Jessica Bayne and Jennifer McCaffrey, my editors at Longman Publishers, have provided invaluable assistance as well. Finally, I would like to thank my wife and academic partner, Rosanne Barker, who was always there for me whenever I needed a thoughtful critique or suggestion.

1

The Intellectual West

The frontier and the wilderness have been sources of fascination to Americans ever since the beginning of the colonial period in the early seventeenth century. Historians were similarly interested. It was impossible not to be, given the amount of energy the American people have invested in the westward movement. For nineteenth-century scholars—such as Frances Parkman and George Bancroft—the wilderness had been a wild place to be conquered, tamed, and subdued. Each forest that was clear cut, each parcel of land that was plowed, each Indian that was killed or assimilated, and each new territory acquired from a foreign country was a mark of progress, proof that a superior civilization was making its way across the continent, bringing to pass the wishes of God. Whether it was the Puritan's "errand into the wilderness" in the seventeenth century or the "Manifest Destiny" of the nineteenth century, the westward movement was predestined, at least in the minds of most Americans, before the twentieth century.

Pointing to 1890 census figures, which showed that no more unsettled land remained in the Great West, Frederick Jackson Turner announced that a key chapter of American history had come to an end, marking a turning point in American history. Beginning with the work of Frederick Jackson Turner, historians have taken a more sophisticated look at the West, although elements of the earlier hero worship have certainly survived among some historians and in the popular culture.

From the 1930s to the 1950s, Walter Prescott Webb modified Turner's work. In perhaps his greatest book, *The Great Plains,* Webb advanced an interpretation that was almost as environmentally deterministic as Turner's, with the arid Great Plains standing in for the humid woodlands of the trans-Appalachian West. But, unlike Turner, who concentrated his focus on the process of westward expansion, Webb suggested that social evolution took place in the region itself. Regardless of their differences, the classical interpretations advanced by Turner and Webb contrast sharply with contemporary scholarship in Western history.

In recent years, the so-called "New History of the West" has generated enormous controversy among scholars and politicians, primarily because the new historians have not seen the history of the American West as the fulfillment of God's will or the triumph of a superior civilization. Instead, they see racism, ethnocentrism, sexism, and environmental exploitation as the legacy of the frontier. To the new historians the word "frontier" is fraught with racist and nationalistic implications, arguing that the term itself lacks sophistication, since it infers that there is some kind of artificial boundary between "savagery and civilization." In his monumental, *"It's Your Misfortune and None of My Own": A New History of the American West,* Richard White spends more than 630 pages examining the history of the American West without ever once mentioning the word, "frontier."

Historian Patricia Limerick takes particular umbrage with the notion of the closing of the frontier. In her groundbreaking and controversial book, *The Legacy of Conquest* (1987), she contends that the West should be viewed as a place rather than a process, that its history did not end in 1890, but continues into the late twentieth century. Limerick cites the persistence of mineral rushes, homesteading, conflict, and environmental destruction in order to link the present-day West with earlier incarnations of the frontier experience. Where Turner saw the history of the West as a procession of European institutions modified by a series of frontier experiences, Limerick sees the West as a "convergence of diverse people," a place where Indians, Europeans, Latin Americans, Asians, and Afro-Americans "interacted with each other and with the environment." A process that continues to this day.

The Turner thesis has proven incredibly resilient over the past century. The requisite repudiation of the Turner thesis in almost every offering from the new historians stands as testimony to the intellectual impact of Turner's 1893 essay. Of course, the last chapter on the history of the American West has not yet been written. In fact, it never will be. The frontier experience is too central to the American character.

Suggestions for Further Reading

Ray Allen Billington, *Frederick Jackson Turner: Historian, Scholar, Teacher* (New York: Oxford University Press, 1973).

John Mack Faragher, *Rereading Frederick Jackson Turner* (New York: H. Holt, 1994).

Wilbur Jacobs, *On Turner's Trail: 100 Years of Writing Western History* (Lawrence: University Press of Kansas, 1994).

Richard White, *"It's Your Misfortune and None of My Own": A New History of the American West* (Norman: University of Oklahoma Press, 1991).

Robert G. Athearn, *The Mythic West in Twentieth Century America* (Lawrence: University Press of Kansas, 1986).

Critical Thinking

1. What does Turner mean by the "Significance of the Frontier in American History?"

2. How does Limerick's West differ from the portraits by Turner and Webb?

3. In which of these essays is the West portrayed as a place rather than a process?

4. How did the census of 1890 impact Turner's thesis?

5. Which interpretation of the West do you feel represents the "true" West, and which portrays the mythic West?

Document 1.1

The Significance of the Frontier in American History

In 1893, historian Frederick Jackson Turner of the University of Wisconsin delivered a scholarly paper to a meeting of the American Historical Association in Chicago, Illinois. The title of the paper was "The Significance of the Frontier in American History." Statistics from the 1890 census had precipitated the essay. The Census Bureau reported that the frontier no longer existed in the United States. An era was over, and Turner wanted to take the measure of it. The essay was an intellectual earthquake that shook the historical discipline to its foundations. In an age when most scholars looked back to Europe for the roots of civilization, Turner faced west, arguing that American democracy, individualism, self-reliance, and hard work were legacies of the frontier west, not the civilized east. The paper was controversial and has spawned three generations of scholarly debate. "The Significance of the Frontier in American History," portions of which appear below, is one of the most significant documents in American intellectual history. Portions of the census report that inspired Turner are also included below.*

In a recent bulletin of the Superintendent of the Census for 1890 appear these significant words: "Up to and including 1880 the country had a frontier of settlement, but at present the unsettled area has been so broken into by isolated bodies of settlement that there can hardly be said to be a frontier line. In the discussion of its extent, its westward movement, etc., it can not, therefore, any longer have a place in the census reports." This brief official statement marks the closing of a great historic movement. Up to our own day, American history has been in a large degree the history of the colonization of the Great West. The existence of an area of free land, its continuous recession, and the advance of American settlement westward explain American development.

Behind institutions, behind constitutional forms and modifications, lie the vital forces that call these organs into life and shape them to meet changing conditions. The peculiarity of American institutions is the fact that they have been compelled to adapt themselves to the changes of an expanding people—to the changes involved in crossing a continent, in winning a wilderness, and in developing at each area of this progress out of the primitive economic and political conditions of the frontier into the complexity of city life. Said Calhoun in 1817, "We are great, and rapidly—I was about to say fearfully— growing!" So saying, he touched the distinguishing feature of American life. All peoples show development; the germ theory of politics has been sufficiently emphasized. In the

---

* Frederick Jackson Turner, *The Frontier in American History* (New York: Henry Holt and Company, 1921), pp. 1-35.

case of most nations, however, the development has occurred in a limited area; and if the nation has expanded, it has met other growing peoples whom it has conquered. But in the case of the United States we have a different phenomenon. Limiting our attention to the Atlantic coast, we have the familiar phenomenon of the evolution of institutions in a limited area, such as the rise of representative government; the differentiation of simple colonial governments into complex organs; the progress from primitive industrial society, without division of labor, up to manufacturing civilization. But we have, in addition to this, a recurrence of the process of evolution in each western area reached in the process of expansion. Thus, American development has exhibited not merely advance along a single line, but a return to primitive conditions on a continually advancing frontier line, and a new development for that area. American social development has been continually beginning over again on the frontier. This perennial rebirth, this fluidity of American life, this expansion westward with its new opportunities, its continuous touch with the simplicity of primitive society, furnish the forces dominating American character. The true point of view in the history of this nation is not the Atlantic coast, it is the Great West. Even the slavery struggle, which is made so exclusive an object of attention by writers like Professor von Holst, occupies its important place in American history because of its relation to westward expansion.

In this advance, the frontier is the outer edge of the wave—the meeting point between savagery and civilization. Much has been written about the frontier from the point of view of border warfare and the chase, but as a field for the serious study of the economist and the historian, it has been neglected.

The American frontier is sharply distinguished from the European frontier—a fortified boundary line running through dense populations. The most significant thing about the American frontier is that it lies at the hither edge of free land. In the census reports, it is treated as the margin of that settlement which has a density of two or more to the square mile. The term is an elastic one, and for our purposes, does not need sharp definition. We shall consider the whole frontier belt, including the Indian country and the outer margin of the "settled area" of the census reports. This paper will make no attempt to treat the subject exhaustively; its aim is simply to call attention to the frontier as a fertile field for investigation, and to suggest some of the problems which arise in connection with it.

In the settlement of America, we have to observe how European life entered the continent, and how America modified and developed that life and reacted on Europe. Our early history is the study of European germs developing in an American environment. Too exclusive attention has been paid by institutional students to the Germanic origins; too little to the American factors. The frontier is the line of most rapid and effective Americanization. The wilderness masters the colonist. It finds him a European in dress, industries, tools, modes of travel, and thought. It takes him from the railroad car and puts him in the birch canoe. It strips off the garments of civilization and arrays him in the hunting shirt and the moccasin. It puts him in the log cabin of the Cherokee and Iroquois and runs an Indian palisade around him. Before long, he has gone to planting Indian corn and plowing with a sharp stick; he shouts the war cry and takes the scalp in orthodox Indian fashion. In short, at the frontier, the environment is at first too strong for the man. He must accept the conditions which it furnishes, or perish, and so he fits himself into the Indian clearings and follows the Indian trails. Little by little he transforms the wilderness, but the outcome is not the old Europe, not simply the development of Germanic germs, any more than the first phenomenon was a case of reversion to the Germanic mark. The fact is that here is a new product that is American. At first, the frontier was the Atlantic coast. It was the frontier of Europe in a very real sense. Moving westward, the frontier became more and more American. As successive terminal moraines result from successive glaciations, so each frontier leaves its traces behind it, and when it becomes a settled area, the region still partakes of the frontier characteristics. Thus the advance of the frontier has meant a steady movement away from the influence of Europe, a steady growth of independence on American lines. And to study this advance, the men who grew up under these conditions, and the political, economic, and social results of it, is to study the really American part of our history.

In the course of the seventeenth century, the frontier was advanced up the Atlantic river courses, just beyond the "fall line," and the tidewater region became the settled area. In the first half of the eighteenth century, another advance occurred. Traders followed the Delaware and Shawnese Indians to the Ohio as early as the end of the first quarter of the century. Gov. Spotswood of Virginia made an expedition in 1714 across the Blue Ridge. The end of the first quarter of the century saw the advance of the Scotch-Irish and the Palatine Germans up the Shenandoah Valley into the western part of Virginia, and along the Piedmont region of the Carolinas. The Germans in New York pushed the frontier of settlement up the Mohawk to German Flats. In Pennsylvania, the town of Bedford indicates the line of settlement. Settlements soon began on the New River, or the Great Kanawha, and on the sources of the Yadkin and French Broad. The King attempted to arrest the advance by his proclamation of 1763, forbidding settlements beyond the sources of the rivers flowing into the Atlantic; but in vain. In the period of the Revolution, the frontier crossed the Alleghanies into Kentucky and Tennessee, and the upper waters of the Ohio were settled. When the first census was taken in 1790, the continuous settled area was bounded by a line which ran near the coast of Maine, and included New England, except a portion of Vermont and New Hampshire, New York along the Hudson and up the Mohawk about Schenectady, eastern and southern Pennsylvania, Virginia well across the Shenandoah Valley, and the Carolinas and eastern Georgia. Beyond this region of continuous settlement were the small settled areas of Kentucky and Tennessee, and the Ohio, with the mountains intervening between them and the Atlantic area, thus giving a new and important character to the frontier. The isolation of the region increased its peculiarly American tendencies, and the need of transportation facilities to connect it with the East called out important schemes of internal improvement, which will be noted farther on. The "West," as a self-conscious section, began to evolve.

From decade to decade, distinct advances of the frontier occurred. By the census of 1820, the settled area included Ohio, southern Indiana and Illinois, southeastern Missouri, and about one-half of Louisiana. This settled area had surrounded Indian areas, and the management of these tribes became an object of political concern. The frontier region of the time lay along the Great Lakes, where Astor's American Fur Company operated in the Indian trade, and beyond the Mississippi, where Indian traders extended their activity even to the Rocky Mountains; Florida also furnished frontier conditions. The Mississippi River region was the scene of typical frontier settlements.

The rising steam navigation on western waters, the opening of the Erie Canal, and the westward extension of cotton culture added five frontier states to the Union in this period. Grund, writing in 1836, declares: "It appears then that the universal disposition of Americans to emigrate to the western wilderness, in order to enlarge their dominion over inanimate nature, is the actual result of an expansive power which is inherent in them, and which by continually agitating all classes of society is constantly throwing a large portion of the whole population on the extreme confines of the State, in order to gain space for its development. Hardly is a new State or Territory formed before the same principle manifests itself again and gives rise to a further emigration; and so is it destined to go on until a physical barrier must finally obstruct its progress."

In the middle of this century, the line indicated by the present eastern boundary of Indian Territory, Nebraska, and Kansas marked the frontier of the Indian country. Minnesota and Wisconsin still exhibited frontier conditions, but the distinctive frontier of the period is found in California, where the gold discoveries had sent a sudden tide of adventurous miners, and in Oregon, and the settlements in Utah. As the frontier had leaped over the Alleghanies, so now it skipped the Great Plains and the Rocky Mountains; and in the same way that the advance of the frontiersmen beyond the Alleghanies had caused the rise of important questions of transportation and internal improvement, so now the settlers beyond the Rocky Mountains needed means of communication with the East, and in the furnishing of these arose the settlement of the Great Plains and the development of still another kind of frontier life. Railroads, fostered by land grants, sent an increasing tide of immigrants into the Far West. The United States Army fought a series of Indian wars in Minnesota, Dakota, and the Indian Territory.

By 1880 the settled area had been pushed into northern Michigan, Wisconsin, and Minnesota, along Dakota rivers, and in the Black Hills region, and was ascending the rivers of Kansas and Nebraska. The development of mines in Colorado had drawn isolated frontier settlements into that region, and Montana and Idaho were receiving settlers. The frontier was found in these mining camps and the ranches of the Great Plains. The superintendent of the census for 1890 reports, as previously stated, that the settlements of the West lie so scattered over the region that there can no longer be said to be a frontier line.

In these successive frontiers we find natural boundary lines which have served to mark and to affect the characteristics of the frontiers, namely: the "fall line;" the Alleghany Mountains; the Mississippi; the Missouri where its direction approximates north and south; the line of the arid lands, approximately the ninety-ninth meridian; and the Rocky Mountains. The fall line marked the frontier of the seventeenth century; the Alleghanies that of the eighteenth; the Mississippi that of the first quarter of the nineteenth; the Missouri that of the middle of this century (omitting the California movement); and the belt of the Rocky Mountains and the arid tract, the present frontier. Each was won by a series of Indian wars.

At the Atlantic frontier, one can study the germs of processes repeated at each successive frontier. We have the complex European life sharply precipitated by the wilderness into the simplicity of primitive conditions. The first frontier had to meet its Indian question, its question of the disposition of the public domain, of the means of intercourse with older settlements, of the extension of political organization, of religious and educational activity. And the settlement of these and similar questions for one frontier served as a guide for the next. The American student needs not to go to the "prim little townships of Sleswick" for illustrations of the law of continuity and development. For example, he may study the origin of our land policies in the colonial land policy; he may see how the system grew by adapting the statutes to the customs of the successive frontiers. He may see how the mining experience in the lead regions of Wisconsin, Illinois, and Iowa was applied to the mining laws of the Sierras, and how our Indian policy has been a series of experimentations on successive frontiers. Each tier of new States has found in the older ones material for its constitutions. Each frontier has made similar contributions to American character, as will be discussed farther on.

But with all these similarities there are essential differences, due to the place element and the time element. It is evident that the farming frontier of the Mississippi Valley presents different conditions from the mining frontier of the Rocky Mountains. The frontier reached by the Pacific Railroad, surveyed into rectangles, guarded by the United States Army, and recruited by the daily immigrant ship, moves forward at a swifter pace and in a different way than the frontier reached by the birch canoe or the pack horse. The geologist traces patiently the shores of ancient seas, maps their areas, and compares the older and the newer. It would be a work worth the historian's labors to mark these various frontiers and in detail compare one with another. Not only would there result a more adequate conception of American development and charasteristics, but invaluable additions would be made to the history of society.

Loria, the Italian economist, has urged the study of colonial life as an aid in understanding the stages of European development, affirming that colonial settlement is for economic science what the mountain is for geology, bringing to light primitive stratifications. "America," he says, "has the key to the historical enigma which Europe has sought for centuries in vain, and the land which has no history reveals luminously the course of universal history." There is much truth in this. The United States lies like a huge page in the history of society. Line by line as we read this continental page from West to East we find the record of social evolution. It begins with the Indian and the hunter; it goes on to tell of the disintegration of savagery by the entrance of the trader, the pathfinder of civilization; we read the annals of the pastoral stage in ranch life; the exploitation of the soil by the raising of unrotated crops of corn and wheat in sparsely settled farming communities; the intensive culture of the denser farm settlement; and finally the manufacturing organization with city and factory system. This page is familiar to the student of census statistics, but how little of it has been used by our historians. Particularly in eastern States this page is a palimpsest. What is now a manufacturing State was in an earlier decade an area of intensive farming. Earlier yet it had been a wheat area, and still earlier the "range" had attracted the cattleherder. Thus Wisconsin, now developing manufacture, is a State with varied agricultural interests. But earlier it was given over to almost exclusive grain-raising, like North Dakota at the present time.

Each of these areas has had an influence in our economic and political history; the evolution of each into a higher stage has worked political transformations. But what constitutional historian has made any adequate attempt to interpret political facts by the light of these social areas and changes?

The Atlantic frontier was compounded of fisherman, fur-trader, miner, cattle-raiser, and farmer. Excepting the fisherman, each type of industry was on the march toward the West, impelled by an irresistible attraction. Each passed in successive waves across the continent. Stand at Cumberland Gap and watch the procession of civilization, marching single file— the buffalo following the trail to the salt springs, the Indian, the fur-trader and hunter, the cattle-raiser, the pioneer farmer—and the frontier has passed by. Stand at South Pass in the Rockies a century later and see the same procession with wider intervals between. The unequal rate of advance compels us to distinguish the frontier into the trader's frontier, the rancher's frontier, or the miner's frontier, and the farmer's frontier. When the mines and the cow pens were still near the fall line the traders' pack trains were tinkling across the Alleghanies, and the French on the Great Lakes were fortifying their posts, alarmed by the British trader's birch canoe. When the trappers scaled the Rockies, the farmer was still near the mouth of the Missouri.

Why was it that the Indian trader passed so rapidly across the continent? What effects followed from the trader's frontier? The trade was coeval with American discovery. The Norsemen, Vespuccius, Verrazani, Hudson, John Smith, all trafficked for furs. The Plymouth pilgrims settled in Indian cornfields, and their first return cargo was of beaver and lumber. The records of the various New England colonies show how steadily exploration was carried into the wilderness by this trade. What is true for New England is, as would be expected, even plainer for the rest of the colonies. All along the coast from Maine to Georgia the Indian trade opened up the river courses. Steadily the trader passed westward, utilizing the older lines of French trade. The Ohio, the Great Lakes, the Mississippi, the Missouri, and the Platte, the lines of western advance, were ascended by traders. They found the passes in the Rocky Mountains and guided Lewis and Clark, Frémont, and Bidwell. The explanation of the rapidity of this advance is connected with the effects of the trader on the Indian. The trading post left the unarmed tribes at the mercy of those that had purchased fire-arms—a truth which the Iroquois Indians wrote in blood, and so the remote and unvisited tribes gave eager welcome to the trader. "The savages," wrote La Salle, "take better care of us French than of their own children; from us only can they get guns and goods." This accounts for the trader's power and the rapidity of his advance. Thus the disintegrating forces of civilization entered the wilderness. Every river valley and Indian trail became a fissure in Indian society, and so that society became honeycombed. Long before the pioneer farmer appeared on the scene, primitive Indian life had passed away. The farmers met Indians armed with guns. The trading frontier, while steadily undermining Indian power by making the tribes ultimately dependent on the whites, yet, through its sale of guns, gave to the Indian increased power of resistance to the farming frontier. French colonization was dominated by its trading frontier; English colonization by its farming frontier. There was an antagonism between the two frontiers as between the two nations. Said Duquesne to the Iroquois, "Are you ignorant of the difference between the king of England and the king of France? Go see the forts that our king has established and you will see that you can still hunt under their very walls. They have been placed for your advantage in places which you frequent. The English, on the contrary, are no sooner in possession of a place than the game is driven away. The forest falls before them as they advance, and the soil is laid bare so that you can scarce find the wherewithal to erect a shelter for the night.

And yet, in spite of this opposition of the interests of the trader and the farmer, the Indian trade pioneered the way for civilization. The buffalo trail became the Indian trail, and this became the trader's "trace," the trails widened into roads, and the roads into turnpikes, and these in turn were transformed into railroads. The same origin can be shown for the railroads of the South, the Far West, and the Dominion of Canada. The trading posts reached by these trails were on the sites of Indian villages which had been placed in positions suggested by nature; and these trading posts, situated so as to command the water systems of the country, have grown into such cities as Albany, Pittsburgh, Detroit, Chicago, St. Louis, Council Bluffs, and Kansas City. Thus civilization in America has followed the arteries made by geology, pouring an ever richer tide through them, until at last the slender paths of aboriginal intercourse have been broadened and interwoven into the complex mazes of modern commercial lines; the wilderness has been interpenetrated by lines of civilization growing ever more numerous. It is like the steady growth of a complex nervous system for the originally simple, inert continent. If one would understand why we are to-day one nation, rather than a collection of isolated states, he must study this economic and social consolidation of the country. In this progress from savage conditions lie topics for the evolutionist.

The effect of the Indian frontier as a consolidating agent in our history is important. From the close of the seventeenth century, various intercolonial congresses have been called to treat with Indians and establish common measures of defense. Particularism was strongest in colonies with no Indian frontier. This frontier stretched along the western border like a cord of union. The Indian was a common danger, demanding united action. Most celebrated of these conferences was the Albany congress of 1754, called to treat with the Six Nations, and to consider plans of union. Even a cursory reading of the plan proposed by the congress reveals the importance of the frontier. The powers of the general council and the officers were, chiefly, the determination of peace and war with the Indians, the regulation of Indian trade, the purchase of Indian lands, and the creation and government of new settlements as a security against the Indians. It is evident that the unifying tendencies of the Revolutionary period were facilitated by the previous coöperation in the regulation of the frontier. In this connection may be mentioned the importance of the frontier, from that day to this, as a military training school, keeping alive the power of resistance to aggression, and developing the stalwart and rugged qualities of the frontiersman.

It would not be possible in the limits of this paper to trace the other frontiers across the continent. Travelers of the eighteenth century found the "cowpens" among the canebrakes and peavine pastures of the South, and the "cow drivers" took their droves to Charleston, Philadelphia, and New York. Travelers at the close of the War of 1812 met droves of more than a thousand cattle and swine from the interior of Ohio going to Pennsylvania to fatten for the Philadelphia market. The ranges of the Great Plains, with ranch and cowboy and nomadic life, are things of yesterday and of to-day. The experience of the Carolina cowpens guided the ranchers of Texas. One element favoring the rapid extension of the rancher's frontier is the fact that in a remote country lacking transportation facilities the product must be in small bulk, or must be able to transport itself, and the cattle raiser could easily drive his product to market. The effect of these great ranches on the subsequent agrarian history of the localities in which they existed should be studied.

The maps of the census reports show an uneven advance of the farmer's frontier, with tongues of settlement pushed forward and with indentations of wilderness. In part this is due to Indian resistance, in part to the location of river valleys and passes, in part to the unequal force of the centers of frontier attraction. Among the important centers of attraction may be mentioned the following: fertile and favorably situated soils, salt springs, mines, and army posts.

The frontier army post, serving to protect the settlers from the Indians, has also acted as a wedge to open the Indian country, and has been a nucleus for settlement. In this connection mention should also be made of the government military and exploring expeditions in determining the lines of settlement. But all the more important expeditions were greatly indebted to the earliest pathmakers, the Indian guides, the traders and trappers, and the French voyageurs, who were inevitable parts of governmental expeditions from the days of Lewis and Clark. Each expedition was an epitome of the previous factors in western advance.

In an interesting monograph, Victor Hehn has traced the effect of salt upon early European development, and has pointed out how it affected the lines of settlement and the form of administration. A similar study might be made for the salt springs of the United States. The early settlers were tied to the coast by the need of salt, without which they could not preserve their meats or live in comfort. Writing in 1752, Bishop Spangenburg says of a colony for which he was seeking lands in North Carolina, "They will require salt & other necessaries which they can neither manufacture nor raise. Either they must go to Charleston, which is 300 miles distant ...Or else they must go to Boling's Point in V^a on a branch of the James & is also 300 miles from here ... Or else they must go down the Roanoke—I know not how many miles—where salt is brought up from the Cape Fear." This may serve as a typical illustration. An annual pilgrimage to the coast for salt thus became essential. Taking flocks or furs and ginseng root, the early settlers sent their pack trains after seeding time each year to the coast. This proved to be an important educational influence, since it was almost the only way in which the pioneer learned what was going on in the East. But when discovery was made of the salt springs of the Kanawha, and the Holston, and Kentucky, and central New York, the West began to be freed from dependence on the coast. It was in part the effect of finding these salt springs that enabled settlement to cross the mountains.

From the time the mountains rose between the pioneer and the seaboard, a new order of Americanism arose. The West and the East began to get out of touch of each other. The settlements from the sea to the mountains kept connection with the rear and had a certain solidarity. But the over-mountain men grew more and more independent. The East took a narrow view of American advance, and nearly lost these men. Kentucky and Tennessee history bears abundant witness to the truth of this statement. The East began to try to hedge and limit westward expansion. Though Webster could declare that there were no Alleghanies in his politics, yet in politics in general they were a very solid factor.

The exploitation of the beasts took hunter and trader to the west, the exploitation of the grasses took the rancher west, and the exploitation of the virgin soil of the river valleys and prairies attracted the farmer. Good soils have been the most continuous attraction to the farmer's frontier. The land hunger of the Virginians drew them down the rivers into Carolina, in early colonial days; the search for soils took the Massachusetts men to Pennsylvania and to New York. As the eastern lands were taken up migration flowed across them to the west. Daniel Boone, the great backwoodsman, who combined the occupations of hunter, trader, cattle-raiser, farmer, and surveyor— learning, probably from the traders, of the fertility of the lands of the upper Yadkin, where the traders were wont to rest as they took their way to the Indians, left his Pennsylvania home with his father, and passed down the Great Valley road to that stream. Learning from a trader of the game and rich pastures of Kentucky, he pioneered the way for the farmers to that region. Thence he passed to the frontier of Missouri, where his settlement was long a landmark on the frontier. Here again he helped to open the way for civilization, finding salt licks, and trails, and land. His son was among the earliest trappers in the passes of the Rocky Mountains, and his party are said to have been the first to camp on the present site of Denver. His grandson, Col. A. J. Boone, of Colorado, was a power among the Indians of the Rocky Mountains, and was appointed an agent by the government. Kit Carson's mother was a Boone. Thus this family epitomizes the backwoodsman's advance across the continent.

The farmer's advance came in a distinct series of waves. In *Peck's New Guide to the West,* published in Boston in 1837, occurs this suggestive passage:

> Generally, in all the western settlements, three classes, like the waves of the ocean, have rolled one after the other. First comes the pioneer, who depends for the subsistence of his family chiefly upon the natural growth of vegetation, called the "range," and the proceeds of hunting. His implements of agriculture are rude, chiefly of his own make, and his efforts directed mainly to a crop of corn and a "truck patch." The last is a rude garden for growing cabbage, beans, corn for roasting ears, cucumbers, and potatoes. A log cabin, and, occasionally, a stable and corn-crib, and a field of a dozen acres, the timber girdled or "dead ened," and fenced, are enough for his occupancy. It is quite immaterial whether he ever becomes the owner of the soil. He is the occupant for the time being, pays no rent, and feels as independent as the "lord of the manor." With a horse, cow, and one or two breeders of swine, he strikes into the woods with his family, and becomes the founder of a new county, or perhaps state. He builds his cabin, gathers around him a few other families of similar tastes and habits, and occupies till the range is somewhat subdued, and hunting a little precarious, or, which is more frequently the case, till the neighbors crowd around, roads, bridges, and fields annoy him, and he lacks elbow room. The preëmption law enables him to dispose of his cabin and cornfield to the next class of emigrants; and, to employ his own figures, he "breaks for the high timber," "clears out for the New Purchase," or migrates to Arkansas or Texas, to work the same process over.
>
> The next class of emigrants purchase the lands, add field to field, clear out the roads, throw rough bridges over the streams, put up hewn log houses with glass windows and brick or stone chimneys, occasionally plant orchards, build mills, school-houses, court-houses, etc., and exhibit the picture and forms of plain, frugal, civilized life.
>
> Another wave rolls on. The men of capital and enterprise come. The settler is ready to sell out and take the advantage of the rise in property, push farther into the interior and become, himself, a man of capital and enterprise in turn. The small village rises to a spacious town

or city; substantial edifices of brick, extensive fields, orchards, gardens, colleges, and churches are seen. Broadcloths, silks, leghorns, crapes, and all the refinements, luxuries, elegancies, frivolities, and fashions are in vogue. Thus wave after wave is rolling westward; the real Eldorado is still farther on.

A portion of the two first classes remain stationary amidst the general movement, improve their habits and condition, and rise in the scale of society.

The writer has traveled much amongst the first class, the real pioneers. He has lived many years in connection with the second grade; and now the third wave is sweeping over large districts of Indiana, Illinois, and Missouri. Migration has become almost a habit in the West. Hundreds of men can be found, not over 50 years of age, who have settled for the fourth, fifth, or sixth time on a new spot. To sell out and remove only a few hundred miles makes up a portion of the variety of backwoods life and manners.

Omitting those of the pioneer farmers who move from the love of adventure, the advance of the more steady farmer is easy to understand. Obviously the immigrant was attracted by the cheap lands of the frontier, and even the native farmer felt their influence strongly. Year by year the farmers who lived on soil whose returns were diminished by unrotated crops were offered the virgin soil of the frontier at nominal prices. Their growing families demanded more lands, and these were dear. The competition of the unexhausted, cheap, and easily tilled prairie lands compelled the farmer either to go west and continue the exhaustion of the soil on a new frontier, or to adopt intensive culture. Thus the census of 1890 shows, in the Northwest, many counties in which there is an absolute or a relative decrease of population. These States have been sending farmers to advance the frontier on the plains, and have themselves begun to turn to intensive farming and to manufacture. A decade before this, Ohio had shown the same transition stage. Thus the demand for land and the love of wilderness freedom drew the frontier ever onward.

Having now roughly outlined the various kinds of frontiers, and their modes of advance, chiefly from the point of view of the frontier itself, we may next inquire what were the influences on the East and on the Old World. A rapid enumeration of some of the more noteworthy effects is all that I have time for.

First, we note that the frontier promoted the formation of a composite nationality for the American people. The coast was preponderantly English, but the later tides of continental immigration flowed across to the free lands. This was the case from the early colonial days. The Scotch-Irish and the Palatine Germans, or "Pennsylvania Dutch," furnished the dominant element in the stock of the colonial frontier. With these peoples were also the freed indented servants, or redemptioners, who at the expiration of their time of service passed to the frontier. Governor Spotswood of Virginia writes in 1717, "The inhabitants of our frontiers are composed generally of such as have been transported hither as servants, and, being out of their time, settle themselves where land is to be taken up and that will produce the necessarys of life with little labour." Very generally these redemptioners were of non-English stock. In the crucible of the frontier the immigrants were Americanized, liberated, and fused into a mixed race, English in neither nationality nor characteristics. The process has gone on from the early days to our own. Burke and other writers in the middle of the eighteenth century believed that Pennsylvania was "threatened with the danger of being wholly foreign in language, manners, and perhaps even inclinations." The German and Scotch-Irish elements in the frontier of the South were only less great. In the middle of the present century the German element in Wisconsin was already so considerable that leading publicists looked to the creation of a German state out of the commonwealth by concentrating their colonization. Such examples teach us to beware of misinterpreting the fact that there is a common English speech in America into a belief that the stock is also English.

In another way the advance of the frontier decreased our dependence on England. The coast, particularly of the South, lacked diversified industries, and was dependent on England for the bulk of its supplies. In the South there was even a dependence on the Northern colonies for articles of food. Governor Glenn, of South Carolina, writes in the middle of the eighteenth century: "Our trade with New York and Philadelphia was of this sort, draining us of all the little money and bills we could gather from other places for their bread, flour, beer, hams, bacon, and other things of their produce, all which, except beer, our new townships begin to supply us with, which are settled with very industrious and thriving Germans. This no doubt diminishes the number of shipping and the appearance of our trade, but it is far from being a detriment to us." Before long the frontier created a demand for merchants. As it retreated from the coast it became less and less possible for England to bring her supplies directly to the consumer's wharfs, and carry away staple crops, and staple crops began to give way to diversified agriculture for a time. The effect of this phase of the frontier action upon the northern section is perceived when we realized how the advance of the frontier aroused seaboard cities like Boston, New York, and Baltimore, to engage in rivalry for what Washington called "the extensive and valuable trade of a rising empire."

The legislation which most developed the powers of the national government, and played the largest part in its activity, was conditioned on the frontier. Writers have discussed the subjects of tariff, land, and internal improvement, as subsidiary to the slavery question. But when American history comes to be rightly viewed it will be seen that the slavery question is an incident. In the period from the end of the first half of the present century to the close of the Civil War slavery rose to primary, but far from exclusive, importance. But this does not justify Dr. von Holst (to take an example) in treating our constitutional history in its formative period down to 1828 in a single volume, giving six volumes chiefly to the history of slavery from 1828 to 1861, under the title "Constitutional History of the United States." The growth of nationalism and the evolution of American political institutions were dependent on the advance of the frontier. Even so recent a writer as Rhodes, in his "History of the United States since the Compromise of 1850," has treated the legislation called out by the western advance as incidental to the slavery struggle.

This is a wrong perspective. The pioneer needed the goods of the coast, and so the grand series of internal improvement and railroad legislation began, with potent nationalizing effects. Over internal improvements occurred great debates, in which grave constitutional questions were discussed. Sectional groupings appear in the votes, profoundly significant for the historian. Loose construction increased as the nation marched westward. But the West was not content with bringing the farm to the factory. Under the lead of Clay—"Harry of the West"—protective tariffs were passed, with the cry of bringing the factory to the farm. The disposition of the public lands was a third important subject of national legislation influenced by the frontier.

The public domain has been a force of profound importance in the nationalization and development of the government. The effects of the struggle of the landed and the landless States, and of the Ordinance of 1787, need no discussion. Administratively the frontier called out some of the highest and most vitalizing activities of the general government. The purchase of Louisiana was perhaps the constitutional turning point in the history of the Republic, inasmuch as it afforded both a new area for national legislation and the occasion of the downfall of the policy of strict construction. But the purchase of Louisiana was called out by frontier needs and demands. As frontier States accrued to the Union, the national power grew. In a speech on the dedication of the Calhoun monument Mr. Lamar explained: "In 1789 the States were the creators of the Federal Government; in 1861 the Federal Government was the creator of a large majority of the States."

When we consider the public domain from the point of view of the sale and disposal of the public lands we are again brought face to face with the frontier. The policy of the United States in dealing with its lands is in sharp contrast with the European system of scientific administration. Efforts to make this domain a source of revenue, and to withhold it from emigrants in order that settlement might be compact, were in vain. The jealousy and the fears of the East were powerless in the face of the demands of the frontiersmen. John Quincy Adams was obliged to confess: "My own system of administration, which was to make the national domain the inexhaustible fund for progressive and unceasing internal improvement, has failed." The reason is obvious; a system of administration was not what the West demanded; it wanted land. Adams states the situation as follows: "The slaveholders of the South have bought the coöperation of the western country by the bribe of the western lands, abandoning to the new Western States their own proportion of the public property and aiding them in the design of grasping all the lands into their own hands. Thomas H. Benton was the author of this system, which he brought forward as a substitute for the American system of Mr. Clay, and to supplant him as the leading statesman of the West. Mr. Clay, by his tariff compromise with Mr. Calhoun, abandoned his own American system. At the same time he brought forward a plan for distributing among all the States of the Union the proceeds of the sales of the public lands. His bill for that purpose passed both Houses of Congress, but was vetoed by President Jackson, who, in his annual message of December, 1832, formally recommended that all public lands should be gratuitously given away to individual adventurers and to the States in which the lands are situated."

"No subject," said Henry Clay, "which has presented itself to the present, or perhaps any preceding, Congress, is of greater magnitude than that of the public lands." When we consider the far-reaching effects of the government's land policy upon political, economic, and social aspects of American life, we are disposed to agree with him. But this legislation was framed under frontier influences, and under the lead of Western statesmen like Benton and Jackson. Said Senator Scott of Indiana in 1841: "I consider the preëmption law merely declaratory of the custom or common law of the settlers."

It is safe to say that the legislation with regard to land, tariff, and internal improvements—the American system of the nationalizing Whig party—was conditioned on frontier ideas and needs. But it was not merely in legislative action that the frontier worked against the sectionalism of the coast. The economic and social characteristics of the frontier worked against sectionalism. The men of the frontier had closer resemblances to the Middle region than to either of the other sections. Pennsylvania had been the seed-plot of frontier emigration, and, although she passed on her settlers along the Great Valley into the west of Virginia and the Carolinas, yet the industrial society of these Southern frontiersmen was always more like that of the Middle region than like that of the tide-water portion of the South, which later came to spread its industrial type throughout the South.

The Middle region, entered by New York harbor, was an open door to all Europe. The tide-water part of the South represented typical Englishmen, modified by a warm climate and servile labor, and living in baronial fashion on great plantations; New England stood for a special English movement—Puritanism. The Middle region was less English than the other sections. It had a wide mixture of nationalities, a varied society, the mixed town and county system of local government, a varied economic life, many religious sects. In short, it was a region mediating between New England and the South, and the East and the West. It represented that composite nationality which the contemporary United States exhibits, that juxtaposition of non-English groups, occupying a valley or a little settlement, and presenting reflections of the map of Europe in their variety. It was democratic and nonsectional, if not national; "easy, tolerant, and contented," rooted strongly in material prosperity. It was typical of the modern United States. It was least sectional, not only because it lay between North and South, but also because with no barriers to shut out its frontiers from its settled region, and with a system of connecting waterways, the Middle region mediated between East and West as well as between North and South. Thus it became the typically American region. Even the New Englander, who was shut out from the frontier by the Middle region, tarrying in New York or Pennsylvania on his westward march, lost the acuteness of his sectionalism on the way.

The spread of cotton culture into the interior of the South finally broke down the contrast between the "tide-water" region and the rest of the State, and based Southern interests on slavery. Before this process revealed its results, the western portion of the South, which was akin to Pennsylvania in stock, society, and industry, showed tendencies to fall away from the faith of the fathers into internal improvement legislation and nationalism. In the Virginia convention of 1829-30, called to revise the constitution, Mr. Leigh, of Chesterfield, one of the tide-water counties, declared:

> "One of the main causes of discontent which led to this convention, that which had the strongest influence in overcoming our veneration for the work of our fathers, which taught us to condemn the sentiments of Henry and Mason and Pendleton, which weaned us from our reverence for the constituted authorities of the State, was an overweening passion for internal improvement. I say this with perfect knowledge, for it has been avowed to me by gentlemen from the West over and over again. And let me tell the gentleman from Albemarle

(Mr. Gordon) that it has been another principal object of those who set this ball of revolution in motion, to overturn the doctrine of State rights, of which Virginia has been the very pillar, and to remove the barrier she has interposed to the interference of the Federal Government in that same work of internal improvement, by so reorganizing the legislature that Virginia, too, may be hitched to the Federal car."

It was this nationalizing tendency of the West that transformed the democracy of Jefferson into the national republicanism of Monroe and the democracy of Andrew Jackson. The West of the War of 1812, the West of Clay, and Benton and Harrison, and Andrew Jackson, shut off by the Middle States and the mountains from the coast sections, had a solidarity of its own with national tendencies. On the tide of the Father of Waters, North and South met and mingled into a nation. Interstate migration went steadily on—a process of cross-fertilization of ideas and institutions. The fierce struggle of the sections over slavery on the western frontier does not diminish the truth of this statement; it proves the truth of it. Slavery was a sectional trait that would not down, but in the West it could not remain sectional. It was the greatest of frontiersmen who declared: "I believe this Government can not endure permanently half slave and half free. It will become all of one thing or all of the other." Nothing works for nationalism like intercourse within the nation. Mobility of population is death to localism, and the western frontier worked irresistibly in unsettling population. The effect reached back from the frontier and affected profoundly the Atlantic coast and even the Old World.

But the most important effect of the frontier has been in the promotion of democracy here and in Europe. As has been indicated, the frontier is productive of individualism. Complex society is precipitated by the wilderness into a kind of primitive organization based on the family. The tendency is anti-social. It produces antipathy to control, and particularly to any direct control. The tax-gatherer is viewed as a representative of oppression. Prof. Osgood, in an able article, has pointed out that the frontier conditions prevalent in the colonies are important factors in the explanation of the American Revolution, where individual liberty was sometimes confused with absence of all effective government. The same conditions aid in explaining the difficulty of instituting a strong government in the period of the confederacy. The frontier individualism has from the beginning promoted democracy.

The frontier States that came into the Union in the first quarter of a century of its existence came in with democratic suffrage provisions, and had reactive effects of the highest importance upon the older States whose peoples were being attracted there. An extension of the franchise became essential. It was *western* New York that forced an extension of suffrage in the constitutional convention of that State in 1821; and it was *western* Virginia that compelled the tide-water region to put a more liberal suffrage provision in the constitution framed in 1830, and to give to the frontier region a more nearly proportionate representation with the tide-water aristocracy. The rise of democracy as an effective force in the nation came in with western preponderance under Jackson and William Henry Harrison, and it meant the triumph of the frontier—with all of its good and with all of its evil elements. An interesting illustration of the tone of frontier democracy in 1830 comes from the same debates in the Virginia convention already referred to. A representative from western Virginia declared:

> "But, sir, it is not the increase of population in the West which this gentleman ought to fear. It is the energy which the mountain breeze and western habits impart to those emigrants. They are regenerated, politically I mean, sir. They soon become *working politicians;* and the difference, sir, between a *talking* and a *working* politician is immense. The Old Dominion has long been celebrated for producing great orators; the ablest metaphysicians in policy; men that can split hairs in all abstruse questions of political economy. But at home, or when they return from Congress, they have negroes to fan them asleep. But a Pennsylvania, a New York, an Ohio, or a western Virginia statesman, though far inferior in logic, metaphysics, and rhetoric to an old Virginia statesman, has this advantage, that when he returns home be takes off his coat and takes hold of the plow. This gives him bone and muscle, sir, and preserves his republican principles pure and uncontaminated."

So long as free land exists, the opportunity for a competency exists, and economic power secures political power. But the democracy born of free land, strong in selfishness and individualism, intolerant of administrative experience and education, and pressing individual liberty beyond its proper bounds, has its dangers as well as its benefits. Individualism in America has allowed a laxity in regard to governmental affairs which has rendered possible the spoils system and all the manifest evils that follow from the lack of a highly developed civic spirit. In this connection may be noted also the influence of frontier conditions in permitting lax business honor, inflated paper currency and wild-cat banking. The colonial and revolutionary frontier was the region whence emanated many of the worst forms of an evil currency. The West in the War of 1812 repeated the phenomenon on the frontier of that day, while the speculation and wild-cat banking of the period of the crisis of 1837 occurred on the new frontier belt of the next tier of States. Thus each one of the periods of lax financial integrity coincides with periods when a new set of frontier communities had arisen, and coincides in area with these successive frontiers, for the most part. The recent Populist agitation is a case in point. Many a State that now declines any connection with the tenets of the Populists, itself adhered to such ideas in an earlier stage of the development of the State. A primitive society can hardly be expected to show the intelligent appreciation of the complexity of business interests in a developed society. The continual recurrence of these areas of paper-money agitation is another evidence that the frontier can be isolated and studied as a factor in American history of the highest importance.

The East has always feared the result of an unregulated advance of the frontier, and has tried to check and guide it. The English authorities would have checked settlement at the headwaters of the Atlantic tributaries and allowed the "savages to enjoy their deserts in quiet lest the peltry trade should decrease." This called out Burke's splendid protest:

"If you stopped your grants, what would be the consequence? The people would occupy without grants. They have already so occupied in many places. You can not station garrisons in every part of these deserts. If you drive the people from one place, they will carry on their annual tillage and remove with their flocks and herds to another. Many of the people in the back settlements are already little attached to particular situations. Already they have topped the Appalachian Mountains. From thence they behold before them an immense plain, one vast, rich, level meadow; a square of five hundred miles. Over this they would wander without a possibility of restraint; they would change their manners with their habits of life; would soon forget a government by which they were disowned; would become hordes of English Tartars; and, pouring down upon your unfortified frontiers a fierce and irresistible cavalry, become masters of your governors and your counselers, your collectors and comptrollers, and of all the slaves that adhered to them. Such would, and in no long time must, be the effect of attempting to forbid as a crime and to suppress as an evil the command and blessing of Providence, 'Increase and multiply.' Such would be the happy result of an endeavor to keep as a lair of wild beasts that earth which God, by an express charter, has given to the children of men."

But the English Government was not alone in its desire to limit the advance of the frontier and guide its destinies. Tide-water Virginia and South Carolina gerrymandered those colonies to insure the dominance of the coast in their legislatures. Washington desired to settle a State at a time in the Northwest; Jefferson would reserve from settlement the territory of his Louisiana Purchase north of the thirty-second parallel, in order to offer it to the Indians in exchange for their settlements east of the Mississippi. "When we shall be full on this side," he writes, "we may lay off a range of States on the western bank from the head to the mouth, and so range after range, advancing compactly as we multiply." Madison went so far as to argue to the French minister that the United States had no interest in seeing population extend itself on the right bank of the Mississippi, but should rather fear it. When the Oregon question was under debate, in 1824, Smyth, of Virginia, would draw an unchangeable line for the limits of the United States at the outer limit of two tiers of States beyond the Mississippi, complaining that the seaboard States were being drained of the flower of their population by the bringing of too much land into market. Even Thomas Benton, the man of widest views of the destiny of the West, at this stage of his career declared that along the ridge of the Rocky mountains "the western limits of the Republic should be drawn, and the statue of the fabled god Terminus should be raised upon its highest peak, never to be thrown down." But the attempts to limit the boundaries, to restrict land sales and settlement, and to deprive the West of its share of political power were all in vain. Steadily the frontier of settlement advanced and carried with it individualism, democracy, and nationalism, and powerfully affected the East and the Old World.

The most effective efforts of the East to regulate the frontier came through its educational and religious activity, exerted by interstate migration and by organized societies. Speaking in 1835, Dr. Lyman Beecher declared: "It is equally plain that the religious and political destiny of our nation is to be decided in the West," and he pointed out that the population of the West "is assembled from all the States of the Union and from all the nations of Europe, and is rushing in like the waters of the flood, demanding for its moral preservation the immediate and universal action of those institutions which discipline the mind and arm the conscience and the heart. And so various are the opinions and habits, and so recent and imperfect is the acquaintance, and so sparse are the settlements of the West, that no homogeneous public sentiment can be formed to legislate immediately into being the requisite institutions. And yet they are all needed immediately in their utmost perfection and power. A nation is being "born in a day... But what will become of the West if her prosperity rushes up to such a majesty of power, while those great institutions linger which are necessary to form the mind and the conscience and the heart of that vast world. It must not be permitted... Let no man at the East quiet himself and dream of liberty, whatever may become of the West... Her destiny is our destiny."

With the appeal to the conscience of New England, he adds appeals to her fears lest other religious sects anticipate her own. The New England preacher and school-teacher left their mark on the West. The dread of Western emancipation from New England's political and economic control was paralleled by her fears lest the West cut loose from her religion. Commenting in 1850 on reports that settlement was rapidly extending northward in Wisconsin, the editor of the *Home Missionary* writes: "We scarcely know whether to rejoice or mourn over this extension of our settlements. While we sympathize in whatever tends to increase the physical resources and prosperity of our country, we can not forget that with all these dispersions into remote and still remoter corners of the land the supply of the means of grace is becoming relatively less and less." Acting in accordance with such ideas, home missions were established and Western colleges were erected. As seaboard cities like Philadelphia, New York, and Baltimore strove for the mastery of Western trade, so the various denominations strove for the possession of the West. Thus an intellectual stream from New England sources fertilized the West. Other sections sent their missionaries; but the real struggle was between sects. The contest for power and the expansive tendency furnished to the various sects by the existence of a moving frontier must have had important results on the character of religious organization in the United States. The multiplication of rival churches in the little frontier towns had deep and lasting social effects. The religious aspects of the frontier make a chapter in our history which needs study.

From the conditions of frontier life came intellectual traits of profound importance. The works of travelers along each frontier from colonial days onward describe certain common traits, and these traits have, while softening down, still persisted as survivals in the place of their origin, even when a higher social organization succeeded. The result is that to the frontier the American intellect owes its striking characteristics. That coarseness and strength combined with acuteness and inquisitiveness; that practical, inventive turn of mind, quick to find expedients; that masterful grasp of material things, lacking in the artistic but powerful to effect great ends; that restless, nervous energy; that dominant individualism, working for good and for evil, and withal that buoyancy and exuberance which comes with freedom—these are traits of the frontier, or traits called out elsewhere because of the existence of the frontier. Since the days when the fleet of Columbus sailed into the waters of the New World, America has been another name for opportunity, and the people of the United States have taken their tone from the incessant expansion which has not only been open but has even been forced upon them. He would be a rash prophet who should assert that the expansive character of American life has now entirely ceased. Movement has been its dominant fact, and, unless this training has no effect upon a people, the American energy will continually demand a wider field for its exercise. But never again will such gifts of free land offer themselves. For a moment, at the frontier, the bonds of custom are broken and unrestraint is triumphant. There is no *tabula rasa*. The stubborn American environment is there with its imperious summons to accept its conditions; the inherited ways of doing things are also there; and yet, in spite of environment, and in spite of custom, each frontier did indeed furnish a new field of opportunity, a gate of escape from the bondage of the past; and freshness, and confidence, and scorn of older society, impatience of its restraints and its ideas, and indifference to its lessons, have accompanied the frontier. What the Mediterranean Sea was to the Greeks, breaking the bond of custom, offering new experiences, calling out new institutions and activities, that, and more, the ever retreating frontier has been to the United States directly, and to the nations of Europe more remotely. And now, four centuries from the discovery of America, at the end of a hundred years of life under the Constitution, the frontier has gone, and with its going has closed the first period of American history.

Document 1.2

The West of Walter Prescott Webb

During the middle decades of the twentieth century, Walter Prescott Webb was the premier historian of the American West. He taught at the University of Texas and wrote a number of major works, including the seminal *The Great Plains* (1931). Webb built on the Turner thesis, arguing that Turner's West, which hinged on axes, water, and the long rifle, had little relevance for the arid Great Plains. On the Great Plains beyond the humid woodlands, settlers adapted to the region with innovations such as the Colt revolver, the windmill, and barbed wire. In the following essay, Webb describes the history of the "Six Shooter." *

Definition or description of a weapon that is known and recognized the world over is hardly necessary. Briefly, the revolver is a pistol with a rotating cylinder containing ordinarily five or six chambers, each of which discharges through a single barrel. It is six pistols encompassed in one, commonly known to its familiars as a "gun," "six-gun," "shooting iron," "six-shooter," or "Colt." The Colt was the original revolver, so far as

---

* Walter Prescott Webb, *The Great Plains* (New York: Grossett & Dunlap, 1931), pp. 167-79.

American history is concerned, and it furnished the principle upon which other models were constructed. This is the story of how the revolver originated, of how it met the peculiar needs of the plainsman, and of the circumstances under which it was adopted.

It has been pointed out that all the combatants the Texans had to meet were mounted; therefore the weapons used by the Texas Rangers, if they were adequately to meet the need, must be suited to mounted combat. This brings us to an examination of the weapons of the Texans and of the Indians.

The arms originally carried by the Texas Ranger were those of the American pioneers east of the Mississippi. The American long rifle has been designated as one of the principal factors in the conquest of America. This weapon, however, was designed for use on the ground, not on horse-back. It developed in the woods for service in the forests and glades when the user had both feet planted firmly on solid earth. The "hair trigger," the "double sights," the "find bead," are terms significant of a weapon nicely adjusted and to be carefully aimed. Moreover, in the decade 1830-1840 the cap-and-ball rifle was still in use, the loading of which was a meticulous and time-consuming task. The powder had to be measured and poured, the ball had to be rammed down the barrel with a long rod, the tube must be "primed," and the cap or flint had to be adjusted. All this took about a minute, and in a fight much can happen in a minute. That the rifle was no horseman's weapon needs no demonstration.

The sword and lance, the horseman's traditional weapons, were outworn relics of the pre-gunpowder era. The Mexicans used the lance, as did the Plains Indians, but the Texans never used either lance or sword. The sword was ineffective against the Mexican, who was an artist with a knife and a rope; it was useless against the Comanche, who refused to engage in close combat. Once when there was talk of equipping the Texas Rangers with swords, an old Texan remarked, "They would doubtless be of great service to the Rangers, especially in a snake country."

The American pioneer did take to Texas with him the pistol—the old single-shot dueling piece, or the smaller derringer-like weapon, or the large horse pistol. The horse pistol could be used on horseback, but a horseman could hardly carry more than two of them. At best it was possible for the early Texan to carry on horseback three shots, one in his rifle and one in each of the two pistols in his belt. The first was practically useless to a mounted man, and the two pistols were bulky and unwieldy and had the same disadvantages of loading as the rifle had.

Let us turn next to an examination of Comanche weapons. For defense, the warrior carried a rawhide shield hung on his left arm; for offense, a fourteen-foot spear, a plain or sinew-backed bow, and a quiver of arrows tipped with flint or steel. These he used effectively on both game and enemy.

Imagine now a battle between the Texans and the Comanches, and observe the relative advantages in weapons possessed by each. In most respects the Indian had the best of it. In the first place, the Texan carried at most three shots; the Comanche carried twoscore or more arrows. It took the Texan a minute to reload his weapon; the Indian could in that time ride three hundred yards and discharge twenty arrows. The Texan had to dismount in order to use his rifle effectively at all, and it was his most reliable weapon; the Indian remained mounted throughout the combat. Apparently the one advantage possessed by the white man was a weapon of longer range and more deadly accuracy than the Indian's bow, but the agility of the Indian and the rapidity of his movements did much to offset this advantage.

Imagine now the three probable issues of an Indian battle. The most common form of encounter was that in which the white men stood and received the attack. Such engagements are often represented in pictures by a body of plumed warriors riding in a circle, the center of which is a group of white men and women huddled together in the open plain and protected by whatever barricades they could hastily improvise. This picture had its justification in practice upon the trans-Plains trails leading from Missouri to Oregon, California, and Santa Fe. The purpose of the Indian tactics was to exhaust the ammunition of the white men by "drawing their fire," and then rush upon them before they could reload. The white men saved themselves by conserving their ammunition, firing slowly and in rotation by the platoon system, so that some of the weapons were always primed. It was a situation which called for great economy and precaution. It gave rise to such admonitions as "Hold your fire," "Take steady aim," "Make every shot tell." The marvelous marksmanship of that early day was due to the fact that the first shot was frequently the only shot.

But let us assume as a second possible procedure in battle that the Indians retreat and the Rangers pursue. In this event the white men would discharge their rifles first, then mount, and go in pursuit. At most they had only two shots each, and these were soon spent. In the meantime the Indian could discharge his arrow from his running horse, and as soon as his adversary's guns were empty could turn upon him with arrows and spear.

As a third possibility the Texans would retreat and the Indians pursue. Here was a situation which the Rangers and all who fought Plains Indians found most dangerous, and one in which escape depended on the speed of one's horse. All the Comanche's weapons were peculiarly adapted to the situation, and he liked nothing better than to have his enemy running before him on the open plain. Arrow would follow arrow from his snapping bow, and if better mounted than his enemy, he could push up and spear him from a distance of ten or twelve feet. Timber to hide in or a fast horse to ride offered the Ranger his only safety. Lacking these, he lost his scalp to the Indian, who left the mangled body to the birds and wolves.

Undoubtedly the Texans needed a new weapon, something with a reserve power and capable of "continuous" action—a weapon more rapid than the Indian's arrows, of longer reach than his spear, and, above all, one adapted to use on horseback. The man who supplied the weapon that fulfilled all these necessities was a Connecticut Yankee by the name of Samuel Colt. The story of Colt's invention, his struggle, confessed failure, and final success—coupled as it was with the Rangers of the Texas republic—is a story which for dramatic interest is perhaps not excelled in the annals of American invention.

Colt found the pistol a single-shooter and left it a six-shooter. Thus judged the Texan rangers, when they coined this new word "six-shooter," to describe a thing no less new among men, an engine which rendered them victorious against fearful odds, and over both Mexicans and Indians.

The close relationship of Texas and the Rangers to the evolution of this distinctive American weapon is exemplified in the very names given to these early revolvers. The first model, "which won its fame and fortune," was called the "Texas." A second model, with certain improvements over the old, was brought out probably about 1842. It was a Texas Ranger who suggested the improvements, and it was for him that the improved weapon was named. This man, Samuel H. Walker, captain of the Rangers, had been sent to New York to purchase a supply of the latest firearms, and while there he arranged to meet the inventor of the Texas.

The Texas, the Walker, and the term "six-shooter," coined by the Rangers—all these names bear evidence that the "Lone Star Republic" had much to do with the development of the new weapon. The exact date at which the revolvers were brought to Texas remains uncertain. The early Texas Rangers, better fighters than scribes, have left but scant record of their border doings. Still there is something—a copy of a signed statement by two Rangers that the revolvers appeared in Texas in 1839. It was in the following year that John C. Hays and his men were stationed in San Antonio, and it was Hays and his men, Walker among them, who proved conclusively the value of the revolvers. Thus we are able to fix the date of introduction before 1840.

The battle of the Pedernales has good claims to being the first battle in which the six-shooter was used on mounted Indians. Hays and fourteen of his men had gone out from San Antonio to look for Indians, and on their return discovered that they were being followed by about seven Comanches. A desperate battle ensued in which the Rangers "shot them down with their pistols." Some of the Rangers and more than thirty Indians were killed.

Soon after this battle Hays found further opportunity to test the value of the revolver in a fight in the Nueces cañon. Here the Indians in superior numbers made the attack, sweeping round the Rangers on both sides and discharging their arrows as they passed. Hays and his men first emptied their rifles and then sprang into their saddles for pursuit. "Never," said an old Indian fighter, "was a band of Indians more surprised than at this charge. They expected the Rangers to remain on the defensive, and to finally wear them out and exhaust their ammunition ... In vain the Comanches tried to turn their horses and make a stand, but such was the wild confusion of running horses, popping pistols, and yelling Rangers that they abandoned the idea of a rally and sought safety in flight." In the pursuit, which covered three miles, the Rangers literally carried out their leader's orders to "powder-burn" them, causing the Indians to drop bows, shields, and lances all along the route. Years later a Comanche chief who was in this fight said that he never wanted to fight Jack Hays and his Rangers again, that they had a shot for every finger on the hand, and that he lost half his warriors, who died for a hundred miles along the trail toward Devil's River.

The evidence thus far seems clear. The revolver had been proved; it had found its place as the perfect weapon for the horseman who waged war on the Plains Indians. In the meantime the American frontier to the north was emerging from the woods and was ready to push into the Plains country or the horse country and the future six-shooter land. Thousands of guns would be demanded each year, factories would arise, and a fortune would be emptied by the plainsmen into the pockets of the ingenious inventor. But it was too late; for disaster had already overtaken Samuel Colt.

Three reasons may be given for Colt's failure. First, the United States government did not recognize the value of his new weapon, and the military experts repeatedly made unfavorable reports upon it. Second, though the Republic of Texas recognized the value of the six-shooter, its corps of fighting men was small and its financial situation so bad that it could not make large purchases. Third, the frontier line of settlement had not yet moved far west of the Mississippi. *It was still in the timber.* Therefore the American frontiersmen were not yet sufficiently in need of a horseman's weapon to buy the revolvers in large quantities.

In the light of what has been said, the rapid spread of the six-shooter over the whole Plains area is easy to understand. It is not difficult to see why people associate the six-shooter with Westerners of the Plains. Some still believe, such is the force of tradition, that the Westerners "wear 'em low on the right leg, and pull 'em smokin'."

In the Mexican War, the revolver had attained a national reputation, for every soldier who saw the Texas Rangers marveled at their general appearance and at the wonderful weapons they wore. When these soldiers returned home they spread the reputation of the Colt revolvers far and near. The treaty of Guadalupe Hidalgo transferred to the United States all the Southwest and the southern portion of the Great Plains corridor. Those who went into the West went on horseback with six-shooters in their belts. How the six-shooter was taken up by the cowboys after the Civil War will be treated in another place. Whatever abuses grew out of the six-shooter—and there were doubtless many—it should be borne in mind that its introduction, rapid spread, and popularity throughout the Plains area, the Indian and cattle country, were in response to a genuine need for a horseman's weapon. Whatever sins the six-shooter may have to answer for, it stands as the first mechanical adaptation made by the American people when they emerged from the timber and met a set of new needs in the open country of the Great Plains. It enabled the white man to fight the Plains Indian on horseback.

Document 1.3

The New Western History

In recent years, a number of historians have moved beyond the West of heroic white men to examine other dimensions of the frontier experience. None of these historians has been more influential than Patricia Limerick of the University of Colorado. Her frontier is inhabited by people of color and women, as well as by white men, and her story is not one of unmitigated progress. The following essay is taken from her influential book *The Legacy of Conquest: The Unbroken Past of the American West* (1987).*

In 1883 Nannie Alderson married, left her home in Virginia, and traveled to her new life on a ranch in Montana. Reminiscing about those years, Mrs. Alderson noted a

---

* Patricia Nelson Limerick, *The Legacy of Conquest: The Unbroken Past of the American West* (New York: W. W. Norton & Company, 1987), pp. 17-32.

particular feature of Montana cuisine and landscape. "Everyone in the country lived out of cans," she said, "and you would see a great heap of them outside every little shack."

Hollywood did not commemorate those heaps in Western movies, and yet, by the common wisdom of archaeologists, trash heaps say a great deal about their creators. Living out of cans, the Montana ranchers were typical Westerners, celebrating independence while relying on a vital connection to the outside world. More important, the cans represented continuity, simply by staying in place. The garbage collector never came. And the evidence of last week's—last year's—meals stayed in sight.

When Western historians yielded to a preoccupation with the frontier and its supposed end, past and present fell apart, divided by the watershed of 1890. But Western reality followed other patterns. Matter, issues, memories, and dilemmas were all conserved. In the mountains of Colorado, miners dug shafts, worked mines, and then gave them up. The miners left; their works remain. One walks with some caution in these historic regions; land that appears solid may be honeycombed, and one would not like to plunge unexpectedly into the legacy of Western history.

The conquest of Western America shapes the present as dramatically—and sometimes as perilously as the old mines shape the mountainsides. To live with that legacy, contemporary Americans ought to be well informed and well warned about the connections between past and present. But here the peculiar status of Western American history has posed an obstacle to understanding. Americans are left to stumble over—and sometimes into—those connections, caught off guard by the continued vitality of issues widely believed to be dead.

Like slavery, conquest tested the ideals of the United States. Conquest deeply affected both the conqueror and the conquered, just as slavery shaped slaveholder and slave. Both historical experiences left deep imprints on particular regions and on the nation at large. The legacy of slavery and the legacy of conquest endure, shaping events in our own time.

Here, however, we reach a principal difference: to most twentieth-century Americans, the legacy of slavery was serious business, while the legacy of conquest was not. Southern historians successfully fought through the aura of moonlight and magnolias, and established slavery, emancipation, and black/white relations as major issues in American history. The Civil War, Reconstruction, the migration of Southern blacks into other regions, and the civil rights movement all guaranteed that the nation would recognize the significance of slavery and the South.

Conquest took another route into national memory. In the popular imagination, the reality of conquest dissolved into stereotypes of noble savages and noble pioneers struggling quaintly in the wilderness. These adventures seemed to have no bearing on the complex realities of twentieth-century America. In Western paintings, novels, movies, and television shows, those stereotypes were valued precisely because they offered an escape from modern troubles. The subject of slavery was the domain of serious scholars and the occasion for sober national reflection; the subject of conquest was the domain of mass entertainment and the occasion for lighthearted national escapism. An element of regret for "what we did to the Indians" had entered the picture, but the dominant feature of conquest remained "adventure." Children happily played "cowboys and Indians" but stopped short of "masters and slaves."

When the history of conquest lost solidity, the history of an entire region suffered the same loss. Just as black/white relations and slavery were particularly associated with the South, so conquest was particularly associated with the West. Of course, the entire New World had been conquered; the West was hardly unique in this regard. But if the American West was mentioned to an American—or, perhaps even more, to a European—frontier wars and pioneering came immediately to mind. For various reasons, the West acquired an identity as the focal point of conquest. In that character, the West enjoyed its few moments of celebrity in mainstream American history as the necessary stage setting for the last big sweep of national expansionism. But when conquest reached the Pacific and filled in the areas in between, attention returned eastward. Historical significance had been a tourist—visiting the West for the peak of adventure and heading home when the action slowed down.

Professional historians of the American West thus became a people locked in an identity crisis, given to brooding about their place in the profession. Reasons for brooding appeared in a variety of forms: the failure of universities to replace older Western historians when they retired; the reluctance of East Coast publishers and reviewers to pay attention to Western history; the occasional remarks revealing that well-established American historians did not have much respect for the field. In 1984, at a conference on American Indian history, I sat in the audience and heard one colonial historian confirm the Western historians' worst fears:

> Yet how important is the "West" (minus California and urban population clusters in the Pacific Northwest) in the twentieth century or even in the nineteenth century?... For, in our role as scholars, we must recognize that the subject of westward expansion itself no longer engages the attention of many, perhaps most, historians of the United States. Surveys of college and university curricula indicate a steady decline in courses dealing with "history of the west," significant numbers of graduate students no longer write dissertations on this subject; and few of the leading members of our profession have achieved their scholarly reputations in this field.

What had happened to Western history? Paradoxically, the problem stemmed from the excess of respect given to the ideas of the field's founder, Frederick Jackson Turner, ideas presented in Turner's famous 1893 address, "The Significance of the Frontier in American History." Turner was a scholar with intellectual courage, an innovative spirit, and a forceful writing style. But respect for the individual flowed over into excessive deference to the individual's ideas. To many American historians, the Turner thesis *was* Western history. If something had gone wrong with the thesis, something had gone wrong with Western history.

The center of American history, Turner had argued, was actually to be found at its edges. As the American people proceeded westward, "the frontier [was] the outer edge of the wave—the meeting point between savagery and civilization" and "the line of most effective and rapid Americanization." The struggle with the wilderness turned Europeans into Americans, a process Turner made the central story of American history: "The existence of an area of free land, its continuous recession, and the advance of American settlement westward, explain American development." But American development came to an unsettling close when the 1890 census revealed that no vast tracts of land remained for American conquest. "And now," Turner noted at the conclusion of his essay, "four centuries from the discovery of America, at the end of a hundred years of life under the Constitution, the frontier has gone, and with its going has closed the first period of American history."

Turner, in 1893, seemed to have the field of Western American history fully corralled, unified under the concept "frontier." Exploration, fur trade, overland travel, farming, mining, town founding, merchandising, grazing, logging—the diverse activities in the nineteenth-century West were all supposed to fit into the category. In fact, the apparently unifying concept of the frontier had arbitrary limits that excluded more than they contained. Turner was, to put it mildly, ethnocentric and nationalistic. English-speaking white men were the stars of his story; Indians, Hispanics, French Canadians, and Asians were at best supporting actors and at worst invisible. Nearly as invisible were women, of all ethnicities. Turner was also primarily concerned with agrarian settlement and folk democracy in the comparatively well watered Midwest. Deserts, mountains, mines, towns, cities, railroads, territorial government, and the institutions of commerce and finance never found much of a home in his model.

Like many historians, Turner was interpreting the past in light of recent events. This presentism had great benefits and also great risks. History was bound to go on. Any definitive statement on the meaning of the West offered in 1893 would soon show its age. On this count, many of Turner's protégés did him a disservice. Their respect for him left the 1893 thesis set in stone. Turner himself moved on. In his later essays and his courses, he kept adding "more history" as it accumulated, noting, for instance, the Western oil boom that occurred after 1890 and yet showed many frontier-like characteristics. But while Turner moved on, the Turner thesis kept its 1893 form. By definition, the twentieth-century West fell outside the 1893 model. The frontier thesis, Howard Lamar wrote in 1968, "implied that a discontinuity existed between America's rural past and its urban-industrial present." Stressing discontinuity and the end of "the first period of American history," the thesis was by its own admission, Lamar pointed out, "useless as a guide for the present and future."

The rigidity of the Turner Thesis left it particularly vulnerable to a great expansion of scholarship, accelerating in the 1960s and afterward. Individual historians simply set aside the Thesis and studied particular Western places, people, and events. The diversity and complexity those studies revealed, especially in the history of the West's "minorities" (some of whom were, in earlier phases, majorities), represented an intellectual revolution. Few of the findings fit the Turnerian conceptual model. Thus, a central irony: the very vitality of Western research, by exploding the model, made mainstream historians declare that the field was dead.

Teachers often encountered the problem in the classroom. If they tried to keep up with the field, read new books and articles, and synthesize those findings for the students, they had no clear way to organize the course. The old Turnerian model of Anglo-Americans purposefully moving westward provided no help. The new Indian history alone rendered old course outlines untenable; the recognition of tribal diversity and of the active role Indians played in shaping history made for a much richer story, but also for one without a simple chronological shape. The breakdown of the old organizing idea fostered chaos; the corral built to contain Western history had been knocked apart.

Conceptual change in Western history occurred slowly: the Turner corral served a variety of functions. Since Turner had given the American frontier national significance, abandoning him threatened the West's place in the mainstream of American history. The Turner concept also was tidy. In identifying an 1890 watershed, Turner labored to create what colonial historians and Southern historians got without effort. The American Revolution periodized colonial history. The Civil War and emancipation periodized Southern history. Both events provided writers of history with graceful ways to begin and end. Historians proceed with a safe conviction that 1776 and 1865 were real watersheds.

Western historians had good reason to envy that windfall. The fact remained: the West never went to war for its independence. There is, of course, plenty of revolutionary rhetoric: complaints of exploitation and colonialism; comparisons of the Department of the Interior to the ministers of George III; laments over autonomy lost to meddling bureaucrats—but no confederation of Western states, no war for independence, and thus no watershed comparable to the Revolution or the Civil War.

Left without a major turning point, Western historians had to create one. The opening and closing of the frontier were set up like hags marking the start and finish of a racecourse, to give the West its significant chronology.

There was no conceptual problem in getting the frontier opened—with the arrival of white people in territory new to them or with the discovery of unexploited resources. The problem came at the other end. There is simply no definition of "the closing of the frontier" that is anything but arbitrary and riddled with exceptions and qualifications.

What did Turner and the director of the census mean by the "end of the frontier"? "Population in the West," Harold Simonson wrote, "had reached the figure of at least two persons per square mile, the basis for calling an area settled." This is an odd definition. If population density is the measure of a frontier condition, then the existence of a city, a town, or even a small mining camp closes the frontier for that site. One could easily argue the opposite—that a sudden concentration of population marks the opening stage and that a population lowered through, for instance, the departure of people from a used-up mining region marks the end of the frontier and its opportunities. Hinging his definition on population density, Turner referred to the fact that most of the frontier had been transformed into individually owned property; and yet in the Far West of 1890, one-half of the land remained federal property.

On a solely agrarian frontier, Turner's definition might make some sense. One could say that when every arable acre was privately owned, if not yet in cultivation, the frontier had closed. In mining or grazing, though, use was never dependent on conventional ownership. Mineral claims on federal lands tended to be transitory, subsurface rights often being detached from surface ownership. Similarly, nerve, enterprise, and finally leasing—not ownership determined grazing rights on the public domain.

Regardless of the percentage of land in private ownership, opportunity in the discovery and development of natural resources reached no clear terminus. If the frontier ended in 1890, what was going on when prospectors and miners rushed to the southern Nevada mining discoveries—in 1900? What of the expansion of irrigated farming following the passage of the Newlands Reclamation Act—in 1902? How does one dismiss the 1901 Spindletop gusher and the boom in Western oil, irregular but persistent through the century? How can one discount the uranium rushes of the late 1940s and 1950s? Are Geiger counters and airplanes less frontier-like than picks and shovels?

The effort to exclude twentieth-century events from the category "frontier" immersed the Western historian in conceptual fog. Hinging the admissions requirement on simple technology seemed arbitrary. Frontiers involve mules, horses, and oxen but not jeeps; pickaxes and pans but not air drills and draglines; provisions in sacks and tins but not in freeze-dried packets; horsedrawn plows but not mechanized combines with air-conditioned drivers' modules; bows and arrows but certainly not nuclear tests in Nevada; amateurs but not engineers. This, is at base, a judgment of sentiment and nostalgia—in favor of tools controllable by one person, and supposedly closer to nature, and against the intrusion of modern machinery. The distinction says a great deal about the emotions of historians but little about Western history.

A frequent, less sentimental strategy for frontier definition involves a focus on symbolic events. This is an intellectually stimulating exercise, but it serves only to accent the intractable diversity of Western events. For this exercise, one selects first a defining characteristic of the frontier and then an associated event. If contiguous territorial acquisition is the key process, 1848 and the acquisition of Oregon and the Mexican territories (or, alternatively, the Gadsden Purchase in 1854) mark the end of the frontier. If individual opportunity is preeminent, the Comstock Lode in the 1860s stands out, signaling the consolidation of industrial underground mining and the shift in aspiration from windfalls to wages. If the workability of the West as a refuge for distinctive societies is deemed essential, the 1890 Mormon concession on polygamy signals the closing. If unrestricted use of the public domain is crucial, the frontier ended in 1934, with the Taylor Grazing Act and the leasing of grazing rights on the public lands. If political dependence in the form of territorial organization is the representative factor, the frontier ended in 1912, with the admission of New Mexico and Arizona to statehood—or, if one includes the noncontiguous territory, in 1959, with the admission of Alaska.

My own preferred entry in the "closing" competition is the popularization of tourism and the quaintness of the folk. When Indian war dances became tourist spectacles, when the formerly scorned customs of the Chinese drew tourists to Chinatown, when former out-groups found that characteristics that had once earned them disapproval could now earn them a living, when fearful, life-threatening deserts became charming patterns of color and light, the war was over and the frontier could be considered closed, even museumized. My nomination has a problem too—it does not come with clear divisions in time. Let the car break down in the desert, or let the Indians file a lawsuit to reassert an old land claim, and the quaint appeal of nature and native can abruptly vanish. The frontier is suddenly reopened.

Frontier, then, is an unsubtle concept in a subtle world. Even so, the idea of the frontier is obviously worth studying as a historical artifact. The idea played an enormous role in national behavior, but so did the ideas of savagery and civilization, concepts that are currently not well respected as analytic terms. I certainly do not discount the power of the concept "frontier" in American history. My point is that the historian is obligated to understand how people saw their own times, but not obligated to adopt their terminology and point of view. That one may study how Westerners depended on the Colt repeating revolver is not an argument for using a gun in professional debate.

If we give up a preoccupation with the frontier and look instead at the continuous sweep of Western American history, new organizing ideas await our attention, but no simple, unitary model. Turner's frontier rested on a single point of view; it required that the observer stand in the East and look to the West. Now, like many scholars in other fields, Western historians have had to learn to live with relativism.

A de-emphasis of the frontier opens the door to a different kind of intellectual stability. Turner's frontier was a process, not a place. When "civilization" had conquered "savagery" at any one location, the process—and the historian's attention—moved on. In rethinking Western history, we gain the freedom to think of the West as a place—as many complicated environments occupied by natives who considered their homelands to be the center, not the edge.

In choosing to stress place more than process, we cannot fix exact boundaries for the region, any more than we can draw precise lines around "the South," "the Midwest," or that most elusive of regions "the East." Allowing for a certain shifting of borders, the West in this book will generally mean the present-day states of California, Oregon, Washington, Idaho, Utah, Nevada, Arizona, New Mexico, Colorado, Kansas, Nebraska, Oklahoma, Texas, Montana, Wyoming, North Dakota, and South Dakota and, more changeably, Iowa, Missouri, Arkansas, and Louisiana. (Many patterns explored here apply also to Alaska, but limits of space and time have prohibited its full inclusion.) This certainly makes for a complicated package, but the West as place has a compensatory, down-to-earth clarity that the migratory, abstract frontier could never have.

Reorganized, the history of the West is a study of a place undergoing conquest and never fully escaping its consequences. In these terms, it has distinctive features as well as features it shares with the histories of other parts of the nation and the planet. Under the Turner thesis, Western history stood alone. An exciting trend in modern scholarship leads toward comparative history—toward Western American history as one chapter in the global story of Europe's expansion. Studies in "comparative conquests" promise to help knit the fragmented history of the planet back together. Western American history can be a prime contributor to that endeavor.

De-emphasize the frontier and its supposed end, conceive of the West as a place and not a process, and Western American history has a new look. First, the American West was an important meeting ground, the point where Indian America, Latin America, Anglo-America, Afro-America, and Asia intersected. In race relations, the West could make the turn-of-the-century Northeastern urban confrontation between European immigrants and American nativists look like a family reunion. Similarly, in the diversity of languages, religions, and cultures, it surpassed the South.

Second, the workings of conquest tied these diverse groups into the same story. Happily or not, minorities and majorities occupied a common ground. Conquest basically involved the drawing of lines on a map, the definition and allocation of ownership (personal, tribal, corporate, state, federal, and international), and the evolution of land from matter to property. The process had two stages: the initial drawing of the lines (which we have usually called the frontier stage) and the subsequent giving of meaning and power to those lines, which is still under way. Race relations parallel the distribution of property, the application of labor and capital to make the property productive, and the allocation of profit. Western history has been an ongoing competition for legitimacy—for the right to claim for oneself and sometimes for one's group the status of legitimate beneficiary of Western resources. This intersection of ethnic diversity with property allocation unifies Western history.

The contest for property and profit has been accompanied by a contest for cultural dominance. Conquest also involved a struggle over languages, cultures, and religions; the pursuit of legitimacy in property overlapped with the pursuit of legitimacy in way of life and point of view. In a variety of matters, but especially in the unsettled questions of Indian assimilation and in the disputes over bilingualism and immigration in the still semi-Hispanic Southwest, this contest for cultural dominance remains a primary unresolved issue of conquest. Reconceived as a running story, a fragmented and discontinuous past becomes whole again.

With its continuity restored, Western American history carries considerable significance for American history as a whole. Conquest forms the historical bedrock of the whole nation, and the American West is a preeminent case study in conquest and its consequences. Conquest was a literal, territorial form of economic growth. Westward expansion was the most concrete, down-to-earth demonstration of the economic habit on which the entire nation became dependent. If it is difficult for Americans to imagine that an economy might be stable and also healthy, many of the forces that fostered that attitude can be traced to the Western side of American history. Cultural pluralism and responses to race form primary issues in American social relations, and the American West—with its diversity of Indian tribes, Hispanics, Euro-Americans of every variety, and blacks—was a crucial case study in American race relations. The involvement of the federal government in the economy and the resulting dependence, resentment, and deficit have become major issues in American history and in contemporary politics, and the American West was the arena in which an expanded role for the federal government first took hold. Cycles of prosperity and recession have long characterized the American economy, and in that long-running game of crack-the-whip, the West has been at the far end of the whip, providing the prime example of the boom/bust instability of capitalism. The encounter of innocence with complexity is a recurrent theme in American culture, and Western history may well be the most dramatic and sustained case of high expectations and naïveté meeting a frustrating and intractable reality. Many American people have held to a strong faith that humans can master the world—of nature and of humans—around them, and Western America put that faith to one of its most revealing tests. A belief in progress has been a driving force in the modern world; as a depository of enormous hopes for progress, the American West may well be the best place in which to observe the complex and contradictory outcome of that faith.

Beyond its national role, Western America has its own regional significance. Remoteness from both New York and Washington, D.C.; the presence of most of the nation's Indian reservations; proximity to Mexico; ports opening to the Pacific Basin and Asia; dependence on natural-resource extraction; the undergoing of conquest at a time when the American nation was both fully formed and fully self-conscious; the association of the region with a potent and persistent variety of nationalistic myth; the aridity of many areas: all these factors give Western America its own, intrinsic historical significance.

In this book, I have undertaken to pull the pieces together, to combine two or three decades of thriving scholarship with a decade of thriving journalism in Western American subjects. Much of the most interesting work in Western history has been done by individuals who consider themselves first and foremost urban, social, business, labor, Chicano, Indian, or environmental historians—not Western historians. Work in these specialties has prospered, but efforts at a regional synthesis have lagged behind. In the same way, journalists and historians often labor in separate spheres, unaware of the themes that unite their work. Their findings fit together to form a revived version of Western history, and this book is therefore an interpretation and a synthesis, not a monograph and not a survey or summary.

This book has taught me why historians might flee the challenge of synthesis. The genre breeds two alternating fears: that one is only echoing platitudes, and that one has gone out on a limb. The second fear has at least a kind of exhilaration; I am sometimes fully convinced that life out on a limb is the only life worth living. Everything I have written here, I believe. But because the field is vital and changing, I anticipate new developments every week; if Western history continues to thrive, I will look back at certain passages and shudder at my shortsightedness.

Despite those moments of exhilaration and because this book, by definition, relies on secondary sources, I am saying some familiar things. Earl Pomeroy has long stressed continuity in Western history and downplayed the frontier. In an essay published in 1959, John Caughey carefully explored the distinction between the West as frontier and the West as place or region. My own adviser, Howard Lamar, has long studied the twentieth-century West. Why repeat their arguments? Because the message has not gotten through. The public holds to the idea of a great discontinuity between the frontier and the Western present. Even in universities, the old perceptions of Western history seem to thrive. Young scholars, hired to teach Western American history, learn that their departments expect their courses to end in 1890. My own courses in Western history at the University of Colorado carry the title "The Early American Frontier" and "The Later American Frontier," while I postpone the labor of going to the committee on courses to explain how the field has changed and why a new title is in order. Others, then, have said much of what I say in this book; nonetheless, the importance of the message and a widespread reluctance to receive it justify the deployment of many messengers.

Just as Turner did, I take my cues from the present. I am thus sure to be overtaken by unplanned obsolescence. A presentist view seems to me, as it did to Turner, worth the risk. In the second half of the twentieth century, every major issue from "frontier" history reappeared in the courts or in Congress. Struggles over Indian resources and tribal autonomy; troubled relations with Mexico; controversy over the origins of Mormonism; conflicts over water allocation; another farm crisis; a drastic swing downward in the boom/bust cycles of oil, copper, and timber; continued heavy migration to some parts of the West, with all the familiar problems of adjusting to growth and sorting out power between natives and newcomers; disputes over the use of the public lands; a determined retreat on federal spending in the West: all these issues were back on the streets and looking for trouble. Historians of the future will find meanings in these events beyond my imagination, but I firmly believe they will find the 1980s to be a key period in Western American history. If the federal government implements the Reagan policy of reversing the historical pattern of using federal money to stabilize Western economies, historians will see the 1980s as a watershed decade.

In countless ways, events in the 1980s suggest a need to reevaluate Western history. Consider the case study offered by Louis L'Amour, author of "88 books about life on the

American frontier" (as of March 1984). L'Amour is the mid-twentieth century's successor to Zane Grey, a writer still intoxicated with the independence, nobility, grandeur, and adventure of the frontier. He remains true to the plot formula of tough men in the tough land. "A century ago," L'Amour wrote in a commentary in 1984, "the Western plains were overrun by buffalo, and many a tear has been shed over their passing, but where they grazed we now raise grain to feed a large part of the world..." This process of progress through conquest reached no terminus: "We are a people born to the frontier, and it has not passed away. Our move into space has opened the greatest frontier of all, the frontier that has no end."

But only a year later, in 1985, circumstances disclosed a different Louis L'Amour. "Louis L'Amour's Real Life Showdown," the headline in the *Denver Post* read, "Western Author, Colorado Ute Duel over Proposed Power-Line." L'Amour's idyllic ranch in southwest Colorado faced the threat of "a 345,000-volt power line," which would frame his view of the mountains "with cables and towering support poles" and which might also trigger "health problems, ranging from headaches and fatigue to birth defects and cancer." L'Amour fought back with the conventional Western American weapon—the lawsuit— not the six-gun.

If L'Amour recognized the irony in his situation, he did not share it with reporters. The processes of Western development do run continuously from past to present, from mining, cattle raising, and farming on to hydroelectric power and even into space. The power line is a logical outcome of the process of development L'Amour's novels celebrate. But in this particular case, the author was facing the costs of development, of conquest, and not simply cheering for the benefits. "People never worry about these things until it's too late," L'Amour said of the power line in 1985. Eight-eight books later, he was at last hot on the trail of the meanings of Western history.

2

A Collision of Worlds

Perhaps the most fundamental reality in the history of the West has been the ongoing confrontation between the values and resources of native Americans and those of the European settlers. Wherever Europeans settled—the Americas, Africa, Asia, Australia, New Zealand, and the Pacific—they encountered indigenous peoples with unique worldviews. Those worldviews often contrasted sharply with those of Europeans, becoming the source of ongoing social and political conflict.

This was especially true of the New World, where Europeans imported a completely different culture. In contrast to the corporate worldview of most Indians, in which the needs of the tribe were more compelling than the demands of any one person, Europeans worshipped at the altar of individualism. Society existed to promote the accumulation of individual wealth and power. While most Native Americans believed in community property, Europeans were capitalists praising the virtues of private property. In contrast to the consensus politics practiced by Indian tribes, European political culture revolved around majority-rule democracy or minority-rule totalitarianism. Finally, most Europeans could not understand Indian reverence for the environment. Instead of seeing the world as a living, conscious entity deserving care and respect, most Europeans viewed the earth as lifeless and inorganic, an inanimate object existing for the benefit of human beings, completely subject to human manipulation for the purpose of converting natural resources into individual wealth. Europeans and Native Americans had a difficult, if not impossible, time understanding one another. The misunderstandings continue today.

There is no consensus as to how many people lived in pre-Columbian America. While historians in the 1940s and 1950s estimated that the population of the entire hemisphere was little more than eight million, recent scholarship suggests that the population of the Americas probably exceeded the combined total of Europe and Russia at the time of Columbus's first voyage in 1492, with eight to twelve million Native Americans living north of the current Mexican border.

When considering the relationship between indigenous peoples and the "West," the concept of region becomes an abstraction. As the celebrated Native American writer M. Scott Momaday has noted, the Indians of Canada see the American West as the South; the indigenous peoples of Mexico see it as the North; and the native peoples of the West explain their relationship with the region through their own complex cosmologies. From the beginning native peoples of the Americas were considered an obstacle to European settlement and expansion. Europeans exploited tribal differences and rivalries and created a dependence on European knives, guns, and horses.

In the years following 1492, Spanish explorers, soldiers, and missionaries left the strongest European imprint on what contemporary Americans consider the western United States. Even if one was to disregard place names with Spanish origins, the "West" would be inconceivable today without the human and environmental transformations wrought by the Spanish settlement of the New World. Spaniards not only introduced familiar domesticated livestock such as cattle, sheep, and horses and the grasses that they subsisted on, but also many virulent diseases that diminished the native populations.

Suggestions for Further Reading

Alfred W. Crosby, Jr., *The Columbian Exchange: Biological and Cultural Consequences of 1492* (Westport, CN: Greenwood Publishing, 1972).

Richard Erdoes and Alfonso Ortiz, eds., *American Indian Myths and Legends* (New York: Pantheon Books, 1984).

Alvin M. Josephy, Jr., ed., *America in 1492: The World of the Indian Peoples before the Arrival of Columbus* (New York: Knopf, 1992).

Edward H. Spicer, *Cycles of Conquest: The Impact of Spain, Mexico, and the United States on the Indians of the Southwest, 1533-1960* (Tucson: University of Arizona Press, 1962).

David Weber, *The Spanish Frontier in North America* (New Haven: Yale University Press, 1992).

Critical Thinking

1. Contrast the creation myths of the Zunis and the Creeks. How are they similar and different? Can these contrasts be explained by their geographical environments?

2. How does Alvar Nunez Cabeza de Vaca depict the native peoples and environment of northern Mexico?

3. Compare the reaction of the Micmacs to the French with the Pueblo response to the Spanish.

4. How did Father Serra regard the native peoples of southern California? Where did they fit into his plans to construct a string of missions in California?

5. How does William Wassell portray the religion of the Sioux? Do most of the European accounts depict native peoples as pagans? If so what do they base their opinions on?

Document 2.1

A Zuñi Creation Legend

The Zuñis are Indian people whose traditional homeland was, and still is, in northwestern New Mexico and northeastern Arizona. For centuries, they have lived as settled, village farmers, raising their crops in an arid environment using sophisticated irrigation techniques. Like the Creeks, and most other peoples of the world, the Zuñis had their own version of the creation of the world.*

Before the beginning of the new-making, Awonawilona (the Maker and Container of All, the All-father Father), solely had being. There was nothing else whatsoever throughout the great space of the ages save everywhere black darkness in it, and everywhere void desolation.

In the beginning of the new-made, Awonawilona conceived within himself and thought outward in space, whereby mists of increase, steams potent of growth; were evolved and uplifted. Thus, by means of his innate knowledge, the All-container made himself in person and form of the Sun whom we hold to be our father and who thus came to exist and appear. With his appearance came the brightening of the spaces with light and with the brightening of the spaces the great mist-clouds were thickened together and fell, whereby was evolved water in water; yea, and the world-holding sea.

With his substance of flesh outdrawn from the surface of his person, the Sun-father formed the seed-stuff of twain worlds, impregnating therewith the great waters, and lo! In the heat of his light these waters of the sea grew green and scums rose upon them, waxing wide and weighty until, behold! They became Awitelin Tsita, the "Four-fold Containing Mother-earth," and Apoyan Tä'chu, the "All-covering Father-sky."

From the lying together of these twain upon the great world-waters, so vitalizing, terrestrial life was conceived; whence began all beings of earth, men and the creatures, in the Fourfold womb of the World.

Thereupon the Earth-mother repulsed the Sky-father, growing big and sinking deep into the embrace of the waters below, thus separating from the Sky-father in the embrace of the waters above. As a woman forebodes evil for her first-born ere born, even so did the Earth-mother forebode, long withholding from birth her myriad progeny and meantime seeking counsel with the Sky-father. "How," said they to one another, "shall our children when brought forth, know one place from another, even by the white light of the Sun-father?"

Now like all the surpassing beings the Earth-mother and the Sky-father were changeable, even as smoke in the wind; transmutable at thought, manifesting themselves in any form at will, like as dancers may be mask-making.

---

* *Thirteenth Annual Report of the Bureau of Ethnology* (Washington, D.C.: U.S. Government Printing Office, 1891), p. 379.

Thus, as a man and woman, spake they, one to the other. "Behold!" said the Earth-mother as a great terraced bowl appeared at hand and within it water, "this is as upon me the homes of my tiny children shall be. On the rim of each world-country they wander in, terraced mountains shall stand, making in one region many, whereby country shall be known from country, and within each, place from place. "Behold, again!" said she as she spat on the water and rapidly smote and stirred it with her fingers. Foam formed, gathering about the terraced rim, mounting higher and higher. "Yea," said she, "and from my bosom they shall draw nourishment, for in such as this shall they find the substance of life whence we were ourselves sustained, for see!" Then with her warm breath she blew across the terraces; white flecks of the foam broke away, and, floating over above the water, were shattered by the cold breath of the Sky-father attending, and forthwith shed downward abundantly fine mist and spray! "Even so, shall white clouds float up from the great waters at the borders of the world, and clustering about the mountain terraces of the horizons be borne aloft and abroad by the breaths of the surpassing of soul-beings, and of the children, and shall hardened and broken be by thy cold, shedding downward, in rain-spray, the water of life, even into the hollow places of my lap! For therein chiefly shall nestle our children mankind and creature-kind, for warmth in thy coldness."

Lo! Even the trees on high mountains near the clouds and the Sky-father crouch low toward the Earth-mother for warmth and protection! Warm is the Earth-mother, cold the Sky-father, even as woman is the warm, man the cold being!

"Even so!" said the Sky-father; "Yet not alone shalt thou helpful be unto our children, for behold!" and he spread his hand abroad with the palm downward and into all the wrinkles and crevices thereof he set the semblance of shining yellow corn-grains; in the dark of the early world-dawn they gleamed like sparks of fire, and moved as his hand was moved over the bowl, shining up from and also moving in the depths of the water therein. "See!" said he, pointing to the seven grains clasped by his thumb and four fingers, "by such shall our children be guided; for behold, when the Sun-father is not nigh, and thy terraces are as the dark itself (being all hidden therein), then shall our children be guided by lights-like to these lights of all the six regions turning round the midmost one-as in and around the midmost place, where these our children shall abide, lie all the other regions of space! Yea! And even as these grains gleam up from the water, so shall seed-grains like to them, yet numberless, spring up from thy bosom when touched by my waters, to nourish our children." Thus and in other ways many devised they for their offspring.

Document 2.2

Alvar Núñez Cabeza de Vaca: "Indians of the Rio Grande" (1528)

In 1528, the expedition of Spanish explorer Panfilo de Navarez was stranded on the Gulf Coast of Florida. Despairing of ever being rescued, they assembled several makeshift boats and headed out into the Gulf of Mexico, but ocean currents carried them to the northwest, not south or southwest, and they shipwrecked on the upper Gulf Coast. Coastal Indians enslaved the crew. In 1534, however, several members of the expedition escaped, including Alvar Núñez Cabeza de Vaca and Estevancio, an African slave. During the next two years, they crossed Texas and eventually made their way all the way south to Mexico City. Cabeza de Vaca later published an account of his journey. An excerpt from his journal follows.*

They are so accustomed to running that, without resting or getting tired, they run from morning till night in pursuit of a deer, and kill a great many, because they follow until the game is worn out, sometimes catching it alive. Their huts are of matting placed over four arches. They carry them on their back and move every two or three days in quest of food; they plant nothing that would be of any use.

They are very merry people, and even when famished do not cease to dance and celebrate their feasts and ceremonials. Their best times are when "tunas" (prickly pears) are ripe, because then they have plenty to eat and spend the time in dancing and eating day and night. As long as these tunas last they squeeze and open them and set them to dry. When dried they are put in baskets like figs and kept to be eaten on the way. The peelings they grind and pulverize.

All over this country there are a great many deer, fowl and other animals which I have before enumerated. Here also they come up with cows: I have seen them thrice and have eaten their meat. They appear to me of the size of those in Spain. Their horns are small, like those of the Moorish cattle; the hair is very long, like fine wool and like a peajacket; some are brownish and others black, and to my taste they have better and more meat than those from here. Of the small hides the Indians make blankets to cover themselves with, and of the taller ones they make shoes and targets. These cows come from the north, across the country further on, to the coast of Florida, and are found all over the land for over four hundred leagues. On this whole stretch, through the valleys by which they come, people who live there descend to subsist upon their flesh. And a great quantity of hides are met with inland.

We remained with the Avavares Indians for eight months, according to our reckoning of the moons. During that time they came for us from many places and said that verily we were children of the sun. Until then Donates and the negro had not made any cures, but we found ourselves so pressed by the Indians coming from all sides, that all of us had to become medicine men. I was the most daring and reckless of all in undertaking cures. We never treated anyone that did not afterwards say he was well, and they had such confidence in our skill as to believe that none of them would die as long as we were among them...

The women brought many mats, with which they built us houses, one for each of us and those attached to him. After this we would order them to boil all the game, and they did it quickly in ovens built by them for the purpose. We partook of everything a little,

---

* A. F. Bandelier, ed., *His Own Narrative: The Journal of Alvar Núñez Cabeza de Vaca and His Companions from Florida to the Pacific, 1528-1536* (New York: A. S. Barnes & Company, 1905), 91-94.

giving the rest to the principal man among those who had come with us for distribution among all. Every one then came with the share he had received for us to breathe on it and bless it, without which they left it untouched. Often we had with us three to four thousand persons. And it was very tiresome to have to breathe on and make the sign of the cross over every morsel they ate or drank. For many other things which they wanted to do they would come to ask our permission, so that it is easy to realize how greatly we were bothered. The women brought us tunas, spiders, worms, and whatever else they could find, for they would rather starve than partake of anything that had not first passed through our hands.

While traveling with those, we crossed a big river coming from the north and, traversing about thirty leagues of plains, met a number of people that came from afar to meet us on the trail, who treated us like the foregoing ones.

Thence on there was a change in the manner of reception, insofar as those who would meet us on the trail with gifts were no longer robbed by the Indians of our company, but after we had entered their homes they tendered us all they possessed, and the dwellings also. We turned over everything to the principals for distribution. Invariably those who had been deprived of their belongings would follow us, in order to repair their losses, so that our retinue became very large. They would tell them to be careful and not conceal anything of what they owned, as it could not be done without our knowledge, and then we would cause their death. So much did they frighten them that on the first few days after joining us they would be trembling all the time, and would not dare to speak or lift their eyes to Heaven.

Those guided us for more than fifty leagues through a desert of very rugged mountains, and so arid that there was no game. Consequently we suffered much from lack of food, and finally forded a very big river, with its water reaching to our chest. Thence on many of our people began to show the effects of the hunger and hardships they had undergone in those mountains, which were extremely barren and tiresome to travel.

The next morning all those who were strong enough came along, and at the end of three journeys we halted. Alonso del Castillo and Estevanico, the negro, left with the women as guides, and the woman who was a captive took them to a river that flows between mountains where there was a village in which her father lived, and these were the first adobes we saw that were like unto real houses. Castillo and Estevanico went to these and, after holding parley with the Indians, at the end of three days Castillo returned to where he had left us, bringing with him five or six of the Indians. He told how he had found permanent houses, inhabited, the people of which ate beans and squashes, and that he had also seen maize.

Of all things upon earth, that caused us the greatest pleasure, and we gave endless thanks to our Lord for this news. Castillo also said that the negro was coming to meet us on the way, near by, with all the people of the houses. For that reason we started, and after going a league and a half met the negro and the people that came to receive us, who gave us beans and many squashes to eat, gourds to carry water in, robes of cowhide, and other things. As those people and the Indians of our company were enemies, and did not understand each other, we took leave of the latter, leaving them all that had been given to us, while we went on with the former and, six leagues beyond, when night was already approaching, reached their houses, where they received us with great ceremonies. Here we remained one day, and left on the next, taking them with us to other permanent houses, where they subsisted on the same food also, and thence on we found a new custom...

Having seen positive traces of Christians and become satisfied they were very near, we gave many thanks to our Lord for redeeming us from our sad and gloomy condition. Anyone can imagine our delight when he reflects how long we had been in that land, and how many dangers and hardships we had suffered. That night I entreated one of my companions to go after the Christians, who were moving through the part of the country pacified and quieted by us, and who were three days ahead of where we were. They did not like my suggestion, and excused themselves from going, on the ground of being tired and worn out, although any of them might have done it far better than I, being younger and stronger.

Seeing their reluctance, in the morning I took with me the negro and eleven Indians and, following the trail, went in search of the Christians. On that day we made ten leagues, passing three places where they slept. The next morning I came upon four Christians on horseback, who, seeing me in such a strange attire, and in company with Indians, were greatly startled. They stared at me for quite awhile, speechless; so great was their surprise that they could not find words to ask me anything. I spoke first, and told them to lead me to their captain, and we went together to Diego de Alcaraz, their commander.

Document 2.3

The Micmacs Describe the French Empire

Of course, it was not just the Europeans who found Native American society strange; the Indians themselves often looked upon European society with bewilderment. European food, clothing, housing, and religion contrasted sharply with the values and institutions of most Indian tribes. Around 1677, Chrestien LaClerq, a Roman Catholic missionary laboring among the Micmacs of eastern Canada, recorded the following reaction of an Indian leader to the arrival and influence of French institutions.*

I am greatly astonished that the French have so little cleverness, as they seem to exhibit in the matter of which thou hast just told me on their behalf, in the effort to persuade us to convert our poles, our barks, and our wigwams into those houses of stone and of wood which are tall and lofty, according to then account, as these trees. Do men of

* William G. Ganong, trans. and ed., *New Relation of Gaspesia, with the Customs and Religion of the Gaspesian Indians* (Toronto: Champlain Society, 1910), pp. 104-06.

five to six feet in height need houses which are sixty to eighty? Thou art not as bold nor as stout as we, because when thou goest on a voyage thou canst not carry upon they shoulders thy buildings and thy edifices. Therefore it is necessary that thou preparest as many lodgings as thou makest changes of residence, or else thou lodgest in a hired house which does not belong to thee. As for us, we find ourselves secure from all these inconveniences, and we can always say, more truly than thou, that we are at home everywhere, because we set up our wigwams with ease wheresoever we go, and without asking permission of anybody. Thou reproachest us, very inappropriately, that our country is a little hell in contrast with France, which thou comparest to a terrestrial paradise, inasmuch as it yields thee, so thou sayest, every kind of provision in abundance. Thou sayest of us also that we are the most miserable and most unhappy of all men, living without religion, without manners, without honour, without social order, and, in a word, without any rules, like the beasts in our woods and our forests, lacking bread, wine, and a thousand other comforts which thou hast in superfluity in Europe. Well, my brother, if thou dost not yet know the real feelings which our Indians have towards thy country and towards all thy nation, it is proper that I inform thee at once. I beg thee now to believe that, all miserable as we seem in thine eyes, we consider ourselves nevertheless much happier than thou in this, that we are very content with the little that we have; and believe also once for all, I pray, that thou deceivest thyself greatly if thou thinkest to persuade us that thy country is better than ours. For if France, as thou sayest, is a little terrestrial paradise, art thou sensible to leave it? And why abandon wives, children, relatives, and friends? Why risk thy life and thy property every year, and why venture thyself with such risk, in any season whatsoever, to the storms and tempests of the sea in order to come to a strange and barbarous country which thou considerest the poorest and least fortunate of the world? Besides, since we are wholly convinced of the contrary, we scarcely take the trouble to go to France, because we fear, with good reason, lest we find little satisfaction there, seeing, in our own experience, that those who are natives thereof leave it every year in order to enrich themselves on our shores. We believe, further, that you are also incomparably poorer than we, and that you are only simple journeymen, valets, servants, and slaves, all masters and grand captains though you may appear, seeing that you glory in our old rags and in our miserable suits of beaver which can no longer be of use to us, and that you find among us, in the fishery for cod which you make in these parts, the wherewithal to comfort your misery and the poverty which oppresses you. As to us, we find all our riches and all our conveniences among ourselves, without trouble and without exposing our lives to the dangers in which you find yourselves constantly through your long voyages. And, whilst feeling compassion for you in the sweetness of our repose, we wonder at the anxieties and cares which you give yourselves night and day in order to load your ship. We see also that all your people live, as a rule, only upon cod which you catch among us. It is everlastingly nothing but cod-cod in the morning, cod at midday, cod at evening, and always cod, until things come to such a pass that if you wish some good morsels, it is at our expense; and you are obliged to have recourse to the Indians, whom you despise so much, and to beg them to go a-hunting that you may be regaled. Now tell me this one little thing, if thou hast any sense: Which of these two is the wisest and happiest-he who labours without ceasing and only obtains, and that with great trouble, enough to live on, or he who rests in comfort and finds all that he needs in the pleasure of hunting and fishing? And if we have not any longer among us any of those old men of a hundred and thirty to forty years, it is only because we are gradually adopting your manner of living, for experience is making it very plain that those of us live longest who, despising your bread, your wine, and your brandy, are content with their natural food of beaver, of moose, of waterfowl, and fish, in accord with the custom of our ancestors and of all the Gaspesian nation. Learn now, my brother, once for all, because I must open to thee my heart: there is no Indian who does not consider himself infinitely more happy and more powerful than the French.

Document 2.4

The Pueblo Revolt (1680)

When the Spaniards ventured north in the sixteenth century from what is today Mexico City into the so-called "borderlands," they hoped to convert the Indians into Christian farmers, establish Spain's claim to much of the New World, and exploit whatever deposits of gold and silver that were available. But in the deserts of the American Southwest, Spanish soldiers and missionary priests encountered a "troublesome" people not anxious to cast off their traditional lifestyle for a European model. The Pueblo peoples of northwestern New Mexico especially resented the heavy Spanish yoke. In 1680, under the leadership of the charismatic Popé they rose up in a bloody rebellion and drove out the Spaniards. It was, however, only a shortlived victory. A few years later, the Spaniards returned in force and reestablished their military control of northern New Mexico.*

The pueblo communities were now to rid themselves for a time of their Spanish masters, whom they regarded as tyrants. Past efforts to shake off their fetters had only shown how tightly they were riveted. They were required to render implicit obedience, and to pay heavy tribute of pueblo products and personal service. Their complaints, however, in this direction are not definitely known. The Spaniards in their later gathering of testimony ignored this element of secular oppression, if, as can hardly be doubted, it existed, and represented the revolt to be founded exclusively, as it was indeed largely, on religious grounds. The New Mexicans seem to have been more strongly attached than most American tribes to their aboriginal faith, and they had secretly continued so far as possible the practice of the old forms of worship. The friars had worked zealously to stamp out every vestige of the native rites; and the authorities had enforced the strictest compliance with Christian regulations, not hesitating to punish the slightest neglect, unbelief, relapse into paganism, so-called witchcraft, or chafing under missionary rule,

---

* Hubert Howe Bancroft, *The Works of Hubert Howe Bancroft. Vol. 17: History of Arizona and New Mexico, 1530-1888* (San Francisco: The History Company, Publishers, 1889), pp. 174-82.

with flogging, imprisonment, slavery, or even death. During the past thirty years large numbers of natives had been hanged for alleged forcery, or communion with the devil, though generally accused also of projected rebellion or plotting with the Apaches. The influence of the native old men, or priests—sorcerers, the Spaniards called them—was still potent; the very superiority of the pueblo organization gave the patriotic conspirators an advantage; past failures had taught caution; and so skillfully was the movement managed that the premature outbreak a few days before the time agreed upon was hardly less successful and deadly than would have been the revolt as planned.

Popé, connected with a former disturbance and accused of many crimes, was the moving spirit now. He was a San Juan Indian, but made Taos the centre of his efforts. Appealing to the popular superstition as well as patriotism, he claimed to have formed an alliance with the Great Spirit, or El Demonio of the Spaniards; and personally or through his agents and associates—chief among whom were Catiti of Santo Domingo, Tupatú of Picurí, and Jaca of Taos—Popé brought into his scheme all the pueblos except those of the Piros in the south, who for some unexplained reason were not invited. The Tanos and the Queres of Ciénega are doubtfully said to have shown some reluctance. A knotted cord was the mysterious calendar sent by swift runners to all the pueblos to make known the date of rising, which seems to have been fixed for the 13th of August, 1680.

Despite the utmost precautions, however—no woman being intrusted with the secret, and Popé killing his own son-in-law on suspicion of treachery—the influence of the friars over certain converts was so strong that the plot was revealed, perhaps as early as the 9th, from several different sources.

The Tanos of San Lázaro and San Cristóbal revealed Popé's plot to Padre Bernal, the custodio. Padre Velasco of Pecos received a like confession from one of his neophytes. The alcalde of Taos sent a warning which caused the governor to arrest two Tesuque Indians who had been sent by the Tehuas to consult with the Tanos and Queres. Otermin sent messengers in all haste to warn padres and settlers south of San Felipe to flee to Isleta, while those of the north were to start for the capital or Santa Cruz de la Cañada. Pope saw that his only hope of success was in immediate action, and by his orders the Taos, Picuríes, and Tehuas attacked the missions and farms of the northern pueblos before dawn on the 10th, "llevandolo todo á sangre y fuego." Apparently hostilities had been committed at Santa Clara a day or two earlier, and some of the more distant pueblo rose a day or two later, as soon as they heard of the premature outbreak. I follow Escalante's version for what is not found in Otermin's journal; but little reliance can be put in the accuracy of details. All agree that the outbreak was on the 10th, day of San Lorenzo, and that it was premature. On that day Alférez Lucero and a soldier arrived at Santa Fé, with news of the rising of the Tehuas, reporting that the alcalde mayor had collected the people at La Cañada, and that the rebels were in force at Santa Clara. Captain Francisco Gomez was sent out to reconoitre, and returned on the 12th with confirmation and a few details of the disaster. The governor on the 13th ordered the alcalde and sargento mayor, Luis Quintana, to bring in the people from La Cañada to Santa Fé, which was probably accomplished. He sent out native scouts, despatched an order to Lieutenant-general Alonso García to send aid from Isleta and prepared to defend the capital.

It was the plan of the New Mexicans to utterly exterminate the Spaniards; and in the massacre none was spared—neither soldier, priest, or settler, personal friend or foe, young or old, man or woman—except that a few beautiful women and girls were kept as captives. From San Felipe south all were warned in time to make their escape. Many settlers of the valley farther north took refuge at La Cañada and were saved; but in all the missions of the north and east and west only the friar at Cochitá, those at Santa Fé, and one in the Zuñi province—who was perhaps absent—escaped death. The number of victims was slightly over 400, including 21 missionaries and 73 men capable of bearing arms; those who escaped were about 1,950, including 11 missionaries and 155 capable of bearing arms. It will be noticed that the friars with few exceptions were new-comers, and that the whole number in the province was less than might have been expected from preceding annals.

On August 14th the scouts returned and reported that 500 Indians from Pecos and the eastern pueblos were approaching; and next morning the foe appeared in San Miguel in the suburbs of the villa. One of the number was induced to enter the town and hold a conference; but he said that nothing could change the determination of his countrymen, who had brought two crosses, one red, as a token of war, the other white, indicating peace; but if the Spaniards should choose the white flag they must immediately quit the country. They said they had killed God and Santa Maria, and the king must yield. The governor sent out a force to attack the enemy before reënforcements could arrive, and soon went out in person. The battle lasted nearly all day, but when the Spaniards seemed on the point of victory, the northern army of Taos, Picuríes, and Tehuas appeared on the field, and Otermin was obliged to retire with his men to protect the palacio, where women and children had taken refuge. The siege of Santa Fé lasted five days. The natives were about 3,000 strong. They soon took and destroyed the suburbs, and indeed all but the plaza and *casas reales.* The church and convent were burned, and the water supply was cut off. Out of a population of 1,000, Otermin had less than 150 men, many of them servants utterly unfit for military service; but the situation was critical, and finally on the 20th with 100 men he made a desperate sortie. Invoking "the sweet name of María," this forlorn hope threw itself against the besiegers and drove them back, killing 300 and bringing 47 captives into the villa, who, after their testimony had been taken, were shot in the plaza. During the whole siege and battles only five Spaniards were killed, though the governor and many others were wounded.

It was decided on the 21st to abandon Santa Fé, or, as the original record puts it, to march to the relief of Isleta; clothing to the value of $8,000 was distributed; and the governor, garrison, women and and children, and three friars—Cadena, Duran, and Farfan—about 1,000 persons in all, began their march on foot, each carrying his own luggage, as the horses were barely sufficient for the sick and wounded. The natives, though watching the fugitives from the hills and sometimes being seen at a distance, made no attack. Perhaps they had not yet the courage to face the desperate valor of Otermin's little band, or they waited for the hardships of the march to render their deadly task less difficult; but it is more likely that they were content to avoid further bloodshed, now that their chief object had been effected in the invaders' retreat.

The route was by Santo Domingo, where were found the bodies of three padres and five other Spaniards who had been murdered, and thence to San Felipe and Sandía, whose Spanish inhabitants had escaped, though all these pueblos had been sacked and partially ruined, all vestiges of Christianity having been destroyed. Several haciendas on the way were found in ruins, with evidence that the occupants had been killed. Isleta was reached on the 27th; but the refugees under Captain García had left this pueblo thirteen days before and gone south to Fra Cristóbal. At Alamillo, in the region of Socorro, the governor met García, who had been overtaken by his messengers and returned. Legal proceedings were begun against him for having left Isleta without orders; out he claimed to have acted from necessity, having neither force nor supplies, and believing that all in the north were dead. Here also, on September 6th, was met Pedro de Leiva with thirty men, part of the escort of Padre Ayeta's supply train, sent up from El Paso by the procurador to aid the fugitives. All went south to Fra Cristóbal, where on the 16th a council determined that under the circumstances it was impracticable to return to Santa Fé; and before the end of September the whole force was encamped in the region of El Paso del Norte, where for twenty years or more the Franciscans had had a mission of Guadalupe.

Document 2.5

Creek Origins

Native American groups enjoyed a wide variety of creation theologies. In fact, there were almost as many creation stories among them as there were tribes. When Europeans arrived in the New World, and then as they migrated across the continent, they tried to convert Indians to their own creation story. Some tribes acquiesced easily, others resisted fiercely, and many took European beliefs, mixed them with their own religions, and developed new, syncretic faiths. In 1735, Chief Chekilli of the Creek Indians shared the following Creek version of the creation of the world.*

At a certain time the Earth opened in the West, where its mouth is. The Earth opened and the Kasihtas came out of its mouth, and settled nearby. But the Earth became angry and ate up their children; therefore they moved farther West. A part of them, however, turned back, and came again to the same place where they had been, and settled there. The greater number remained behind, because they thought it best to do so. Their children, nevertheless, were eaten by the Earth, so that, full of dissatisfaction, they journeyed toward the sunrise.

They came to a thick, muddy, slimy river-came there, camped there, rested there, and stayed overnight there. The next day they continued their journey and came, in one day, to a red, bloody river. They lived by this river, and ate of its fishes for two years; but there were low springs there; and it did not please them to remain. They went toward the

* Albert S. Gatschet, *A Migration Legend of the Creek Indians* (Philadelphia: D. G. Brinton, 1884), Vol. 1, pp. 244-51.

end of this bloody river, and heard a noise as of thunder. They approached to see whence the noise came. At first they perceived a red smoke, and then a mountain which thundered; and on the mountain was a sound as of singing. They sent to see what this was; and it was a great fire which blazed upward, and made this singing noise. This mountain they named the King of Mountains. It thunders to this day; and men are very much afraid of it.

They here met a people of three different Nations. They had taken and saved some of the fire from the mountain; and, at this place, they also obtained a knowledge of herbs and of other things.

From the East, a white fire came to them; which, however, they would not use. From the South came a fire which was [blue?]; neither did they use it. From the West, came a fire which was black; nor would they use it. At last, came a fire from the North, which was red and yellow. This they mingled with the fire they had taken from the mountain; and this is the fire they use today; and this, too, sometimes sings. On the mountain was a pole which was very restless and made a noise, nor could any one say how it could be quieted. At length they took a motherless child, and struck it against the pole; and thus killed the child. They then took the pole, and carry it with them when they go to war. It was like a wooden tomahawk, such as they now use, and of the same wood.

Here they also found four herbs or roots, which sang and disclosed their virtues: first, Pasaw, the rattlesnake root; second Micoweanochaw, red-root; third Sowatchko, which grows like wild fennel; and fourth, Eschalapootchke, little tobacco. These herbs, especially the first and third, they use as the best medicine to purify themselves at their Busk. At this Busk, which is held yearly, they fast, and make offerings of the first fruits. Since they have learned the virtues of these herbs, their women, at certain times, have a separate fire, and remain apart from the men five, six, and seven days, for the sake of purification. If they neglected this, the power of the herbs would depart; and the women would not be healthy.

About this time a dispute arose, as to which was the oldest, and which should rule; and they agreed, as they were four Nations, they would set up four poles, and make them red with clay which is yellow at first, but becomes red by burning. They would go to war; and whichever Nation should first cover its pole, from top to bottom, with the scalps of their enemies, should be oldest.

They all tried, but the Kasihtas covered their pole first, and so thickly that it was hidden from sight. Therefore, they were looked upon, by the whole Nation, as the oldest. The Chickasaws covered their pole next; then the Alabamas; but the Abihkas did not cover their pole higher than to the knee.

At that time there was a bird of large size, blue in color, with a long tail, and swifter than an eagle, which came every day and killed and ate their people. They made an image in the shape of a woman, and placed it in the way of this bird. The bird carried it off, and kept it a long time, and then brought it back. They left it alone, hoping it would bring something forth. After a long time, a red rat came forth from it, and they believed the bird was the father of the rat. They took council with the rat how to destroy its father. Now the bird had a bow and arrows; and the rat gnawed the bowstring, so that the bird could not defend itself, and the people killed it. They called this bird the King of Birds. They think the eagle is a great King; and they carry its feathers when they go to War or make Peace; the red mean War; the white, Peace. If an enemy approaches with white feathers and a white mouth, and cries like an eagle, they dare not kill him.

After this they left that place, and came to a white footpath. The grass and everything around were white; and they plainly perceived that people had been there. They crossed the path, and slept near there. Afterward they turned back to see what sort of path that was, and who the people were who had been there, in the belief that it might be better for them to follow that path. They went along it to a creek called Coloose-hutche, that is, Coloose-creek, because it was rocky there and smoked.

They crossed it, going toward the sunrise, and came to a people and a town named Coosa. Here they remained four years. The Coosas complained that they were preyed upon by a wild beast, which they called man-eater or lion, which lived in a rock.

The Kasihtas said they would try to kill the beast. They dug a pit and stretched over it a net made of hickory-bark. They then laid a number of branches, crosswise, so that the lion could not follow them, and, going to the place where he lay, they threw a rattle into his den. The lion rushed forth in great anger, and pursued them through the branches. Then they thought it better that one should die rather than all; so they took a motherless child, and threw it before the lion as he came near the pit. The lion rushed at it, and fell in the pit, over which they threw the net, and killed him with blazing pine-wood. His bones, however, they keep to this day; on one side, they are red, on the other blue.

The lion used to come every seventh day to kill the people; therefore, they remained there seven days after they had killed him. In remembrance of him, when they prepare for War, they fast six days and start on the seventh. If they take his bones with them, they have good fortune.

After four years they left the Coosas, and came to a river which they called Nowphawpe, now Callasi-hutche. There they tarried two years; and, as they had no corn, they lived on roots and fishes, and made bows, pointing the arrows with beaver teeth and flint-stones, and for knives they used split canes.

They left this place, and came to a creek, called Wattoola-hawka-hutche, Whooping-creek, so called from the whooping of cranes, a great many being there; they slept there one night. They next came to a river, in which there was a waterfall; this they named the Owatunka-river. The next day they reached another river, which they called the Aphoosa pheeskaw.

The following day they crossed it, and came to a high mountain, where were people who, they believed, were the same who made the white path. They, therefore, made white arrows and shot at them, to see if they were good people. But the people took their white arrows, painted them red, and shot them back. When they showed these to their chief, he said that it was not a good sign; if the arrows returned had been white, they could have gone there and brought food for their children, but as they were red they must not go. Nevertheless, some of them went to see what sort of people they were; and found their houses deserted. They also saw a trail which led into the river; and, as they could not see the trail on the opposite bank, they believed that the people had gone into the river, and would not again come forth.

At that place is a mountain, called Moterelo, which makes a noise like beating on a drum; and they think this people live there. They hear this noise on all sides when they go to war.

They went along the river, till they came to a waterfall, where they saw great rocks, and on the rocks were bows lying; and they believed the people who made the white path had been there.

They always have, on their journeys, two scouts who go before the main body. These scouts ascended a high mountain and saw a town. They shot white arrows into the town; but the people of the town shot back red arrows. Then the Kasihtas became angry, and determined to attack the town, and each one have a house when it was captured.

They threw stones into the river until they could cross it, and took the town (the people had flattened heads) and killed all but two persons. In pursuing these they found a white dog, which they slew. They followed the two who escaped, until they came again to the white path, and saw the smoke of a town, and thought that this must be the people they had so long been seeking. This is the place where now the tribe of Apalachicolas live, from whom Tomochichi is descended.

The Kasihtas continued bloody-minded; but the Apalachicolas gave them black drink, as a sign of friendship, and said to them: "Our hearts are white, and yours must be white, and you must lay down the bloody tomahawk, and show your bodies as a proof that they shall be white." Nevertheless, they were for the tomahawk; but the Apalachicolas got it by persuasion, and buried it under their beds. The Apalachicolas likewise gave them white feathers, and asked to have a chief in common. Since then they have always lived together.

Some settled on one side of the river, some on the other. Those on one side are called Kasihtas, those on the other, Cowetas; yet they are one people, and the principal towns of the Upper and Lower Creeks.

Document 2.6

Father Serra Reports on Mission Labor (1772)

In 1749 the Roman Catholic missionary, Father Junipero Serra (1713-1784), gave up a promising future at home to seek martyrdom among the Indians of the New World, first in Mexico than in California. Serra personally founded nine out of the twenty missions that would dot the El Camino Real, or King's Highway every thirty miles. The following passage is an extract from a biography of Serra written by his friend Father Francisco Palou. This portrait of the mission system hints at a darker side of the Franciscan order, which relied on California's Native American population for both supplies and back-breaking labor.*

---

* *Francisco Palou's Life and Apostolic Labors of the Venerable Father Junipero Serra,* (Pasadena, CA.: George Wharton James, 1913), 133-135.

The principal sources of supply for our people have been the pagans. Through their kindness we are alive, because God willed it so. To be sure the milk from the cows and the few vegetables from the garden have been two great sources of sustenance for these establishments, but both of these are daily becoming scantier. Not for that account do I feel any concern, nor should your Reverence grieve that these Missions have been founded as it is in no way a cause for grief to any one of those who have come to occupy these Missions. The discomfort is found only in the fact that the lack of workers among us makes it impossible to proceed with the founding of the new Missions. The Fathers of San Luis have at last been relieved of the tension of fourteen long months of waiting by the news of the abundant provisions which the vessels have brought, and the Mission will soon be founded. All the necessary things for it are already at hand.

If for the foundation of the Mission here we may have to wait for such a time as supplies can be sent up from below, and if the progress has to depend upon the coming of a ship, many years may pass without anything being done, on account of the difficulties of reaching these remote regions with the necessary succor, in view of the difficulties which your Reverence feels and understands even better than myself. All the Missionaries are groaning and we all deplore the vexations, the hardships and the delays which we have to endure, but no one desires or thinks of leaving his Mission. The fact is that, hardship or no hardship, there are many souls saved in heaven, and souls converted in Monterey, in San Antonio and San Diego and perhaps in San Gabriel, though I have not heard of any yet. There is quite a considerable number of Christians who praise God, and His Holy Name is in the mouth of these same gentiles more frequently than in that of many Christians. And although some have declared that these apparently gentle lambs will some day all of them turn into tigers and lions, indeed it might be so if God would permit it, but speaking of those of Monterey, we have now had experience of them for three years and with those of San Antonio, two years, and we can say that every day they grow better.

And above all, the promise which God made in these last days to our Father San Francisco (as the Seraphic Mother Mary of Jesus says), that the pagans have only to look upon his sons in order to be converted to our Holy Catholic Faith is something which I have seen and felt in my own experience for if, indeed, there are any here that are not Christians it is in my judgment simply because of our ignorance of the language. This learning of a new language is not new to me, but I imagine I have very little grace for it, on account of my sins, and in lands such as these where it is not possible to secure an interpreter nor a teacher, humanly speaking, until some one of these people can learn to use the Castilian, necessarily some time must be allowed to pass before one can accomplish much.

This difficulty has already been overcome in San Diego and adults are being baptized and marriages celebrated; and here we are preparing to do the same thing because the young men are beginning to make explanations of things in the Castilian. As to the rest, if some help comes now, it will not be long before it will matter very little to us whether the vessels come or not as far as provisions are concerned, but as things are now, the Missions can make little headway. But withal I trust in God that all is to be remedied.

But now we come to the matter of principal importance. I am going to San Diego with Commander Don Pedro Fages, and if it should happen that your Reverence should undertake to explore the stretch of country lying between San Fernando Vellicat and that port in order to distribute in it the five new Missions, and it might be that you are doing that thing now, the occasion might arise in which we could personally embrace each other in the middle or toward the end of September, and so our mutual communication would take the place of many letters, and we could discuss at our leisure how best to carry on this great work which, without deserving it, the God, our Lord, has put into our hands. The great comfort which such a meeting with you would bring to me I leave to the imagination of your Reverence, but please do not come just for my sake, but only in case you think it wise for the greatest good of all. We could make our plans to return each one to his own field before the rainy season, and it seems to me there would be time for it all. But above all, I do ask most earnestly that, either with your Reverence or else by themselves, two more friars be allowed to come at this time, in order to secure the founding of San Buenaventura or to take the place of the Missionaries at San Gabriel who, on account of sickness, had to leave. If these two were to come to take the place of the two sick ones who have gone I will understand that I am not to ask for any more help, except it be from the College itself. Try to see to it that those who are to come are well provided with patience and charity and in that case they will have a joyous time and will here become very rich,-I say, rich in hardships; but then, whither goes the ox that does not plow? And if he does not plow, how can there be harvest?

During my absence Father Pieras, with one of the Fathers from San Luis [Obispo], will take charge of the administration of this Mission and another one will go to San Antonio, where Father Fr. Buenaventura Sitjar has been left alone, in order that he may be so much nearer the place in which he is to begin his Mission. The Mission of San Antonio which, on San Buenaventura's day, celebrated its first anniversary, has been suffering the lack of the necessities of life and has had recourse entirely to the grains harvested by the pagans and to the native cornmeal. This Mission owes the good Father Pieras the charity of more than four mule-loads of provision of this sort as on his last visit to me he brought me three. From Father Fr. Juan [Crespi] I send you no word because from his letters you will know all about his trip; in short, I will not write further; if we see each other, we can talk it all over (with the favor of God); and if not, I hope I can write again more at length.

Document 2.7

The Religion of the Sioux

During the sixteenth, seventeenth, eighteenth, and nineteenth centuries, powerful religious impulses drove European explorers, priests, and settlers throughout the world. To please their monarchs, they launched the imperial adventures of Spain, France, England, and Portugal, and to please their god, they brought a zealous Christianity with them. When they encountered indigenous peoples in the Americas, Africa, Asia, Australia, and the Pacific, Europeans often looked askance at the local religious beliefs. Usually, they found the indigenous religions to be inferior and "barbaric," which only increased European enthusiasm for converting native peoples. The following document describes the Sun Dance religion of the Sioux peoples of North America.*

To the Sioux of the past, religion was truly a mystery. From the simple growth of the blade of grass to the complex phenomena of the thunder-storm, all life, power, and strength were interpreted as the physical acts of unknown gods. The Great Spirit is a name given us by the interpreter, for the Sioux had no conception of a single spirit, however great, capable of ruling the universe. Lightning was the anger of a thunder god, an awful bird, whose structure varied from wings containing only six quills to wings with four joints each, according to the imagination of the medicine-man. The moving god, he whose aid it was most difficult to invoke, was too subtle to be likened to any known form, but he controlled the intellect, passions, and mental faculties, abstractions for which the Sioux has not even a name. The Hayoka was the contrary god, who sat naked, and fanned himself in the coldness of a Dakota blizzard, and huddled shivering over a fire in the heat of summer, who cried for joy and laughed in his sorrow. Rocks and bowlders were the hardest and strongest things; hence they belonged to the oldest gods-smaller rocks were fetiches. On the barren buttes of the Dakotas may be seen many a crumbling pile of stones erected in by-gone days to propitiate an unknown god. Many a forgotten chief has gone to the highest hill when his son was sick, and amidst fastings and incantations reared a mound of little stones in the hope that his loved one's life might be spared. And still another relic of the savage belief of the old Sioux is found on the bodies of the warriors themselves. Take almost any man who is thirty years old or more, and he can show you long scars on his back or breast, and dozens of smaller scars on his arms, all inflicted by himself in fulfilling his vows to the sun. The sun-dance was one of the great religious and political events of the Sioux life. Whole villages assembled and feasted, while the worshippers fasted and exhausted the strength they were to need so badly in the coming test of endurance. On the appointed day none but virgins were allowed to cut down and trim the tree that was to be used, while only chiefs and warriors of exceptional bravery were allowed to carry it to its place in the centre of the village. Here, with mysterious pipe-smokings and unintelligible incantations, the pole is planted, ropes of buffalo-hide having been fastened to its top, one rope for each worshipper. The men, already half dead from exhaustion, are then brought out and laid on the ground around the pole, always ready knives thrust through the muscles of their chests or backs, and in the holes thus made wooden skewers thrust, to which are fastened the loose ends of the ropes. Then round and round dance the worshippers, their eyes fixed on the blazing sun, while the jerk, jerk, jerk of the bleeding flesh beats a sickening time to the hi-yas of a Dakota song. Friends and relatives, men, women, and children, gash their arms and breasts to stimulate the dancers and keep up their courage. When the flesh is

* William H. Wassell, "The Religion of the Sioux," *Harper's New Monthly Magazine*, 89 (1894), pp. 945-46.

torn apart the dancer is released, his vow fulfilled, his bravery, his manhood, unquestioned... These and a thousand other monstrous customs were what the early missionary had to combat.

The Sioux hereafter, was a particularly happy idea, in the main in keeping with the advanced views of some of their white brothers of the present day. There were happy hunting-grounds, but there were no unhappy ones. When a Methodist minister, attending one of the Indian commissions in the 70's, painted a hell with colors of fire and brimstone, the only necessity for such a future abode was, as an old chief expressed it, for all the whites. Some Indians might lie, steal, or commit murder, but these were tangible offences receiving prompt punishment, and as such were violations of a social rather than a religious code. And, in fact, to kill a Crow Indian, steal his ponies, or lie to him and get him into trouble, were things that made the plenteous game, the clear waters, and the rich grass all the more abundant for the Sioux in the happy hunting-grounds. The medicine-man was not a priest, for their religion had no conception of such. He was self-appointed. Who could displace him or doubt his power! By some shrewdness he predicted a coming event, or by luck he performed an unheard-of act, and then his greatness was assured. Sitting-Bull, medicine-man rather than chief, once predicted rain in a season of drought. With mysterious pipe-smokings and vague incantations he prayed for rain, and sure enough it came. When the crops again needed water he was applied to, but he cautiously answered: "Too much rain will drown you. I can easily make it rain, but no one can make it stop."

3

Acquiring a Continental Empire

In pursuit of a continental empire, the United States acquired lands from other countries through a variety of treaties. The Treaty of Paris, signed in 1783, resulted in the acquisition of lands lying between the Appalachian Mountains and the Mississippi River. Like other land purchases made by the federal government, these new lands became part of the public domain, lands owned by the United States government. Under the terms of the 1783 treaty, 225 million acres of public lands came under control of the federal government.

Over the following years the government drafted policies for the administration and disposal of its lands, culminating in the development of a territorial system. According to the new system devised by Thomas Jefferson in the 1780s, when a sufficient population developed, territories would be established that would eventually become states northeast of the Ohio River.

The Land Ordinance of 1785 laid the foundations for the public land system that would survive almost intact until the passage of the Homestead Act in 1862. The ordinance established the system of land sale based on the rectilinear survey of one mile square sections. The new system would open the way for the sale of huge tracts of land at auction with the profits benefitting the desperately depleted United States Treasury. Following the passage of the Northwest Ordinance in 1787, which provided for the structure of government for the territories prior to statehood, the basic framework of the American territorial system was in place.

The encroachment of American settlement into the trans-Appalachian territories between 1790 and 1800 led indirectly to the purchase of the Louisiana territory in 1803. The prosperity of the Northwest Territory was closely linked to its access to the Mississippi River. Although the Mississippi River was still controlled by Spain, farmers in the region envisioned a time in the not too distant future when they could ship produce to markets on the East Coast and Europe via the Gulf of Mexico. Following the Spanish transferral of the region to France in 1800, President Thomas Jefferson directed negotiations that resulted in the purchase of the region for $15 million. The acquisition of this vast area initiated an expansionist psychology among the American people that found its greatest expression in the late 1840s culminating in the War with Mexico. In addition, the land purchase set a precedent for the new government under the Constitution to acquire land by purchase as well as ended the presence of powerful foreign adversaries on the western frontier.

American expansion in the early nineteenth century is indelibly linked with the life of Andrew Jackson, the first president born in the West. Jackson's land policies during his presidency would result in the opening up of new land for settlement, but this time at the expense of Indian peoples rather than foreign nations such as England and Spain. Following his first presidential address in 1829, in which he paid lip service to humanitarian interests, Jackson embarked on a campaign that led to the removal of Indians from the southeast to west of the Mississippi River in 1830. Clearing out the Indian occupants from several regions of the frontier, the Removal Act of 1830 added large tracts of lands to the public domain.

After the deaths of Davy Crockett and James Bowie and 185 comrades at the Alamo in March 1836, "Remember the Alamo" became the rallying cry for Texans as they drove the Mexican army across the border the following month. After its defeat in just eighteen minutes at the hands of the Texas army at the Battle of San Jacinto, Mexico ceased to challenge the legitimacy of Texan independence. In the process, Mexico lost a million square miles of territory and the Republic of Texas became a recognized nation until 1845 when it joined the Union.

Suggestions for Further Reading

Gibson, James R., *Imperial Russia in Frontier America: The Changing Geography of Supply of Russian America, 1784-1867* (New York: Oxford University Press, 1976).

Donald Jackson, *Thomas Jefferson and the Stony Mountains: Exploring the West from Monticello* (Urbana, Ill.: University of Illinois Press, 1981).

Roy M. Robbins, *Our Landed Heritage: The Public Domain, 1776-1970* (Lincoln: University of Nebraska Press, 2nd ed., 1976).

Malcolm J. Rohrbough, *The Land Office Business: The Settlement and Administration of American Public Lands, 1789-1837,* (New York: Oxford University Press, 1968)

Jack M. Sosin, *The Revolutionary Frontier, 1763-1783* (New York: Holt, Rinehart and Winston, 1967).

Critical Thinking

1. What were the provisions of the Louisiana Purchase?

2. Translate the poem "The Men of the Alamo" into historical prose. How does this poem jibe with the reality of this historical event?

3. Under what conditions was Texas allowed to join the Union?

4. What stipulations concerning Western lands were included in the Land Ordinance of 1785 and the Northwest Ordinance?

5. What was President Andrew Jackson's solution to the "Indian problem?"

Document 3.1

The Land Ordinance of 1785 (1785)

The Land Ordinance of 1785 was one of the most important laws in the history of westward expansion. It established the system of land sale based on a rectilinear survey which divided the land into 640 acre (one mile square) sections. According to the ordinance, the land would be sold at auction, with minimum prices fixed at one dollar per acre. Initially designed for the Northwest Territory, the plan's Jeffersonian passion for symmetry would prove unsuitable for the diverse physical landscape of the trans-Mississipi West.*

An Ordinance for ascertaining the mode of disposing of Lands in the Western Territory.

Be it ordained by the United States in Congress assembled, that the territory ceded by individual States to the United States, which has been purchased of the Indian inhabitants, shall be disposed of in the following manner:

A surveyor from each state shall be appointed by Congress or a Committee of the States, who shall take an oath for the faithful discharge of his duty, before the Geographer of the United States ...

The Surveyors, as they are respectively qualified, shall proceed to divide the said territory into townships of six miles square, by lines running due north and south, and others crossing these at right angles, as near as may be, unless where the boundaries of the late Indian purchases may render the same impracticable...

The first line, running due north and south as aforesaid, shall begin on the river Ohio, at a point that shall be found to be due north from the western termination of a line, which has been run as the southern boundary of the State of Pennsylvania; and the first line, running east and west, shall begin at the same point, and shall extend throughout the whole territory. Provided, that nothing herein shall be construed, as fixing the western boundary of the State of Pennsylvania. The geographer shall designate the townships, or fractional parts of townships, by numbers progressively from south to north; always beginning each range with No. 1; and the ranges shall be distinguished by their progressive numbers to the westward. The first range, extending from the Ohio to the lake Erie, being marked No. 1. The Geographer shall personally attend to the running of the first east and west line; and shall take the latitude of the extremes of the first north and south line, and of the mouths of the principal rivers.

The lines shall be measured with a chain; shall be plainly marked by chaps on the trees, and exactly described on a plat; whereon shall be noted by the surveyor, at their proper distances, all mines, salt-springs, salt-licks and mill-seats, that shall come to his

---

* *Journal of the Continental Congress*, ed. by J. C. Fitzpatrick, Vol. XXVIII, 375.

knowledge, and all water-courses, mountains and other remarkable and permanent things, over and near which such lines shall pass, and also the quality of the lands.

The plats of the townships respectively, shall be marked by subdivisions into lots of one mile square, or 640 acres, in the same direction as the external lines, and numbered from 1 to 36; always beginning the succeeding range of the lots with the number next to that with which the preceding one concluded…

…And the geographer shall make… returns, from time to time, of every seven ranges as they may be surveyed. The Secretary of War shall have recourse thereto, and shall take by lot therefrom, a number of townships… as will be equal to one seventh part of the whole of such seven ranges… for the use of the late Continental army…

The board of treasury shall transmit a copy of the original plats, previously noting thereon the townships and fractional parts of townships, which shall have fallen to the several states, by the distribution aforesaid, to the commissioners of the loan-office of the several states, who, after giving notice… shall proceed to sell the townships or fractional parts of townships, at public vendue, in the following manner, viz.: The township or fractional part of a township No. 1, in the first range, shall be sold entire; and No. 2, in the same range, by lots; and thus in alternate order through the whole of the first range… provided, that none of the lands, within the said territory, be sold under the price of one dollar the acre, to be paid in specie, or loan-office certificates, reduced to specie value, by the scale of depreciation, or certificates of liquidated debts of the United States, including interest, besides the expense of the survey and other charges thereon, which are hereby rated at thirty six dollars the township… on failure of which payment, the said lands shall again be offered for sale.

There shall be reserved for the United States out of every township the four lots, being numbered 8, 11, 26, 29, and out of every fractional part of a township, so many lots of the same numbers as shall be found thereon, for future sale. There shall be reserved the lot No. 16, of every township, for the maintenance of public schools within the said township; also one-third part of all gold, silver, lead and copper mines, to be sold, or otherwise disposed of as Congress shall hereafter direct…

And Whereas Congress… stipulated grants of land to certain officers and soldiers of the late Continental army… for complying with such engagements, Be it ordained, That the secretary of war… determine who are the objects of the above resolutions and engagements… and cause the townships, or fractional parts of townships, hereinbefore reserved for the use of the late Continental army, to be drawn for in such manner as he shall deem expedient…

Document 3.2

The Northwest Ordinance (1787)

With the signing of the Treaty of Paris in 1783, in which the United States acquired from Great Britain all the territory lying between the

Appalachian Mountains and the Mississippi River, the prospects of a western land rush became very real. At the time, there were thirteen states, but Congress was concerned about just how new regions would be incorporated into the Union. After considerable debate during the Articles of Confederation period, in 1787 Congress passed the Northwest Ordinance. The legislation provided the model for the process by which the next thirty-seven states became part of the United States.*

Article I.

No person, demeaning himself in a peaceable and orderly manner, shall ever be molested on account of his mode of worship, or religious sentiments, in the said territories.

Article II.

The inhabitants of the said territory shall always be entitled to the benefits of the writ of *habeas corpus,* and of the trial by jury; of a proportionate representation of the people in the legislature, and of judicial proceedings according to the course of common law. All persons shall be bailable, unless for capital offences, where the proof shall be evident, or the presumption great. All fines shall be moderate; and no cruel or unusual punishments shall be inflicted. No man shall be deprived of his liberty or property, but by the judgment of his peers, or the law of the land, and should the public exigencies make it necessary, for the common preservation, to take any person's property, or to demand his particular services, full compensation shall be made for the same. And, in the just preservation of rights and property, it is understood and declared, that no law ought ever to be made or have force in the said territory, that shall, in any manner whatever, interfere with or affect private contracts, or engagements, *bona fide,* and without fraud previously formed.

Article III.

Religion, morality, and knowledge being necessary to good government and the happiness of mankind, schools and the means of education shall forever be encouraged. The utmost good faith shall always be observed towards the Indians; their lands and property shall never be taken from them without their consent; and in their property, rights, and liberty they never shall be invaded or disturbed, unless in just and lawful wars authorized by Congress; but laws founded in justice and humanity shall, from time to time, be made, for preventing wrongs being done to them, and for preserving peace and friendship with them.

---

* William MacDonald, *Select Documents Illustrative of the History of the United States 1776-1861* (London: The Macmillan Company, 1920), pp. 22-29.

Article IV.

The said territory, and the States which may be formed therein, shall forever remain a part of this confederacy of the United States of America, subject to the Articles of Confederation, and to such alterations therein as shall be constitutionally made; and to all the acts and ordinances of the United States in Congress assembled, conformable thereto. The inhabitants and settlers in the said territory shall be subject to pay a part of the Federal debts, contracted, or to be contracted, and a proportional part of the expenses of government to be apportioned on them by Congress, according to the same common rule and measure by which apportionments thereof shall be made on the other States; and the taxes for paying their proportion shall be laid and levied by the authority and direction of the legislatures of the district, or districts, or new States, as in the original States, within the time agreed upon by the United States in Congress assembled. The legislatures of those districts, or new States, shall never interfere with the primary disposal of the soil by the United States in Congress assembled, nor with any regulations Congress may find necessary for securing the title in such soil to the *bona fide* purchasers. No tax shall be imposed on lands the property of the United States; and in no case shall non-resident proprietors be taxed higher than residents. The navigable waters leading into the, Mississippi and Saint Lawrence, and the carrying places between the same, shall be common highways, and forever free, as well to the inhabitants of the said territory as to the citizens of the United States, and those of any other States that may be admitted into the confederacy, without any tax, impost, or duty therefor.

Article V.

There shall be formed in the said territory not less than three nor more than five States; and the boundaries of the States, as soon as Virginia shall alter her act of cession and consent to the same, shall become fixed and established as follows, to wit: The western State, in the said territory, shall be bounded by the Mississippi, the Ohio, and the Wabash Rivers; a direct line drawn from the Wabash and Post Vincents, due north, to the territorial line between the United States and Canada; and by the said territorial line to the Lake of the Woods and Mississippi. The middle State shall be bounded by the said direct line, the Wabash from Post Vincents to the Ohio, by the Ohio, by a direct line drawn due north from the mouth of the Great Miami to the said territorial line, and by the said territorial line. The eastern State shall be bounded by the last-mentioned direct line, the Ohio, Pennsylvania, and the said territorial line: *Provided, however,* And it is further understood and declared, that the boundaries of these three States shall be subject so far to be altered, that, if Congress shall hereafter find it expedient, they shall have authority to form one or two States in that part of the said territory which lies north of an east and west line drawn through the southerly bend or extreme of Lake Michigan. And whenever any of the said States shall have sixty thousand free inhabitants therein, such State shall be admitted, by its delegates, into the Congress of the United States, on an equal footing with the original States, in all respects whatever; and shall be at liberty to form a permanent constitution and State government: *Provided,* The constitution and government, so to be formed, shall be republican, and in conformity to the principles contained in these articles, and, so far as it can be consistent with the general interest of the confederacy, such admission shall be allowed at an earlier period, and when there may be a less number of free inhabitants in the State than sixty thousand.

Article VI.

There shall be neither slavery nor involuntary servitude in the said territory, otherwise than in the punishment of crimes, whereof the party shall have been duly convicted: *Provided always,* That any person escaping into the same, from whom labor or service is lawfully claimed in any one of the original States, such fugitive may be lawfully reclaimed, and conveyed to the person claiming his or her labor or service as aforesaid.

Be it ordained by the authority aforesaid, That the resolutions of the 23d of April, 1784, relative to the subject of this ordinance, be, and the same are hereby, repealed, and declared null and void.

Done by the United States, in Congress assembled, the 13th day of July, in the year of our Lord 1787, and of their sovereignty and independence the twelfth.

Document 3.3

The Louisiana Purchase

It was only a matter of time before American settlers began crossing the Mississippi River in their search for land. But France and Spain, and later Mexico, would have something to say about that phenomenon. France claimed sovereignty over the Louisiana Territory, which included what is today Louisiana, Oklahoma, Kansas, Nebraska, part of Minnesota, North Dakota, South Dakota, Wyoming, Montana, and Iowa. Spain controlled what is today Texas, Arizona, New Mexico, California, Colorado, Utah, and Nevada. In 1803, President Thomas Jefferson resolved the issue with France, purchasing the Louisiana territory for $15 million and, with the stroke of a pen, doubling the size of the United States. The treaty negotiating the transfer of Louisiana from French to American sovereignty follows.*

ARTICLE I. Whereas, by the article the third of the treaty concluded at St. Idelfonso, the 9th Vendémiaire, an. 9 (1st October, 1800) between the First Consul of the French Republic and his Catholic Majesty, it was agreed as follows: "His Catholic Majesty promises and

---

* William MacDonald, *Select Documents Illustrative of the History of the United States 1776-1861* (London: The Macmillan Company, 1920), pp. 279-82.

engages on his part, to cede to the French Republic, six months after the full and entire execution of the conditions and stipulations herein relative to his royal highness the duke of Parma, the colony or province of Louisiana, with the same extent that it now has in the hands of Spain, and that it had when France possessed it; and such as it should be after the treaties subsequently entered into between Spain and other states." And *whereas,* in pursuance of the treaty, and particularly of the third article, the French Republic has an incontestible title to the domain and to the possession of the said territory: The First Consul of the French Republic desiring to give to the United States a strong proof of his friendship, doth hereby cede to the said United States, in the name of the French Republic, forever and in full sovereignty, the said territory with all its rights and appurtenances, as fully and in the same manner as they have been acquired by the French Republic, in virtue of the above-mentioned treaty, concluded with his Catholic Majesty.

ART. II. In the cession made by the preceding article are included the adjacent islands belonging to Louisiana, all public lots and squares, vacant lands, and all public buildings, fortifications, barracks, and other edifices which are not private property.-The archives, papers, and documents, relative to the domain and sovereignty of Louisiana, and its dependencies, will be left in the possession of the commissaries of the United States, and copies will be afterwards given in due form to the magistrates and municipal officers, of such of the said papers and documents as may be necessary to them.

ART. III. The inhabitants of the ceded territory shall be incorporated in the Union of the United States, and admitted as soon as possible, according to the principles of the Federal constitution, to the enjoyment of all the rights, advantages and immunities of citizens of the United States; and in the mean time they shall be maintained and protected in the free enjoyment of their liberty, property, and the religion which they profess.

ART. V. Immediately after the ratification of the present treaty by the President of the United States, and in case that of the First Consul shall have been previously obtained, the commissary of the French Republic shall remit all the military posts of New Orleans, and other parts of the ceded territory, to the commissary or commissaries named by the President to take possession; the troops, whether of France or Spain, who may be there, shall cease to occupy any military post from the time of taking possession, and shall be embarked as soon as possible, in the course of three months after the ratification of this treaty.

ART. VI. The United States promise to execute such treaties and articles as may have been agreed between Spain and the tribes and nations of Indians, until, by mutual consent of the United States and the said tribes or nations, other suitable articles shall have been agreed upon.

ART. VII. As it is reciprocally advantageous to the commerce of France and the United States to encourage the communication of both nations for a limited time in the country ceded by the present treaty, until general arrangements relative to the commerce of both nations may be agreed on; it has been agreed between the contracting parties, that the French ships coming directly from France or any of her colonies, loaded only with the produce and manufactures of France or her said colonies; and the ships of Spain coming directly from Spain or any of her colonies, loaded only with the produce or manufactures of Spain or her colonies, shall be admitted during the space of twelve years in the ports of New Orleans, and in all other legal ports of entry within the ceded territory, in the same manner as the ships of the United States coming directly from France or Spain, or any of their colonies, without being subject to any other or greater duty on merchandize, or other or greater tonnage than that paid by the citizens of the United States.

During the space of time above mentioned, no other nation shall have a right to the same privileges in the ports of the ceded territory:... it is however well understood that the object of the above article is to favor the manufactures, commerce, freight and navigation of France and of Spain, so far as relates to the importations that the French and Spanish shall make into the said ports of the United States, without in any sort affecting the regulations that the United States may make concerning the exportation of the produce and merchandize of the United States, or any right they may have to make such regulations.

ART. VIII. In future and forever after the expiration of the twelve years, the ships of France shall be treated upon the footing of the most favored nations in the ports above mentioned.

ART. IX. The particular convention signed this day by the respective ministers, having for its object to provide for the payment of debts due to the citizens of the United States by the French Republic, prior to the 30th of September, 1800, (8th Vendémiaire, an. 9,) is approved, and to have its execution in the same manner as if it had been inserted in this present treaty; and it shall be ratified in the same form and in the same time, so that the one shall not be ratified distinct from the other.

Another particular convention signed at the same date as the present treaty relative to a definitive rule between the contracting parties is in the like manner approved, and will be ratified in the same form, and in the same time, and jointly.

Document 3.4

Opposition to the Louisiana Purchase (1803)

Some Federalists were bitterly opposed to the Louisiana Purchase. Among the most impassioned voices of opposition was Senator Samuel White of Delaware. To Federalists like White, the acquisition of this territory offered the possibility that the lure of this vast wilderness would draw so many settlers west that it would diminish the power of the federal government while strengthening the frontier agrarian constituency in national politics.*

... Mr. [Samuel] WHITE [Delaware] rose and made the following remarks:
... Admitting then, Mr. President, that His Catholic Majesty [The King of Spain] is hostile to the cession of this territory to the United States, and no honorable gentleman

---

* *The Debates and Proceedings in the Congress of the United States, First to Eighteenth Congress, March 3, 1789, to May 27, 1824*, (Washington, D.C.: Gales and Seaton, 1852), XIII, pp. 31-35.

will deny it, what reasons have we to suppose that the French Prefect, provided the Spaniards should interfere, can give to us peaceable possession of the country? He is acknowledged there in no public character, is clothed with no authority, nor has he a single soldier to enforce his orders. I speak now, sir, from mere probabilities. I wish not to be understood as predicting that the French will not cede to us the actual and quiet possession of the territory. I hope to God they may, for possession of it we must have-I mean of New Orleans, and of such other positions on the Mississippi as may be necessary to secure to us forever the complete and uninterrupted navigation of that river. This I have ever been in favor of; I think it essential to the peace of the United States, and to the prosperity of our Western country. But as to Louisiana, this new, immense, unbounded world, if it should ever be incorporated into this Union, which I have no idea can be done but by altering the Constitution, I believe it will be the greatest curse that could at present befall us; it may be productive of innumerable evils, and especially of one that I fear even to look upon. Gentlemen on all sides, with very few exceptions, agree that the settlement of this country will be highly injurious and dangerous to the United States; but as to what has been suggested of removing the Creeks and other nations of Indians from the eastern to the western banks of the Mississippi, and of making the fertile regions of Louisiana a howling wilderness, never to be trodden by the foot of civilized man, it is impracticable. The gentleman from Tennessee (Mr. COCKE) has shown his usual candor on this subject, and I believe with him, to use his strong language, that you had as well pretend to inhibit the fish from swimming in the sea as to prevent the population of that country after its sovereignty shall become ours. To every man acquainted with the adventurous, roving, and enterprising temper of our people, and with the manner in which our Western country has been settled, such an idea must be chimerical. The inducements will be so strong that it will be impossible to restrain our citizens from crossing the river. Louisiana must and will become settled, if we hold it, and with the very population that would otherwise occupy part of our present territory. Thus our citizens will be removed to the immense distance of two or three thousand miles from the capital of the Union, where they will scarcely ever feel the rays of the General Government; their affections will become alienated; they will gradually begin to view us as strangers; they will form other commercial connexions, and our interests will become distinct.

These, with other causes that human wisdom may not now foresee, will in time effect a separation, and I fear our bounds will be fixed nearer to our houses than the waters of the Mississippi. We have already territory enough, and when I contemplate the evils that may arise to these States, from this intended incorporation of Louisiana into the Union, I would rather see it given to France, to Spain, or to any other nation of the earth, upon the mere condition that no citizen of the United States should ever settle within its limits, than to see the territory sold for an hundred millions of dollars, and we retain the sovereignty. But however dangerous the possession of Louisiana might prove to us, I do not presume to say that the retention of it would not have been very convenient to France, and we know that at the time of the mission of Mr. Monroe, our Administration had never thought of the purchase of Louisiana, and that nothing short of the fullest conviction on the part of the First Consul that he was on the very eve of a war with England; that this being the most defenceless point of his possessions, if such they could be called, was the one at which the British would first strike, and that it must inevitably fall into their hands, could ever have induced his pride and ambition to make the sale. He judged wisely, that he had better sell it for as much as he could get than lose it entirely. And I do say that under existing circumstances, even supposing that this extent of territory was a desirable acquisition, fifteen millions of dollars was a most enormous sum to give. Our Commissioners were negotiating in Paris-they must have known the relative situation of France and England-they must have known at the moment that a war was unavoidable between the two countries, and they knew the pecuniary necessities of France and the naval power of Great Britain. These imperious circumstances should have been turned to our advantage, and if we were to purchase, should have lessened the consideration. Viewing, Mr. President, this subject in any point of light-either as it regards the territory purchased, the high consideration to be given, the contract itself, or any of the circumstances attending it, I see no necessity for precipitating the passage of this bill; and if this motion for postponement should fail, and the question on the final passage of the bill be taken now, I shall certainly vote against it.

Document 3.5

Andrew Jackson, First Annual Message to Congress (1829)

A former frontiersman and Indian fighter, President Andrew Jackson was the architect of America's Indian removal policy, which was designed to relocate Indians peoples out west, beyond the Mississippi River. In his first annual message to Congress in 1829, he cloaks his intentions for removal in a rhetoric rich in concern and altruism. The following year, Jackson would support the Removal Act of 1830, which displaced many of the eastern Indians to lands west of the Mississippi and opened up new lands for white settlement.*

The condition and ulterior destiny of the Indian tribes within the limits of some of our states have become objects of much interest and importance. It has long been the policy of government to introduce among them the arts of civilization, in the hope of gradually reclaiming them from a wandering life. This policy has, however, been coupled with another wholly incompatible with its success. Professing a desire to civilize and settle them, we have at the same time lost no opportunity to purchase

---

* *Messages and Papers of the Presidents*, ed. J.D. Richardson, (National Archives and Records Administration, 1896), II, 456-459 (December 8, 1829).

their lands and thrust them farther into the wilderness. By this means they have not only been kept in a wandering state, but been led to look upon us as unjust and indifferent to their fate...

Our conduct toward these people is deeply interesting to our national character. Their present condition, contrasted with what they once were, makes a most powerful appeal to our sympathies. Our ancestors found them the uncontrolled possessors of these vast regions. By persuasion and force they have been made to retire from river to river and from mountain to mountain, until some of the tribes have become extinct and others have left but remnants to preserve for awhile their once terrible names. Surrounded by the whites with their arts of civilization, which, by destroying the resources of the savage, doom him to weakness and decay, the fate of the Mohegan, the Narragansett, and the Delaware is fast overtaking the Choctaw, the Cherokee, and the Creek. That this fate surely awaits them if they remain within the limits of the states does not admit of a doubt. Humanity and national honor demand that every effort should be made to avert so great a calamity...

As a means of effecting this end, I suggest for our consideration the propriety of setting apart an ample district west of the Mississippi, and without [outside] the limits of any state or territory now formed, to be guaranteed to the Indian tribes as long as they shall occupy it, each tribe having a distinct control over the portion designated for its use. There they may be secured in the enjoyment of governments of their own choice, subject to no other control from the United States than such as may be necessary to preserve peace on the frontier and between the several tribes. There the benevolent may endeavor to teach them the arts of civilization, and, by promoting union and harmony among them, to raise up an interesting commonwealth, destined to perpetuate the race and to attest the humanity and justice of this government.

This emigration should be voluntary, for it would be as cruel as unjust to compel the aborigines to abandon the graves of their fathers and seek a home in a distant land. But they should be distinctly informed that if they remain within the limits of the states they must be subject to their laws.

Document 3.6

"Men of the Alamo" (1836)

Late in February 1836, a ragtag army of Spanish-speaking Tejanos and American immigrants moved into the Alamo, a mission and presidio in what is today San Antonio, Texas. They were determined to hold out there, in the name of Texas liberty, against the much larger Mexican army of General Antonio López de Santa Anna, which was just as determined to prevent Texas from gaining its independence. On the morning of March 6, 1836, Santa Anna's army attacked, annihilating the

Texans. But in death, the defenders of the Alamo became icons to freedom and liberty. A month later, when General Sam Houston's Texas army defeated the Mexicans at the Battle of San Jacinto and captured Santa Anna, the clarion call of "Remember the Alamo" had inspired the victory. The following poem, written by James Jeffrey Roche in 1888, captures the reverence most nineteenth-century Americans felt for the "heroes of the Alamo."*

To Houston at Gonzales town, ride, Ranger, for your life,
Nor stop to say good-by to-day to home or child or wife;
But pass the word from ranch to ranch, to every Texan sword,
That fifty hundred Mexicans have crossed the Nueces ford,
With Castrillon and perjured Cos, Sesmá and Almonté
And Santa Anna ravenous for vengeance and for prey.
They smite the land with fire and sword; the grass shall never grow
Where northward sweeps that locust horde on San Antonio.
Now who will bar the foeman's path to gain a breathing space,
Till Houston and his scattered men shall meet him face to face?
Who holds his life as less than naught when home and honor call,
And counts the guerdon full and fair for liberty to fall?
Oh, who but Barrett Travis, the bravest of them all!
With sevenscore of riflemen to play the rancher's game,
And feed a counter-fire to halt the sweeping prairie flame:
For Bowie of the broken blade is there to cheer them on,
With Evans of Concepeion, who conquered Castrillon,
And o'er their heads the Lone Star flag defiant floats on high.
And no man thinks of yielding, and no man fears to die.

But ere the siege has held a week a cry is heard without,
A clash of arms, a rifle peal, the Rangers' ringing shout.
And two-and-thirty beardless boys have bravely hewed their way
To die with Travis if they must to conquer if they may.
Was ever bravery so cheap in Glory's mart before
In all the days of chivalry, in all the deeds of war?

But once again the foemen gaze in wonderment and fear
To see a stranger break their lines and hear the Texans cheer.
God! how they cheered to welcome him, those spent and starving men!
For Davy Crockett by their side was worth an army then.
The wounded ones forgot their wounds; the dying drew a breath
To hail the king of border men, then turned to laugh at death.
For all knew Davy Crockett, blithe and generous as bold,
And strong and rugged as the quartz that hides its heart of gold.

---

* James Jeffrey Roche, "Men of the Alamo," *Harper's New Monthly Magazine*, 78 (December 1888), 463.

His simple creed for word or deed true as the bullet sped,
And rung the target straight: "Be sure you're right, then go ahead!"

And were they right who fought the fight for Texas by his side?
They questioned not; they faltered not; they only fought and died.
Who hath an enemy like these, God's mercy slay him straight!-
A thousand Mexicans lay dead outside the Convent gate,
And half a thousand more must die before the fortress falls.
And still the tide of war beats high around the 'leaguered walls.

At last the bloody breach is won; the weakened lines give way;
The wolves are swarming in the court; the lions stand at bay.
The leader meets them at the breach, and wins the soldier's prize;
A foeman's bosom sheathes his sword when gallant Travis dies.
Now let the victor feast at will until his crest be red-
We may not know what raptures fill the vulture with the dead.
Let Santa Anna's valiant sword right bravely hew and back
The senseless corse; its hands are cold; they will not strike him back.
Let Bowie die, but 'ware the hand that wields his deadly knife;
Four went to slay, and one comes back, so dear he sells his life. And last of all let
     Crockett fall, too proud to sue for grace,
So grand in death the butcher dared not look upon his face.

But far on San Jacinto's field the Texan toils are set,
And Alamo's dread memory the Texan steel shall whet.
And Fame shall tell their deeds who fell till all the years be run.
"Thermopylae left one alive-the Alamo left none."

Document 3.7

The Annexation of Texas

Early in the 1820s, white southerners began migrating into East Texas at the invitation of the Mexican government, which had recently won its independence from Spain. They brought slaves with them and transplanted the cotton culture of the Old South. But during the next decade, the immigrants, now known as "Texicans," became increasingly restive under Mexican sovereignty, and in 1836 they rebelled, fighting the famous battles of the Alamo and San Jacinto.

They succeeded, declaring their independence from Mexico. But when Texas applied for admission to the Union, Congress rejected them. Texas was a slave state, and many abolitionist northerners feared that making Texas part of the Union would only strengthen what was already an evil institution. For nearly a decade, Texas was the independent Lone Star Republic. But in 1845, with American-Mexican relations rapidly deteriorating, Congress moved ahead and approved the annexation of Texas.*

Resolved... That Congress doth consent that the territory properly included within, and rightfully belonging to the Republic of Texas, may be erected into a new State, to be called the State of Texas, with a republican form of government, to be adopted by the people of said republic, by deputies in convention assembled, with the consent of the existing government, in order that the same may be admitted as one of the States of this Union.

2. *And be it further resolved,* That the foregoing consent of Congress is given upon the following conditions, and with the following guarantees, to wit: *First,* Said State to be formed, subject to the adjustment by this government of all questions of boundary that may arise with other governments; and the constitution thereof, with the proper evidence of its adoption by the people of said Republic of Texas, shall be transmitted to the President of the United States, to be laid before Congress for its final action, on or before the first day of January, one thousand eight hundred and forty-six. *Second,* Said State, when admitted into the Union, after ceding to the United States, all public edifices, fortifications, barracks, ports and harbors, navy and navy-yards, docks, magazines, arms, armaments, and all other property and means pertaining to the public defence belonging to said Republic of Texas, shall retain all the public funds, debts, taxes, and dues of every kind, which may belong to or be due and owing said republic; and shall also retain all the vacant and unappropriated lands lying within its limits, to be applied to the payment of the debts and liabilities of said Republic of Texas, and the residue of said lands, after discharging said debts and liabilities, to be disposed of as said State may direct; but in no event are said debts and liabilities to become a charge upon the Government of the United States. *Third.* New States, of convenient size, not exceeding four in number, in addition to said State of Texas, and having sufficient population, may hereafter, by the consent of said State, be formed out of the territory thereof, which shall be entitled to admission under the provisions of the federal constitution. And such States as may be formed out of that portion of said territory lying south of thirty-six degrees thirty minutes north latitude, commonly known as the Missouri compromise line, shall be admitted into the Union with or without slavery, as the people of each State asking admission may desire. And in such State or States as shall be formed out of said territory north of said Missouri compromise line, slavery, or involuntary servitude, (except for crime,) shall be prohibited.

3. *And be it further resolved,* That if the President of the United States shall in his judgment and discretion deem it most advisable, instead of proceeding to submit the

---

* William MacDonald, *Select Documents Illustrative of the History of the United States 1776-1861* (London: The Macmillan Company, 1920), pp. 369-70.

foregoing resolution to the Republic of Texas, as an overture on the part of the United States for admission, to negotiate with that Republic; then,

Be it resolved, That a State, to be formed out of the present Republic of Texas, with suitable extent and boundaries, and with two representatives in Congress, until the next apportionment of representation, shall be admitted into the Union, by virtue of this act, on an equal footing with the existing States, as soon as the terms and conditions of such admission, and the cession of the remaining Texian territory to the United States shall be agreed upon by the Governments of Texas and the United States: And that the sum of one hundred thousand dollars be, and the same is hereby, appropriated to defray the expenses of missions and negotiations, to agree upon the terms of said admission and cession, either by treaty to be submitted to the Senate, or by articles to be submitted to the two houses of Congress, as the President may direct.

4

Exploring the New Empire

When the Louisiana Purchase was consummated in 1803, little was known about the lands west of the Mississippi River. Over the next century a procession of fur traders, mountain men, scientists, artists, and government sponsored expeditions would survey the new lands in the West.

Following the Louisiana Purchase, President Thomas Jefferson selected his private secretary, Captain Meriwether Lewis, to direct an expedition to explore the Louisiana Territory and search for the mythic northwest Passage to the Pacific Ocean. Lewis chose an old friend, William Clark, to share the command. By 1804, the two commanders had picked twenty-seven permanent members to accompany them on the historic journey, including Clark's slave York, who left perhaps the greatest impression on the Indian cultures they encountered.

On May 14 the "Corps of Discovery" left St. Louis for the unmapped West. Travelling up the Missouri River, they averaged almost fifteen miles per day. Within the year, the expedition had added several more members, including the remarkable Shoshoni woman, Sacagawea and her interpreter-husband Toussaint Charbonneau. In late fall of 1805 the expedition reached the Pacific Ocean via the Columbia River. Returning to St. Louis more than two years after its initial departure, the Corps of Discovery had covered over 8,000 miles and had opened the trans-Mississippi West to fur trading and settlement. Despite numerous encounters with the indigenous cultures, only one was of a violent nature. What is even more incredible is that only one man died on the expedition, from a ruptured appendix, a condition that probably would have taken his life even if he had remained at home.

Following Mexico's independence from Spain in 1821, the new government relaxed trade restrictions, which had formerly barred foreigners from Spain's frontier territories in the Southwest. Although other merchants had been arrested by Spanish authorities and had their merchandise confiscated, Missouri entrepreneur William Becknell embarked for Santa Fe in the fall of 1821. After an encounter with Mexican soldiers he learned that Mexico had been granted independence and that Santa Fe was now receptive to foreign trade. After pocketing a healthy profit for his troubles, Becknell returned to Missouri. Subsequently, Becknell would return, trailblazing a better route across the Cimarron Desert and in the process earn the title "Father of the Santa Fe Trail."

The Lewis and Clark Expedition inaugurated the western fur trade, when it was reported that the journey had traversed the richest beaver country in the nation. Over the next twenty years a fur trade system developed in the Northwest and along the Missouri River that revolved around trading posts owned by companies such as the American Fur Company, the Missouri Fur Company, and Hudson's Bay Company. This system was designed to lure the Indians away from trading with the British in the Northwest. At these posts, or factories as they were better known, the United States government exchanged goods with Indians for fur.

As fur trapping expanded into the Rocky Mountains in the 1820s, this factory trading system became obsolete because the Indians in this region were unconcerned with trapping, preferring to spend their time in more traditional pursuits. In 1825, General William Ashley organized the first American rendezvous, an annual event for the next fifteen years, where Indians and fur trappers met to trade, receive news from home, and cut loose after many months in the wilderness.

Laying the groundwork for future commerce, settlement, and emigration routes, the contributions of fur traders and mountain men such as Jedediah Smith to the geographical and scientific knowledge of the West cannot be overestimated.

Less familiar names than John C. Fremont and Lewis and Clark contributed mightily to our knowledge of the West as well, including Randolph Barnes Marcy, who conducted five major expeditions through the West and sketched the first accurate maps of the Southwest. And among the most enduring images of the early nineteenth century West were those created by the artist George Catlin and the naturalist and wildlife painter John James Audubon. Traveling widely in the trans-Mississippi West in the 1830s and 40s, both men made significant contributions to our knowledge of Indian and frontier life.

Suggestions for Further Reading

Stephen E. Ambrose. *Undaunted Courage: Meriwether Lewis, Thomas Jefferson, and the Opening of the American West* (New York: Simon and Schuster, 1996).

William Goetzmann, Army *Exploration in the American West, 1803-1863,* (New Haven: Yale University Press, 1959).

David Lavender, *The Way to the Western Sea: Lewis and Clark across the Continent* (New York: Harper and Row, 1988).

David J. Weber, *The Mexican Frontier, 1821-1846: The American Southwest under Mexico* (Albuquerque: University of New Mexico Press, 1982).

David Wishart, *The Fur Trade of the American West, 1807-1840* (Lincoln: University of Nebraska Press, 1979).

Critical Thinking

1. How did Native Americans react to York during the Lewis and Clark expedition?

2. Describe the activities of a typical Rocky Mountain rendezvous.

3. Compare Audubon's concern for the buffalo with George Catlin's account of an Indian buffalo hunt. Does Catlin's account conflict with the popular conception of the Indian as the "perfect environmentalist/conservationist?"

4. Contrast the geographical obstacles that confronted expeditions led by John C. Fremont and Randolph Marcy. What physical features were prototypically western?

5. What did President Jefferson learn from Meriwether Lewis's report about the trans-Mississippi West?

Document 4.1

Lewis's Initial Report to the President (1806)

On September 26, 1806, Meriwether Lewis and William Clark returned to St. Louis after having completed the most significant mission of exploration in American history. Leaving Missouri in the spring of 1804, the Lewis and Clark expedition set off in several flat-bottomed boats on what would prove to be a twenty-eight month, eight thousand mile adventure. This "Corps of Discovery" was composed of forty-five men, twenty-nine of whom would be permanent members of the expedition. In a venture conceived and partially financed by President Thomas Jefferson, Lewis and Clark were entrusted with exploring vast lands obtained in the Louisiana Purchase, and in the process with locating a water route or the Pacific and collect scientific information. The Lewis and Clark expedition achieved more than anyone could have possibly imagined and in doing so "opened the door to the West." In the following passage, Lewis reports to Jefferson on the success of the expedition.*

It is with pleasure that I announce to you the safe arrival of myself and party at 12 o'clock today at this place with our papers and baggage. In obedience to your orders we have penetrated the continent of North America to the Pacific Ocean, and sufficiently

---

* Reuben Gold Thwaites, ed., *Original Journals of the Lewis and Clark Expedition* (New York, 1904-1905), Vol. 7, pp. 334-37.

explored the interior of the country to affirm with confidence that we have discovered the most practicable route which does exist across the continent by means of the navigable branches of the Missouri and Columbia Rivers...

We view this passage across the continent as affording immense advantages to the fur trade, but fear that the advantages which it offers as a communication for the productions of the East Indies to the United States and thence to Europe will never be found equal on an extensive scale to that by way of the Cape of Good Hope; still we believe that many articles not bulky, brittle nor of a very perishable nature may be conveyed to the United States by this route with more facility and at less expense than by that at present practiced.

The Missouri and all its branches from the Cheyenne upwards abound more in beaver and common otter, than any other streams on earth, particularly that proportion of them lying within the Rocky Mountains. The furs of all this immense tract of country including such as may be collected on the upper portion of the River St. Peters, Red River, and the Assinniboin with the immense country watered by the Columbia, may be conveyed to the mouth of the Columbia by the 1st of August in each year and from thence be shipped to, and arrive in Canton [China] earlier than the furs at present shipped from Montreal annually arrive in London...

If the government will only aid, even in a very limited manner, the enterprise of her citizens I am fully convinced that we shall shortly derive the benefits of a most lucrative trade from this source, and that in the course of ten to twelve years a tour across the continent by the route mentioned will be undertaken by individuals with as little concern as a voyage across the Atlantic is at present...

I have brought with me several skins of the sea otter, two skins of the native sheep of America, five skins and skeletons complete of the Bighorn or mountain ram, and a skin of the mule deer besides the skins of several other quadrapeds and birds native of the countries through which we have passed. I have also preserved a pretty extensive collection of plants, and collected nine other vocabularies [of Indian tribes].

I have prevailed on the great chief of the Mandan nation to accompany me to Washington; he is now with my friend and colleague Capt. Clark at this place, in good health and spirits, and very anxious to proceed...

Document 4.2

Ben York (1804)

One of the best known members of the Lewis and Clark Expedition, York (b. c. 1770-?) was born a slave and willed to William Clark upon his father's death. Possessing prodigious strength and a keen wit, York was with Clark the entire expedition, to the Pacific Ocean and back to

St. Louis. Upon their return he was freed by Clark. He later moved to Louisville, where he married and worked in the hauling business. According to one account he later fell victim to cholera, probably in the early 1830s. In the following entries from Clark's diary of the expedition, Indians come to their camp, where they see a black man for the first time. York, ever the ham, impresses them with feats of strength and tells the visitors that he had once been a wild animal but was caught and tamed by his master.*

[Clark:]   River Maropa 9th of October 1804. Tuesday—

a windey rainey night, and cold, So much So we Could not speek with the Indians to day the three great Chiefs and many others Came to see us to day, we gave them some tobacco and informed them we would Speek on tomorrow, the day continued Cold & windey some rain Sorry Canoos of Skins passed down from the 2 Villages a Short distance above, and many Came to view us all day, much astonished at my black Servent, who did not lose the opportunity of [displaying-ED.] his powers Strength &c. &c. this nation never Saw a black man before.
    Several hunters Came in with loades of meat, I observed Several Canoos made of a Single Buffalow Skin with 3 thre squars Cross the river to day in waves as high as I ever Saw them on this river, quite uncomposed I have a Slite Plursie this evening verry cold &c. &c.

10th of October Wednesday 1804. —

a fine morning wind from the S.E. at about 11 oClock the wind Shifted, to the N. W. we prepare all things ready to Speak to the Indians, M[r]. Tabo & M[r.] Gravolin came to brackfast with us the Cheefs &c. came from the lower Town, but none from the 2 upper Towns, which is the largest, we Continue to delay & waite for them at 12 oClock Despatchd Gravelin to envite them to come down, we have every reason to believe that a gellousy exists between the Villages for fear of our makeing the 1st. Cheif from the lower Village, at one oClock the Cheifs all assembled & after Some little Cerremony the council Commenced, we inform[d] them what we had told the others before i. e. Ottoes & Seaux. made 3 Cheif I for each Village; gave them presents. after the Council was over we Shot the air guns which astonished them much, the[y] then Departed and we rested Secure all night, Those Indians wer much astonished at my Servent, they never Saw a black man before, all flocked around him & examin[d] him from top to toe, he Carried on the joke and made himself more turribal than we wished him to doe. Those Indians are not fond of Spirt[a] Licquer. of any kind

---

* Reuben Gold Thwaites, ed., *Original Journals of the Lewis and Clark Expedition, 1804-1806*, Vol. 1, (1905), pp. 185-186; 243.

Fort Mandan on the NE bank of the Missouries 1600 Miles up Tuesday
January the 1st 1805.—

The Day was ushered in by the Descharge of two Cannon, we Suffered 16 men with
their Musick to visit the 1st. Village for the purpose of Danceing, by as they Said the
perticular request of the Chiefs of that Village, about 11 oClock I with an inturpeter &
two men walked up to the Village, (my views were to alay Some little Miss
understanding which had taken place thro jelloucy and mortification as to our treatment
towards them I found them much pleased at the Danceing of our men, I ordered my black
Servent to Dance which amused the Croud Verry much, and Somewhat astonished them,
that So large a man should be active &c. &c. I went into the lodges of all the men of
note. except two, whome I heard had made Some expressions not favourable towards us,
in Compareing us with the traders from the north,-those Chiefs observed (to us that) what
they Sayed was in just (in jest) & laftur. just as I was about to return, the 2^d. Chief a(nd)
the Black man, also a Chief return^d from a Mission on which they had been Sent to meet
a large party (150) of Gross Ventres who were on their way down from their Camps 10
Miles above to revenge on the Shoe tribe an injury which they had received by a Shoe
man Steeling a Gross Ventres Girl, those Chiefs gave the pipe [and] turned the party
back, after Delivering up the Girl, which the Shoe Chief had taken and given to them for
that purpose."

Document 4.3

Sacajawea (1805)

Sacajawea, (c. 1780-1812/1884) was a Shoshone woman, captured by
either the Crows or the Hidatsas. Outside the journals kept by Lewis
and Clark, little is known about Sacajawea. In 1805 she married a
French-Canadian trapper named Toussaint Charbonneau. Joining the
Lewis and Clark expedition as an interpreter, Charbonneau brought
along his wife and young son. According to the diaries kept by Lewis
and Clark, she proved to be one of the most valuable members of the
expedition. Despite giving birth while the expedition was still in winter
quarters, she served as an interpreter, guide, and peacemaker with
various tribes, and on one occasion saved Clark's diary and other
supplies that were almost lost in the river. For her great service to the
expedition, Lewis recorded in his diary naming a river in honor of "Bird
Woman," her Shoshone name. The historic Sacajawea passed from the

scene when her husband decided to leave the expedition when it prepared to return to the east. In the first passage, Sacajawea recognizes land she had traveled in her youth. The second excerpt describes her departure from the expedition.*

Along these roads there were also appearances of old buffalo paths, and some old heads of buffaloes; and as these animals evince wonderful sagacity in the choice of their routes, the coincidence of a buffalo with an Indian track affords the strongest evidence that it is the best. In the afternoon they passed along the hill side, north of the creek, for six miles, when they entered an extensive level plain. Here the Indian tracks scattered so much that they were wholly at a loss which to follow; but Sacajaweah recognised the plain immediately. She had travelled it often during her childhood, and informed them that it was greatly resorted to by the Shoshonees, who came here for the purpose of gathering *quamash* and of taking beaver, with which the plain abounded; that Glade Creek was a branch of Wisdom River, and that, on reaching the more elevated part of the plain, they would see a gap in the mountains, on the route to the canoes, and from that gap the high point of a mountain covered with snow.

August 17. The principal chiefs of the Minnetarees now came down to bid us farewell, as none of them could be prevailed on to go with us. This circumstance induced our interpreter, Chaboneau, to remain here with his wife and child, as he could no longer be of use to us, and, although we offered to take him with us to the United States, he declined, saying that there he had no acquaintance, and no chance of making a livelihood, and preferred remaining among the Indians. This man had been very serviceable to us, and his wife was particularly useful among the Shoshonees: indeed, she had borne with a patience truly admirable the fatigues of so long a route, encumbered with the charge of an infant, who was then only nineteen months old. We therefore paid him his wages, amounting to five hundred dollars and thirty-three cents, including the price of a horse and a lodge purchased of him, and soon afterward dropped down to the village of Big White, attended on shore by all the Indian chiefs, who had come to take leave of him. We found him surrounded by his friends, who sat in a circle smoking, while the women were crying. He immediately sent his wife and son, with their baggage, on board, accompanied by the interpreter and his wife, and two children; and then, after distributing among his friends some powder and ball which we had given him, and smoking a pipe, he went with us to the river side. The whole village crowded about us, and many of the people wept aloud at the departure of their chief.

---

* Archibald M'Vikar. ed., *History of the Expedition Under the Command of Captain Lewis and Clarke*, (New York: Harper and Brothers, 1842), pp. 283; 315-316.

Document 4.4

The Santa Fe Trail (1821)

Prior to Mexico's independence from Spain in 1821, American traders who had dared to venture into the Southwest risked Imprisonment and the confiscation of goods by Spanish officials. In 1821, a Missouri Indian trader by the name of William Becknell learned from Mexican soldiers on the southern Plains that Mexico had won independence and that there was a huge demand for American trade goods in Santa Fe. The following year, Becknell pioneered a trail from Missouri across the Cimarron Desert to Santa Fe, inaugurating the Santa Fe Trail. The following excerpt describes the often treacherous process of bringing goods from Franklin, Missouri, to Santa Fe in the early years of the trail.*

Four men, starting with their goods in 1812, and manfully pushing their way to Santa Fe, returned only in 1821, having been imprisoned during nearly all the intermediate time. The next year, however, marked the opening of the Santa Fe Trail, that wonderful road, some eight hundred miles in length, rising so imperceptibly for three-quarters of this distance as to seem absolutely level, and without bridge from end to end. There it stretched away toward the sunset half a century ago, and there it stretches today; and what poet's dream, what prophetic vision of the ardent patriot, steadfastly believing in the future greatness of his country, is commensurate with either the romance or the reality of the march over and beside it, during those fifty years, of the pioneer, the trader, the soldier, the Free-State champion, the settler, and the railroad engineer?

The first traders carried their merchandise on pack horses or mules, and it was in 1824 that it was decided to use wagons, a number of which reached Santa Fe with much less difficulty than might have been expected. The practicability of this method being established, the trade began steadily to increase, and in a few years a large amount of capital was embarked therein. Its initial point was first Franklin, some one hundred and fifty miles west of St. Louis; then Independence; then Westport-all these towns being on the Missouri River, and thus easily reached during the season of navigation. Here were found motley crowds-traders, out-fitters, dealers in supplies of all kinds, tourists, invalids hoping to regain their health by a trip on the plains, drivers, and "roughs" in abundance. The covered wagons were drawn first by horses, then by mules, then by both mules and oxen, and were carefully loaded. Besides the merchandise, supplies for the men were carried-say, bacon, flour, coffee, sugar, and a little salt, it being expected that enough buffaloes would be killed to furnish fresh meat. Starting off in detached parties, the wagons would rendezvous at Council Grove, on a branch of the Neosho River, twenty miles north of the present town of Emporia, and here an organization would be effected

---

* "The Santa Fe Trail," *Harper's New Monthly Magazine*, (July 1880), 186-90.

for mutual aid and protection during the long journey. In such a caravan there would be, perhaps, one hundred wagons, and a "captain of the caravan" would divide them into four divisions, with a lieutenant to each. Every individual in the caravan was compelled to stand his watch at night, and this guard must have presented a motley assortment of clothing and arms. When all was ready, the start was made. Every night a hollow square and temporary corral were made with the wagons, and the camp fires lighted outside of this square. Across swamps, quagmires, and even rivers, the teams were driven, men being sent ahead to make temporary bridges over the first two of brush or long grass covered with earth, and sometimes, for crossing streams, to fabricate "buffalo boats" of hides stretched over frames of poles, or empty wagon bodies.

When the caravans were within a moderate distance of Santa Fe, runners were forwarded to send back supplies, engage store-houses, and make arrangements with the customs officers-arrangements not unlike, probably, those made with (some) customs officers in other parts of the world and in later days. And then, at last, the long valleys traversed and the high hills crossed, the goal appeared in sight. Loud cheers rang out, guns were discharged, and demonstrations of the greatest joy abounded on every side.

"The arrival produced a great deal of bustle and excitement among the natives. 'Los Americanos!' 'Los carros!' 'La entrada de la caravana!' were to be heard in every direction; and crowds of women and boys flocked around to see the newcomers, while crowds of *leperos* hung about, as usual, to see what they could pilfer. The wagoners were by no means free from excitement on this occasion. Informed of the 'ordeal' they had to pass, they had spent the previous morning in 'rubbing up,' and now they were prepared, with clean faces, sleek combed hair, and their choicest Sunday suit, to meet the 'fair eyes' of glistening black that were sure to stare at them as they passed. There was yet another preparation to be made in order to 'show off' to advantage. Each wagoner must tie a brand-new 'cracker' to the lash of his whip, for on driving through the streets and the *plaza publicas* every ????

Document 4.5

Rendezvous and the Rocky Mountain Fur Trade

In 1825, General William H. Ashley revolutionized the Rocky Mountain fur trade by introducing the rendezvous system as a replacement for the fortified trading post. Over the next fifteen years, trappers left their camps to trade at the annual rendezvous. Each year, one meeting was held at the close of the spring hunt in the Rocky Mountains. The rendezous created more accessible trading centers for Indians and mountain men and provided not only a location where furs could be traded, but a source for supplies and an opportunity for social intercourse. The following passage depicts the carnival-like atmosphere where free trappers and company trappers intermingled with Indians, picked up letters from home, and received news from members of the freight caravans. For many, the annual meeting was an unrestrained debauch, which often included racing, duelling, gambling, drinking, and shooting matches.*

The Green River Valley was at his time the scene of one of those general gatherings of traders, trappers, and Indians, that we have already mentioned. The three rival companies, which, for a year past had been endeavoring to out-trade, out-trap, and out-wit each other, were here encamped in close proximity, awaiting their annual supplies. About four miles from the rendezvous of Captain Bonneville was that of the American Fur Company, hard by which, was that also of the Rocky Mountain Fur Company.

After the eager rivalry and almost hostility displayed by these companies in their late campaigns, it might be expected that, when thus brought in juxtaposition, they would hold themselves warily and sternly aloof from each other, and, should they happen to come in contact, brawl and bloodshed would ensue.

No such thing! Never did rival lawyers, after a wrangle at the bar, meet with more social good humor at a circuit dinner. The hunting season over, all past tricks and maneuvers are forgotten, all feuds and bickerings buried in oblivion. From the middle of June to the middle of September, all trapping is suspended; for the beavers are then shedding their furs, and their skins are of little value. This, then, is the trapper's holiday, when he is all for fun and frolic, and ready for a saturnalia among the mountains.

At the present season, too, all parties were in good humor. The year had been productive. Competition, by threatening to lessen their profits, had quickened their wits, roused their energies, and made them turn every favorable chance to the best advantage; so that, on assembling at their respective places of rendezvous, each company found itself in possession of a rich stock of peltries.

The leaders of the different companies, therefore, mingled on terms of perfect good fellowship; interchanging visits, and regaling each other in the best style their respective camps afforded. But the rich treat for the worthy captain was to see the "chivalry" of the various encampments, engaged in contests of skill at running, jumping, wrestling, shooting with the rifle, and running horses. And then their rough hunters' feastings and carousals. They drank together, they sang, they laughed, they whooped; they tried to outbrag and outlie each other in stories of their adventures and achievements. Here the free trappers were in all their glory; they considered themselves the "cocks of the walk," and always carried the highest crests. Now and then familiarity was pushed too far, and would effervesce into a brawl, and a "rough and tumble" fight; but it all ended in cordial reconciliation and maudlin endearment.

The presence of the Shoshonie tribe contributed occasionally to cause temporary jealousies and feuds. The Shoshonie beauties became objects of rivalry among some of the amorous mountaineers. Happy was the trapper who could muster up a red blanket, a

* Washington Irving, *The Adventures of Captain Bonneville, J.S.A. in the Rocky Mountains and the Far West*, (New York: G.P. Putnam's Sons, 1885), 215-218.

string of gay beads, or a paper of precious vermilion, with which to win the smiles of a Shoshonie fair one.

The caravans of supplies arrived at the valley just at this period of gallantry and good-fellowship. Now commenced a scene of eager competition and wild prodigality at the different encampments. Bales were hastily ripped open, and their motley contents poured forth. A mania for purchasing spread itself throughout the several bands,-munitions for war, for hunting, for gallantry, were seized upon with equal avidity-rifles, hunting knives, traps, scarlet cloth, red blankets, garish beads, and glittering trinkets, were bought at any price, and scores run up without any thought how they were ever to be rubbed off. The free trappers, especially, were extravagant in their purchases. For a free mountaineer to pause at a paltry consideration of dollars and cents, in the attainment of any object that might strike his fancy, would stamp him with the mark of the beast in the estimation of his comrades. For a trader to refuse one of these free and flourishing blades a credit, whatever unpaid scores might stare him in the face, would be a flagrant affront scarcely to be forgiven.

Now succeeded another outbreak of revelry and extravagance. The trappers were newly fitted out and arrayed, and dashed about with their horses caparisoned in Indian style. The Shoshonie beauties also flaunted about in all the colors of the rainbow. Every freak of prodigality was indulged to its full extent, and in a little while most of the trappers, having squandered away all their wages, and perhaps run knee-deep in debt, were ready for another hard campaign in the wilderness.

Document 4.6

A Buffalo Hunt (1832)

While recent films such as *Dances With Wolves* portray Plains Indians as almost perfect environmentalists, western artist George Catlin (1796-1872) recorded a different portrait of Indian hunting techniques during the 1830s. One of the first artists of note to document American Indian culture, Catlin describes the destruction of a herd of buffalo in less than a half hour's time in the following passage.*

The Minatarees, as well as the Mandans, had suffered for some months past for want of meat, and had indulged in the most alarming fears, that the herds of buffaloes were emigrating so far off from them, that there was great danger of their actual starvation, when it was suddenly announced through the village one morning at an early hour, that a

* *George Catlin, Letters and Notes on the Manners, Customs, and Condition of the North American Indians,* Vol I., (1841), pp. 199-202.

herd of buffaloes was in sight, when an hundred or more young men mounted their horses with weapons in hand and steered their course to the prairies... The plan of attack, which in this country is familiarly called a *"surround,"* was explicitly agreed upon, and the hunters who were all mounted on their "buffalo horses" and armed with bows and arrows or long lances, divided into two columns, taking opposite directions, and drew themselves gradually around the herd at a mile or more distance from them; thus forming a circle of horsemen at equal distances apart, who gradually closed in upon them with a moderate pace, at a signal given. The unsuspecting herd at length "got the wind" of the approaching enemy and fled in a mass in the greatest confusion. To the point where they were aiming to cross the line, the horsemen were seen at full speed, gathering and forming in a column, brandishing their weapons and yelling in the most frightful manner, by which means they turned the black and rushing mass which moved off in an opposite direction where they were again met and foiled in a similar manner, and wheeled back in utter confusion; by which time the horsemen had closed in from all directions, forming a continuous line around them, whilst the poor affrighted animals were eddying about in a crowded and confused mass, hooking and climbing upon each other; when the work of death commenced...

In this grand turmoil, a cloud of dust was soon raised, which in parts obscured the throng where the hunters were galloping their horses around and driving the whizzing arrows or their long lances to the hearts of these noble animals; which in many instances, becoming infuriated with deadly wounds in their sides, erected their shaggy manes over their blood-shot eyes and furiously plunged forwards at the sides of their assailants' horses, sometimes goring them to death at a lunge, and putting their dismounted riders to flight for their lives; sometimes their dense crowd was opened, and the blinded horsemen, too intent on their prey amidst the cloud of dust, were hemmed and wedged in amidst the crowding beasts, over whose backs they were obliged to leap for security, leaving their horses to the fate that might await them in the results of this wild and desperate war. Many were the bulls that turned upon their assailants and met them with desperate resistance; and many were the warriors who were dismounted, and saved themselves by the superior muscles of their legs; some who were closely pursued by the bulls, wheeled suddenly around and snatching the part of a buffalo robe from around their waists, threw it over the horns and the eyes of the infuriated beast, and darting by its side drove the arrow or the lance to its heart. Others suddenly dashed off upon the prairies by the side of the affrighted animals which had escaped from the throng, and closely escorting them for a few rods, brought down their hearts blood in streams, and their huge carcasses upon the green and enamelled turf.

In this way this grand hunt soon resolved itself into a desperate battle: and in the space of fifteen minutes, resulted in the total destruction of the whole herd, which in all their strength and fury were doomed, like every beast and living thing else, to fall before the destroying hands of mighty man.

I had sat in trembling silence upon my horse, and witnessed this extraordinary scene, which allowed not one of these animals to escape out of my sight. Many plunged off upon the prairie for a distance, but were overtaken and killed; and although I could not distinctly estimate the number that were slain, yet I am sure that some hundreds of these noble animals fell in this grand mêlée.

The scene after the battle was over was novel and curious in the extreme; the hunters were moving about amongst the dead and dying animals, leading their horses by their halters, and claiming their victims by their private marks upon their arrows, which they were drawing from the wounds in the animals' sides.

Amongst the poor affrighted creatures that had occasionally dashed through the ranks of their enemy, and sought safety in flight upon the prairie (and in some instances, had undoubtedly gained it), I saw them stand awhile, looking back, when they turned, and, as if bent on their own destruction, retraced their steps, and mingled themselves and their deaths with those of the dying throng. Others had fled to a distance on the prairies, and for want of company, of friends or of foes, had stood and gazed on till the battle-scene was over; seemingly taking pains to stay, and hold their lives in readiness for their destroyers, until the general destruction was over, when they fell easy victims to their weapons-making the slaughter complete.

After this scene, and after arrows had been claimed and recovered, a general council was held, when all hands were seated on the ground, and a few pipes smoked; after which, all mounted their horses and rode back to the village.

Document 4.7

Audubon's Western Journey (1843)

The wildlife painter and naturalist John James Audubon (1785-1851) was born in Haiti and educated in France. Settling in Kentucky in 1803, he first worked as a taxidermist before devoting himself to the pictorial documentation of American wildlife after an 1820 trip on the Mississippi River. In 1843 at the age of fifty-eight he undertook a long deferred expedition to the Far West. During the eight-month journey he kept a journal and for fifty years it was feared lost until one of his granddaughters reacquired it from an old secretary in 1896. The following letter to Spencer Baird Audubon outlines Audubons' final plans for the western journey. In the second passage he forsees the departure of the buffalo.*

NEW YORK, Nov. 29, 1842.

MY DEAR YOUNG FRIEND,

* Francis Hobart Herrick, *Audubon the Naturalist: A History of his Life and Time*, (New York: D. Appleton, 1917), pp. 248-249; 255-256.

It seems to me as if an age had already elapsed since I have heard from you or your whereabouts. Neither do I know clearly whether in the way of correspondence, you are in my debt, or I am in yours. Nevertheless I now write to you, and request you to read this letter more than once, and think deeply on the purport of its contents that you may be the [more] able to form a true Idea of what I intend to say [to] you, and for yourself to give me a true answer, on which I can depend, no matter whether it is to my liking or not.

It is now determined that I shall go towards the Rocky Mountains at least to the Yellowstone River, and up the latter Stream four hundred miles, and perhaps go across the Rocky Mountains. I have it in my power to proceed to the Yellowstone by Steamer from St. Louis on the 1st day of April next; or to go to the "Mountains of the Wind" in the very heart and bosom of the Rocky Mountains in the company of Sir William Drommond Stewart, Baronet who will leave on the 1st of May next also from St. Louis.

It has occurred to me that perchance you would like to spare a few months of your life, to visit the great Western Wilderness, and perhaps again prefer going in my Company in preference to that of any other person? Of this of course I cannot Judge without your answer to this. I thought that you would have been in New York long ere this, but not a Word of you has reached any friend of yours here for several months. I have had an abundance of applications from different sections of the country, from Young Gents who proffer much efficiency, etc., but I do not know them as I know you, and if the terms which I am about to propose to you will answer your own views, I wish you to write to me at once so that I may know how to prepare myself for such a Journey, and under such circumstances.

Would you like to go with me at any rate? By which I mean, whether by Land, or by Water, and undertake, besides acting towards me as a friend, to prepare whatever skins of Birds or Quadrupeds, I may think fit for us to bring home. The Birds, you might have one half as your own, the Quadrupeds, (should you wish it) you might have a 4th or every 4th specimen of the same species, reserving to myself all that is new or exceedingly rare.

I will procure and furnish all the materials for skinning, preparing, and saving whatever we may find in Ornithology and in Mammalia, and in all probability (if you think it absolutely necessary) pay one half your expenses from the time we leave St. Louis until our return to that city. You will have to work hard, of course, but then I trust to that the knowledge alone which you must acquire would prove a sufficient compensation, and as you already know me pretty well, I need not say to you that I am not "hard on the trigger."

It will be necessary for you to provide a good double barrelled Gun, and an excellent Rifle, Shot bag, powder flask, &c, a good hatchet, and a sufficiency of clothes for something like a 12 month's Campaign. But if you will write me at once upon the subject, I can give you a more and a better a/c of all my intentions, than is at present necessary...

Yours Always,

John J. Audubon.

On the 15th of July they started up the shore of the Yellowstone in a cart. The party soon had had enough of buffalo hunting, and on one day the naturalist was nearly speared by a charging bull that had been wounded. "What a terrible destruction of life," he says, "as it were for nothing, or next to it, as the tongues only were brought in, and the flesh of these fine animals was left to beasts and birds of prey, or to rot on the spots where they fell. The prairies are literally covered with the skulls of the victims, and the roads the Buffalo make in crossing the prairies have all the appearance of heavy wagon tracks." Foreseeing the departure of the buffalo, he wrote:

One can hardly conceive how it happens, notwithstanding these many deaths and the immense numbers that are murdered almost daily on these boundless wastes called prairies, besides the hosts that are drowned in the freshets, and the hundreds of young calves who die in early spring, so many are yet to be found. Daily we see so many that we hardly notice them more than the cattle in our pastures about our homes. But this cannot last; even now there is a perceptible difference in the size of the herds, and before many years the Buffalo, like the Great Auk, will have disappeared.

Document 4.8

Fremont's Expedition to the Rocky Mountains (1846)

A noted explorer, politician, and soldier, John Charles Fremont (1813-1890) embarked on his first expedition to the trans-Mississippi West in 1838 when he was commissioned in the United States Corps of Topographical Engineers. By the time he was forty his narratives of western exploration had earned him the moniker "pathfinder." In the following passage Fremont encounters the legendary mountain man Jim Beckwourth (c. 1800-1866). Son of a minor Irish aristocrat and a black slave woman, Beckwourth became a familiar fixture at rendezvous time during the heyday of the Rocky Mountain fur trade.*

JULY 9.-This morning we caught the first faint glimpse of the Rocky mountains, about sixty miles distant. Though a tolerable bright day, there was a slight mist, and we were just able to discern the snowy summit of "Long's peak" (*"les deux oreilles"* of the Canadians,) showing like a cloud near the horizon. I found it easily distinguishable, there being a perceptible difference in its appearance from the white clouds that were floating about the sky. I was pleased to find that among the traders the name of "Long's peak" had been adopted and become familiar in the country. In the ravines near this place, a light brown sandstone made its first appearance. About 8, we discerned several persons on horseback a mile or two ahead, on the opposite side of the river. They turned in towards the river, and we rode down to meet them. We found them to be two white men,

---

* John C. Fremont, *Narrative of the Exploring Expedition to the Rocky Mountains in the Year 1842; And to Oregon and North California in the Years 1843-44*, (Syracuse: L.W. Hall, 1846), 30-31.

and a mulatto named Jim Beckwith, who had left St. Louis when a boy, and gone to live with the Crow Indians. He had distinguished himself among them by some acts of daring bravery, and had risen to the rank of chief, but had now, for some years, left them. They were in search of a band of horses that had gone off from a camp some miles above, in charge of Mr. Chabonard. Two of them contained down the river, in search of the horses, and the American turned back with us, and we rode on towards the camp. About eight miles from our sleeping place, we reached Bijou's fork, an affluent of the right bank. Where we crossed it, a short distance from the Platte, it has a sandy bed about four hundred yards broad; the water in various small streams, a few inches deep. Seven miles further brought us the camp of some four or five whites (New Englanders, I believe,) who had accompanied Captain Wyeth to the Columbia river, and were independent trappers. All had their squaws with them, and I was really surprised at the number of little fat, buffalo-fed boys that were tumbling about the camp, all apparently of the same age, about three or four years old. They were encamped on a rich bottom, covered with a profusion of rich grass, and had a large number of fine-looking horses and mules. We rested with them a few minutes, and in about two miles arrived at Chabonard's camp, on an island in the Platte. On the heights above, we met the first Spaniard I had seen in the country. Mr. Chabonord was in the service of Bent and St. Vrain's company, and had left their fort some forty or fifty miles above, in the spring, with boats laden with the furs of the last year's trade. He had met the same fortune as the voyageurs of the North fork; and, finding it impossible to proceed, had taken up his summer's residence on this island, which he had named St. Helena. The river hills appeared to be composed entirely of sand, and the Platte had lost the muddy character of its waters, and here was tolerably clear. From the mouth of the South fork, I had found it occasionally broken up by small islands; and at the time of our journey, which was at a season of the year when the water were at a favorable stage, it was not navigable for any thing drawing six inches water. The current was very swift-the bed of the stream a coarse gravel. From the place at which we had encountered the Arapahoes, the Platte had been tolerably well fringed with timber, and the island here had a fine grove of very large cottonwoods, under whose broad shade the tents were pitched. There was a large drove of horses in the opposite prairie bottom; smoke was rising from the scattered fires, and the encampment had quite a patriarchal air. Mr. C. received us hospitably. One of the people was sent to gather mint, with the aid of which he concocted very good julep; and some boiled buffalo tongue, and coffee with the luxury of sugar, were soon set before us. The people in his employ were generally Spaniards, and among them I saw a young Spanish woman from Taos, whom I found to be Beckwith's wife.

Document 4.9

Comanche Hostility to Negroes (1852)

Although he conducted five major expeditions through the West and was the first explorer to trace the Red River to its source (1852), Randolph Barnes Marcy (1812-1887) never received the recognition of Lewis and Clark, Fremont, and other contemporaries. During his Red River expedition, Marcy was accompanied by his son-in-law George B. McClellan, the future commander of Union forces during the Civil War. In the following passage Marcy comments on how Comanches received strangers and the curious hostility reserved for black Americans.*

The mode of life of the prairie tribes, owing to their unsettled and wandering habits, is such as to render their condition one of constant danger and apprehension. The security of their numerous animals from the encroachments of their enemies, and their constant liability to attacks, make it imperatively necessary for them to be at all times upon the alert. Their details for herdsmen are made with as much regularity as the guard-details at a military post; and even in times of the most profound peace, they guard their animals both night and day, while scouts are often patrolling upon the adjoining heights to give notice of the approach of strangers, when their animals are hurried to a place of security, and everything made ready for defence. The manner in which they salute a stranger is somewhat peculiar, as my own reception at one of their encampments will show. The chief at this encampment was a very corpulent old man, with exceedingly scanty attire, who, immediately on our approach, declared himself a great friend of the Americans, and persisted in giving me evidence of his sincerity by an embrace, which, to please him, I forced myself to submit to, although it was far from agreeable to my own feelings. Seizing me in his brawny arms while we were yet in the saddle, and laying his greasy head upon my shoulder, he inflicted upon me a most bruinlike squeeze, which I endured with a degree of patient fortitude worthy of the occasion; and I was consoling myself upon the completion of the salutation, when the savage again seized me in his arms, and I was doomed to another similar torture, with his head on my other shoulder, while at the same time he rubbed his greasy face against mine in the most affectionate manner; all of which proceeding, he gave me to understand, was to be regarded as a most distinguished and signal mark of affection for the American people in general, whom, as he expressed it, he loved so much that it almost broke his heart; and in particular for myself, who, as their representative, can bear testimony to the strength of his attachment. On leaving his camp, the chief shook me heartily by the hand, telling me at the same that he was not a

---

* Randolph B. Marcy, *Exploration of the Red River of Louisiana in the Year 1852*, Senate Ex. Doc., 33d Congress, 1st Sess., (Washington: Beverly Tucker, Senate Printer, 1854), '109-111.

Comanche, but an American; and as I did not feel disposed to be outdone in politeness by an Indian, I replied in the same spirit, that there was not a drop of Anglo-Saxon blood in my veins, but that I was wholly and absolutely a Comanche, at which he seemed delighted, duly understanding and appreciating the compliment. These people are hospitable and kind to all with whom they are not at war; and on the arrival of a stranger at their camps a lodge is prepared for him, and he is entertained as long as he chooses to remain among them. They are also kind and affectionate to each other, and as long as anything comestible remains in the camp all are permitted to share alike; but with these exceptions, they are possessed of but few virtues. Polygamy is sanctioned, and is very common among them, every man being allowed as many wives as he can support.

Within the past few years the Comanches have (for what reason I could not learn) taken an inveterate dislike to the negroes, and have massacred several small parties of those who attempted to escape from the Seminoles and cross the plains for the purpose of joining Wild Cat upon the Rio Grande. Upon inquiring of them the cause of their hostility to the blacks, they replied that it was because they were slaves to the whites; that they were sorry for them. I suspect however, that they were actuated by other motives than they cared about acknowledging, and that instead of wishing to better their condition by sending them to another world, where they would be released from the fetters of bondage, they were apprehensive, if they permitted them to pass quietly, that in time Wild Cat's followers upon the Rio Grande would augment to such a degree that he would interfere with their marauding operations along the Mexican borders. During the past year they have also been hostile towards the Delawares and Shawnees, and have killed several individuals who have been into their country in small parties. The Creek Indians, who exercise a good influence over the prairie tribes, have counselled them to commit no further acts of hostility upon these Indians, and I presume they will take measures to enforce a strict adherence to their wishes in this respect. These people, who ware so extremely jealous of their own freedom that they will often commit suicide rather than be taken prisoners, are the more prone to enslave others, and this dominant principle is carried to the greatest extreme so far as regards their women. A beast of burden and a slave to the will of her brutal master, yet, strange as it may appear, the Comanche woman seems contented with her lot, and submits to her fate without a murmur. The hardships imposed upon the females are most severe and cruel. The distance of rank and consideration which exists between the black slave and his master is not greater than between the Comanche warrior and his wife. Every degrading office that is imposed upon the black by the most tyrannical master, falls, among the Comanches, to the lot of the wretched female. They, in common with other Indians, are not a prolific race; indeed, it is seldom that a woman has more tan three or four children. Many of these, owing to unavoidable exposure, die young; the boys, however, are nurtured with care and treated with great kindness by their mothers, while the girls are frequently beaten and abused unmercifully. I have never seen an idiot, or one that was naturally deformed, among them.

5

Life in the Antebellum West

The year 1848 was a seminal year in the history of the West. The discovery of gold in California in January inaugurated the great westward migration, luring tens of thousands of gold seekers by sea and over land to the Pacific Coast. Most followed the central overland trail, while others opted for southern routes through Santa Fe and northern Mexico. The years of the California Gold Rush, 1848-1850, were marked by a terrible cholera pandemic that followed the course of emigration from the old World to New Orleans, and then up the important navigable rivers heading to St. Louis and the Missouri River jumping-off towns. Cholera infected overlanders who then carried the disease to California.

In February 1848, the War with Mexico War was terminated when the vanquished nation ceded 1.2 million square miles of territory to the United States including California in the Treaty of Guadalupe Hidalgo. Although it was one of the most important territorial additions in the entire history of the United States, it would go a long way toward fanning the flames of the developing sectional conflict.

By 1850 the nation faced a crisis over the disposal of the new territories won from Mexico. Many saw the issue of slavery in the southwest as an artificial issue since the land was inhospitable to the plantation agricultural economy that made slavery profitable. Subsequently the Utah and New Mexico territories were organized under popular sovereignty with the hope that nature would stop the spread of slavery there.

The question of slavery in the territories was reopened just four years later with the passage of the Kansas-Nebraska Act. Hostility to the bill's provisions led to early bloodshed in Kansas, a harbinger of what was to come within the next seven years. The Kansas-Nebraska Act exacerbated the sectional discord between the North and the South. The bill nullified the Missouri Compromise and applied popular sovereignty to the two territories, opening the possible expansion of slavery in an area where it had been prohibited by law for more than thirty years.

With the passage of Kansas-Nebraska, settlers from proslavery Missouri and neighboring free states rushed into Kansas attempting to influence the outcome of the vote over slavery. Free-state men and proslavery factions established separate governments and organized militias, and in one of the most notorious examples of sectional violence in the West, the abolitionist John Brown and several followers hacked five southerners to death near Pottawatomie Creek in 1856.

The western overland experience is one of the most chronicled episodes in American history. Hundreds of diaries, letters, and journals testify to the mid-nineteenth century western migration. Most traditional accounts of the trek reflect the experiences of white families heading West to farm or of single men under the spell of the gold fever. Despite the existence of slavery many black families sought their futures in the antebellum West including at least one thousand African Americans who participated in the California Gold Rush in 1850. Some were slaves who accompanied their masters with the promise of freedom for stalwart service in the gold fields. Others were free men or runaway slaves. Black gold seekers occasionally banded together and formed their own companies for protection and still others belonged to integrated units. And when blacks found themselves barred from other mining frontiers because of discriminatory mining laws they headed for western urban centers, where the prospects were probably much better.

Suggestions for Further Reading

Eugene Berwanger, *The Frontier Against Slavery: Western Anti-Negro Prejudice and the Slavery Extension Controversy* (Urbana: University of Illinois Press, 1967).

John Mack Faragher, *Women and Men on the Overland Trail,* (New Haven: Yale University Press, 1979).

William Loren Katz, *The Black West,* (New York: Simon Schuster, 1987).

Lillian Schlissel, *Women's Diaries of the Westward Journey* (New York: Schocken Books, 1982).

John D. Unruh, Jr., *The Plains Across: The Overland Emigrants and the Trans-Mississippi West, 1840-1860,* (Urbana: University of Illinois Press. 1979).

Critical Thinking

1. What conditions could "Forty-Niners" expect to encounter in the California goldfields?

2. How did the California argonauts contract cholera? Was there anything they could have done to protect themselves from the disease?

3. What impact did western territorial politics have on the sectional crisis leading up to the Civil War?

4. Discuss the treatment of African Americans in the West in the years before the Civil War.

5. Although slavery was prohibited in most Western states and territories, did racial and ethnic minorities actually have more opportunities in this region than in other regions?

Document 5.1

The Forty-Niners

In January 1848, James W. Marshall detected the gleam of gold at the bottom of a stream about forty miles from Sutter's Fort, California, inaugurating the California Gold Rush. By the end of 1849, perhaps twenty-five thousand gold seekers had reached California by the sea routes, but these numbers paled in comparison with the thousands who chose the overland trek. In that year alone, more than 80,000 "Forty-Niners" reached California, with over 35,000 traveling by way of the central overland route. The following passages include an account of conditions in the gold fields, where high expectations yielded to broken dreams, and extracts from the journal of William Ives Morgan, who reached California by ship at the beginning of 1850.*

By whatever route the adventurers arrived in California, once there the cry was "On to the diggings!" The miner stopped only long enough in San Francisco to procure his outfit. This consisted of a pick, pan, shovel, rocker, dipper, wooden basket, blankets, and a few simple cooking and eating utensils. Thus furnished, he hurried on to join the throng of eager prospectors all pressing forward to satisfy the master passion for gold. With frantic oaths teamsters lashed their struggling mules, raising thick clouds of dust. Horsemen with heavy packs on their saddles passed them. Tented ox-carts were a common sight. And sprinkled through this toiling mass, almost lost in the dust and the crowd, were many footsore bearers of their own burdens of tools, arms, and supplies.

Sutter's Fort was the goal of these endless caravans. Here was assembled a throng of traders and miners, rough, sunburned, unkempt men in red or blue woolen shirts, deerskin suits, or oilskins, with now and then a Mexican with his picturesque short-jacketed suit, spurs and sombrero. This crowd was constantly changing as from day to day there came in new arrivals on one side and on the other there were new departures for the gold fields.

But even when the gold fields themselves were finally reached it was not the end of the journey. Overcrowded camps, rumors of great finds elsewhere, and most of all the cravings of a fevered imagination, led the seeker after yellow wealth on and on and on. Sometimes he was led to fortune, sometimes to utter wreck, often to both.

The conditions had a strange effect upon the country. Often several thousand people would congregate in one place in a few weeks after a rich find had been made. Tents gave place to houses of wood and brick. Newspapers, sewers, even gas works sprang into existence seemingly out of nothing. A city charter was obtained and a municipal administration organized and then-a new find farther on and the new city's population vanished in a day, leaving silence and desolation over the erstwhile aspiring metropolis.

* Henry K. Norton, *The Story of California*, (Chicago: A. C. McClurg and Co., 1913), pp. 222-229.

But this was not the only peculiar condition in the social status in California in 1849 and the following years which go to make up the period widely known as the "Days of '49." The population of the state was a motley aggregation in every respect. There were collected in a comparatively small section people from every part of the world and representing every known system of law, manners and morals. Less than eight per cent of the total population of the state were women, and in the mining districts this proportion was in many instances as low as two per cent. And the men were all young men; there were no gray heads among them.

This great, unruly, and unruled mob was one seething mass of excitement in the wild chase for gold. And of this excitement San Francisco was the center. Here were brought together the newly arrived Argonaut, the newly rich miner, and the scores of human leeches that preyed upon both. The number of men in the city who were not striving for sudden riches was negligible. The Argonaut was pressing on to the gold fields; the returned miner spent his time and his pile of gold-dust at the gaming table in an effort to make more without even going to the trouble of picking it off the ground; and the leeches were watching every chance to rob and cheat both of these classes of all that could be taken from them.

The man who had sold his all in the East to go to California found that he must waste no time in San Francisco, or his little capital would quickly vanish. The rapid production of gold, and the prevalent use of the dust as money, depreciated its value at one time as low as $4 an ounce. Prices were fabulous. Picks and shovels sold for from $5 to $15 each; a tin pan or a wooden bowl for $5; a butcher knife for $30; beef with one potato, for $1.25; baked beans "greased" for $1; hash, low-grade, 75c; hash, "18 carats," $1; roast grizzly bear for $1; "square meal" for $3; wine and spirits for $10 to $40 a quart bottle; washing was done for $15 a dozen pieces. The smallest coin tendered for any service was a fifty cent piece. The quarter was seldom used even in the purchase of the smallest articles. Everything, even boot-blacking, was done on a grand scale. Wages for ordinary laborers were at the rate of $1 an hour. Terms at "Delmonico's Hotel" were $50 a week for "plenty to eat, if one was not too fastidious, and a good bunk to sleep in." The bar made things a little noisy and an occasional free fight furnished excitement. Such were the conditions which the goldseekers had to face in San Francisco. Few remained more than one day.

The work at the mines was extremely hard. As one of the early preachers in San Francisco, Reverend William Taylor says, "there was more hard work than has ever been done in any country by the same number of men in the same length of time, since the world was made." The hardships were real as well as imaginary. The work had to be carried on under the blazing rays of the summer sun and at the same time in the ice-cold waters from the snow-covered Sierras. The strain of these conditions was hard on the strongest. This and the steady working in the wet drifts and tunnels was necessarily injurious to health. The food too was poor. Salt meat and no vegetables for long periods of time caused many to contract scurvy. The illness brought on by these conditions laid the foundation for crime by depriving many of the means of earning a livelihood. In October of 1850 an epidemic of cholera took off about a tenth of the population.

It is probable that the same amount of work as was performed by these miners in California, if it had been done in their own homes in their old employments, would have brought as large returns, but of course without the incentive of possible big strikes. Many averaged $100 a day; some as high as $500 and $700. This bred a strong hope in those who were not so fortunate, and each man worked to his utmost capacity with the thought in his mind that it would be his turn next, and another day would see him a wealthy man.

At first operations were confined to surface picking and shallow digging along streams and ravines. These sources of supply failing, the streams were turned aside and their beds worked for the precious metal. This was supplemented by "dry-washing," a process of sifting out the gold. The surface gold was soon exhausted and more elaborate methods were introduced. These necessitated the use of machinery of a simple kind. Almost all of the eastern-made contrivances for mining were utterly useless, but one of them, the "cradle," came into very common use. It consisted of a long box which was constantly rocked while "pay-dirt" was flushed through with water. The gold sank to the bottom and the dirt was washed out.

In its result mining was much like gambling, and in the eager pursuit for gold was born the miners' passion for speculation which lost for many of them in the gambling halls of San Francisco all they had earned in the gold fields. The miner became restless and even when in possession of a good claim would drop it and hasten on at the rumor of a better find. The whole life was a lottery. Land adjoining extremely rich claims was often worthless. And the wild rough uncertain character of the life itself made patient industry distasteful and even contemptible. A Mexican dug the gold-dust from his claim with a horn spoon from nine o'clock in the morning until four o'clock in the afternoon. In that short space of time he had taken out thousands of dollars. With his newly acquired wealth he set up a monte bank and bought a bottle of whiskey. By ten o'clock that night he was penniless and drunk.

The novelty and irresponsibility of the life led to much disorder and some crime, but the typical miner was a fair, square, sensible man. Most of the miners were influenced to some extent by their environment, but with few exceptions retained their manliness. In the early part of the rush to the mines gold-dust was often left in the tents unguarded with no thought of the possibility of theft. This sense of security was due to the determined attitude of the miners toward thieves. Quarreling was of course frequent but it was seldom attended with serious results. Every man knew his opponent was armed and drawing a gun usually meant death to one or the other, and often to both. Under these circumstances men hesitated to draw their weapons and most small matters were settled with fists.

Most of the mining was done in the summer months. With the October rains the cold became too severe for work in the gold fields, and a rush for San Francisco and the other towns set in with such strength as to rival the rush for the mines. Some, content with their gains, returned home.

Document 5.2

Cholera in Missouri (1849)

European immigrants brought cholera to American port cities in 1848. From New Orleans this deadly epidemic was carried by both immigrants and gold seekers up the Mississippi River to St. Louis where it did its most deadly work, killing more than 7,000 of the inhabitants in a matter of months. California-bound emigrants next carried it to the jumping-off towns along the Missouri River where preparations were made for the overland journey to California. The following documents testify to the impact of cholera on the Missouri frontier.*

May 4 4 A.M. at *Jefferson City* but as I was in the arms of Morpheus I did not see it weather warm and some rain 2 Cases of Colera reported on board which followed the boat from St. Louis when it is some what fatal but no one cares for it but those who are attached as the Fables from morning to night are surrounded by card players who enjoy betting 4°C at Boonville a pretty vilage county site Boon County 1 Death to day from colera

5
weather still cloudy and some rain on this river there are numerous vilages which I do not mention from their smallness and unfavorable appearance but yet some appear to do considerable business also some pretty residences to day I have been reading a book entitled Lorenzo Dow who was a stranger escentric singular and good man and who laye down many good rules by which we should be governed, and plausibly argues many important parts of scripture & at 4°C burried a victim of Colera

9
Our horses are sold at an average of about 40$ but oxen are worth from 40 to 50$ pr yoke Colera in camps a great many backing out in the frontier towns there are about from 10 to 12 Thousand and fresh arrivals every day and also some backing out some failing to go to Calaf are directing their course to Texas- and some to other places west great mertality on steam boats owing to the crowd of passengers by the colera.

15
For several days rain, cloudy weather and nearly cold enough for frost, the colera is raging to a fearful extent among the Emigrants daily they are dieing and as much cared for as beast much less than oxen or mules as men bewail the loss of property but not

---

* *Diary of J.W. Chatham*, May 4, 5, 9, 15, 1849, typescript, The Center for American History, University of Texas at Austin; "California in 1849," *John Hudgins Papers*, 2 pp. typescript, Western Historical Manuscript Collection, University of Missouri at Columbia.

companions here is the most unprincipled heartless & courteous people that can be found I think setled in any country, to day a young virginian paid 25$ dollars for his Brother dieing on a bed, heartless monster unprincipled Republican unworthy of a freemans name, many dies but no name is know[n] and many a widow will mourn for her husbands return and think themselves forsaken while they are laying under the cold sod Calafornias golden inducement will cause a many a tender females heart to bleed, but man man you will pursue your greatest enemy, your greatest curse. All is confusion in camp prepareing to start tomorrow Dr Steck is labouring under a slight attack of the Colera thankful am I for escapeing so far I have been among the Colera for one month but thank God I have yet escaped and by his Divine mer[cy] hope to do so no one knows but he may be the next victim as some go to bed well and by tomorrows noon are in the icy arms of death frail humanity, how this should teach you to prepare for a future life but such is the thought of but few as vice is the reigning monarch.

CALIFORNIA IN 1849

On the 6th day of May, 1849, I, John Hudgins, Mooresville, Livingston County, Missouri, drove out of my father's yard with eight yoke of oxen hitched to a large Kentucky Turnpike wagon loaded with about 6,000 pounds of provisions, mostly flour, bacon, sugar, coffee, with 10 gallons of alcohol and 1 gallon of cholera medicine. I owned three quarters of the outfit and Warren M. Hudgins, a cousin, owned one-fourth. My two brothers, James and Humphrey, aged respectively 17 and 15, accompanied us.

The first day out we joined six other wagons belonging to the following parties from this county; Stone Bro's and McCrosky, two; Lawson, one; Patrick, one; Gobin and Shafer, one; and Woolfcale, one.

We expected to go the South Pass route, and intended to cross the Missouri River at St. Joseph. The soring was cold and wet which made the grass late and traveling slow. On the 11th we were in the west part of Clinton County. We sent a man ahead to see about crossing the river. [He reported that the ferry was two weeks behind, and the people there were dying with the cholera like hogs.] We heard that there was a small boat at Westport landing, or Kansas City, as it is now called.

We turned south through Smithville and Barry, drove up the bottom to the ferry, and crossed, ourselves with the negro boss who had charge of the boat, which was a small one and would only take one wagon and one yoke of oxen at a load. It took two trips for each outfit. We cordelled the boat up against the current each trip on the south side about one fourth mile so as to make up for what she drifted down each trip.

There was a ledge of rock 5 or 6 feet above the water on the south of Jackson County side. Along the edge of the water was a lot of clothing that had been thrown away, the cholera having run out or killed all but three persons that we saw, one merchant, one blacksmith, and the negro ferryman. We got everything across and got out past Westport. (Kansas City)

Next morning, the 13th, Uncle Antony (Patrick's servant), took the cholera. We gave all the medicine and nursing that we could but we were camped out on the prairie out of sight of timber. John Stone and I rode some 5 or 6 miles and found some dead willows which the prairie fires had killed. We cut a large bundle each and carried them to the camp to build a fire for the sick man, but it did no good. He died in the tent with mud and water all around. The oxen, chained to the wagon, were up to their knees in mud. We laid by two days. Antony died in the night and as soon as it was light, we yoked up the oxen and started the wagons, and left a detail of four men to bury the dead, myself one of them.

We had spades but no picks. The ground was so soft that we did not think that we would need them. When we got down about two feet we come to hard pan that we could not dig with the spade so we hollowed and fitted it as well as we could, rolled him in his blankets and covered him up. Then we cut sods and raised a mound four feet high over him. His master and comrade from childhood had gone on with the wagons and I never saw more sincere grief. They had been more than brothers from early childhood.

Next day we camped at Big John Spring, still cloudy and raining showers, four cases of cholera but we cured them with frequent doses of medicine. Here a train overtook us with the horse, saddle, and saddle bags of Bouben McCroskie, who had started to overtake his wagon horses. Back three days after we left home our change in our route had put him one day more behind. He left an old acquaintance's camp after eating a hearty breakfast, and was found before noon dead beside the road. So Stone, his partner, sold his horse to Patrick and that night she was stolen by the Kaw Indians. I found their trail and wanted to follow to their village, take the best horse that we could find and keep it until they brought the stolen horse back. Patrick was afraid we would get into trouble with the Indian agents at Council Grove.

Document 5.3

Slavery in the Western Territories (1850)

In a speech before the Senate in 1850, Daniel Webster eloquently states his opposition to slavery in the western lands won from Mexico. Webster recognizes the artificiality of the slavery debate in the arid West, which was not conducive to the plantation economy. Since nature would stop the spread of slavery in Utah and New Mexico.*

Now, as to California and New Mexico, I hold slavery to be excluded from those territories by a law even superior to that which admits and sanctions it in Texas. I mean the law of nature, of physical geography, the law of the formation of the earth. That law settles for ever, with a strength beyond all terms of human enactment, that slavery cannot exist in California or New Mexico. Understand me, Sir; I mean slavery as we regard it; the slavery of the colored race as it exists in the Southern States… It is as impossible that African slavery, as we see it among us, should find its way, or be introduced, into California and New Mexico, as any other natural impossibility. California and New

---

* Daniel Webster, *Works*, (Boston, 1851), V., pp. 350-353.

Mexico are Asiatic in their formation and scenery. They are composed of vast ridges of mountains, of great height, with broken ridges and deep valleys. The sides of these mountains are entirely barren; their tops capped by perennial snow. There may be in California, now made free by its constitution, and no doubt there are, some tracts of valuable land. But it is not so in New Mexico... What is there in New Mexico that could, by any possibility, induce any body to go there with slaves? There are some narrow strips of tillable land on the borders of the rivers; but the rivers themselves dry up before midsummer is gone. All that the people can do in that region is to raise some little articles, some little wheat for their tortillas, and that by irrigation. And who expects to see a hundred black men cultivating tobacco, corn, cotton, rice, or anything else, on lands in New Mexico, made fertile only by irrigation?

I look upon it, therefore, as a fixed fact, to use the current expression of the day, that both California and New Mexico are destined to be free, ... free by the arrangement of things ordained by the Power above us. I have therefore to say, in this respect also, that this country is fixed for freedom, to as many persons as shall ever live in it, by a less repealable law than that which attaches to the right of holding slaves in Texas; and I will say further, that, if a resolution or a bill were now before us, to provide a territorial government for New Mexico, I would not vote to put any prohibition into it whatever. Such a prohibition would be idle, as it respects any effect it would have upon the territory; and I would not take pains uselessly to reaffirm an ordinance of nature, nor to reenact the will of God...

Sir, wherever there is a substantive good to be done, wherever there is a foot of land to be prevented from becoming slave territory, I am ready to assert the principle of the exclusion of slavery. I am pledged to it from the year 1837; I have been pledged to it again and again; and I will perform those pledges; but I will not do a thing unnecessarily that wounds the feelings of others, or that does discredit to my own understanding.

Document 5.4

The Compromise of 1850

The slavery question was once again brought into national politics following new territorial acquisitions resulting from the Mexican War in 1848. Since 1846, every northern state legislature endorsed the Wilmot Proviso which prohibited slavery from any territories won from Mexico. However, this resolution was never passed by Congress. With the Southern states threatening to secede, various compromise resolutions were considered. Henry Clay's Omnibus Bill covering the organization of the territories contained the basis for what became known as the Compromise of 1850. Ultimately, California was admitted as a free state, slavery was outlawed in the nation's capital, a harsher slave law was enacted, and the Utah and New Mexico territories were organized with popular sovereignty.*

I. CLAY'S RESOLUTIONS

It being desirable, for the peace, concord, and harmony of the Union of these States, to settle and adjust amicably all existing questions of controversy between them arising out of the institution of slavery upon a fair, equitable and just basis: therefore,

1. *Resolved,* That California, with suitable boundaries, ought, upon her application to be admitted as one of the States of this Union, without the imposition by Congress of any restriction in respect to the exclusion or introduction of slavery within those boundaries.

2. *Resolved,* That as slavery does not exist by law, and is not likely to be introduced into any of the territory acquired by the United States from the republic of Mexico, it is inexpedient for Congress to provide by law either for its introduction into, or exclusion from, any part of the said territory; and that appropriate territorial governments ought to be established by Congress in all of the said territory, not assigned as the boundaries of the proposed State of California, without the adoption of any restriction or condition on the subject of slavery.

3. *Resolved,* That the western boundary of the State of Texas ought to be fixed on the Rio del Norte, commencing one marine league from its mouth, and running up that river to the southern line of New Mexico; thence with that line eastwardly, and so continuing in the same direction to the line as established between the United States and Spain, excluding any portion of New Mexico, whether lying on the east or west of that river.

4. *Resolved,* That it be proposed to the State of Texas, that the United States will provide for the payment of all that portion of the legitimate and bona fide public debt of that State contracted prior to its annexation to the United States, and for which the duties on foreign imports were pledged by the said State to its creditors, not exceeding the sum of -dollars, in consideration of the said duties so pledged having been no longer applicable to that object after the said annexation, but having thenceforward become payable to the United States; and upon the condition, also, that the said State of Texas shall, by some solemn and authentic act of her legislature or of a convention, relinquish to the United States any claim which it has to any part of New Mexico.

5. *Resolved,* That it is inexpedient to abolish slavery in the District of Columbia whilst that institution continues to exist in the State of Maryland, without the consent of that State, without the consent of the people of the District, and without just compensation to the owners of slaves within the District.

6. *But, resolved,* That it is expedient to prohibit, within the District, the slave trade in slaves brought into it from States or places beyond the limits of the District, either to be sold therein as merchandise, or to be transported to other markets without the District of Columbia.

7. *Resolved,* That more effectual provision ought to be made by law, according to the requirement of the constitution, for the restitution and delivery of persons bound to

---

* U. S. *Senate Journal*, 31st Congress, 1st Session, January 29, 1850, p. 118
  U. S. *Statutes at Large*, Vol. IX, p. 446; 453; 462.

service or labor in any State, who may escape into any other State or Territory in the Union. And,

8. *Resolved,* That Congress has no power to promote or obstruct the trade in slaves between the slaveholding States; but that the admission or exclusion of slaves brought from one into another of them, depends exclusively upon their own particular laws.

2. THE TEXAS AND NEW MEXICO ACT

September 9, 1850

An Act proposing to the State of Texas the Establishment of her Northern and Western Boundaries, the Relinquishment by the said State of all Territory claimed by her exterior to said Boundaries, and of all her claims upon the United States, and to establish a territorial Government for New Mexico.

Be it enacted, That the following propositions shall be, and the same hereby are, offered to the State of Texas, which, when agreed to by the said State, and in an act passed by the general assembly, shall be binding and obligatory, upon the United States, and upon the said State of Texas: *Provided,* The said agreement by the said general assembly shall be given on or before the first day of December, eighteen hundred and fifty:

FIRST. The State of Texas will agree that her boundary on the north shall commence at the point at which the meridian of one hundred degrees west from Greenwich is intersected by the parallel of thirty-six degrees thirty minutes north latitude, and shall run from said point due west to the meridian of one hundred and three degrees west from Greenwich; thence her boundary shall run due south to the thirty-second degree of north latitude; thence on the said parallel of thirty-two degrees of north latitude to the Rio Bravo del Norte, and thence with the channel of said river to the Gulf of Mexico.

SECOND. The State of Texas cedes to the United States all her claim to territory exterior to the limits and boundaries which she agrees to establish by the first article of this agreement.

THIRD. The State of Texas relinquishes all claim upon the United States for liability of the debts of Texas, and for compensation or indemnity for the surrender to the United States of her ships, forts, arsenals, customhouses, custom-house revenue, arms and munitions of war, and public buildings with their sites, which became the property of the United States at the time of the annexation.

FOURTH. The United States, in consideration of said establishment of boundaries, cessation of claim to territory, and relinquishment of claims, will pay to the State of Texas the sum of ten millions of dollars in a stock bearing five per cent. interest, and redeemable at the end of fourteen years, the interest payable half-yearly at the treasury of the United States...

Sec. 2. And that all that portion of the Territory of the United States bounded as follows (boundaries)... is hereby erected into a temporary government, by the name of the Territory of New Mexico: *Provided,* That nothing in this act contained shall be construed to inhibit the government of the United States from dividing said Territory into two or more Territories, in such manner and at such times as Congress shall deem convenient and proper, or from attaching any portion thereof to any other Territory or State: *And provided, further,* That, when admitted as a State. the said Territory, or any portion of the same, shall be received into the Union, with or without slavery, as their constitution may prescribe at the time of their admission.

3. THE UTAH ACT

September 9, 1850

An Act to establish a Territorial Government for Utah
Be it enacted, That all that part of the territory of the United States included within the following limits, to wit: bounded on the west by the State of California, on the north by the Territory of Oregon, and on the east by the summit of the Rocky Mountains, and on the south by the thirty-seventh parallel of north latitude, be, and the same is hereby, created into a temporary government, by the name of the Territory of Utah; and, when admitted as a State, the said Territory, or any portion of the same, shall be received into the Union, with or without slavery, as their constitution may prescribe at the time of their admission: *Provided,* That nothing in this act contained shall be construed to inhibit the government of the United States from dividing said Territory into two or more Territories, in such manner and at such times as Congress shall deem convenient and proper, or from attaching any portion of said Territory to any other State or Territory of the United States...

Document 5.5

People v. George W. Hall (1854)

In the following 1854 decision the Supreme Court of the State of California refused to allow the testimony of Chinese in court. Subsequently, numerous Chinese residents became robbery and murder victims since whites recognized they would be immune from prosecution. It is noteworthy in this decision that the Chinese were lumped together with blacks and Indians, who were also barred from testifying againts whites in court.*

The People, Respondent, v. George W. Hall, Appellant
Witness-Persons Incompetent-Section 394 of the Civil Practice Act provides: "No Indian or Negro shall be allowed to testify as a witness in any action in which a white person is a party."
Idem.-Section 14 of the Criminal Act provides: "No Black, or Mulatto person, or Indian shall be allowed to give evidence in favor of, or against a White man." *Held,* that

---

* *People v. George W. Hall*, 4 Cal. 399 (1854).

the words, Indian, Negro, Black, and White, are generic terms, designating race. That, therefore, Chinese and all other peoples not white, are included in the prohibition from being witnesses against Whites.

Mr. Chief Justice Murray delivered the opinion of the Court. Mr. J. Heydenfeldt concurred.

The Appellant, a free white citizen of this State, was convicted of murder upon the testimony of Chinese witnesses.

The point involved in this case, is the admissibility of such evidence.

The three hundred ninety-fourth section of the Act Concerning Civil Cases, provides that no Indian or Negro shall be allowed to testify as a witness in any action or proceeding in which a White person is a party.

The fourteenth section of the Act of April 16, 1850, regulating Criminal Proceedings, provides that "No Black or Mulatto person, or Indian, shall be allowed to give evidence in favor of, or against a white man."

The true point at which we are anxious to arrive is, the legal significance of the words, "Black, Mulatto, Indian and White person," and whether the Legislature adopted them as generic terms, or intended to limit their application to specific types of the human species...

The words of the Act must be construed in *pari materia.* It will not be disputed that "White" and "Negro" are generic terms, and refer to two of the great types of mankind. If these, as well as the word "Indian," are not to be regarded as generic terms, including the two great races which they were intended to designate, but only specific, and applying to those whites and Negroes who were inhabitants of this continent at the time of the passage of the Act, the most anomalous consequences would ensue. The European white man who comes here would not be shielded from the testimony of the degraded and demoralized caste, while the Negro, fresh from the coast of Africa, or the Indian of Patagonia, the Kanaka, South Sea Islander, or New Hollander, would be admitted, upon their arrival, to testify against white citizens in our courts of law.

To argue such a proposition would be an insult to the good sense of the Legislature.

The evident intention of the Act was to throw around the citizen a protection for life and property, which could only be secured by removing him above the corrupting influences of degraded castes.

It can hardly be supposed that any Legislature would attempt this by excluding domestic Negroes and Indians, who not unfrequently have correct notions of their obligations to society, and turning loose upon the community the more degraded tribes of the same species, who have nothing in common with us, in language, country, or laws.

In using the words "no Black or Mulatto person, or Indian shall be allowed to give evidence for or against a White person," the Legislature, if any intention can be ascribed to it, adopted the most comprehensive terms to embrace every known class or shade of color, as the apparent design was to protect the white person from the influence of all testimony other than that of persons of the same caste. The use of these terms must, by every sound rule of construction, exclude every one who is not of white blood...

The word "White" has a distinct signification, which *ex vi termini,* excludes black, yellow, and all other colors. It will be observed, by reference to the first section of the second Article of the Constitution of the State, that none but white males can become electors... On examination of the constitutional debates, it will be found that not a little difficulty existed in selecting these precise words, which were finally agreed upon as the most comprehensive that could be suggested to exclude all inferior races...

The same rule which would admit them to testify, would admit them to all the equal rights of citizenship, and we might soon see them at the polls, in the jury box, upon the bench, and in our legislative halls.

This is not a speculation which exists in the excited and over-heated imagination of the patriot and statesman, but it is an actual and present danger.

The anomalous spectacle of the distinct people, living in our community, recognizing no laws of this State, except through necessity, bringing with them their prejudices and national feuds, in which they indulge in open violation of law; whose mendacity is proverbial; a race of people whom nature has marked as inferior, and who are incapable of progress or intellectual development beyond a certain point, as their history has shown; differing in language, opinions, color, and physical conformation; between whom nature has placed an impassable difference, is now presented, and for them is claimed, not only the right to swear away the life of a citizen, but the further privilege of participating with us in administering the affairs of our Government.

For these reasons, we are of the opinion that the testimony was inadmissible.

Document 5.6

Slave Women in the West

In the years prior to the Civil War, black women were an uncommon sight in the American West. While Anglo women left hundreds of diaries and letters recording their western lives, few accounts have surfaced telling of the black woman's experience in the trans-Mississippi region. During the 1930s, members of the Oklahoma Writer's Project interviewed former slaves, most then in their nineties, and recorded their stories for posterity. In the first two passages, a former slave woman recounts her overland trip from Missouri to Texas, and an Oklahoma woman recalls her mother's passage to the Indian Territory as a slave to a Creek family. In the concluding excerpt 90-year old Chaney Richardson remembers her years as a slave in a Cherokee family.*

We rides the wagons all the way, how many days. I dunno. The country was wild most of the way, and I know now that we come through the same country where I lives now, only it was to the east... And we keeps on riding and comes to the big river that's all

* George P. Rawick, ed., *The American Slave*, (Westport, Conn.: Greenwood Publishing Co., 1972), Vol. 7, pp. 90–91; 115–117; 257–261.

brown and red looking, (Red River) and the next thing I was sold to Mrs. Vaughn at Bonham, Texas, and there I stays till after the slaves is free.

The new Mistress was a widow, no children round the place, and she treat me mighty good. She was good white folks-like old Master Ben, powerful good.

When the word get to us that the slaves is free, the Mistress says I is free to go anywheres I want. And I tell her this talk about being free sounds like foolishment to me-anyway, where can I go? She just pat me on the shoulder and say I better stay right there with her, and that's what I do for a long time. Then I hears about how the white folks down at Dallas pays big money for house girls and there I goes.

That's all I ever do after that-work at the houses till I gets too old to hobble on these tired old feets and legs, then I just sits down.

Just sits down and wishes for old master Ben to come and get me, and take care of this old woman like he use to do when she is just a little black child on the plantation in Missouri!

God Bless old Master Ben-he was good white folks!

MARY GRAYSON
Age 83 yrs.
Tulsa, Oklahoma

I am what we colored people call a "native." That means that I didn't come into the Indian country from somewhere in the Old South, after the War, like so many negroes did, but I was born here in the old Creek Nation, and my master was a Creek Indian. That was eighty three years ago, so I am told.

My mammy belonged to white people back in Alabama when she was born-down in the southern part I think, for she told me that after she was a sizeable girl her white people moved into the eastern part of Alabama where there was a lot of Creeks. Some of them Creeks was mixed up with the whites, and some of the big men in the Creeks who come to talk to her master was almost white, it looked like. "My white folks moved around a lot when I was a little girl," she told me.

When mammy was about 10 or 12 years old, some of the Creeks begun to come out to the Territory in little bunches. They wasn't the ones who was taken out here by the soldiers and contractor men—they come on ahead by therselves and most of them had plenty of money, too. A Creek come to my mammy's master and bought her to bring out here, but she heard she was being sold and run off into the woods. There was an old clay pit, dug way back into a high bank, where the slaves had been getting clay to mix with hog hair scrapings to make chinking for the big log houses that they built for the master and the cabins they made for themselves. Well, my mammy run and hid way back in that old clay pit, and it was way after dark before the master and the other man found her.

The Creek man that bought her was a kind sort of a man, mammy said, and wouldn't let the master punish her. He took her away and was kind to her, but he decided she was too young to breed and he sold her to another Creek who had several slaves already, and he brought her out to the Territory.

The McIntosh men was the leaders in the bunch that come out at that time, and one of the bunch, named Jim Perryman, bought my mammy and married her to one of his "boys," but after he waited a while and she didn't have a baby he decided she was no good breeder and he sold her to Mose Perryman.

Mose Perryman was my master, and he was a cousin to Legus Perryman, who was a big man in the Tribe. He was a lot younger than Mose, and laughed at Mose for buying my mammy, but he got fooled, because my mammy got married to Mose's slave boy Jacob, the way the slaves was married them days, and went ahead and had ten children for Mr. Mose.

Mose Perryman owned my pappy and his older brother, Hector, and one of the McIntosh men, Oona, I think his name was, owned my pappy's brother William. I can remember when I first heard about there was going to be a war. The older children would talk about it, but they didn't say it was a war all over the country. They would talk about a war going to be "back in Alabama," and I guess they had heard the Creeks talking about it that way.

When I was born we lived in the Choaka bottoms, and Mr. Mose Perryman had a lot of land broke in all up and down the Arkansas river along there. After the War, when I had got to be a young woman, there was quite a settlement grew up at Choska (pronounced Choe-skey) right across the river east of where Haskell now is, but when I was a child before the War all the whole bottoms was marshy kind of wilderness except where farms had been cleared out. The land was very rich, and the Creeks who got to settle there were lucky. They always had big crops. All west of us was high ground, toward Gibson station and Fort Gibson, and the land was sandy. Some of the McIntoshes lived over that way, and my Uncle William belonged to one of them.

We slaves didn't have a hard time at all before the War. I have had people who were slaves of white folks back in the old states tell me that they had to work awfully hard and their masters were cruel to them sometimes, but all the Negroes I knew who belonged to Creeks always had plenty of clothes and lots to eat and we all lived in good log cabins we built. We worked the farm and tended to the horses and cattle and hogs, and some of the older women worked around the owner's house, but each Negro family looked after a part of the fields and worked the crops like they belonged to us.

When I first heard talk about the War the slaves were allowed to go and see one another sometimes and often they were sent on errands several miles with a wagon or on a horse, but pretty soon we were all kept at home, and nobody was allowed to come around and talk to us. But we heard what was going on.

The McIntosh men got nearly everybody to side with them about the War, but we Negroes got word somehow that the Cherokees over back of Ft. Gibs was not going to be in the War, and that there were some Union people over there who would help slaves to get away, but we children didn't know anything about what we heard our parents whispering about, and they would stop if they heard us listening. Most of the Creeks who lived in our part of the country, between the Arkansas and the Verdigris, and some even south of the Arkansas, belonged to the Lower Creeks and sided with the South, but down below us along the Canadian River they were Upper Creeks and there was a good deal of talk about them going with the North. Some of the Negroes tried to get away and go down to them, but I don't know of any from our neighborhood that want to them.

CHANEY RICHARDSON
Age 90 years
Fort Gibson, Okla.

I was born in the old Caney settlement southeast of Tahlequah on the banks of Caney Creek. Off to the north we could see the big old ridge of Sugar Mountain when the sun shine on him first thing in the morning when we all getting up.

I didn't know nothing else but some kind of war until I was a grown women, because when I first can remember my old Master, Charley Rogers, was always on the lockout for somebody or other he was lined up against in the big feud.

My master and all the rest of the folks was Cherokees, and they'd been killing each other off in the feud ever since long before I was borned, and jest because old Master have a big farm and three-four families of Negroes them other Cherokees keep on pestering his stuff all the time. Us children was always afeared to go any place less'n some of the grown folks was along.

We didn't know what we was a-feared of, but we heard the Master and Mistress keep talking 'tout "another Party killing" and we stuck close to the place.

When I was about 10 years old that feud got so bad the Indians was always talking about getting their horses and cattle killed and their slaves harmed. I was too little to know how bad it was until one morning my own mammy went off somewhere down the road to git some stuff to dye cloth and she didn't come back.

Lots of the young Indian bucks on both sides of the feud would ride around the woods at night, and old Master got powerful oneasy about my mammy and had all the neighbors and slaves out looking for her, but nobody find her.

It was about a week later that two Indian men rid up and ask old master wesn't his gal Ruth gone. He says yes, and they take one of the slaves along with a wagon to show where they seen her.

They find her in some bushes where she'd been getting bark to set the dyes, and she been dead all the time. Somebody done hit her in the head with a club and shot her through and through with a bullet too. She was so swole up they couldn't lift her up and jest had to make a deep hole right along side of her and roll her in it she was so bad mortified.

Old Master nearly go crazy he was so mad, and the young Cherokee man ride the woods every night for about a month, but they never catch on to who done it.

I think old Master sell the children or give them out to somebody then, because I never see my sisters and brother for a long time after the Civil War, and for me, I have to go live with a new mistress that was a Cherokee neighbor. Her name was Hannah Ross, and she raised me until I was grown.

When the Civil War come along we seen lots of white soldiers in then brown butternut suits all over the place, and about all the Indian men was in it too. Old master Charley Rogers' boy Charley went along too. Then pretty soon-it seem like about a year-a lot of the Cherokee men come back home and say they not going back to the War with that General Cooper and some of them go off the Federal side because the captain go to the Federal side too.

Somebody come along and tell me my own pappy have to go in the war and I think they say he on the Cooper side, and then after while Kiss Hannah tell me he git kill over in Arkansas.

I was so grieved all the time I don't remember much what went on, but I know pretty soon my Cherokee folks had all the stuff they had at up by the soldiers and they was jest a few wagons and mules left.

All the slaves was piled in together and some of the grown ones walking, and they took us way down across the big river and kept us in the bottoms a long time until the War was over.

We lived in a kind of a camp, but I was too little to know where they got the grub to feed us with. Most all the Negro men was off somewhere in the War.

Then one day they had to bust up the camp and some Federal soldiers go with us and we all start back home. We git to a place where all the houses is burned down and I ask what is that place. Miss Hannah say: "Skullyville, child. That's where they had part of the War."

All the slaves was set out when we git to Fort Gibson, and the soldiers say we all free now. They give us grub and clothes to the Negroes at that place. It wasn't no town but a fort place and a patch of big trees.

Miss Hannah take me to her place and I work there until I was grown. I didn't git any money that I seen, but I got a good place to stay.

Pretty soon I married Ran Lovely and we lived in a double log house here at Fort Gibson. Then my second husband was Henry Richardson, but he's been dead for years, too. We had six children, but they all dead but one.

I didn't went slavery to be over with, mostly because we had the War I reckon. All that trouble made me the loss of my mammy and pappy, and I was always treated good when I was a slave. When it was over I had rather be at home like I was. None of the Cherokees ever whipped us, and my mistress give me some mighty fine rules to live by to git along in this world, too.

The Cherokee didn't have no jail for Negroes and no jail for themselves either. If a man done a crime he come back to take his punishment without being locked up.

Document 5.7

The Kansas-Nebraska Act (1854)

In 1854, Stephen A. Douglas proposed legislation to organize territorial governments in Kansas and Nebraska. His solution to the expansion of slavery into federal territory was to allow territorial residents themselves to decide the issue, a process later known as popular sovereignty. The passage of this legislation probably did more than any other issue to inflame actional dissension and ignite the Civil War seven years later. At the heart of the Kansas-Nebraska Act was Douglas's intention to connect the imminent transcontinental railroad to his home state of Illinois. He gave little consideration to the fact at this land had already been promised to tribes just recently forcibly relocated from the east. In one fell swoop, Kansas-Nebraska repealed the Missouri Compromise, upset the political balance between the North and the South, and created the Republican Party.*

CHAP. LIX.-An Act to Organize the Territories of Nebraska and Kansas.
May 30, 1854.

Be it enacted by the Senate and House of Representatives of the United States of America in Congrees assembled, That all that part of the territory of the United States included within the following limits, except such portions thereof as are hereinafter expressly exempted from the operations of this act, to wit: beginning at a point in the Missouri River where the fortieth parallel of north latitude crosses the same; thence west on said parallel to the east boundary of the Territory of Utah, on the summit of the Rocky Mountains; thence on said summit northward to the forty-ninth parallel of north latitude; thence east on said parallel to the western boundary of the territory of Minnesota; thence southward on said boundary to the Missouri River; thence down the main channel of said river to the place of beginning, be, and the same is hereby, created into a temporary government by the name of the Territory of Nebraska; and when admitted as a State or States, the said Territory, or any portion of the same, shall be received into the Union with or without slavery, as their constitution may prescribe at the time of their admission: Provided, That nothing in this act contained shall be construed to inhibit the government of the United States from dividing said Territory into two or more Territories, in such manner and at such times as Congress shall deem convenient and proper, or from attaching any portion of said Territory to any other State or Territory of the United States: Provided further, That nothing in this act contained shall be construed to impair the rights of person or property now pertaining to the Indians in said Territory, so long as such rights shall remain unextinguished by treaty between the United States and such Indians, or to include any territory which, by treaty with any Indian tribe, is not, without the consent of said tribe, to be included within the territorial limits or jurisdiction of any State or Territory; but all such territory shall be excepted out of the boundaries, and constitute no part of the Territory of Nebraska, until said tribe shall signify their assent to the President of the United States to be included within the said Territory of Nebraska, or to affect the authority of the government of the United States to make any regulations respecting such Indians, their lands, property, or other rights, by treaty, law, or otherwise, which it would have been competent to the government to make if this act had never passed.

SEC. 2. And be it further enacted, That the executive power and authority in and over said Territory of Nebraska shall be vested in a Governor, who shall hold his office for four years, and until his successor shall be appointed and qualified, unless sooner removed by the President of the United States. The Governor shall reside within said Territory, and shall be commander-in-chief of the militia thereof. He may grant pardons

---

* "Kansas-Nebraska Act," Thirty-Third Congress, Sess. I., 59, (May 30, 1854), pp. 277–284, 287.

and respites for offences against the laws of said Territory, and reprieves for offences against the laws of the United States, until the decision of the President can be made known thereon; he shall commission all officers who shall be appointed to office under the laws of the said Territory, and shall take care that the laws be faithfully executed.

SEC. 5. And be it further enacted, That every free white male inhabitant above the age of twenty-one years who shall be an actual resident of said Territory, and shall possess the qualifications hereinafter prescribed, shall be entitled to vote at the first election, and shall be eligible to any office within the said Territory; but the qualifications of voters, and of holding office, at all subsequent elections, shall be such as shall be prescribed by the Legislative Assembly: Provided, That the right of suffrage and of holding office shall be exercised only by citizens of the United States and those who shall have declared on oath their intention to become such, and shall have taken an oath to support the Constitution of the United States and the provisions of this act: And provided further, That no officer, soldier, seaman, or marine, or other person in the army or navy of the United States, or attached to troops in the service of the United States, shall be allowed to vote or hold office in said Territory, by reason of being on service therein.

SEC. 18. And be it further enacted, That all officers to be appointed by the President, by and with the advice and consent of the Senate, for the Territory of Nebraska, who, by virtue of the provisions of any law now existing, or which may be enacted during the present Congress, are required to give security for moneys that may be intrusted with them for disbursement, shall give such security, at such time and place, and in such manner, as the Secretary of the Treasury may prescribe.

SEC. 19. And be it further enacted, That all that part of the Territory of the United States included within the following limits, except such portions thereof as are hereinafter expressly exempted from the operations of this act, to wit, beginning at a point on the western boundary of the State of Missouri, where the thirty-seventh parallel of north latitude crosses the same; thence west on said parallel to the eastern boundary of New Mexico; thence north on said boundary to latitude thirty-eight; thence following said boundary westward to the east boundary of the Territory of Utab, on the summit of the Rocky Mountains; thence northward on said summit to the fortieth parallel of latitude; thence east on said parallel to the western boundary of the State of Missouri; thence south with the western boundary of said State to the place of beginning, be, and the same is hereby, created into a temporary government by the name of the Territory of Kansas; and when admitted as a State or States, the said Territory, or any portion of the same, shall be received into the Union with or without slavery, as their Constitution may prescribe at the time of their admission: Provided, That nothing in this act contained shall be construed to inhibit the government of the United States from dividing said Territory into two or more Territories, in such manner and at such times as Congress shall deem convenient and proper, or from attaching any portion of said Territory to any other State or Territory of the United States: Provided further, That nothing in this act contained shall be construed to impair the rights of person or property now pertaining to the Indians in said Territory, so long as such rights shall remain unextinguished by treaty between the United States and such Indians, or to include any territory which, by treaty with any Indian tribe, is not, without the consent of said tribe, to be included within the territorial limits or jurisdiction of any State or Territory; but all such territory shall be excepted out of the boundaries, and constitute no part of the Territory of Kansas, until said tribe shall signify their assent to the President of the United States to be included within the said Territory of Kansas, or to affect the authority of the government of the United States to make any regulation respecting such Indians, their lands, property, or other rights, by treaty, law, or otherwise, which it would have been competent to the government to make if this act had never passed.

SEC. 28. And be it further enacted, That the provisions of the act entitled "An act respecting fugitives from justice, and persons escaping from the service of their masters," approved February twelfth, seventeen hundred and ninety-three, and the provisions of the act entitled "An act to amend, and supplementary to, the aforesaid act," approved September eighteenth, eighteen hundred and fifty, be, and the same are hereby, declared to extend to and be in full force within the limits of the said Territory of Kansas.

Document 5.8

Texas Slave Insurrection (1860)

In the study of the American West, Texas offers a study in contrasts with its southern and western characteristics. During the antebellum years, Texas was the only state in the southwest with a significant slave population. Every southern state had a tradition of supressing slave insurrections, both real and rumored, with harsh sanctions. In July 1860 much of Dallas's business center was burned to the ground. Subsequent fires in seven other Texas cities fanned rumors of an abolitionist inspired plot to free the slaves. Coming on the heels of John Brown's raid on Harpers Ferry the previous year, many Texans were panic stricken. Ensuing vigilante violence led to the deaths of up to a hundred blacks and northern abolitionists. The following letter to the editor of a northern paper from a southern white offers insight into the anti-abolitionist hysteria in Texas.*

The wildest excitement prevails throughout the north-western, north-eastern, and the central portions of Texas, in consequence of *Abolition incendiarism.* I have no doubt but you have seen, ere this reaches you, the burning of Dallas, Denton, Black Jack Grove, and quite a large number of stores and mills. Loss estimated at between $1,500,000 and $2,000,000. Since then the *Abolitionists* have been detected in attempts to fire a number of other towns South of the above, and in an extensive plan of insurrection among the negros, headed by these demons of hell. On some plantations the negros have been

---

* John Townsend, *The Doom of Slavery in the Union; its Safety out of it,* (1860).

examined, and arms and ammunition in considearble amount have been found in their possession; they all admit they were given to them by these *Lincolnites.* Every day we hear of the burning of some town, mill, store, or farmhouse. Henderson was burnt to ashes on the 6th instant, being the general election day for State and county officers. We hear of two or three other towns burnt on the same day. *Women and children* have been so frightened by these burnings and threatened rebellion of the negros, that in several instances they have *left their homes in their fright, and when found were almost confirmed maniacs!* Military companies are organized all over the state, and one-half of our citizens do constant patrol duty. But unfortunately up to this time Judge Lynch has had the honor to preside only in ten cases of whites (northern Lincolnites) and about sixty-five of negros, all of whom were hung or burnt, as to the degree of their implication in the rebellion and burning. The plan was to burn all of the towns, thereby destroy the arms and ammunition, also country stores, mills, farms, and corn cribs, &c. Then on election day they were to be headed by John Browns, and march south for Houston and Galveston city, where they would all unite, and after pillaging and burning those two cities, the negros were promised by these devils incarnate, that they would have in readiness a number of vessels, and would take them forthwith to Mexico, where they would be free. The *credulity of the negro* is so great, that he can be *induced to believe almost anything,* no matter how impossible it may be, particularly when he is informed by a shrewd white man that the thing can be done, and that he will lead them on and accomplish the object. But the end is not yet. I believe that the northern churches are at the bottom of this whole affair-in fact the fanatics have already acknowledged it. They say that this Texas raid is in revenge for the expulsion of some of their brethren of the Methodist church from Texas, about twelve or eighteen months ago, for preaching and teaching Abolition incendiarism to the negros in northern Texas. Unless the churches send out new recruits of John Browns, I fear the boys will have nothing to do this winter (as they have hung all that can be found), the school boys have become so excited by the sport in hanging Abolitionists, that the schools are completely deserted, they having formed companies, and will go seventy-five or one handred miles on horseback to participate in a single execution of the sentence of Judge Lynch's Court. It has now become a settled conviction in the South *that this Union cannot subsist one day after Abe Lincoln has been declared President,* if God, in his infinite wisdom, should permit him to live that long, for they (the people of the South) have made up their minds that they had rather die, sword in hand, in defence of their homes, their wives, their children and slaves, in defence of the Constitution, the laws, and their sacred honor, than *tamely submit to an organized system of robbery, a degraded and loathsome scheme of amalgamation,* a breakleg up of the compromises of the Constitution, and a total exclusion of the south from the common territories of the country won by their blood and treasure.

6

The Ideology of Westward Expansion

Rudimentary policies governing land sales were established soon after the American Revolution. Over the next century, the national land system was gradually modified. Minimum prices for lands were established and public lands were to be surveyed and then put up for sale at public auctions. One rule that was established early on, but was often violated, was the prohibition against settlement or squatting on public lands prior to purchase.

By the first decades of the nineteenth century, a growing number of residents in the western states and territories were dissatisfied with the current system of land disposal. In past years settlers were able to range over the public domain before selecting a land site that suited them. Many settlers claimed property before they had title and had begun improvements, only to be evicted by officials before they could complete the purchase procedures. While settlers considered the minimum land prices too high, speculators bought up large tracts of land and withheld them from settlement until they could make the greatest profit. Too often these lands belonged to squatters.

American expansion and land acquisition in the 1840s was fueled by a variety of motives, rationalizations, and federal land policies. In 1845 New York journalist John L. O'Sullivan coined the phrase "manifest destiny," a slogan that has become inextricably linked to the expansion of the 1840s, when America annexed Texas, acquired Oregon from Great Britain, and purchased California and the Southwest from Mexico. Although it is not a sharply defined idea, inherent in the concept of manifest destiny is the notion that Americans were destined by divine providence to expand their national domain to its natural borders. This expansion was justified by rhetoric heralding American superiority.

Westward expansion was accomplished with the help of federal land policies, which enabled settlers to carve out 160-acre sections through a variety of programs, ranging from pre-emption to the Homestead Act passed in 1862. Settlement was accelerated by the expansion of railroad system into the Far West in the late 1860s.

Fleeing persecution and mob violence, members of the Church of Latter-day Saints, commonly known as Mormons, led by Brigham Young, sought refuge and security in the vast wilderness of the Great Basin region of the West. Following the Treaty of Guadalupe Hidalgo, the Great Basin and its Mormon stronghold at Salt Lake City became a part of the United States. With the discovery of gold in 1848, the region reaped economic benefits from the overland traffic to California. Mormon settlers, skilled in the techniques of irrigation, had made this arid region prosper since their arrival in 1847, but were still considered squatters by the federal government. Until the United States government opened up a land office in the Utah Territory in 1869, officials of the

Mormon church managed land distribution and settlement. But once the federal system was established in 1869, Mormon settlers set to formalize their occupation of the Great Basin using procedures established by the Preemption Act and the Homestead Act.

Westward expansion was spearheaded by an unwavering sense of American superiority. The rhetoric of expansionism led to fateful consequences for non-Anglo cultures. American expansionists ignored Indian and Mexican land claims as well as countless treaties such as the Treaty of Fort Laramie, as they carved out an empire that would expand from coast to coast and south to the Rio Grande River following the Treaty of Guadalupe Hidalgo and the Gadsden Purchase. The ideological underpinnings of expansionism had repercussions that would reverberate into the 1880s when Californians led a campaign to end Chinese immigration into the American West.

Suggestions for Further Reading

Arnoldo De Leon, *They Called Them Greasers: Anglo Attitudes Toward Mexicans in Texas, 1821–1900* (Austin: University of Texas Press. 1983).

John S. D. Eisenhower, *So Far from God: The U.S. War with Mexico* (New York: Random House, 1989).

Reginald Horsman, *Race and Manifest Destiny,* (Cambridge: Harvard University Press, 1981).

Robert W. Johannsen, *To the Halls of the Montezumas: The Mexican War in the American Imagination* (New York: Oxford University Press. 1985).

Frederick Merk, *Manifest Destiny and Mission in American History: A Reinterpretation* (New York: Knopf, 1963).

Critical Thinking

1. What was the penalty for violating anti-polygamy legislation?

2. What was the difference between the Homestead and Preemption Acts?

3. According to John L. O'Sullivan, what characteristics of the American nation determine its future? How is the United States different from other nations? How could O'Sullivan's rhetoric drive expansion?

4. Compare President Polk's War Message with the subsequent Treaty of Guadalupe Hidalgo. Did the treaty reflect Polk's initial goals?

5. What was the impact of the Chinese Exclusion Act on Chinese immigration to the United States?

Document 6.1

The Preemption Act (1841)

Central to Whig politics in the 1830s and 1840 was the idea of using the proceeds from western land sales to finance internal improvements. Cheap land sales would encourage westward expansion, and the money from those land sales would improve the national infrastructure. Southerners generally opposed the idea because they were convinced that most of the improvements would be built in the North and West, not in the South. But in 1841, Congress passed the Preemption Act over southern objections. The law allowed a prospective settler to stake out a land claim before the sale and then pay $1.25 an acre for that same land when the sale commenced. Proceeds from the sale would then be distributed to the states for constructing internal improvements. In 1842, the distribution part of the law was repealed, but the preemption provisions continued, and they greatly accelerated the westward movement. The following document contains relevant portions of the Preemption Act of 1841.*

SEC. 10. *And be it further enacted,* That from and after the passage of this act, every... man, over the age of twenty-one years, and being a citizen of the United States, or having filed his declaration of intention to become a citizen... who since the first day of June, A. D. eighteen hundred and forty, has made... a settlement in person on the public lands to which the Indian title had been... extinguished, and which... shall have been, surveyed prior thereto, and who shall inhabit and improve the same, and who... shall erect a dwelling thereon, ... is hereby, authorized to enter with... the land office... any number of acres not exceeding one hundred and sixty, or a quarter section of land, to include the residence of such claimant, upon paying to the United States the minimum price of such land, subject, however, to the following limitations and exceptions: No person shall be entitled to more than one pre-emptive right by virtue of this act; no person who is the proprietor of three hundred and twenty acres of land in any State or Territory of the United States, and no person who shall quit or abandon his residence on his own land to reside on the public land in the same State or Territory, shall acquire any right of pre-emption under this act; no lands included in any reservation... no lands reserved for the support of schools, nor the lands... to which the title has been or may be extinguished by the United States at any time during the operation of this act; no sections of land reserved to the United States alternate to other sections granted to any of the States for the construction of any... public improvement; no sections... included within

---

* *Public Statutes at Large of the United States* (Washington, D.C.: U.S. Government Printing Office, 1922), Vol. 5, pp. 455-56.

the limits of any incorporated town; no portions of the public lands which have been selected as the site for a city or town; no parcel or lot of land actually settled and occupied for the purposes of trade and not agriculture; and no lands on which are situated any known salines or mines, shall be liable to entry under and by virtue of the provisions of this act...

SEC. 11. *And be it further enacted,* That when two or more persons shall have settled on the same quarter section of land, the right of pre-emption shall be in him or her who made the first settlement, provided such persons shall conform to the other provisions of this act; and all questions as to the right of pre-emption arising between different settlers shall be settled by the register and receiver of the district within which the land is situated, subject to an appeal to and a revision by the Secretary of the Treasury of the United States.

SEC. 12. *And be it further enacted,* That prior to any entries being made under and by virtue of the provisions of this act, proof of the settlement and improvement thereby required, shall be made to the satisfaction of the register and receiver of the land district in which such lands may lie... and all assignments and transfers of the right hereby secured, prior to the issuing of the patent, shall be null and void.

SEC. 13. *And be it further enacted,* That before any person claiming the benefit of this act shall be allowed to enter such lands, he or she shall make oath before the receiver or register of the land district in which the land is situated... that he or she has never had the benefit of any right of pre-emption under this act; that he or she is not the owner of three hundred and twenty acres of land in any State or Territory of the United States, nor hath he or she settled upon and improved said land to sell the same on speculation, but in good faith to appropriate it to his or her own exclusive use or benefit; and that he or she has not, directly or indirectly, made any agreement or contract, in any way or manner, with any person or persons whatsoever, by which the title which he or she might acquire from the government of the United States, should ensure in whole or in part, to the benefit of any person except himself or herself...

Document 6.2

John L. O'Sullivan, "The Great Nation of Futurity" (1845)

The New York newspaperman John L. O'Sullivan coined the phrase "manifest destiny" in 1845. Manifest destiny was more a slogan than any well-defined idea. At its core was the notion that America's destiny was to expand its borders from the Atlantic Ocean west to the Pacific Ocean and southwest to the Rio Grande River. In this selection,

O'Sullivan demonstrates that as early as 1839 he foresaw the territorial expansion that would accompany the 1840s.*

The American people having derived their origin from many other nations, and the Declaration of National Independence being entirely based on the great principle of human equality, these facts demonstrate at once our disconnected position as regards any other nation; that we have, in reality, but little connection with the past history of any of them and still less with all antiquity, its glories, or its crimes. On the contrary, our national birth was the beginning of a new history, the formation and progress of an untried political system, which separates us from the past and connects us with the future only; and so far as regards the entire development of the natural rights of man, in moral, political, and national life, we may confidently assume that our country is destined to be the great nation of futurity.

It is so destined, because the principle upon which a nation is organized fixes its destiny, and that of equality is perfect, is universal. It presides in all the operations of the physical world, and it is also the conscious law of the soul-the self-evident dictate of morality, which accurately defines the duty of man to man, and consequently man's rights as man. Besides, the truthful annals of any nation furnish abundant evidence that its happiness, its greatness, its duration, were always proportionate to the democratic equality in its system of government.

How many nations have had their decline and fall because the equal rights of the minority were trampled on by the despotism of the majority; or the interests of the many sacrificed to the aristocracy of the few; or the rights and interests of all given up to the monarchy of one? These three kinds of government have figured so frequently and so largely in the ages that have passed away that their history, through all time to come, can only furnish a resemblance. Like causes produce like effects, and the true philosopher of history will easily discern the principle of equality, or of privilege, working out its inevitable result. The first is regenerative, because it is natural and right; and the latter is destructive to society, because it is unnatural and wrong.

What friend of human liberty, civilization, and refinement can cast his view over the past history of the monarchies and aristocracies of antiquity, and not deplore that they ever existed? What philanthropist can contemplate the oppressions, the cruelties, and injustice inflicted by them on the masses of mankind and not turn with moral horror from the retrospect?

America is destined for better deeds. It is our unparalleled glory that we have no reminiscences of battlefields, but in defense of humanity, of the oppressed of all nations, of the rights of conscience, the rights of personal enfranchisement. Our annals describe no scenes of horrid carnage, where men were led on by hundreds of thousands to slay one another, dupes and victims to emperors, kings, nobles, demons in the human form called heroes. We have had patriots to defend our homes, our liberties, but no aspirants to crowns or thrones; nor have the American people ever suffered themselves to be led on by wicked ambition to depopulate the land, to spread desolation far and wide, that a human being might be placed on a seat of supremacy.

---

* John L. O'Sullivan, "The Great Nation of Futurity," *The United States Magazine and Democratic Review*, (November, 1839), 2-3, 6.

We have no interest in the scenes of antiquity, only as lessons of avoidance of nearly all their examples. The expansive future is our arena and for our history. We are entering on its untrodden space with the truths of God in our minds, beneficent objects in our hearts, and with a clear conscience unsullied by the past. We are the nation of human progress, and who will, what can, set limits to our onward march? Providence is with us, and no earthly power can. We point to the everlasting truth on the first page of our national declaration, and we proclaim to the millions of other lands that "the gates of hell-the powers of aristocracy and monarchy-shall not prevail against it."

The far-reaching, the boundless future, will be the era of American greatness. In its magnificent domain of space and time, the nation of many nations is destined to manifest to mankind the excellence of divine principles; to establish on earth the noblest temple ever dedicated to the worship of the Most High, the Sacred, and the True. Its floor shall be a hemisphere, roof the firmament of the star-studded heavens, and its congregation of Union of many Republics, comprising hundreds of happy millions, calling owning no man master, but governed by God's natural and moral law of equality, the law of brotherhood-of "peace and good will amongst men."

Yes, we are the nation of progress, of individual freedom, of universal enfranchisement. Equality of rights is the cynosure of our union of states, the grand exemplar of the correlative equality of individuals; and, while truth sheds its effulgence, we cannot retrograde without dissolving the one and subverting the other. We must onward to the fulfillment of our mission-to the entire development of the principle of our organization-freedom of conscience, freedom of person, freedom of trade and business pursuits, universality of freedom and equality. This is our high destiny, and in nature's eternal, inevitable decree of cause and effect we must accomplish it. All this will be our future history, to establish on earth the moral dignity and salvation of man-the immutable truth and beneficence of God. For this blessed mission to the nations of the world, which are shut out from the lifegiving light of truth, has America been chosen; and her high example shall smite unto death the tyranny of kings, hierarchs, and oligarchs and carry the glad tidings of peace and good will where myriads now endure in existence scarcely more enviable than that of beasts of the field. Who, then, can doubt that our country is destined to be the great nation of futurity?

Document 6.3

The Mexican War (1846)

The annexation of Texas in 1845 and the spirit of Manifest Destiny, which argued for a God-given American right to exercise sovereignty over the entire continent, put the United States and Mexico on a collision course. President James K. Polk was determined to add

California, Utah, Nevada, Colorado, Arizona, and New Mexico to the United States. Mexico was just as determined to keep its territory. After a clash between United States and Mexican troops north of the Rio Grande River early in 1846, Polk sent a war message to Congress. Excerpts from this message are included below.*

In my message at the commencement of the present session, I informed you that, upon the earnest appeal both of the congress and convention of Texas, I had ordered an efficient military force to take a position "between the Nueces and the Del Norte." This had become necessary, to meet a threatened invasion of Texas by the Mexican forces, for which extensive military preparations had been made. The invasion was threatened solely because Texas had determined, in accordance with a solemn resolution of the Congress of the United States, to annex herself to our Union; and, under these circumstances, it was plainly our duty to extend our protection over her citizens and soil.

This force was concentrated at Corpus Christi, and remained there until after I had received such information from Mexico as rendered it probable, if not certain, that the Mexican government would refuse to receive our envoy.

Meantime Texas, by the final action of our Congress, had become an integral part of our Union. The Congress of Texas, by its act of December 19, 1836, had declared the Rio del Norte to be the boundary of that republic. Its jurisdiction had been extended and exercised beyond the Nueces. The country between that river and the Del Norte had been represented in the congress and in the convention of Texas; had thus taken part in the act of annexation itself; and is now included within one of our congressional districts. Our own Congress had, moreover, with great unanimity, by the act approved December 31, 1845, recognised the country beyond the Nueces as a part of our territory, by including it within our own revenue system; and a revenue officer, to reside within that district, has been appointed, by and with the advice and consent of the senate. It became, therefore, of urgent necessity to provide for the defence of that portion of our country. Accordingly, on the 13th of January last, instructions were issued to the general in command of these troops to occupy the left bank of the Del Norte. This river, which is the southwestern boundary of the state of Texas, is an exposed frontier; from this quarter invasion was threatened; upon it, and in its immediate vicinity, in the judgment of high military experience, are the proper stations for the protecting forces of the government. In addition to this important consideration, several others occurred to induce this movement. Among these are the facilities afforded by the ports at Brazos Santiago and the mouth of the Del Norte, for the reception of supplies by sea; the stronger and more healthful military positions; the convenience for obtaining a ready and a more abundant supply of provisions, water, fuel, and forage; and the advantages which are afforded by the Del Norte in forwarding supplies to such posts as may be established in the interior and upon the Indian frontier.

The movement of the troops to the Del Norte was made by the commanding general, under positive instructions to abstain from all aggressive acts toward Mexico or Mexican

---

* William MacDonald, *Select Documents Illustrative of the History of the United States 1776-1861* (London: The Macmillan Company, 1920), pp. 346-53.

citizens, and to regard the relations between that republic and the United States as peaceful, unless she should declare war, or commit acts of hostility indicative of a state of war. He was specially directed to protect private property, and respect personal rights.

The army moved from Corpus Christi on the 11th of March, and on the 28th of that month arrived on the left bank of the Del Norte, opposite to Matamoras, where it encamped on a commanding position, which has since been strengthened by the erection of field works. A depot has also been established at Point Isabel, near the Brazos Santiago, thirty miles in rear of the encampment. The selection of his position was necessarily confided to the judgment of the general in command.

The Mexican forces at Matamoras assumed a belligerent attitude, and, on the 12th of April, General Ampudia, then in command, notified General Taylor to break up his camp within twenty-four hours, and to retire beyond the Nueces river, and, in the event of his failure to comply with these demands, announced that arms, and arms alone, must decide the question. But no open act of hostility was committed until the 24th of April. On that day, General Arista, who had succeeded to the command of the Mexican forces, communicated to General Taylor that "he considered hostilities commenced, and should prosecute them." A party of dragoons, of sixty-three men and officers, were on the same day despatched from the American camp up the Rio del Norte, on its left bank, to ascertain whether the Mexican troops had crossed, or were preparing to cross, the river, "became engaged with a large body of these troops, and, after a short affair, in which some sixteen were killed and wounded, appear to have been surrounded and compelled to surrender."

The grievous wrongs perpetrated by Mexico upon our citizens throughout a long period of years remain unredressed; and solemn treaties, pledging her public faith for this redress, have been disregarded. A government either unable or unwilling to enforce the execution of such treaties, fails to perform one of its plainest duties.

Our commerce with Mexico has been almost annihilated. It was formerly highly beneficial to both nations; but our merchants have been deterred from prosecuting it by the system of outrage and extortion which the Mexican authorities have pursued against them, whilst their appeals through their own government for indemnity have been made in vain. Our forbearance has gone to such an extreme as to be mistaken in its character. Had we acted with vigor in repelling the insults and redressing the injuries inilicted by Mexico at the commencement, we should doubtless have escaped all the difficulties in which we are now involved.

Instead of this, however, we have been exerting our best efforts to propitiate her good-will. Upon the pretext that Texas, a nation as independent as herself, thought proper to unite its destinies with our own, she has affected to believe that we have severed her rightful territory, and in official proclamations and manifestoes has repeatedly threatened to make war upon us, for the purpose of reconquering Texas. In the meantime, we have tried every effort at reconciliation. The cup of forbearance had been exhausted, even before the recent information from the frontier of the Del Norte. But now, after reiterated menaces, Mexico has passed the boundary of the United States, has invaded our territory, and shed American blood upon the American soil. She has proclaimed that hostilities have commenced, and that the two nations are now at war.

As war exists, and, notwithstanding all our efforts to avoid it, exists by the act of Mexico herself, we are called upon by every consideration of duty and patriotism to vindicate with decision the honor, the rights, and the interests of our country.

Anticipating the possibility of a crisis like that which has arrived, instructions were given in August last, "as a precautionary measure" against invasion, or threatened invasion, authorizing General Taylor, if the emergency required, to accept volunteers, not from Texas only, but from the States of Louisiana, Alabama, Mississippi, Tennessee, and Kentucky; and corresponding letters were addressed to the respective governors of those states. These instructions were repeated; and, in January last, soon after the incorporation of "Texas into our union of states," General Taylor was further "authorized by the President to make a requisition upon the executive of that State for such of its militia force as may be needed to repel invasion, or to secure the country against apprehended invasion." On the second day of March he was again reminded, "in the event of the approach of any considerable Mexican force, promptly and efficiently to use the authority with which he was clothed to call to him such auxiliary force as he might need." War actually existing, and our territory having been invaded, General Taylor, pursuant to authority vested in him by my direction, has called on the governor of Texas for four regiments of state troops-two to be mounted, and two to serve on foot; and on the governor of Louisiana for four regiments of infantry, to be sent to him as soon as practicable.

In further vindication of our rights, and defence of our territory, I invoke the prompt action of Congress to recognise the existence of the war, and to place at the disposition of the Executive the means of prosecuting the war with vigor, and thus hastening the restoration of peace. To this end I recommend that authority should be given to call into the public service a large body of volunteers, to serve for not less than six or twelve months, unless sooner discharged. A volunteer force is beyond question more efficient than any other description of citizen soldiers; and it is not to be doubted that a number far beyond that required would readily rush to the field upon the call of their country. I further recommend that a liberal provision be made for sustaining our entire military force and furnishing it with supplies and munitions of war.

The most energetic and prompt measures, and the immediate appearance in arms of a large and overpowering force, are recommended to Congress as the most certain and efficient means of bringing the existing collision with Mexico to a speedy and successful termination.

In making these recommendations, I deem it proper to declare that it is my anxious desire not only to terminate hostilities speedily, but to bring all matters in dispute between this government and Mexico to an early and amicable adjustment; and, in this view, I shall be prepared to renew negotiations, whenever Mexico shall be ready to receive propositions, or to make propositions of her own.

I transmit herewith a copy of the correspondence between our envoy to Mexico and the Mexican minister for foreign affairs; and so much of the correspondence between that envoy and the Secretary of State, and between the Secretary of War and the general in command on the Del Norte, as is necessary to a full understanding of the subject.

Document 6.4

The Oregon Treaty (1846)

War with Mexico was looming on the horizon in the spring of 1846, and diplomatic pressures also mounted with Great Britain over the legal status of the Pacific Northwest. The British laid claim to the Pacific Northwest all the way south to what is today the Oregon-California boundary, but American settlers already vastly outnumbered English settlers in the region. For his part, President James K. Polk claimed American sovereignty over what is today Oregon, Washington, and a good deal of British Columbia. The United States wanted the issue resolved as soon as possible. The possibility of a simultaneous war with Mexico and Great Britain appealed to very few Americans. Negotiations began between British and American diplomats, and an agreement was reached in June 1846. The United States acquired political sovereignty over what is today the Pacific Northwest states of Washington, Oregon, and parts of Idaho. The so-called Oregon Treaty is included below.*

The United States of America and Her Majesty the Queen of the United Kingdom of Great Britain and Ireland, deeming it to be desirable for the future welfare of both countries that the state of doubt and uncertainty which has hitherto prevailed respecting the sovereignty and government of the territory on the northwest coast of America, lying westward of the Rocky or Stony Mountains, should be finally terminated by an amicable compromise of the rights mutually asserted by the two parties over the said territory, have respectively named Plenipotentiaries to treat and agree concerning the terms of such settlement, that is to say:

The President of the United States of America has, on his part, furnished with full powers James Buchanan, Secretary of State of the United States, and Her Majesty the Queen of the United Kingdom of Great Britain and Ireland has, on her part, appointed the Right Honorable Richard Pakenham, a member of Her Majesty's Most Honorable Privy Council, and Her Majesty's Envoy Extraordinary and Minister Plenipotentiary to the United States;

Who, after having communicated to each other their respective full powers, found in good and due form, have agreed upon and concluded the following articles:

---

* William MacDonald, *Select Documents Illustrative of the History of the United States 1776-1861* (London: The Macmillan Company, 1920), pp. 356-58.

Article I.

From the point on the forty-ninth parallel of north latitude, where the boundary laid down in existing treaties and conventions between the United States and Great Britain terminates, the line of boundary between the territories of the United States and those of Her Britannic Majesty shall be continued westward along the said forty-ninth parallel of north latitude to the middle of the channel which separates the continent from Vancouver's Island, and thence southerly through the middle of the said channel, and of Fuca's Straits, to the Pacific Ocean: Provided, however, that the navigation of the whole of the said channel and straits, south of the forty-ninth parallel of north latitude, remain free and open to both parties.

Article II.

From the point at which the forty-ninth parallel of north latitude shall be found to intersect the great northern branch of the Columbia River, the navigation of the said branch shall be free and open to the Hudson's Bay Company, and to all British subjects trading with the same, to the point where the said branch meets the main stream of the Columbia, and thence down the said main stream to the ocean, with free access into and through the said river or rivers, it being understood that all the usual portages along the line thus described shall, in like manner, be free and open. In navigating the said river or rivers, British subjects, with their goods and produce, shall be treated on the same footing as citizens of the United States; it being, however, always understood that nothing in this article shall be construed as preventing, or intended to prevent, the Government of the United States from making any regulations respecting the navigation of the said river or rivers not inconsistent with the present treaty.

Article III.

In the future appropriation of the territory south of the forty-ninth parallel of north latitude, as provided in the first article of this treaty, the possessory rights of the Hudson's Bay Company, and of all British subjects who may be already in the occupation of land or other property lawfully acquired within the said territory, shall be respected.

Article IV.

The farms, lands, and other property of every description belonging to the Puget's Sound Agricultural Company, on the north side of the Columbia River, shall be confirmed to the said company. In case, however, the situation of those farms and lands should be considered by the United States to be of public and political importance, and the United States Government should signify a desire to obtain possession of the whole, or of any part thereof, the property so required shall be transferred to the said Government, at a proper valuation, to be agreed upon between the parties.

Article V.

The present treaty shall be ratified by the President of the United States, by and with the advice and consent of the Senate thereof, and by Her Britannic Majesty; and the ratifications shall be exchanged at London, at the expiration of six months from the date hereof, or sooner if possible.

In witness whereof the respective Plenipotentiaries have signed the same, and have affixed thereto the seals of their arms.

Done at Washington the fifteenth day of June, in the year of our Lord one thousand eight hundred and forty-six.

James Buchanan. [l.s.]
Richard Pakenham. [l.s.]

Document 6.5

The Treaty of Guadalupe Hidalgo (1848)

At the conclusion of the so-called Mexican War, the United States dictated difficult terms to Mexico. President James K. Polk achieved his goal of expanding American sovereignty all the way to the Pacific Ocean. In return for a payment of $15 million, Mexico agreed to cede to the United States what is today New Mexico, Arizona, California, Utah, Nevada, and Colorado. The treaty guaranteed the religious and property-rights of the Mexican citizens living in the region, if they decided to accept American citizenship. Most of them did. Included below are the main articles of the Treaty of Guadalupe Hidalgo.*

In the name of Almighty God:
The United States of America and the United Mexican States, animated by a sincere desire to put an end to the calamities of the war which unhappily exists between the two Republics, and to establish upon a solid basis relations of peace and friendship, which shall confer reciprocal benefits upon the citizens of both, and assure the concord, harmony, and mutual confidence wherein the two peoples should live, as good neighbours, have for that purpose appointed their respective plenipotentiaries, that is to say:

---

* William MacDonald, *Select Documents Illustrative of the History of the United States 1776-1861* (London: The Macmillan Company, 1920), pp. 366-72.

The President of the United States has appointed Nicholas P. Trist, a citizen of the United States, and the President of the Mexican Republic has appointed Don Luis Gonzaga Cuevas, Don Bernardo Couto, and Don Miguel Atristain, citizens of the said Republic;

Who, after a reciprocal communication of their respective full powers, have, under the protection of Almighty God, the author of peace, arranged, agreed upon, and signed the following Treaty of Peace, Friendship, Limits, and Settlement between the United States of America and the Mexican Republic.

ARTICLE I.

There shall be firm and universal peace between the United States of America and the Mexican Republic, and between their respective countries, territories, cities, towns, and people, without exception of places or persons...

ARTICLE V.

The boundary line between the two Republics shall commence in the Gulf of Mexico, three leagues from land, opposite the mouth of the Rio Grande, otherwise called Rio Bravo del Norte, or opposite the mouth of its deepest branch, if it should have more than one branch emptying directly into the sea; from thence up the middle of that river, following the deepest channel, where it has more than one, to the point where it strikes the southern boundary of New Mexico; thence, westwardly, along the whole. Southern boundary of New Mexico (which runs north of the town called Paso) to its western termination; thence, northward, along the western line of New Mexico, until it intersects the first branch of the river Gila; (or if it should not intersect any branch of that river, then to the point on the said line nearest to such branch, and thence in a direct line to the same;) thence down the middle of the said branch and of the said river, until it empties into the Rio Colorado; thence across the Rio Colorado, following the division come between Upper and Lower California, to the Pacific Ocean...

ARTICLE VI.

The vessels and citizens of the United States shall, in all time, have a free and uninterrupted passage by the Gulf of California, and by the river Colorado below its confluence with the Gila, to and from their possessions situated north of the boundary line defined in the preceding article; it being understood that this passage is to be by navigating the Gulf of California and the river Colorado, and not by land, without the express consent of the Mexican Government.

If, by the examinations which may be made, it should be ascertained to be practicable and advantageous to construct a road, canal, or railway, which should in whole or in part run upon the river Gila, or upon its right or its left bank, within the space of one marine league from either margin of the river, the Governments of both republics will form an agreement regarding its construction, in order that it may serve equally for the use and advantage of both countries.

ARTICLE VII.

The river Gila, and the part of the Rio Bravo del Norte lying below the southern boundary of New Mexico, being, agreeably to the fifth article, divided in the middle between the two republics, the navigation of the Gila and of the Bravo below said boundary shall be free and common to the vessels and citizens of both countries; and neither shall, without the consent of the other, construct any work that may impede or interrupt, in whole or in part, the exercise of this right; not even for the purpose of favoring new methods of navigation. Nor shall any tax or contribution, under any denomination or title, be levied upon vessels or persons navigating the same, or upon merchandise or effects transported thereon, except in the case of landing upon one of their shores. If, for the purpose of making the said rivers navigable, or for maintaining them in such state, it should be necessary or advantageous to establish any tax or contribution, this shall not be done without the consent of both Governments.

The stipulations contained in the present article shall not impair the territorial rights of either republic within its established limits.

ARTICLE VIII.

Mexicans now established in territories previously belonging to Mexico, and which remain for the future within the limits of the United States, as defined by the present treaty, shall be free to continue where they now reside, or to remove at any time to the Mexican Republic, retaining the property which they possess in the said territories, or disposing thereof, and removing the proceeds wherever they please, without their being subjected, on this account, to any contribution, tax, or charge whatever.

Those who shall prefer to remain in the said territories may either retain the title and rights of Mexican citizens, or acquire those of citizens of the United States. But they shall be under the obligation to make their election within one year from the date of the exchange of ratifications of this treaty; and those who shall remain in the said territories after the expiration of that year, without having declared their intention to retain the character of Mexicans, shall be considered to have elected to become citizens of the United States.

In the said territories, property of every kind, now belonging to Mexicans not established there, shall be inviolably respected. The present owners, the heirs of these, and all Mexicans who may hereafter acquire said property by contract, shall enjoy with respect to it guarantees equally ample as if the same belonged to eitizens of the United States.

ARTICLE IX.

The Mexicans who, in the territories aforesaid, shall not preserve the character of citizens of the Mexican Republic, conformably with what is stipulated in the preceding article, shall be incorporated into the Union of the United States, and be admitted at the proper time (to be judged of by the Congress of the United States) to the enjoyment of all the rights of citizens of the United States, according to the principles of the Constitution;

and in the mean time, shall be maintained and protected in the free enjoyment of their liberty and property, and secured in the free exercise of their religion without restriction.

ARTICLE XII.

In consideration of the extension acquired by the boundaries of the United States, as defined in the fifth article of the present treaty, the Government of the United States engages to pay to that of the Mexican Republic the sum of fifteen millions of dollars.

Immediately after this treaty shall have been duly ratified by the Government of the Mexican Republic, the sum of three millions of dollars shall be paid to the said Government by that of the United States, at the city of Mexico, in the gold or silver coin of Mexico. The remaining twelve millions of dollars shall be paid at the same place, and in the same coin, in annual installments of three millions of dollars each, together with interest on the same at the rate of six per centum per annum. This interest shall begin to run upon the whole sum of twelve millions from the day of the ratification of the present treaty by the Mexican Government, and the first of the installments shall be paid at the expiration of one year from the same day. Together with each annual installment, as it falls due, the whole interest accruing on such installment from the beginning shall also be paid.

ARTICLE XIII.

The United States engage, moreover, to assume and pay to the claimants all the amounts now due them, and those hereafter to become due, by reason of the claims already liquidated and decided against the Mexican Republic, under the conventions between the two republics severally concluded on the eleventh day of April, eighteen hundred and thirty-nine, and on the thirtieth day of January, eighteen hundred and forty-three; so that the Mexican Republic shall be absolutely exempt, for the future, from all expense whatever on account of the said claims.

ARTICLE XIV.

The United States do furthermore discharge the Mexican Republic from all claims of citizens of the United States, not heretofore decided against the Mexican Government, which may have arisen previously to the date of the signature of this treaty; which discharge shall be final and perpetual, whether the said claims be rejected or be allowed by the board of commissioners provided in the following article, and whatever shall be the total amount those allowed...

Document 6.6

The Treaty of Fort Laramie (1851)

Between 1789 and 1871, a total of 370 formal, written treaties were negotiated between the United States and various Indian tribes. As far as the United States was concerned, these treaties were no different legally than other treaties negotiated with sovereign nations. The treaties dealt with a variety of concerns, including land cessions, territorial boundaries, hunting and fishing rights, trade, rights of way across Indian land, education, and peace. Approximately 230 of the treaties concerned land cessions; ninety-six dealt with issues of peace and allegiance; seventy-six involved removal and resettlement of various tribes; nineteen revolved around payment of debts; and fifteen established annuity payments for various tribes. Some treaties, of course, dealt with one or more of these issues. The Treaty of Fort Laramie of 1851—negotiated between the United States and the Teton Sioux, Cheyennes, Gros Ventres, Crows, Arikaras, and Arapahos—was typical.*

Article I

The aforesaid nations, parties to this treaty, having assembled for the purpose of establishing and confirming peaceful relations amongst themselves, do hereby covenant and agree to abstain in future from all hostilities whatever against each other, to maintain good faith and friendship in all their mutual intercourse, and to make an effective and lasting peace.

Article II

The aforesaid nations do hereby recognize the right of the United States Government to establish roads, military and other posts, within their respective territories.

Article III

In consideration of the rights and privileges acknowledged in the preceding article, the United States bind themselves to protect the aforesaid Indian nations against the commission of all depredations by the people of the said United States, after the ratification of this treaty.

---

* *A Compendium of Indian Treaties* (Washington, D.C.: U.S. Government Printing Office, 1955), pp. 2478-80.

Article IV

The aforesaid Indian nations do hereby agree and bind themselves to make restitution or satisfaction for any wrongs committed, after the ratification of this treaty, by any band or individual of their people, on the people of the United States, whilst lawfully residing in or passing through their respective territories.

Article V

The aforesaid Indian nations do hereby recognize and acknowledge the following tracts of country, included within the metes and boundaries hereinafter designated, as their respective territories, viz:

The territory of the Sioux or Dahcotah Nation, commencing the mouth of the White Earth River, on the Missouri River; thence in a southwesterly direction to the forks of the Platte River; thence up the north fork of the Platte River to a point known as the Red Bute, or where the road leaves the river; thence along the range of mountains known as the Black Hills, to the head-waters of Heart River; thence down Heart River to its mouth; and thence down the Missouri River to the place of beginning.

The territory of the Gros Ventre, Mandans, and Arrickaras Nations, commencing at the mouth of Heart River; thence up the Missouri River to the mouth of the Yellowstone River; thence up the Yellowstone River to the mouth of Powder River in a southeasterly direction, to the head-waters of the Little Missouri River; thence along the Black Hills to the head of Heart River, and thence down Heart River to the place of beginning.

The territory of the Assinaboin Nation, commencing at the mouth of Yellowstone River; thence up the Missouri River to the mouth of the Muscle-shell River; thence from the mouth of the Muscle-shell River in a southeasterly direction until it strikes the head-waters of Big Dry Creek; thence down that creek to where it empties into the Yellowstone River, nearly opposite the mouth of Powder River, and thence down the Yellowstone River to the place of beginning.

The territory of the Blackfoot Nation, commencing at the mouth of Muscle-shell River; thence up the Missouri River to its source; thence along the main range of the Rocky Mountains, in a southerly direction, to the head-waters of the northern source of the Yellowstone River; thence down the Yellowstone River to the mouth of Twenty-five Yard Creek; thence across to the head-waters of the Muscle-shell River, and thence down the Muscle-shell River to the place of beginning.

The territory of the Crow Nation, commencing at the mouth of Powder River on the Yellowstone; thence up Powder River to its source; thence along-the main range of the Black Hills and Wind River Mountains to the head-waters of the Yellowstone River; thence down the Yellowstone River to the mouth of Twenty-five Yard Creek; thence to the head-waters of the Muscle-shell River; thence down the Muscle-shell River to its mouth; thence to the head-waters of Big Dry Creek, and thence to its mouth.

The territory of the Cheyennes and Arrapahoes, commencing at the Red Bute, or the place where the road leaves the north fork of the Platte River; thence up the north fork of the Platte River to its source; thence along the main range of the Rocky Mountains to the head-waters of the Arkansas River; thence down the Arkansas River to the crossing of

the Santa F, road; thence in a northwesterly direction to the forks of the Platte River, an
thence up the Platte River to the place of beginning.

It is, however, understood that, in making this recognition and acknowledgement,
the aforesaid Indian nations do not hereby abandon or prejudice any rights or claims they
may have to other lands; and further, that they do not surrender the privilege of hunting,
fishing, or passing over any of the tracts of country heretofore described.

Article VI

The parties to the second part of this treaty having selected principals or head-chiefs
for their respective nations, through whom all national business will hereafter be
conducted, do hereby bind themselves to sustain said chiefs and their successors during
good behavior.

Article VII

In consideration of the treaty stipulations, and for the damages which have or may
occur by reason thereof to the Indian nations, parties hereto, and for their maintenance
and the improvement of their moral and social customs, the United States bind
themselves to deliver to the said Indian nations the sum of fifty thousand dollars per
annum for the term of ten years, with the right to continue the same at the discretion of
the President of the United States for a period not exceeding five years thereafter, in
provisions, merchandise, domestic animals, and agricultural implements, in such
proportions as may be deemed best adapted to their condition by the President of the
United States, to be distributed in proportion to the population of the aforesaid Indian
nations.

Article VIII

It is understood and agreed that should any of the Indian nations, parties to this
treaty, violate any of the provisions thereof, the United States may withhold the whole or
a portion of the annuities mentioned in the preceding article from the nation so offending,
until, in the opinion of the President of the United States, proper satisfaction shall have
been made.

Document 6.7

The Mormons (1862)

During the first half of the nineteenth century, the Mormons (members
of The Church of Jesus Christ of Latter-day Saints) found themselves
persecuted for religious reasons and driven from New York to Ohio to

Missouri to Illinois, before their founder, Joseph Smith, was assassinated in 1844. Brigham Young then assumed the mantle of Mormon leadership and led the Latter-day Saints in a journey across the continent, where they settled in the isolated valleys of northern Utah. Although Mormon religious beliefs were quite distinct, it was their practice of polygamy that raised the ire of Protestants and led to their systematic persecution. In response to considerable political pressure, Congress passed several anti-polygamy statutes, outlawing the practice. In 1896, the Mormons finally acquiesced and abandoned the practice. The following is an example of early federal anti-polygamy legislation.*

An Act to punish and prevent the Practice of Polygamy in the Territories of the United States and other Places, and disapproving and annulling certain Acts of the Legislative Assembly of the Territory of Utah.

Be it enacted… That every person having a husband or wife living, who shall marry any other person, whether married or single, in a Territory of the United States, or other place over which the United States have exclusive jurisdiction, shall, except in the cases specified in the proviso to this section, be adjudged guilty of bigamy, and, upon conviction thereof, shall be punished by a fine not exceeding five hundred dollars, and by imprisonment for a term not exceeding five years: [certain cases excepted].

SEC. 2. And be it further enacted, That the following ordinance of the provisional government of the State of Deseret, so called, namely: "An ordinance incorporating the Church of Jesus Christ of Latter Day Saints," passed February eight, in the year eighteen hundred and fifty-one, and adopted, reënacted, and made valid by the governor and legislative assembly of the Territory of Utah by an act passed January nineteen, in the year eighteen hundred and fifty-five, entitled "An act in relation to the compilation and revision of the laws and resolutions in force in Utah Territory, their publication, and distribution," and all other acts and parts of acts heretofore passed by the said legislative assembly of the Territory of Utah, which establish, support, maintain, shield, or countenance polygamy, be, and the same hereby are, disapproved and annulled: Provided, That this act shall be so limited and construed as not to affect or interfere with the right of property legally acquired under the ordinance heretofore mentioned with the right "to worship God according to the dictates of conscience," but only to annul all acts and laws which establish, maintain, protect, or countenance the practice of polygamy, evasively called spiritual marriage, however disguised by legal or ecclesiastical solemnities, sacraments, ceremonies, consecrations, or other contrivances.

SEC. 3. And be it further enacted, That it shall not be lawful for any corporation or association for religious or charitable purposes to acquire or hold real estate in any Territory of the United States during the existence of the territorial government of a greater value than fifty thousand dollars; and all real estate acquired or held by any such corporation or association contrary to the provisions of this act shall be forfeited and

---

* William MacDonald, ed., *Select Statutes and Other Documents Illustrative of the History of the United States* (New York: The Macmillan Company, 1922), pp. 43-45.

escheat to the United States: Provided, That existing vested rights in real estate shall not be impaired by the provisions of this section.
APPROVED, July 1, 1862.

Document 6.8

The Homestead Act (1862)

By the mid-nineteenth century, northern politicians competed for votes by promising ever lower land prices in the public domain. That process reached its logical conclusion in 1862, when Congress passed the Homestead Act. The Homestead Act allowed an American citizen to stake out a claim to 160 acres of land in the public domain. If the settler lived on the land for five years and made a major improvement on it each year, he was awarded title to the property at the end of the five-year period. With passage of the Homestead Act of 1862, the era of free land had finally arrived in the United States.*

BE *it enacted by the Senate and House of Representatives of the United States of America in Congress assembled,* That any person who is the head of a family, or who has arrived at the age of twenty-one years, and is a citizen of the United States, or who shall have filed his declaration of intention to become such, ... and who has never borne arms against the United States Government or given aid and comfort to its enemies, shall, from and after the first January, eighteen hundred and sixty-three, be entitled to enter one-quarter section or a less quantity of unappropriated public lands, ... to be located in a body, in conformity to the legal subdivisions of the public lands, and after the same shall have been surveyed...

SEC. 2. *And be it further enacted,* That the person applying for the benefit of this act shall, ... make affidavit before the said register or receiver that he or she is the head of a family, or is twenty-one years or more of age, or shall have performed service in the army or navy of the United States, and that he has never borne arms against the Government of the United States or given aid and comfort to its enemies, and that such application is made for his or her exclusive use and benefit, and that said entry is made for the purpose of actual settlement and cultivation, and not either directly or indirectly for the use or benefit of any other person or persons whomsoever; and upon filing the said affidavit with the register or receiver, and on payment of ten dollars, he or she shall

* *Public Statutes at Large of the United States* (Washington, D.C.: U.S. Government Printing Office, 1922), Vol. 12, pp. 392-93.

thereupon be permitted to enter the quantity of land specified: *Provided, however,* That no certificate shall be given or patent issued therefore until the expiration of five years from the date of such entry; and if, at the expiration of such time, or at any time within two years thereafter, the person making such entry; ... shall prove by two credible witnesses that he, she, or they have resided upon or cultivated the same for the term of five years immediately succeeding the time of filing the affidavit aforesaid, and shall make affidavit that no part of said land has been alienated, and that he has borne true allegiance to the Government of the United States; then, in such case, he, she, or they, if at that time a citizen of the United States, shall be entitled to a patent, as in other cases provided for by law:...

SEC. 4. *And be it further enacted,* That no lands acquired under the provisions of this act shall in any event become liable to the satisfaction of any debt or debts contracted prior to the issuing of the patent therefor.

SEC. 5. *And be it further enacted,* That if, at any time after the filing of the affidavit, as required in the second section of this act, and before the expiration of the five years aforesaid, it shall be proven, after due notice to the settler, to the satisfaction of the register of the land office, that the person having filed such affidavit shall have actually changed his or her residence, or abandoned the said land for more than six months at any time, then and in that event the land so entered shall revert to the government.

SEC. 6. *And be it further enacted,* That no individual shall be permitted to acquire title to more than one quarter section under the provisions of this act; ... That no person who has served, or may hereafter serve, for a period of not less than fourteen days in the army or navy of the United States, either regular or volunteer, under the laws thereof, during the existence of an actual war, domestic or foreign, shall be deprived of the benefits of this act on account of not having attained the age of twenty-one years.

Document 6.9

The First Transcontinental Railroad (1869)

On May 10, 1869, the Union Pacific and Central Pacific railroads successfully linked the eastern United States with the Pacific Coast. Other railroads had been chartered and granted aid by Congress and the states, but these two were the first to complete a transcontinental railroad. With a predominantly Chinese workforce, the Central Pacific was constructed heading eastward from California, just as 10,000 Union Pacific workers, many of whom were Irish, spiked rails to wooden ties westward from Omaha, Nebraska. With great pomp and circumstance, the symbolic last spike was driven at Promontory Summit, Utah. However, much of the line was poorly constructed. According to at least one observer, by the time the two rail heads met, many sections of the track could not safely support a locomotive.*

The whole country now awoke to the contest that the Union Pacific and the Central Pacific were entering upon. Which should reach Salt Lake first, and which should win the big government subsidies, ranging through the mountains from $64,000 to $96,000 a mile?

The Union Pacific chief engineer, after a New York conference during the winter of 1867-8, returned to Omaha, called his staff around him, and laid out his plans. These centered upon Ogden, Utah, 502 miles west of the end of the track, as the objective point for 1868, and Humboldt Wells, 216 miles west of Ogden, for the spring of 1869. Preliminary lines had been run, but no final location had been made west of Laramie City, where town lots were sold in April, 1868. General Dodge had already solved the vital problem of the pass across the Rockies by getting lost one afternoon in the Black Hills-if it is fair so to describe the accident which led to the remarkable discovery. For over two years all explorations had failed to reveal a satisfactory crossing of this secondary range known as the Black Hills, which, on account of their short approaches and their great height, is the most difficult of all the ranges to get over. On this occasion General Dodge, returning from a Powder River campaign, leaving his troops, with a scout and a few men rode up Lodge Pole Creek along the overland trail, and struck south along the crest of the mountains. Indians beset the little party before noon, and got between them and their trains. Holding the Indians at bay with their Winchesters, they retreated. It was nearly night when they finally escaped the enemy, and meantime they had ridden down an unknown ridge that led out of the hills and clear to the plains without a break. That night General Dodge told his guide that if they saved their scalps he believed they had found the crossing of the Black Hills: over this pass the trains of the Union Pacific run to-day.

This engineering work of running the lines through the Black Hills, then, had in 1867 already been done; but beyond that point absolutely everything remained to be done. Engineering parties were distributed during the winter months to be on the ground when spring opened, and those destined for Utah crossed the Wasatch Mountains on sledges, with the snow over the tops of the telegraph poles. The track was laid across the Black Hills, and this gave an opportunity of running ties down the mountain streams instead of bringing them 800 miles from the Missouri River. Even after the builders had reached the Hills the country afforded nothing but the road-bed and ties, and it took forty carloads of material a day to supply "the front." In April, graders were at Laramie working from daylight till dark, and from the start to the season's finish the construction crews worked every day without an hour's loss of time. Every man, from the chief of construction to the water-carriers, seemed pitted for a finish heat, and that season the contractors actually pushed their grade to Green River, to Ogden, to Salt Lake, and to far Humboldt Wells.

---

* Frank H. Spearman, "The First Transcontinental Railroad," *Harper's Monthly Magazine,* (October 1904), 711, 719-20.

Winter caught the builders at the foot of the Wasatch Range, but it no longer stayed them. The spirit of the fight had got beyond that, and the frozen earth was dynamited like rock. Track was laid across the Wasatch on a bed covered with snow and ice, and one of General Casement's track-laying trains, track and all, slid bodily off the ice into the ditch! Even the Mormons roused themselves, and under Brigham Young's exhortation turned mightily into the race. In railroading then, as in politics later, the watchword was, "Claim everything," and the Central Pacific people astonished the Eastern builders by filing a map "claiming" to build as far east as Echo, some distance east of Ogden.

The two companies had 20,000 men at work. The Casement brothers of the Union Pacific construction forces rose to the occasion. Eastern newspapers were carrying daily head-lines, "The Union Pacific built-miles to-day." In the beginning a mile a day was considered good work, but the Casements had long been laying two miles a day, and now were working seven days in the week and every hour that light gave them, and they crowned their supreme efforts by laying in one day nearly eight miles of track between daylight and dark.

The Central Pacific people meantime stayed not for stake or stopped not for stone. They had fourteen tunnels to build, but they did not wait to finish them. Supplies, even to engines, were hauled over the Sierras, and the work was pushed until in the spring of 1869 the opposing track-layers met at Promontory, Utah: the moment at which the law had declared a junction must be made had arrived.

On May 10, Leland Stanford, Governor of California and president of the Central Pacific and Durant, Duff, and Sidney, Dillon of the Union Pacific, assembled with their friends to drive the spike that was to signalize the completion of the great undertaking. A little company of regular soldiers with a garrison band from Fort Douglas preserved the military atmosphere of the long struggle. The Mormons who had helped so faithfully with the road-bed were there, and the coolies from San Francisco and the Irish track-layers from the Atlantic seaboard faced each other. Strawbridge and Reed, the rival superintendents of construction, placed under the rails the last tie of California laurel. Spikes of silver and of gold from Montana, Idaho, and Nevada were presented and driven into it and Dr. Harkness, on behalf of the great Pacific State, presented the last spike, wrought of California gold.

Document 6.10

Chinese Exclusion Act (1882)

Chinese immigrants were drawn to the United States following the California gold rush. Most of them intended to return home with their newfound wealth. But with the mining frontier extending into the Rocky Mountains and the building of the transcontinental railroad, new opportunities convinced many immigrants to stay. Stereotypes and cultural misconceptions along with white fears of job competition escalated tension between white and Chinese workers and led to violence and discrimination in the 1850s and 1860s. By the next decade, the California Workingmen's Party was leading agitation to end Chinese immigration into the United States. Their platform was not lacking in precedents since several judicial decisions had already been handed down by the Supreme Court of the United States and the Supreme Court of the State of California over the past three decades. In 1880, almost 105,000 Chinese people lived in the United States. Two years later Congress passed the exclusion act that barred Chinese laborers for a period of ten years.*

Whereas, in the opinion of the Government of the United States the coming of Chinese laborers to this country endangers the good order of certain localities within the territory: Therefore,

Be it enacted by the Senate and House of Representatives of the United States of America in Congress assembled, That from and after the expiration of ninety days next after the passage of this act, and until the expiration of ten years next after the passage of this act, the coming of Chinese laborers to the United States be, and the same is hereby, suspended; and during such suspension it shall not be lawful for any Chinese laborer to come, or, having so come after the expiration of said ninety days, to remain within the United States.

SEC. 2. That the master of any vessel who shall knowingly bring within the United States on such vessel, and land or permit to be landed, any Chinese laborer, from any foreign port or place, shall be deemed guilty of a misdemeanor, and on conviction thereof shall be punished by a fine of not more than five hundred dollars for each and every such Chinese laborer so brought, and may be also imprisoned for a term not exceeding one year.

SEC. 3. That the two foregoing sections shall not apply to Chinese laborers who were in the United States on the seventeenth day of November, eighteen hundred and eighty, or who shall have come into the same before the expiration of ninety days next after the

---

* *Chinese Exclusion Act,* May 6, 1882, U.S. Statutes at Large, XXII, pp. 58-61.

passage of this act, and who shall produce to such master before going on board such vessel, and shall produce to the collector of the port in the United States at which such vessel shall arrive, the evidence hereinafter in this act required of his being one of the laborers in this section mentioned; nor shall the two foregoing sections apply to the case of any master whose vessel, being bound to a port not within the United States, shall come within the Jurisdiction of the United States by reason of being in distress or in stress of weather, or touching at any port of the United States on its voyage to any foreign port or place: *Provided,* That all Chinese laborers brought on such vessel shall depart with the vessel on leaving port.

SEC. 6. That in order to the faithful execution of articles one and two of the treaty in this act before mentioned, every Chinese person other than a laborer who may be entitled by said treaty and this act to come within the United States, and who shall be about to come to the United States, shall be identified as so entitled by the Chinese Government in each case, such identity to be evidenced by a certificate issued under the authority of said government, which certificate shall be in the English language or (if not in the English language) accompanied by a translation into English, stating such right to come, and which certificate shall state the name, title, or official rank, if any, the age, height, and all physical peculiarities, former and present occupation or profession, and place of residence in China of the person to whom the certificate is issued and that such person is entitled conformably to the treaty in this act mentioned to come within the United States. Such certificate shall be prima-facie evidence of the fact set forth therein, and shall be produced to the collector of customs, or his deputy, of the port in the district in the United States at which the person named therein shall arrive.

SEC. 7. That any person who shall knowingly and falsely alter or substitute any name for the name written in such certificate or forge any such certificate, or knowingly utter any forged or fraudulent certificate, or falsely personate any person named in any such certificate, shall be deemed guilty of a misdemeanor; and upon conviction thereof shall be fined in a sum not exceeding one thousand dollars, and imprisoned in a penitentiary for a term of not more than five years.

SEC. 10. That every vessel whose master shall knowingly violate any of the provisions of this act shall be deemed forfeited to the United States, and shall be liable to seizure and condemnation in any district of the United States into which such vessel may enter or in which she may be found.

SEC. 11. That any person who shall knowingly bring into or cause to be brought into the United States by land, or who shall knowingly aid or abet the landing in the United States from any vessel of any Chinese person not lawfully entitled to enter the United States, shall be deemed guilty of a misdemeanor, and shall, on conviction thereof, be fined in a sum not exceeding one thousand dollars, and imprisoned for a term not exceeding one year.

SEC. 12. That no Chinese person shall be permitted to enter the United States by land without producing to the proper officer of customs the certificate in this act required of Chinese persons seeking to land from a vessel. And any Chinese person found unlawfully within the United States shall be caused to be removed therefrom to the country from whence he came, by direction of the President of the United States, and at the cost of the United States, after being brought before some justice, judge, or commissioner of a court of the United States and found to be one not lawfully entitled to be or remain in the United States.

SEC. 14. That hereafter no State court or court of the United States shall admit Chinese to citizenship; and all laws in conflict with this act are hereby repealed.

SEC. 15. That the words "Chinese laborers," wherever used in this act, shall be construed to mean both skilled and unskilled laborers and Chinese employed in mining.

7

Conflict in the West

The classic image of western violence remains in the clash of cultures between Indians and whites. Indeed, between 1840 and 1890, the West was the scene of more than sixty Indian wars. However, violence was much more variegated than this. The West provided the backdrop for vigilante actions, range wars, labor conflict, outlaw banditry, racial violence, Indian Wars, and all kinds of personal violence, typically between young men carrying weapons and under the influence of alcohol.

Racial and ethnic minorities were too often the targets of western violence, as exemplified by the 1871 anti-Chinese riot in Los Angeles and the 1885 Rock Springs Massacre in Wyoming. Tensions between the Chinese and Anglo communities in the West were amplified by job competition and objections over Chinese customs.

In the early 1840s Indians aided overland pioneers on the western trails, with bloody conflict being the exception rather than the rule. Conflict between Indian and white settlers in the West began in earnest in the years following the California Gold Rush and with the crush of settlers heading west following the passage of the 1862 Homestead Act, which added to tension as thousands competed for the shrinking Indian lands.

During the 1860s the Indian Wars were concentrated on the Great Plains and in the Southwest. One of the most brutal campaigns erupted in Minnesota when Sioux warriors responded to the corruption of local Indian agents and the misery of reservation life, leading to the deaths of between 400 and 800 settlers. In turn, the government eventually sentenced dozens of Indians to be hanged, culminating in the largest mass hanging in American history.

Violence often overstepped the boundary between war and massacre as fighting escalated in the 1860s. While massacres were carried out by both sides during the Indian wars, most often it was the Indians who took the brunt of the casualties. The Sand Creek Massacre in 1864 left 200 men, women, and children butchered to death in eastern Colorado. And in one of the last violent incidents of the Indian wars, more than 150 Sioux were slaughtered at Wounded Knee, South Dakota, although most history books would refer to this incident as a battle well into the late twentieth century. The Plains Indian wars climaxed with the Battle of the Little Big Horn in 1876. Paradoxically, while this battle involved two forces of well armed warriors, rather than wo   .a and children, because Custer and his Seventh cavalry was wiped out, for many years this battle was referred to as a slaughter as evidenced by the contemporary account *Harper's Weekly*. With the death of Sitting Bull in 1890 followed by the carnage at Wounded Knee, the Indian Wars in the West had ended.

According to army statistics there were 1,065 Indian-white engagements between 1865 and 1891, including both civilians and soldiers combatants. The peak years of the fighting followed the Civil War, between 1867 and 1869. An official army compilation suggested that the army lost 932, killed between 1866 and 1891. It is unknown how many Indians were killed in battle. Whatever the toll of lives extinguished in the Western Indian Wars, it must have paled in comparison to the thousands of young men who died in saloon gunfights in cattle towns and mining towns throughout the West.

Suggestions for Further Reading

Richard Maxwell Brown, *No Duty to Retreat: Violence and Values in American History and Society* (Norman: University of Oklahoma Press, 1991).

W. Eugene Hollon, *Frontier Violence: Another Look,* (New York: Oxford University Press, 1974).

Philip D. Jordan, *Frontier Law and Order,* (Lincoln: University of Nebraska Press, 1970).

Clare V. McKanna, *Homicide, Race, and Justice in the American West, 1880-1920,* (Tucson: University of Arizona Press, 1997).

Robert Utley, *The Indian Frontier of the American West, 1846-1890,* (Albuquerque: The University of New Mexico Press, 1982).

Critical Thinking

1. Why was the carnage at Sand Creek considered a massacre rather than a battle? Why did many Americans consider the bloodshed at Wounded Knee a battle instead of a massacre?

2. What conditions led to the conflict at Wounded Knee?

3. Was the Johnson County War sparked by rustling or was it an example of class conflict? Discuss the complex interactions behind this "range war."

4. Was the mass hanging of Sioux Indians warranted following the Minnesota uprising? If you were President Lincoln, what would you have done?

5. Compare the Rock Springs Massacre, Sand Creek Massacre, and Los Angeles riot. What do these incidents tell us about race relations in the West?

Document 7.1

The Sioux Uprising in Minnesota (1862)

In the following passage Mary Schwandt describes her narrow escape during the Santee Sioux Uprising in Minnesota. According to her account she left for New Ulm on August 18, 1862. On the following day and then on August 23, settlers at New Ulm repulsed several Sioux attacks, but not without suffering thirty-four deaths and sixty wounded. The town of New Ulm was virtually destroyed before the depradations were finally ended on September 23.*

On the morning of the 18th of August, Mattie Williams, Mary Anderson, Mr. Patoile, Mr. L. Davis, a Frenchman, and myself, put our clothing into a two-horse wagon and started for New Ulm. When we arrived at John Moore's, a half-breed, we were informed that the Indians were killing all the whites on Beaver Creek and Sacred Heart, and were advised to keep off from the road and follow Mr. Reynolds, who had gone on ahead of us...

When we arrived opposite the fort, Mr. Patoile, supposing we could not cross the river, as there was no ferry there, continued down on the New Ulm road. The horses were now very tired, and we frequently got out and walked. When within about eight miles of New Ulm, some fifty Indians, with horses and wagons, and barrels full of flour, and all sorts of goods and pictures, taken from the houses, came from the direction of that town. They seemed to be all drunk, were very noisy, and perfectly naked, and painted all over their bodies. Two of them, on horseback, came on ahead of the rest, one on each side of us, and ordered us to stop. The team was turned out of the road, and all but Patoile jumped out of the wagon. They came up and shot him, some four balls entering his body, and he fell out of the wagon dead, and they left him lying there.

The rest of us ran toward the woods and hid in a slough, in the tall grass. The men were both killed in the slough. When we jumped from the wagon, Davis exclaimed, "We are lost!" I heard nothing said by any one else. The Frenchman ran in a different direction from where we were. I have a faint recollection of seeing him fall when he was shot. Mr. Davis was with us, and was shot about the same time. Mary Anderson was away behind us, and was shot through the lower part of the body, the ball entering at the hip and coming out through the abdomen. She was not killed, and the Indians must have carried her to the wagon, as, when I again saw her, she was in a wagon, being drawn by one of the savages. As they came toward us we screamed, when one of them took hold of Mattie and tore off her "shaker," and two took hold of me, one hold of each arm, and

---

* Charles S. Bryant, *A History of the Great Massacre by the Sioux Indians*, (Cincinnati: Rickey and Carroll, 1864), pp. 336, 338-341.

forced us back to the wagon. They put Mattie in the wagon with Mary, and me in another, driven by the negro Godfrey. The wagon with Mattie and Mary went toward the Agency, and the one I was in went off into the prairie.

I asked Godfrey what they were going to do with me. He said he did not know. He told me they had chased Mr. and Mrs. Reynolds, and, he thought, had killed them. About two or three miles out on the prairie, we came to the squaws, for whom Godfrey told me they were looking. Here we all sat down, and the squaws took bread from the wagons, and all ate; and the Indians fixed up their hair, and tied it up with ribbons.

It was now about five o'clock. We remained where we were about one hour, and then went on to the house of Waucouta, a chief of the Wapekuta tribe, about half a mile from the Agency. Here I found Mrs. J. W. De Camp, who, with her two children, was captured at the Lower Agency. It was about eight o'clock when we arrived at Waucouta's house, and the buildings were still burning at the Agency when we got there. We could see them plainly from where we were. I had been there about half an hour when an Indian came, whom Mrs. De Camp supposed to be friendly, as he was a farmer Indian, and, fearing others would come and abuse us, she asked him to stay. After awhile a number more came, and, after annoying me with their loathsome attentions for a long time, one of them laid his hands forcibly upon me, when I screamed, and one of the fiends struck me on my mouth with his hand, causing the blood to flow very freely. They then took me out by force, to an unoccupied tepee, near the house, and perpetrated the most horrible and nameless outrages upon my person. These outrages were repeated, at different times during my captivity...

At ten or eleven o'clock, Mattie and Mary Anderson came. The ball was yet in Mary's body, and Waucouta tried to cut it out, but failed. Mary then took the knife from the hand of Waucouta, and removed it herself. We remained here some four days. Cold water was poured upon corn-meal for Mary to drink, but we had nothing to eat, except some potatoes we dug in the garden, for those four days. On the fourth day we went to the camp of Little Crow. Mary Anderson was taken along, but died at about four o'clock on the morning of the 22d of August. We had some chicken here, but no bread. Mary ate of the chicken, and drank some of the broth. This was the last she ever ate. I was with her when she died. It rained very hard a part of the night, and the water ran through and under the tepee, on the ground, and Mary was wet, and had no bed-clothing to keep her dry or warm. She was very thirsty, calling for water all the time, but otherwise did not complain, and said but very little. I watched while Mattie slept, and she watched while I slept. I was awake when she died, and she dropped away so gently that I thought she was asleep, until Mattie told me she was dead.

Document 7.2

The Hanging of Thirty-Eight Indians (1862)

With the nation's attention focused on the Civil War, tension between Minnesota's settlers and the Santee Sioux continued to mount as the Indians saw their ancestral lands dwindle. Starvation and crop failures along with the reluctance of the federal government to pay annuities to the Sioux in a timely fashion led to the murder of white settlers in August 1862. This incident ignited the Minnesota uprising which resulted in the deaths of close to five hundred settlers and property damage of over one million dollars. After federal troops under General John Pope put an end to the conflict, a military court sentenced 303 Sioux to death. However, President Lincoln intervened and selected the thirty-eight that he deemed most culpable to death. On December 26, 1862 they were executed in the largest mass hanging in American history in Mankato, Minnesota.*

As those at the head of the procession came out of the basement we heard a sort of death-wail sounded which was immediately caught up by all the condemned and was chanted in unison until the foot of the scaffold was reached. At the foot of the steps there was no delay. Captain Redfield mounted the drop, at the head, and the Indians crowded after him as if it were a race to see who would get up first. They actually crowded on each other's heels and as they got to the top each took his position without any assistance from those detailed for that purpose. They still kept up a mournful wail and occasionally there would be a piercing scream.

The ropes were soon arranged around their necks, not the least resistance being offered. One or two, feeling the noose uncomfortably tight, attempted to loosen it, and although their hands were tied, they partially succeeded. The movement, however, was noticed by the assistants and the cords rearranged. The white caps which had been placed on the top of their heads were now drawn down over their faces, shutting out forever the light of day from their eyes.

Then ensued a scene that can hardly be described and which can never be forgotten. All joined in shouting and singing, as it appeared to those who were ignorant of the language. The tones seemed somewhat discordant and yet there was harmony in it. Their bodies swayed to and fro and their every limb seemed to be keeping time. The drop trembled and shook as if all were dancing. The most touching scene on the drop was their attempts to grasp each other's hands, fettered as they were. They were very close to each other and many succeeded. Three or four in a row were hand in hand swaying up and

---

* *St. Paul Pioneer*, December 28, 1862.

down with the rise and fall of their voices. One old man reached out on each side but could not grasp a hand. His struggles were piteous and affected many beholders.

We were informed by those who understood the language that their singing and dancing was only to sustain each other, that there was nothing defiant in their last moments, and that no death-song, strictly speaking, was chanted on the gallows. Each one shouted his own name and called the name of his friend, saying in substance, "I'm here! I'm here!"

Captain Burt hastily scanned all the arrangements for the execution and motioned to Major Brown, the signal officer, that all was ready. There was one tap of the drum, almost drowned by the voices of the Indians, then another and the stays of the drop were knocked away, the rope cut and with a crash down came the drop. One rope broke but not until the neck of the victim was dislocated. His body came down on the drop with a heavy thud and a crash of the boards. There was no struggling by any of the Indians for the space of half a minute; the only movements were the natural vibrations occasioned by the fall. In the meantime a new rope was placed around the neck of the one who fell and it having been thrown over the beam he was soon hanging with the others.

After the lapse of a minute several drew up their legs once or twice and there was some movement of the arms. One Indian, at the expiration of ten minutes, still breathed but the rope was better adjusted and life was soon extinct. It is unnecessary to speak of the awful sight of thirty-eight human beings suspended in the air. Imagination will readily supply what we refrain from describing.

After the bodies had hung for about half an hour the physicians of the several regiments reported that life was extinct. Soon after, several United States mule teams appeared and the bodies were taken down and dumped into the wagons without much ceremony. They were carried down to the sandbar in front of the city and all buried in the same hole. The half-breeds were buried in one corner of the hole so they would be disinterred by their friends. Everything was conducted in the most orderly and quiet manner.

As the drop fell the citizens could not repress a shout of exultation, in which the soldiers joined, but that was the only demonstration of feeling. As the wagons bore the bodies of the murderers off to burial the people quietly dispersed, and few, we take it, who witnessed the awful scene will voluntarily look upon its like again.

Document 7.3

The Sand Creek Massacre (1864)

Incoming white settlers to Colorado early in the 1860s created new tensions with many Native American tribes, particularly the Cheyennes. Col. John M. Chivington, a Methodist minister and leader of a Colorado militia unit, believed that Indians were vermin who should be exterminated. In November 1864, his militia force attacked a peaceful

Cheyenne settlement at Sand Creek, Colorado. They killed and then mutilated men, women, and children. The massacre precipitated a bitter debate in the United States over Indian policy. The following documents describing the Sand Creek massacre from different points of view were printed in the *New York. Tribune* in 1879.*

LETTER I

In June, 1864, Governor Evans, of Colorado, sent out a circular to the Indians of the Plains, inviting all friendly Indians to come into the neighborhood of the forts, and be protected by the United States troops. Hostilities and depredations had been committed by some bands of Indians, and the Government was about to make war upon them. This circular says:

"In some instances they (the Indians) have attacked and killed soldiers, and murdered peaceable citizens. For this the Great Father is angry, and will certainly hunt them out and punish them; but he does not want to injure those who remain friendly to the whites. He desires to protect and take care of them. For this purpose I direct that all friendly Indians keep away from those who are at war, and go to places of safety. Friendly Arapahoes and Cheyennes belonging to the Arkansas River will go to Major Colby, United States Agent at Fort Lyon, who will give them provisions and show them a place of safety."

In consequence of this proclamation of the governor, a band of Cheyennes, several hundred in number, came in and settled down near Fort Lyon. After a time they were requested to move to Sand Creek, about forty miles from Fort Lyon, where they were still guaranteed "perfect safety" and the protection of the Government. Rations of food were issued to them from time to time. On the 27th of November, Colonel J. M. Chivington, a member of the Methodist Episcopal Church in Denver, and Colonel of the First Colorado Cavalry, led his regiment by a forced march to Fort Lyon, induced some of the United States troops to join him, and fell upon this camp of friendly Indians at daybreak. The chief, White Antelope, always known as friendly to the whites, came running toward the soldiers, holding up his hands and crying "Stop! stop!" in English. When he saw that there was no mistake, that it was a deliberate attack, he folded his arms and waited till he was shot down. The United States flag was floating over the lodge of Black Kettle, the head chief of the tribe; below it was tied also a small white flag as additional security-a precaution Black Kettle had been advised by United States officers to take if he met troops on the Plains. In Major Wynkoop's testimony, given before the committee appointed by Congress to investigate this massacre, is the following passage:

"Women and children were killed and scalped, children shot at their mothers' breasts, and all the bodies mutilated in the most horrible manner. * * * The dead bodies of females profaned in such a manner that the recital is sickening, Colonel J. M. Chivington all the time inciting his troops to their diabolical outrages."

Another man testified as to what he saw on the 30th of November, three days after the battle, as follows:

* Helen Hunt Jackson, *A Century of Dishonor* (Boston: Little, Brown, and Company, 1917), pp. 343-50.

"I saw a man dismount from his horse and cut the ear from the body of an Indian, and the scalp from the head of another. I saw a number of children killed; they had bullet-holes in them; one child had been cut with some sharp instrument across its side. I saw another that both ears had been cut off. * * * I saw several of the Third Regiment cut off fingers to get the rings off them. I saw Major Sayre scalp a dead Indian. The scalp had a long tail of silver hanging to it."

Robert Bent testified:

"I saw one squaw lying on the bank, whose leg had been broken. A soldier came up to her with a drawn sabre. She raised her arm to protect herself; he struck, breaking her arm. She rolled over, and raised her other arm; he struck, breaking that, and then left her without killing her. I saw one squaw cut open, with an unborn child lying by her side."

Major Anthony testified:

"There was one little child, probably three years old, just big enough to walk through the sand. The Indians had gone ahead, and this little child was behind, following after them. The little fellow was perfectly naked, travelling in the sand. I saw one man get off his horse at a distance of about seventy-five yards and draw up his rifle and fire. He missed the child. Another man came up and said, 'Let me try the son of a b—. I can hit him.' He got down off his horse, kneeled down, and fired at the little child, but he missed him. A third man came up, and made a similar remark, and fired, and the little fellow dropped."

The Indians were not able to make much resistance, as only a part of them were armed, the United States officers having required them to give up their guns. Luckily they had kept a few.

When this Colorado regiment of demons returned to Denver they were greeted with an ovation. *The Denver News* said: "All acquitted themselves well. Colorado soldiers have again covered themselves with glory;" and at a theatrical performance given in the city, these scalps taken from Indians were held up and exhibited to the audience, which applauded rapturously.

After listening, day after day, to such testimonies as these I have quoted, and others so much worse that I may not write and *The Tribune* could not print the words needful to tell them, the committee reported: "It is difficult to believe that beings in the form of men, and disgracing the uniform of United States soldiers and officers, could commit or countenance the commission of such acts of cruelty and barbarity;" and of Colonel Chivington: "He deliberately planned and executed a foul and dastardly massacre, which would have disgraced the veriest savage among those who were the victims of his cruelty."

This was just fifteen years ago, no more. Shall we apply the same rule of judgment to the white men of Colorado that the Government is now applying to the Utes? There are 130,000 inhabitants of Colorado; hundreds of them had a hand in this massacre, and thousands in cool blood applauded it when it was done. There are 4000 Utes in Colorado. Twelve of them, desperate, guilty men, have committed murder and rape, and three or four hundred of them did, in the convenient phrase of our diplomacy, "go to war against the Government;" *i. e.,* they attempted, by force of arms, to restrain the entrance upon their own lands—lands bought, owned and paid for—of soldiers that the Government had sent there, to be ready to make war upon them, in case the agent thought it best to do so! This is the plain English of it. This is the plain, naked truth of it.

And now the Secretary of the Interior has stopped the issue of rations to 1000 of these helpless creatures; rations, be it understood, which are not, and never were, a charity, but are the Utes' rightful dues, on account of lands by them sold; dues which the Government promised to pay "annually forever." Will the American people justify this? There is such a thing as the conscience of a nation-as a nation's sense of justice. Can it not be roused to speak now? Shall we sit still, warm and well fed, in our homes, while five hundred women and little children are being slowly starved in the bleak, barren wildernesses of Colorado? Starved, not because storm, or blight, or drouth has visited their country and cut off their crops; not because pestilence has laid its hand on them and slain the hunters who brought them meat, but because it lies within the promise of one man, by one word, to deprive them of one-half their necessary food for as long a term of years as he may please; and "the Secretary of the Interior cannot consistently feed a tribe that has gone to war against the Government."

We read in the statutes of the United States that certain things may be done by "executive order" of the President. Is it not time for a President to interfere when hundreds of women and children are being starved in his Republic by the order of one man? Colonel J. M. Chivington's method was less inhuman by far. To be shot dead is a mercy, and a grace for which we would all sue, if to be starved to death were our only other alternative.

New York, Jan, Slat, 1880.
H. H.

This letter drew from the former editor of the *Rocky Mountain News,* a Denver newspaper, the following reply:

LETTER II.

To the Editor of the Tribune:
Sir, —In your edition of yesterday appears an article, under the above caption, which arraigns the people of Colorado as a community of barbarous murderers, and finally elevates them above the present Secretary of the Interior, thereby placing the latter gentleman in a most unenviable light if the charges averred be true. "The Sand Creek Massacre" of 1864 is made the text and burden of the article; its application is to the present condition of the White River band of Utes in Colorado. Quotations are given from the testimony gathered, and the report made thereon by a committee of Congress charged with a so-called investigation of the Sand Creek affair. That investigation was made for a certain selfish purpose. It was to break down and ruin certain men. Evidence was taken upon one side only. It was largely false, and infamously partial. There was no answer for the defence.

The Cheyenne and Arapahoe Indians assembled at Sand Creek were not under the protection of a United States fort. A few of them had been encamped about Fort Lyon and drawing supplies therefrom, but they had gradually disappeared and joined the main camp on Dry Sandy, forty miles from the fort, separated from it by a waterless desert, and entirely beyond the limit of its control or observation. While some of the occupants were still, no doubt, occasional visitors at the fort, and applicants for supplies and ammunition, most of the warriors were engaged in raiding the great Platte River Road, seventy-five miles farther north, robbing and burning trains, stealing cattle and horses, robbing and destroying the United States mails, and killing white people. During the summer and fall they had murdered over fifty of the citizens of Colorado. They had stolen and destroyed provisions and merchandise, and driven away stock worth hundreds of thousands of dollars. They had interrupted the mails, and for twenty-two consecutive days none were allowed to pass their lines. When satiated with murder and arson, and loaded with plunder, they would retire to their sacred refuge on Sand Creek to rest and refresh themselves, recruit their wasted supplies of ammunition from Fort Lyon-begged under the garb of gentle, peaceful refuges-and then return to the road to relieve their tired comrades, and riot again in carnage and robbery. These are facts; and when the "robbers' roost" was cleaned out, on that sad but glorious 27th day of November, 1864, they were sufficiently proven. Scalps of white men not yet dried; letters and photographs stolen from the mails; bills of lading and invoices of goods; bales and bolts of the goods themselves, addressed to merchants in Denver; half-worn clothing of white women and children, and many other articles of like character, were found in that poetical Indian camp, and recovered by the Colorado soldiers. They were brought to Denver, and those were the scalps exhibited in the theatre of that city. There was also an Indian saddle-blanket entirely fringed around the edges with white women's scalps, with the long, fair hair attached. There was an Indian saddle over the pommel of which was stretched skin stripped from the body of a white woman. Is it any wonder that soldiers flushed with victory, after one of the hardest campaigns ever endured by men, should indulge-some of them-in unwarranted atrocities after finding such evidence of barbarism, and while more than forty of their comrades were weltering in their own blood upon the field?

If "H. H." had been in Denver in the early part of that summer, when the bloated, festering bodies of the Hungate family-father, mother, and two babes-were drawn through the streets naked in an ox-wagon, cut, mutilated, and scalped-the work of those same red fiends who were so justly punished at Sand Creek; if, later, "H. H." had seen an upright and most estimable business man go crazy over the news of his son's being tortured to death a hundred miles down the Platte, as I did; if "H. H." had seen one-half the Colorado homes made desolate that fateful season, and a tithe of the tears that were caused to flow, I think there would have been one little word of excuse for the people of Colorado-more than a doubtful comparison with an inefficient and culpable Indian policy. Bear in mind that Colorado had no railroads then. Her supplies reached her by only one road—along the Platte—in wagons drawn by oxen, mules, or horses. That line was in full possession of the enemy. Starvation stared us in the face. Hardly a party went or came without some persons being killed. In some instances whole trains were cut off and destroyed. Sand Creek saved Colorado and taught the Indians the most salutary lesson they had ever learned. And now, after fifteen years, and here in the shadow of the Nation's Capitol, with the spectre of "H. H.'s" condemnation staring me in the face, I am neither afraid nor ashamed to repeat the language then used by *The Denver News:* "All acquitted themselves well. Colorado soldiers have again covered themselves with glory."

Thus much of history is gone over by "H. H." to present in true dramatic form the deplorable condition of the White River Utes, 1000 in number, who are now suffering the pangs of hunger and the discomfort of cold in the wilds of Western Colorado, without any kind agent to issue rations, provide blankets, or build fires for them. It is really too bad. A painful dispensation of Providence has deprived them of their best friend, and they are desolate and bereaved. He placed his life and its best efforts, his unbounded enthusiasm for their good, his great Christian heart—all at their service. But an accident befell him, and he is no more. The coroner's jury that sat upon his remains found that his dead body had a barrel stave driven into his mouth, a log-chain around his neck, by which it had been dragged about like a dead hog, and sundry bullet-holes through his body. The presumption was that from the effect of some one of these accidents he died; and, alas! he is no longer to serve out weekly rations to his flock of gentle Utes. There is no sorrow over his death or the desolation it wrought, but there is pity, oceans of pity, for the Indians who are hungry and cold. True, at the time he died they took the flour, the pork, and salt, and coffee, and sugar, and tobacco, and blankets, and all the other supplies that he would have issued to them through all this long winter had he lived. With his care these would have lasted until spring, and been sufficient for their wants; but, without it, "H. H." is suspicious that they are all gone, and yet it is but just past the middle of winter. Can "H. H." tell why this is thus? It is also true that they drove away the large herd of cattle from the increase of which that same unfortunate agent and his predecessors had supplied them with beef for eleven years past, and yet the consumption did not keep pace with the natural increase. They took them all, and are presumed to have them now. True, again, they had at the beginning of winter, or at the period of the melancholy loss of their best friend, about 4000 horses that were rolling fat, and three acres of dogs-not bad food in an emergency, or for an Indian thanksgiving feast-some of which should still remain.

THE WHOLE WHITE RIVER BAND GUILTY.

But "H. H." intimates that there is an alleged excuse for withholding rations from these poor, persecuted red angels. "Twelve" of them have been bad, and the tyrant at the head of the Interior Department is systematically starving all of the 1000 who constitute the band, and their 4000 horses, and 1800 cattle, and three acres of dogs, and six months' supplies, because those twelve bad Indians cannot conscientiously pick themselves out and be offered up as a burnt-offering and a sacrifice to appease the wrath of an outraged and partly civilized nation. This is the present indictment, and the Secretary and the President are commanded to stand up and plead "Guilty or not guilty, but you know you are guilty, d—n you." Now I challenge and defy "H. H.," or any other person living, to pick out or name twelve White River male Utes, over sixteen years of age, who were *not* guilty directly or indirectly, as principals or accomplices before the fact, in the Thornburgh attack or in the Agency massacre. I know these Indians well enough to know that these attacks were perfectly understood and deliberately planned. I cannot be made to believe that a single one of them, of common-sense and intelligence, was ignorant of what was to take place, and that knowledge extended far beyond the White River band. There were plenty of recruits from both the Los Pinos and the Uintah bands. In withholding supplies from the White River Utes the Secretary of the Interior is simply obeying the law. He cannot, except upon his own personal responsibility, issue supplies to a hostile Indian tribe, and the country will hold him accountable for a departure from his line of duty. Inferentially the Indians are justified by "H. H." in their attack upon Thornburgh's command. Their object was to defend "their own lands-lands bought, owned, and paid for." Bought of whom, pray? Paid for by whom? To whom was payment made? The soldiers were making no attack; they contemplated none. The agent had no authority to order an attack. He could not proclaim war. He could have no control whatever over the troops. But his life was in danger. The honor of his family was at stake. He asked for protection, "H. H." says he had no right to it. His life and the honor of his aged wife and of his virgin daughter are gone, and "H. H." is the champion of fiends who wrought the ruin.

Wm. N. Byers.

Document 7.4

An Anti-Chinese Riot in Los Angeles (1871)

California continued to lure immigration from China following the California Gold Rush. By 1870 the predominately male Chinese community of California stood at 50,000. Friction between the Chinese and anglo communities was augmented by job competition and objections over Chinese customs. Assaults on Chinese residents were commonplace in California's coastal towns. Many of the Chinese belonged to competing Tong fraternal societies. In 1871, rival Tongs came to blows on the streets of Los Angeles. In the resulting fray, several police officers were wounded and a civilian killed while attempting to restore order. A mob descended on the Tongs as they attempted to erect a barricade. Before the day was out the white mob had killed eighteen or nineteen of the Chinese. The following contemporary newspaper account describes in graphic detail the lynching and shooting of Chinese residents during this episode.*

The difficulty which occurred yesterday at Negro Alley, between two opposition Chinese companies, in which pistols were then freely used, again broke out afresh about five o'clock last evening. The difficulty of yesterday had been taken into court where it was supposed that it would be properly disposed of. It appears, however, that after coming from Justice Gray's Court where the preliminary examination was commenced yesterday afternoon, they renewed their quarrel and again resorted to the pistol for settlement. Immediately after the first shots were fired, officers and citizens rushed to the scene, and an attempt was made to arrest the parties engaged in the melee. Instead of surrendering, these miscreants at once turned to bay, and discharged the contents of their revolvers at those attempting to arrest them. This dispersed the crowd quicker than it had

---

* *Los Angeles Daily News,* October 25, 1871.

collected; but two of the Chinese still stood at the door of one of their dens, and discharged their weapons at the retreating crowds. One of the officers Bilderrain in a gallant attempt, with one or two others of the officers and some volunteers, to enter this den, was shot in the right shoulder and badly wounded. His brother, a boy about 15 years of age, received a ball in his right leg below the knee. Another man, a well known and respected citizen-named Robert Thompson, who was called upon to assist-while endeavoring to enter was confronted by a Chinaman with a loaded pistol in each hand. These he placed against Thompson's breast, and fired, one of the balls entering the right breast, the wound resulting fatally in about an hour and a half. This repeated firing was the signal for the closing of the iron shutters of neighboring stores.

Knots of men congregated at the street corners; and, in less time than it takes to be told, the entire block was surrounded, so as to permit none to escape. A string of men extended across Los Angeles Street along the east side of Negro Alley and on the western side of the block along Sanchez Street; and an unbroken line formed around the Plaza connecting with both the ends of the lines on Sanchez Street and Negro Alley. The wildest excitement prevailed. The mob was demoralized and uncontrollable. No definite organization existed. There seemed to be an understanding on the part of some few to drive the inmates of the blockaded houses up to the upper end of the block and allow them to escape into the Plaza where parties were stationed to receive them.

A Capture-The Captive Lynched

Shortly after the line had been formed, one of the inmates of the den in which these Chinamen had taken refuge was observed endeavoring to escape across Los Angeles Street. The cry was raised; and he was quickly captured by one Romo Sortorel. He had evidently made up his mind to cut his way through the circle, being armed at the time with a hatchet. When arrested, someone made an attempt to stab him with a knife, cutting the hand of Sortorel. Others took him in charge, with the view of placing him in jail. The infuriated mob followed. Cries of "Hang him!" Take him from Harris!" "Shoot him!" rose in every direction. The officers proceeded safely with their prisoner until they arrived at the junction of Temple and Spring Streets. Here they were surrounded, and the Chinaman forcibly taken from them, and dragged up Temple Street to New High Street. The frame of the sliding doors of a corral at the corner of his street afford a convenient gallows. A rope was soon at hand, and amid is own wailings and the hootings and imprecations of the crowd, he was elevated. The cord broke, however, but another was at hand, and he was regain hoisted to the beam, and there left to swing.

The Multitude Maddened

Returning to the scene, efforts were made by the Sheriff to organize a body of men to watch the place until morning, when more efficient means would be used for capturing those remaining in the houses. But all his efforts failed. Parties then proceeded on the roofs of the Chinese dens, breaking them in with axes, and discharging their pistols into the interior, hoping thereby to succeed in driving them out. In the center of the block, behind the Chinese residences, is a corral. Last evening this contained some seven or eight horses, behind which some of the Chinamen were discovered secreting themselves, and four of them were summarily despatched. The demoniacal desire to set the block on fire and burn them out was broached, but a better spirit prevailed, and the repeated cries of "Burn the S— of B—s out," were answered by more numerous ones, in the negative. The dread of a conflagration was, providentially, predominant in the minds of the majority. Two attempts, nevertheless, were made by throwing fireballs into the open doorways, and through the holes in the roofs, but they were expeditiously extinguished.

For three hours, that portion of the city was a pandemonium. Yells, shouts, curses, and pistol shots rent the air in every direction. A novel idea at last suggested itself to some-one's mind, viz.: that water through the firemen's hose be brought to play upon their retreat, to try and drive them out in that manner. The effort was made, but was unsuccessful, as it was impossible to get any concert of action.

Ferreted Out

About half past nine, some person ventured to enter one of the houses, and presently emerged with a prisoner. The crowd instantly seized him, and hurried him off down to Los Angeles Street to the point south of Commercial Street. At this point were several empty wagons; and in lieu of any more convenient place, a rope was attached to his neck, and he was raised from the ground. Further search resulted in the capture, as far as we could ascertain, of fourteen others, who were similarly dealt with, four of them being taken to the place of execution on New High Street and the other ten to Los Angeles and Commercial Streets. The dwellings on Los Angeles Street, where these scenes were enacted, have an awning projecting over the sidewalk. Six of these Chinamen-one a mere child-swung from it in a row, three hanging together in a bunch. An empty wagon close by had four others hanging to its sides. So furious had the mob become, that they placed the ropes around the necks of their captives as soon as they got them into their hands, and then dragged them along the street to the places of execution, where, more dead than alive, their existence was ended. An effort to stay the proceedings, as possible innocence was being sacrificed for guilt, was squelched, and the humanitarian, threatened with having a place given him among the ghastly row of victims hanging there before him. Such was the terrible vengeance that overtook these men. The bodies of those who were shot were lying on the street and sidewalk last night...

As might be expected, thieves were not idle. Upon breaking open the Chinese establishment, and obtaining complete mastery over the inmates, they commenced to ply their trade, helping themselves to everything they could lay their hands upon. "Help yourself, boys," was the advice boldly given by one, who was actively putting same into practice. When he proceeded to retire, however, the crowd marched him back and forced him to disgorge.

It was currently reported that during the melee about forty of the opposition party of Chinamen, or the Yo Hing Company had decamped, crossing the Los Angeles River, and going in an eastward direction.

Latest

At the time of going to press, seventeen bodies are reported at the jail, and three wounded, besides a large number of women and children in custody.

Everything is now quiet in Negro Alley and the neighborhood, and strong special force will keep guard throughout the rest of the night.

Document 7.5

The Rock Springs Massacre (1885)

During the 1870s and 1880s economic unrest and racial harassment culminated in a series of violent anti-Chinese riots in the West. One of the most notorious incidents occurred in the coal mines of Wyoming. Prior to 1875, the mines in Rock Springs, Wyoming were worked by white miners, most of whom were immigrants from Scandinavia and the British Isles. However, when the miners struck for higher wages in 1875, the mine owners imported 150 Chinese to replace the recalcitrant laborers. Resentment against the Chinese workers was further fueled by white bitterness over the Chinese predilection to work longer hours for lower wages. On September 2, 1885 tension between white and Chinese coal miners erupted into violence resulting in the deaths of at least twenty-eight Chinese coal miners and laborers and the wounding of fifteen others. Following the riot, President Grover Cleveland sent in federal troops at the request of the Wyoming Governor and averted further bloodshed.*

Situated in the south-western part of the Territory, Rock Springs is a place of six hundred or seven hundred inhabitants. The chief industry is coal-mining, and the mines are owned by the Union Pacific Railway Company. For some time the company, through agents, have employed Chinamen in these mines; and on the day of the massacre there were five hundred Celestials [i.e. Chinese] in the Chinese colony, which was located in the east section of the town.

All summer long among the white miners there has been developing a feeling of bitterness against the Chinese, nothing but a pretext being wanted to make an attack. This pretext came Wednesday morning, Sept. 2, when a quarrel arose in the mines, between a white miner and two Chinamen, over the possession of a "room." The fight in the mines became general, and did not end until one Chinaman had been killed, four severely wounded, and several white men badly hurt. All the work in the mines then ceased; the

---

* Isaac Hill Bromley, *The Chinese Massacre at Rock Springs, Wyoming Territory*, September 2, 1885 (Boston: Franklin Press, 1886), pp. 50-52, 54-55.

Chinamen going to their settlement, and the white miners returning to town, and arming themselves with any thing that would carry ball or shot. In the mean time, the Chinese had raised a flag of danger in Chinatown, and every Celestial in Rock Springs was making for his quarters. They appeared to realize the danger of their position, and were actively preparing to depart. No sooner had the miners finished their dinners, than they began to assemble in the streets, and "Vengeance on the Chinese!" was the universal cry, even some of the women joining in the demonstration. A vote was then taken, and the immediate expulsion of the Mongolians was determined upon. Seventy-five armed men, followed by a crowd of boys armed with clubs, shovels, picks, and drills, took up their march for Chinatown, proceeding down the railroad-track. There was a party of Chinamen at work beside the railroad, and the shooting opened on them; but they cleared the way in season to escape serious injury. When within a short distance of the settlement, the mob halted, and sent forward a committee to warn the Chinese that they must leave the place within an hour. A reply was received that they would go in that time; but hardly had thirty minutes elapsed before the crowd moved on toward the enemy, yelling like wild men, and shooting every Chinaman who was in sight. The terrible scene that followed cannot be overdrawn. Without making a show of resistance, the Chinese fled towards the mountains, some hatless, some shoeless, and all without their effects. Running after them, firing indiscriminately, came the white miners, now crazed by the reports of the firearms, and groans of the wounded and dying Chinamen who had been shot before they could escape from the settlement, some even before they left their doors.

Fleeing for their lives, the Chinamen shaped their course in the direction of Bitter Creek, the miners in hot pursuit, and shooting as rapidly as the weapons could be loaded. After the Celestials reached the hills, the shooting ceased, and the inhuman mob marched back to Chinatown, and began looting the houses, of which there were about forty-the property of the Union Pacific, and worth probably five hundred dollars each. Every thing of value was taken from the houses, and they were then set on fire. The flames forced out quite a number of Chinamen who had, until then, eluded detection. These poor fellows were either murdered outright, or fatally wounded and thrown into the burning buildings there to be roasted alive. Not less than fifteen met their fate in this way; and there is not but little doubt that there were at least fifty Chinamen killed altogether. All the afternoon and throughout the night, pistol-shots could be heard in the direction of Chinatown. The burning buildings gave the picture a weird coloring, and the first forcible crusade against the Chinese in America will long be remembered by those who participated in or witnessed it.

During the night, guards were placed about the town to protect the property of the citizens, while the expelled Chinamen rested their limbs on the hills several miles distant, but not too far to witness the destruction of their homes. Thursday morning, Chinatown presented a terrible sight. Protruding from the smouldering ruins were the charred remains of eleven Chinamen, and a sickening odor permeated the entire settlement. Clothing, bedding, household utensils, and provisions were scattered about in confusion, and traces of the preceding day's bloody work could be noticed at every turn. To the east of the town, several bodies were recovered of Chinamen who had been shot while endeavoring to escape, and who were left by their companions to suffer and die where they fell. In the morning the Chinamen who sought refuge in the hills came down to the railroad, and Division Superintendent George W. Dickinson ordered them brought to Evanston on a freight-train. The refugees, about four hundred and fifty in number, arrived at Evanston about four o'clock, Thursday afternoon, half starved, and half frightened to death. They were quartered at the Chinese settlement in Evanston, their fellow-countrymen doing every thing possible to provide for their comfort.

Ah Kuhn, an intelligent Chinaman, speaking English after a fashion, and acting accordingly as interpreter and business manager for the Chinese miners, was called, and answered inquiries as follows:-

GOV. DIR. SAVAGE: Where were you on the day this difficulty occurred?

ANS.: I was in No. 3 mine.

GOV. DIR. SAVAGE: When did you first hear that there was any trouble?

ANS.: About half-past nine I hear there was trouble over in No. 6 mine. I go down Rock Springs with China boy to office. I ask for Mr. Evans. I ask him, "You know trouble over in No. 6 mine?" He say yes. He go No. 3 mine; he stop about hour; I wait for him, I want see him again. He drive wagon up to No. 4 mine. I see lots white men (pretty near a hundred) come across from saloon, and go in section-house. White man he knock China boy down with brick on head; boy he holler and come to Chinatown. I stop him, I tell him "Keep still." About a hundred white men go up to No. 3 mine with rifles. All boys get scared and run away. I say, "Come back." Fellow on hill with rifle stop and shot good many times and come down.

GOV. DIR. SAVAGE: Did you see some of the Chinamen shot?

ANS.: No, I down in cellar, no see 'em. I tell Mr. Evans all boys scared. About eight o'clock some boy he come in and take old boxes and pile 'em all together; he say to another boy, "You get some matches?" I feel awful sorry; not know how to get out. He go out about five minutes; I tell him, "Boy better go." Chinese boy he would not go in house; boys hit him; he fall down on the ground, and boys get scared and run. I stay in cellar from three to eight o'clock. About half-past ten I see lots of men coming down from No. 6 mine. Good many have rifles. I go up to No. 3 mine, and tell Mr. Miller he drive wagon over Chinatown. I tell him, "White man make much trouble, driving Chinamen away." Mr. Miller say, "No get scared." Chinamen work in No. 4 room, No. 5 entry; white man come in and drive Chinaman out. Knock China boys down on the ground; boss he send car down and bring China boy out, and send for wagon and take boy back to his camp. About eight o'clock I saw all houses burning up. I come out of cellar. Three or four white men came along and kick door, and say, "You better come out, or we drag you out." I come out, and run about two hundred yards. I turn my head, I look back and see three or four white men standing. He see me, and shot me four times; I fall down and drop the money, and ran up to No. 4 mine. I went down the track across the river. I walk up the track, and see good many China boys, about seventy or eighty. I walk up to the railroad section-house, knock at the door, and say, "Mr., you better open door and let me in." He say, "Who's that?" I say, China boy." He open the door, and let me come into that house. I say, "I am nearly dead, I got nothing to eat." I ask him, "You give me some bread?" He say, "You got some bread." He say, "What's the matter at Rock Springs?" I say, "Lots trouble, drive China boys out." I sat down and took nip of water; took piece of bread and eat 'em; I feel much better; I say, "Mr., you let me have hand-car I go next station." He say, "I have no hand-car." In morning I started back. He say, "You better not go back to Rock Springs," and I went back to Evanston, and came back on the seventh of the month.

Document 7.6

The Death of Sitting Bull (1890)

The Ghost Dance movement of 1890 was a manifestation of Sioux discontent over the erosion of Sioux culture. The return of Sitting Bull (1831?-1890) to the Standing Rock Agency in 1883 represented a threat to white hegemony on the reservation. Indian agent James McLaughlin feared that the return of the great chief, combined with the outbreak of the Ghost Dance, could lead to another war. Since Sitting Bull still exerted significant influence on the reservation, McLaughlin ordered the Indian police to arrest the old chief at his cabin on Grand River. This passage offers the establishment spin on the subsequent melee that ended in the deaths of Sitting Bull, his son, and twelve others.*

The arrest of Sitting Bull was, no doubt, a measure necessary to prevent further spreading of a revolt which largely emanated from him. Concerning his own dangerous intentions there can be no doubt. The evidence on this point is abundant and specific. The arrest was attempted under telegraphic instructions from General Ruger, at St. Paul, to Colonel Drum, commanding Port Yates, the military post adjoining the Standing Rock Agency, under date of December 12th. It was the expressed wish of General Ruger that the military and the civil agent should co-operate in effecting the arrest. Fortunately entire harmony existed between Colonel Drum and Major McLaughlin. The agent wished to effect the arrest by means of the Indian police, so as to avoid unnecessary irritation to the followers of Sitting Bull, and at a time when the majority of these Indians would be absent from their camp drawing rations at the agency. This rise intention was frustrated by the unexpected attempt of Sitting Bull to save the reservation. Therefore the arrest, instead of being attempted December 20th, was precipitated December 14th. Sitting Bull evidently intended to submit to his captors peaceably, but, while dressing, in his tent for the journey, he was incited to resistance by the outcries of his son, who berated the Indian policemen and exhorted his father not to allow himself to be taken. Upon coming out of his tent, under charge of the police, Sitting Bull yielded to his son's advice and called on his people to rescue him. In an instant a savage crowd of one hundred and fifty

---

* Herbert Welsh, "The Meaning of the Dakota Outbreak," *Scribner's Magazine*, (April, 1891), 451.

Indians attacked and fired upon the police. Almost immediately six of the police were killed or mortally wounded, and Sitting Bull was himself killed by one of the wounded police. The fight lasted about half an hour. The police soon drove the Indians, who far outnumbered them, from around the adjoining buildings and into the surrounding woods. During the fight women attacked the police with knives and clubs, but in every instance the latter simply disarmed and placed them under guard until the troops arrived, after which they were given their liberty. The highest praise for courage and ability was accorded the police for their part in this affair by the military officer commanding the troops who supported them.

Document 7.7

Wounded Knee (1890)

The last confrontation between United States soldiers and the Plains Indians resulted in the deaths of 146 Indian men, women, and children and twenty-five army soldiers at Wounded Knee Creek, South Dakota, in December 1890. As a result of the allotment program and the mass influx of European-American settlers in the West, Native Americans lost most of their land and were relocated to reservations, where non-Indians could exercise greater control over them. The adjustment to reservation life proved extremely difficult for many tribes, and in order to deal with their new situations, some tribes developed new religious ideas. One of those developments was the Ghost Dance religion that spread across the Great Plains in the late nineteenth century, promising. Indians that if they performed the Ghost Dance and were faithful to its principles, they would soon experience a great act of redemption at the hands of the great spirit of the universe. Dead Indians would be resurrected and rejoin their living comrades, white people would be erased from the face of the earth, and the great buffalo herds would be restored. Life would resume as it had been before the Europeans ever arrived. Many whites felt threatened by the Ghost Dance, and tensions between the Sioux peoples and non-Indians escalated, leading to what is known today as the Wounded Knee incident. Whether it was a massacre or a battle certainly depends upon one's perspective. The following excerpt is taken from anthropologist James Mooney's description of the Ghost Dance.*

On the morning of December 29, 1890, preparations were made to disarm the Indians preparatory to taking them to the agency and thence to the railroad. In obedience to instructions the Indians had pitched their tipis on the open plain a short distance west of the creek and surrounded on all sides by the soldiers. In the center of the camp the Indians had hoisted a white flag as a sign of peace and a guarantee of safety. Behind them was a dry ravine running into the creek, and on a slight rise in the front was posted the battery of four Hotchkiss machine guns, trained directly on the Indian camp. In front, behind, and on both flanks of the camp were posted the various troops of cavalry, a portion of two troops, together with the Indian scouts, being dismounted and drawn up in front of the Indians at the distance of only a few yards from them. Big Foot himself was ill of pneumonia in his tipi, and Colonel Forsyth, who had taken command as senior officer, had provided a tent warmed with a camp stove for his reception.

Shortly after 8 oclock in the morning the warriors were ordered to come out from the tipis and deliver their arms. They came forward and seated themselves on the ground in front of the troops. They were then ordered to go by themselves into their tipis and bring out and surrender their guns. The first twenty went and returned in a short time with only two guns. It seemed evident that they were unwilling to give them up and after consultation of the officers part of the soldiers were ordered up to within ten yards of the group of warriors, while another detachment of troops was ordered to search the tipis. After a thorough hunt these last returned with about forty rifles, most of which, however, were old and of little value. The search had consumed considerable time and created a good deal of excitement among the women and children, as the soldiers found it necessary in the process to overturn the beds and other furniture of the tipis and in some instances drove out the inmates. All this had its effect on their husbands and brothers, already wrought up to a high nervous tension and not knowing what might come next. While the soldiers had been looking for the guns Yellow Bird, a medicine-man, had been walking about among the warriors, blowing on an eagle-bone whistle, and urging them to resistance, telling them that the soldiers would become weak and powerless, and that the bullets would be unavailing against the sacred "ghost shirts," which nearly every one of the Indians wore. As he spoke in the Sioux language, the officers did not at once realize the dangerous drift of his talk, and the climax came too quickly for them to interfere. It is said one of the searchers now attempted to raise the blanket of a warrior. Suddenly Yellow Bird stooped down and threw a handful of dust into the air, when, as if this were the signal, a young Indian, said to have been Black Fox from Cheyenne river, drew a rifle from under his blanket and fired at the soldiers, who instantly replied with a volley directly into the crowd of warriors and so near that their guns were almost touching. From the number of sticks set up by the Indians to mark where the dead fell, as seen by the author a year later, this one volley must have killed nearly half the warriors. The survivors sprang to their feet, throwing their blankets from their shoulders as they rose, and for a few minutes there was a terrible hand to hand struggle, where every man's

---

* James Mooney, "The Ghost-Dance Religion and the Sioux Outbreak of 1890," *in Fourteen Annual Report of the Bureau of Ethnology, Part 2* (Washington, D.C.: Government Printing Office, 1896), pp. 868-880.

thought was to kill. Although many of the warriors had no guns, nearly all had revolvers and knives in their belts under their blankets, together with some of the murderous warclubs still carried by the Sioux. The very lack of guns made the fight more bloody, as it brought the combatants to closer quarters.

At the first volley the Hotchkiss guns trained on the camp opened fire and sent a storm of shells and bullets among the women and children, who had gathered in front of the tipis to watch the unusual spectacle of military display. The guns poured in 2-pound explosive shells at the rate of nearly fifty per minute, mowing down everything alive. The terrible effect may be judged from the fact that one woman survivor, Blue Whirlwind, with whom the author conversed, received fourteen wounds, while each of her two little boys was also wounded by her side. In a few minutes 200 Indian men, women, and children, with 60 soldiers, were lying dead and wounded on the ground, the tipis had been torn down by the shells and some of them were burning above the helpless wounded, and the surviving handful of Indians were flying in wild panic to the shelter of the ravine, pursued by hundreds of maddened soldiers and followed up by a raking fire from the Hotchkiss guns, which had been moved into position to sweep the ravine.

There can be no question that the pursuit was simply a massacre, where fleeing women, with infants in their arms, were shot down after resistance had ceased and when almost every warrior was stretched dead or dying on the ground. On this point such a careful writer as Herbert Welsh says: "From the fact that so many women and children were killed, and that their bodies were found far from the scene of action, and as though they were shot down while flying, it would look as though blind rage had been at work, in striking contrast to the moderation of the Indian police at the Sitting Bull fight when they were assailed by women." The testimony of American Horse and other friendlies is strong in the same direction. Commissioner Morgan in his official report says that "Most of the men, including Big Foot, were killed around his tent, where he lay sick. The bodies of the women and children were scattered along a distance of two miles from the scene of the encounter."

This is no reflection on the humanity of the officer in charge. On the contrary, Colonel Forsyth had taken measures to guard against such an occurrence by separating the women and children, as already stated, and had also endeavored to make the sick chief, Big Foot, as comfortable as possible, even to the extent of sending his own surgeon. Dr Glennan, to wait on him on the night of the surrender. Strict orders had also been issued to the troops that women and children were not to be hurt. The butchery was the work of infuriated soldiers whose comrades had just been shot down without cause or warning. In justice to a brave regiment it must be said that a number of the men were new recruits fresh from eastern recruiting stations, who had never before been under fire, were not yet imbued with military discipline, and were probably unable in the confusion to distinguish between men and women by their dress.

After examining all the official papers bearing on the subject in the files of the War Department and the Indian Office, together with the official reports of the Commissioner of Indian Affairs and of the Secretary of War and the several officers engaged; after gathering all that might be obtained from unofficial printed sources and from conversation with survivors and participants in the engagement on both sides, and after going over the battle-ground in company with the interpreter of the scouts engaged, the author arrives at the conclusion that when the sun rose on Wounded Knee on the fatal morning of December 29, 1890, no trouble was anticipated or premeditated by either Indians or troops; that the Indians in good faith desired to surrender and be at peace, and that the officers in the same good faith had made preparations to receive their surrender and escort them quietly to the reservation; that in spite of the pacific intent of Big Foot and his band, the medicine-man, Yellow Bird, at the critical moment urged the warriors to resistance and gave the signal for the attack; that the first shot was fired by an Indian, and that the Indians were responsible for the engagement; that the answering volley and attack by the troops was right and justifiable, but that the wholesale slaughter of women and children was unnecessary and inexcusable.

Authorities differ as to the number of Indians present and killed at Wounded Knee. General Ruger states that the band numbered about 340, including about 100 warriors, but Major Whitside, to whom they surrendered, reported them officially as numbering 120 men and 250 women and children, a total of 370. This agrees almost exactly with the statement made to the author by Mr Asay, a trader who was present at the surrender. General Miles says that there were present 106 warriors, a few others being absent at the time in search of the party under Kicking Bear and Short Bull. Among those who surrendered were about 70 refugees from the bands of Sitting Bull and Hump. No exact account of the dead could be made immediately after the fight, on account of a second attack by another party of Indians coming up from the agency. Some of the dead and wounded left on the field were undoubtedly carried off by their friends before the burial party came out three days later, and of those brought in alive a number afterward died of wounds and exposure, but received no notice in the official reports. The Adjutant-General, in response to a letter of inquiry, states that 128 Indians were killed and 33 wounded. Commissioner Morgan, in his official report, makes the number killed 146. Both these estimates are evidently too low. General Miles, in his final report, states that about 200 men, women, and children were killed. General Colby, who commanded the Nebraska state troops, says that about 100 men and over 120 women and children were found dead on the field, a total of about 220. Agent Royer telegraphed immediately after the fight that about 300 Indians had been killed, and General Miles, telegraphing on the same day, says, "I think very few Indians have escaped." Fifty-one Indians were brought in the same day by the troops, and a few others were found still alive by the burial party three days later. A number of these afterward died. No considerable number got away, being unable to reach their ponies after the light began. General Miles states that 98 warriors were killed on the field. The whole number killed on the field, or who later died from wounds and exposure, was probably very nearly 300.

According to an official statement from the Adjutant-General, 31 soldiers were killed in the battle. About as many more were wounded, one or two of whom afterward died. All of the killed, excepting Hospital Steward Pollock and an Indian scout named High Backbone, belonged to the Seventh cavalry, as did probably also nearly all of the wounded. The only commissioned officer killed was Captain Wallace. He received four bullet wounds in his body and finally sank under a hatchet stroke upon the head. Lieutenant E. A. Garlington, of the Seventh cavalry, and Lieutenant H. L. Hawthorne, of the Second artillery, were wounded. The last-named officer owed his life to his watch, which deflected the bullet that otherwise would have passed through his body.

On New Year's day of 1891, three days after the battle, a detachment of troops was sent out to Wounded Knee to gather up and bury the Indian dead and to bring in the wounded who might be still alive on the field. In the meantime there had been a heavy snowstorm, culminating in a blizzard. The bodies of the slaughtered men, women, and children were found lying about under the snow, frozen stiff and covered with blood. Almost all the dead warriors were formed lying near where the light began, about Big Foot's tipi, but the bodies of the women and children were found scattered along for 2 miles from the scene of the encounter, showing that they had been killed while trying to escape. A number of women and children were found still alive, but all badly wounded or frozen, or both, and most of them died after being brought in. Four babies were found alive under the snow, wrapped in shawls and lying beside their dead mothers, whose last thought had been of them. They were all badly frozen and only one lived. The tenacity of life so characteristic of wild people as well as of wild beasts was strikingly illustrated in the case of these wounded and helpless Indian women and children who thus lived three days through a Dakota blizzard, without food, shelter, or attention to their wounds. It is a commentary on our boasted Christian civilization that although there were two or three salaried missionaries at the agency not one went out to say a prayer over the poor mangled bodies of these victims of war. The Catholic priests had reasons for not being present, as one of them, Father Craft, was lying in the hospital with a dangerous wound received on the battlefield while bravely administering to the lying wants of the soldiers in the heat of the encounter, and the other, Father Jutz, an old man of 70 years, was at the mission school 5 miles away, still attending to his little flock of 100 children as before the trouble began, and unaware of what was transpiring at the agency.

A long trench was dug and into it were thrown all the bodies, piled one upon another like so much cordwood, until the pit was full, when the earth was heaped over them and the funeral was complete. Many of the bodies were stripped by the whites, who went out in order to get the "ghost shirts," and the frozen bodies were thrown into the trench stiff and naked. They were only dead Indians. As one of the burial party said, "It was a thing to melt the heart of a man, if it was of stone, to see those little children, with their bodies shot to pieces, thrown naked into the pit." The dead soldiers had already been brought in and buried decently at the agency. When the writer visited the spot the following winter, the Indians had put up a wire fence around the trench and smeared the posts with sacred red medicine paint.

A baby girl of only three or four months was found under the snow, carefully wrapped up in a shawl, beside her dead mother, whose body was pierced by two bullets. On her head was a little cap of buckskin, upon which the American flag was embroidered in bright beadwork. She had lived through all the exposure, being only slightly frozen, and soon recovered after being brought in to the agency. Her mother being killed, and, in all probability, her father also, she was adopted by General Colby, commanding the Nebraska state troops. The Indian women in camp gave her the poetic name of Zitkala-noni, "Lost Bird," and by the family of her adoption she was baptized under the name of Marguerite (figure 80). She is now (1896) living in the general's family at Washington, a chubby little girl 6 years of age, as happy with her dolls and playthings as a little girl of that age ought to be.

Another little girl about 5 years of age was picked up on the battlefield and brought in by the Indian police on the afternoon of the fight. She was adopted by George Sword, captain of the Indian police, and is now living with him under the name of Jennie Sword, a remarkably pretty little girl, gentle and engaging in her manners (figure 81).

A little boy of four years, the son of Yellow Bird, the medicine-man, was playing on his pony in front of a tipi when the firing began. As he described it some time ago in lisping English: "My father ran and fell down and the blood came out of his mouth [he was shot through the head], and then a soldier put his gun up to my white pony's nose and shot him, and then I ran and a policeman got me."

Document 7.8

Johnson County Range War (1892)

In 1892, Wyoming cattlemen were forced to resort to extralegal means to end cattle rustling on their ranges. Nowhere was the problem more intense than in Johnson County. The Wyoming Stock Growers' Association concocted a plan to eliminate those homesteaders suspected of stealing cattle. In order to put their plan into action, they conspired to recruit a vigilante army of almost fifty men, composed of Texas gunmen, stock detectives, and other cattlemen. Accompanied by several newspaper reporters, this motley group, known as the "Regulators" or "Invaders," descended on northern Wyoming, where they summarily executed several suspects before local citizenry panded together to end this incursion. Several hundred citizens surrounded the Regulators at a ranch before the U.S. Cavalry intervened and ended the bloodletting. The Johnson County War proved a pyrrhic victory for the Regulators, having only killed two actual rustlers. In addition, two of the Texas gunmen were killed accidentally. This dramatic episode would eventually cost the Johnson County Invaders more than $100,000 in legal expenses.*

The last of the important cattle wars was the somewhat famous "rustler war" of 1892, in which a campaign was made by the cattle men of Wyoming against the rustlers of Johnson County, Wyoming. This "war" was not without its opera-bouffe aspects, though it was ventilated for each day for over three weeks in the daily press, and heralded to the corners of the world. It was very much an affair of going after rustlers with a brass band, and it did not result so successfully as

* E. Hough, *The Story of the Cowboy*, (New York: D. Appleton and Company, 1898), pp. 309-318.

was hoped by the leaders of the project. Only two men were killed in this "war," yet the matter attracted far more attention than any similar clash that ever occurred in the cattle country. This was simply because of the newspaper notoriety it had. An old cowman covered the case perfectly when he said: "There might be twenty-five men killed each day down in Lincoln County in the old times, and it wouldn't make half the stir that is made nowadays if one man shoots at another in Wyoming. The newspapers make all the difference." The full force of such a remark can never be felt unless it has been one's fortune to live, at some time or other in his life, in a country where there were no newspapers and no law. He is then back at the beginning of the world, antedating civilization, and in a position to see the crude and grim forces underlying this human nature which pretends later to compose itself with the ways of society, but which has really a snarl and a claw not far away.

The newspaper accounts of the rustler war of 1892 were in many respects incorrect, the despatches coming from Buffalo, in Johnson County, the seat of the rustler element, being entirely contradictory to those emanating from Cheyenne, the headquarters of the big cowmen concerned in the raid. One gathers his beliefs in regard to the situation not from the newspaper accounts, but from thorough review of the matter upon one hand with a cowman who was one of the participants in the raid, and upon the other hand with some rustlers who were at Buffalo and thoroughly concerned in all the incidents which occurred on that side of the "war."

For a long time the rustlers had been making life a burden to the legitimate cowmen of the counties of Johnson, Natrona, and Converse, until they had nearly brought to a standstill all the proper operations of the cattle industry. Before the establishment of the live stock commission and the brand inspectors, it was impossible for a ranchman to tell whether he was going to come out at the end of the year with any cattle left or not. Practically the whole country was living on stolen beef, and not content with this and with serving notice on the cattle companies that they would no longer be allowed to hold their round-ups, the rustlers began to ship beef by car-load lots to the markets of the East. As there were no brand inspectors there to detect the fraudulent nature of such shipments, there was imminent danger that the illegal cattle men would entirely ruin the legal ones. The extent of the losses suffered by the cattle men may be inferred from the fact that within the first year after the appointment of the brand inspectors at the markets they sent back to the commissioners of the State $127,000 of "estray money" on cattle passing to market from the Wyoming range. The commissioners found proper ownership for all but $11,000 of this, but refused some of the funds to rustlers who openly claimed dues therein. This appearance of the action of the new cattle laws was extremely unsatisfactory to the rustlers, and it resulted in a practical solidification of the various rustler factions, and made of the county of Johnson a rustler settlement, where the cattle men had no voice. In four years the cattle men brought one hundred and eighty suits in Johnson County against rustlers for stealing beef or calves, but no jury could be found which would convict a man, and the only case in which a rustler was ever punished was one in which a thief had killed a cow and taken home a quarter of the beef, for which he was convicted of petty larceny and assessed the value of the beef, about eighteen dollars.

The rustlers posed as small stockmen, and did all they could to array the interests of the actual small stockmen against those of the "barons," or ranch capitalists, claiming that the fight was one of wealth against men in moderate circumstances, and asserting that as to the methods practised in acquiring cattle, the big ranchmen were no better than they should be. In this latter statement there was colour of truth in many instances, for the fortune of more than one man engaged in the raid against the rustlers was more than probably laid in the early and active efforts of their foremen with the branding iron. When such foremen sought to carry on the old methods for themselves which they had practised for their employers, the latter made objection, feeling that there had been a change in the former relations of *meum* and *tuum*. There is large undercurrent of unwritten history on both sides of the question in this rustler war. Be that as it may, there was much bitterness felt on both sides, and no doubt both sides thought they had some partial justification in many things which they did or attempted to do.

Early in the spring of 1892 a number of the large cattle owners met at Cheyenne and resolved upon a general raid against the rustlers, they having the names of about one hundred and twenty-five men whom they claimed to know were engaged in the rustling business, some thirty-five of whom they agreed among themselves either to kill or drive out of the country. In this movement to invoke the old-time ways of the range were several men prominent in State affairs, a member of the Legislature, a member of the stock commission, and some two dozen wealthy cattle men, several of whom were practically non-resident Easterners who had large holdings of cattle in Wyoming. There never was a more select, or a more inefficient, lynching party started out across the plains. Nearly all the cowmen of the movement were men of culture and refinement. Two Harvard graduates were among the outfit. There was a young Englishman along to see the fun—which he saw—and all in all the gathering was, socially speaking, everything that could be asked. It was incidentally remarked in one of the newspaper reports that one of the select lynchers while asleep in camp one day chanced to toss out his hand over his blankets, thus displaying two large diamond rings which he wore as part of his range costume. It is not justly to be said of these men that they were not brave and determined, and it probably never occurred to them that they would fail of carrying out their programme as arranged in detail without experiencing any great hindrance on the part of the men they were intending to hang, shoot, or drive out of the country. They had read of such things being done, and agreed that it was desirable they should do some of those things for themselves. That one of their number who tells this story of the raid admits frankly that they made a great mistake. They were all new at that sort of business, Eastern men who had not been reared in the hard school of the old times, and who, while they might have been fit for privates in such an enterprise, were absolutely unfit for leaders; in which latter capacity there seems to have been a general willingness to serve. The men who should have been in charge were the men who were hired by the day to serve as privates—twenty fighting Texans, cowpunchers from the lower range, who were imported for this purpose and paid five dollars a day and expenses to go along and see or assist in the hanging, shooting, and driving out. Had the leader of the cowboys been the leader of the party, the result might have been, at least in some respects, different; for here was a man with followers who, though they had not accumulated enough funds to afford to wear diamond rings when going to a lynching, had none the less served in the rude apprenticeship of Western life on the plains, and knew far more about partisan campaigning than all the men who acted as the leaders of this raid.

The party as finally organized numbered forty-three men, including the twenty Texans, and their outfit was as perfect as money could buy. They had three wagons and plenty of cooks, and evidently intended to travel in perfect comfort. Secretly embarking their outfit on a train at Cheyenne at night, early in April, 1892, they went by rail to Casper, Wyoming, arriving there the following night. Thence they started with their horses and wagons overland across the wild country, something like one hundred and thirty miles, which lay between them and the seat of war. The first serious business of the expedition was at the K. C. ranch, occupied by two well-known rustlers, Nate Champion and Nick Ray. The raiders held up this ranch at day-break, and early in the morning took prisoners two freighters who happened to be stopping at the house, and who came out of the house to go toward the barn. The house was then surrounded by a firing party of twelve men, it being supposed that Champion and Ray would soon miss the other men and come out to see what had become of them. Presently one of the rustlers, Ray, stepped to the door, and at once fell under the rifle fire of the men who lay concealed and waiting for him. The participants in this raid are very reticent in regard to the names of those who did any shooting, but one of the freighters taken prisoner afterward said that it was a smooth-faced boy, one of the Texas fighters, who took the first hurried aim and shot Ray down. Ray was shot again as he crawled back into the house. The other rustler, Champion, remained game till the last and refused to come out, keeping up his fire upon his besiegers whenever opportunity offered. Champion was finally driven out by means of fire. A wagon load of hay was pushed up against the ranch house and set on fire, so that the cabin was burned over the head of the rustler defending it. The body of Ray was later found burned and charred.

When the heat became too much for him, Champion ran from the burning house, endeavouring to reach a little gully near by. He was shot as he ran, and it was later said that twenty-eight wounds were found in his body. The rustler side in this war claim that when Champion was first shot down he was only wounded, and asked the men who came up to him not to shoot again, but that one of the party placed his rifle to Champion's face and deliberately shot him as he lay upon the ground. The body of Champion was left with a card pinned to it bearing the inscription, "Cattle Thieves, beware." In Champion's pocket, after his death, there was found a roughly written memorandum of the events of the day as they appeared to him as he was shut in his cabin by the invading party. He told of the suffering of his comrade Ray, stated the hour of Ray's death, mentioned his efforts to get a shot at the men who were firing at him, stated calmly that he did not think he could hold out much longer, and mentioned the appearance of the wagon-load of hay which he knew was to burn him out. Then, as though in deliberate address to his fellows of the range, he wrote, "Boys, I guess it is all up. Good-bye." Had the fact not been established clearly enough otherwise, it might have been seen from the simple nature of this pitiful little scrawl that the rustler Champion was a brave man. He had long been known and dreaded by the cattle men.

While the siege of the K. C. ranch was in progress, two men came along the trail with a wagon, and owing to the poor management by the leaders of the raiders, these men were allowed to escape, which they did at full speed on the horses which they took from the wagon. It happened that one of these men was Jack Flagg, a man whose brand, Â, was odious in the eyes of more than one of the cattle men who could here have held him prisoner. Flagg was one of the prominent men among the resident range people who were accused of rustling. His escape meant the ruin of the raiders' expedition. Flagg never drew rein until he had alarmed his friends from the K. C. ranch to the town of Buffalo. In twelve hours all Rustlerdom was alarmed and hurrying to the combat. The town of Buffalo, the county seat of Johnson County, and the headquarters of the free-range element, was at once aroused into that deadly fury which among Western men means but one thing. Immediate war was to be given those who had carried war into this country.

Nor was this war upon the side of the rustlers to be without show of legal justice. It is all very well to say that the principle of the majority is a dangerous principle in the hands of dangerous men; yet how can this principle legally be set aside in any of the forms of this Government, whether in the election of officers national or municipal? Legally speaking, the county of Johnson was as regularly organized as any, and a man who lived there had as good a right to vote for the officers of that county as has any man of any part of the Union. The residents of Johnson County had legally elected as their sheriff Red Angus, who therefore was the recognised agent of the law. As sheriff, Angus summoned about him a posse of the citizens of Buffalo and vicinity, in numbers sufficient, as he thought, to accomplish the arrest of the invading party of raiders, who of course had no legal status whatever in that country, and who were breaking laws of a nature always held to be higher than those laws which they accused the rustlers of violating. Surely a more dramatic or more involved situation never appeared upon the cow range than this, when two armies, each armed, each able and anxious to kill, met each other to decide an issue-an issue in which both were wrong! In no country but the West of the cattle days could any such situation ever have arisen.

The sheriff had a vast posse at his back when he started forth from Buffalo to arrest the band of cattle men. The latter, knowing what would be the result of their mistake in allowing the two men to escape and spread the news, pushed on as fast as they could into the country where they expected to find others of the men whom they had upon their list as men to be shot, hung, or driven out of the country. They seem little to have known the seriousness of their undertaking, or the sternness of the men against whom they were proceeding, among whom, wrong as they were, were some of the best cowpunchers and hardiest plainsmen of the entire cattle range. The raiders kept their wagons with them as long as they could, and then pushed on ahead, leaving their supplies behind them. In a little while after that the rustlers swarmed in upon the trail, seized the wagons, and took prisoners the teamsters. From that time the invaders ceased to be the pursuers and became themselves the pursued. They stopped at the T. A. ranch, by this time discovering what the circumstances really were. Here they stood at bay and were surrounded by the forces of the rustlers.

8

Life in the West After The Civil War

While the Civil War had little visible impact on the West, it did indeed effect the lives of people living in the trans-Mississippi region. Few military engagements were fought in the West and the major cities were left undisturbed. Despite the protracted four year struggle, settlement patterns in the West continued as before with little political change.

During the Civil War an ephemeral Pony Express delivered mail between California and St. Joseph, Missouri. However, the completion of the first transcontinental telegraph in 1861 and the inauguration of the Overland Mail Company, which began delivering mail to California that same year, spelled the end of the short-lived Pony Express almost as soon as it had begun.

In 1862 Congress passed legislation to begin construction of the transcontinental railroad. Prior to the Civil War, the plans for such a railroad languished because of the sectional crisis. Both the North and the South lobbied for the railroad to traverse their regions, recognizing the economic benefits that could be accrued. When the Southern states seceded from the Union in 1861, there was little question that the route would avoid the South.

Two of the most enduring symbols of the American West have been the stagecoach and the cowboy. Stagecoach travel was introduced to the West as early as the late 1840s. Following the discovery of gold in California in 1848, cross country mail and passenger service was introduced. In 1857 the Butterfield Overland Mail Company entered into an agreement with the government to deliver mail between St. Louis and Los Angeles. Other stagecoach enterprises soon joined the competition, including Wells Fargo and Company. The completion of the transcontinental railroad in 1869 signalled the decline of stagecoach travel by the 1870s.

In the years following the Civil War the cattle drive, a familiar staple of Western films and literature, became the dominant method of moving stock in the cattle business. Following old Indian and pioneer trails from Texas to Kansas railheads, legendary trailblazers such as Charles Goodnight, Oliver Loving, and Jesse Chisholm delivered tens of thousands of head of cattle north to the Great Plains. The following account of the Chisholm Trail chronicles the predominant route that reached from San Antonio, Texas to Abilene, Kansas. By the 1870s a proliferation of cattle trails and the westward movement of the railroad towns led to the decline of Abilene as a destination and the concomitant dwindling of traffic on the Chisholm Trail.

The increasing importance of cattle culture and the growth in communication and travel in the West during the post-Civil War era introduced new words and traditions to the American lexicon and popular culture. Besides the techniques of a rich ranching tradition, Texan cowboys borrowed many words from the Mexican vaquero, including cinch, chaps, and lariat. The language of Americans was continually enriched as settlers moved West, adopting Spanish and Native American jargon every step of the way.

Decades of Chinese immigration and tension with the predominantly white work force culminated in a series of anti-Chinese riots in the West in the 1870s and 80s. Economic strife and racial antagonism led to the introduction of the "Chinese Question" into national politics and in 1882 Congress passed Chinese exclusion legislation, the first immigration restriction law in the nation's history.

Some of best chroniclers of the post-war West were women, further testifying to their participation in most aspects of frontier life. Francis M. A. Roe and Elizabeth "Libby" Custer were both wives of western military officers. Libby Custer's books on life with her husband, the legendary General George Armstrong Custer, during the Plains Indian wars are Western classics and Francis Roe's letters offer a vivid first-hand depiction of the sacrifices and contributions made by women living in a male-dominated military setting. Isabella Bird renders a different slice of women's life in the West, as she bucked convention to travel by herself through the late nineteenth- century frontier.

Although Frederick Jackson Turner and the Eleventh census pronounced the demise of the frontier in 1890, settlers were still battling to scratch out an existence on the arid Great Plains in the early 1900s. Building a sod hut was a marketable skill and irrigation a fact of life. With the completion of the transcontinental railroad and the telegraph, and the invention of the telephone in 1876, news traveled faster, a trend that would continue undiminished into the current information age.

Suggestions for Further Reading

Anne M. Butler, *Daughters of Joy, Sisters of Misery: Prostitutes in the American West, 1865-90* (Urbana: University of Illinois Press, 1985).

Robert R. Dykstra, *The Cattle Towns: A Social History of the Kansas Cattle Trading Centers, Abilene, Ellsworth, Wichita, Dodge City and Caldwell, 1867-85* (New York: Atheneum, 1976).

Gilbert C. Fite, *The Farmer's Frontier, 1865-1900* (New York: Holt, Rinehart and Winston, 1966).

Richard E. Lingenfelter, *The Hardrock Miners: A History of the Mining Labor Movement in the American West, 1863-90* (Berkeley: University of California Press, 1974).

Joanna L. Stratton, *Pioneer Women: Voices from the Kansas Frontier* (New York: Simon and Schuster, 1981).

Critical Thinking

1. What factors combined to bring an end to the Texas cattle drives to Kansas?

2. What was life like for women married to military officers in the West? Contrast the writings of Libby Custer and Francis Roe.

3. How has the western experience enhanced the American lexicon?

4. What obstacles did homesteaders face in northwestern Montana in the early nineteenth century?

5. Describe conditions endured by passengers on the Overland Stage to California. Contrast these hardships with those endured by cowboys on the Chisholm Trail.

Document 8.1

The Overland Stage to California (1860s)

The 1867 completion of the first transcontinental railroad linking the east coast of the United States with San Francisco dramatically changed life in the West. Mail, supplies, news, rumors, and people could cross the continent in record time, which greatly reduced the price of manufactured goods consumed in the West. In the following essay, Frank Root describes one of the last stagecoach trips across the Great Plains. After the construction of transcontinental railroads, the era of the wagon trains, hand carts, Pony Express, and stagecoaches came to an end.*

There was unusual activity among the stage company's officials in Denver who were making the necessary preparations to reopen the overland route to Atchison. Stages were coming every day from California and Salt Lake. A heavy mail for the East from Utah and Colorado had been accumulating for several weeks at the Denver post-office, and the first stage-coach, with a load of passengers, was started out for Atchison on March 1. At ten o'clock on the morning of the 2d the second coach departed. This was a big Concord, loaded with mail, and, in addition, there were seven passengers, besides the driver and myself. It was the largest mail I ever accompanied between the Rockies and the Missouri river.

---

* Frank A. Root, *The Overland Stage to California* (Topeka, Kansas: Published by the Authors, 1901), pp. 382-384.

The journey for the first nine miles out was necessarily slow and tedious, on account of the road in many places being drifted full of snow. Like Jordan, it was a "hard road to travel," with no sign of a track in sight. We got along as well as could be expected under the circumstances, and ate supper that night at Living Springs, thirty-five miles down the toll-road, and then continued eastward. The wind was blowing quite hard, the night was dark, and the atmosphere cool and disagreeable. The snow was over a foot deep on the level, and still no sign of a broken track, owing to the suspension of all travel for some time previous, because of the Indian depredations.

We had not gone over ten miles from Living Springs before we realized we were lost. We were on the sandy, treeless plains, and no landmarks were in sight. The team had wandered away from the telegraph line. There was not a fence for hundreds of miles along the stage road. It was so dark we couldn't see the mountains west of us, usually visible four or five times the distance. To add to our discomfort, the team had wandered from the road, and, as we ascertained later, were making a circle. The driver, realizing that something was wrong, stopped, and a consultation was held. One of the coach lamps was lighted, and three persons, including myself, volunteered to hunt the road. It was like hunting for a "needle in a haymow"; it was found, however, but not until after an hour's search, nearly a mile away. With a pocket compass I always carried, the discovery was also made that the team, when stopped, was headed towards Denver. After turning around, and in due time getting into the road, once more we moved off in the direction of the Missouri river, but were obliged to travel slowly all night-not going out of a walk-on account of the deep snow.

It was daylight on the morning of the 3d when we reached Bijou ranch. All of us being thoroughly chilled, we went into the house, stood before the fire-place, and tried to thaw out. I had had a fearful, outdoor, all-night ride, with a cold northwest wind. It was impossible to get warm with the accommodations in sight. This ranch, located on the cut-off toll-road, was noted for being one of the coldest on the overland route; but there was a good fire in the grate, and, while almost roasted on one side, the wind whistling through the cracks in the building nearly froze us on the other side. We tarried here an hour, while the team was feeding; thence proceeded on the journey, reaching Junction ranch at eleven o'clock the next morning. Here we prepared our own breakfast, and there was a grand rally around the substantial spread, which consisted of hardtack, bacon, slapjacks, and coffee. Nearly eighteen hours had passed since we had eaten, and seldom was anything on the plains relished more.

At noon we proceeded, with a fresh team, and soon caught up with, and joined, a coach full of passengers that left Denver twenty-four hours ahead of us. Junction was ninety miles from Denver, at the east end of the cut-off toll-road, and here we were furnished with a mounted escort of four boys belonging to the Colorado militia. One of the drivers jokingly suggested that an extra escort ought to be sent along to protect the mounted boys, none of whom were out of their 'teens.

All went well as we journeyed down the South Platte; but it was a glorious sight during the day to meet, about midway between Junction and Godfrey's ranch-since supplies were getting short in Denver-a train of 165 wagons loaded with groceries, provisions, etc., bound for the coming city near the eastern base of the Rockies.

We reached Godfrey's at five o'clock on the second day after leaving Denver, and here stopped a little over sixteen hours. On leaving this ranch, at nine o'clock on the morning of the 4th, we had an escort of ten mounted soldiers. All the regular stage stations and a great many buildings belonging to the ranchmen in the valley had been destroyed by the Indians, and the overland route presented a sad and gloomy appearance.

We stopped that evening for supper and stayed all night at Washington ranch, where a meal was prepared in good style. There was no unnecessary or special ceremony indulged in at this place, but when "grub" was ready an invitation was given to "pitch in," and all did so like a pack of hungry wolves, helping ourselves to the ample supply of substantials nicely prepared and spread before us.

Document 8.2

The Chisholm Trail (1869)

During the Civil War, a Union blockade prevented cattle drives to markets outside of Texas. As a result, longhorns rapidly multiplied on the Texas prairies. By 1866, there were perhaps five million head of cattle. While the value of the livestock had plummeted to four dollars a head in Texas, Eastern markets would pay ten times this amount. The demand for cattle was no less in the North and the West. Confederate veterans returned home to Texas, where they traded the battlefield for the cattle trails, one of the few economic outlets left for the defeated soldiers. The Chisholm Trail was perhaps the most famous of all the trails leading to the trailheads in Kansas. Between 1867 and 1871, more than one million head of cattle were driven to the stockyards at Abilene along the trail originally established by cattleman Jesse Chisholm.*

In 1860, Texas, as it had been for many years before, was the chief producer of live-stock in the Western States. Upon all its widespread ranges were feeding herds by the thousand, and no other industry approached that of cattle-raising in importance or extent. The few hundred thousand cattle of Spanish blood which had been placed there during the State's life as a Mexican province, were multiplied until three and a half million head were estimated as Texas's belongings. They had been somewhat improved in breed, but were still wiry, nervous, long-limbed creatures, with slender, branching horns and restless eyes. They could run like deer, and were almost as wild.

The peculiarly favorable climate of Texas gave the State almost a monopoly of the business. The pastures were green the year around, and the proximity to market, either at points on the Mississippi River, to which herds from the eastern part of the State could

* Charles Moreau Harger, "Cattle-Trails of the Prairies," *Scribner's Magazine,* (June, 1892), 732-736.

easily be driven, or by water from points on the Gulf, gave a distinct advantage. Mexico had in times past been a valuable consumer, but was now nearly deserted, and the nearer selling-places were able to handle the supply. The fine, hair-like "buffalo grass" that covers the prairies for four hundred miles east of the mountains, and wherever found is as nourishing in winter as in summer, flourished in abundance, and the mesquit was not to be despised as a change of diet for the herds.

The outbreak of the war brought upon the ranch-owners a peculiar embarrassment of riches. With the Northern market cut off, and Southern business life demoralized, no disposition could be made of the rapidly increasing herds. Occasional fugitive sales along the Mississippi became almost the only markets. Prices declined, and for a time two to four dollars a head would purchase the best animals on the ranges. Driving northward had not been much practised, and now, with the sharp skirmishing along the Kansas and Missouri frontier, there was no opportunity to begin it. Stock was neglected as valueless. Men were "cattle-poor," and it was a time of discouragement to those who had looked for fortunes in their enterprises.

In 1865 and 1866 the ranch-owners determined to seek Northern markets at any cost, and thousands of animals were massed in the northeast portion of the State preparatory to driving to Missouri railroad stations. The summer of 1866 saw this movement begin. Fully two hundred and seventy thousand head were pushed northward. There was little regularity in the courses taken. The Rock Bluffs ford, on the Red River, was the starting place for many. Up the Kinishi Valley, across the plains to Fort Smith, Ark., then, with a circuitous route among the Ozarks, across southeastern Missouri-that was the line most followed.

In 1867 the old Kansas Pacific Railroad, now the Kansas Division of the Union Pacific, was being built from Kansas City along the valley of the Kaw due west across the State. It had reached half way from the Missouri to the mountains before the possibilities it offered became apparent. The country traversed was but sparsely settled; the towns consisted for the most part of a few rude cabins, including the inevitable saloon. But the tide of emigration was pushing westward, and there was a magnificent empire for it to conquer.

One of the first comers was an Illinois stock-dealer, Joseph G. McCoy, to whom is due the honor of originating the Kansas and Texas cattle-trails. He was familiar with the situation in the Lone Star State, and conceived the idea of forming a great shipping-point on the new railroad. He was encouraged by the officials, and arrangements were made for the location of the proper yards at Abilene, a station one hundred and sixty-five miles from Kansas City, situated in the midst of a richly-grassed prairie section, admirably adapted for grazing grounds of incoming herds. The town had less than a dozen houses, and was within less than thirty miles of the end of the road, as then completed. Yards were built and steps were taken to induce the cattle-men to make this a point from which to ship their herds...

By this time well-defined trails had been located, and for two decades those trunk-lines connecting the great producing and consuming points held their supremacy. The most famous of these was the "Chisholm Trail." It was named after John Chisholm, an eccentric frontier stockman, who was the first to drive over it. Chisholm lived at Paris, Tex., was a bachelor, and had many thousand head of cattle on the ranges in the southern part of the State. Later he removed to New Mexico, and died a few years ago, leaving almost uncounted droves upon his ranches. There was through Texas, reaching down from the Red River, the irregular "Southern Texas Trail," ending at the north near Cooke County. From the Red River, Chisholm broke the way to Kansas, riding ahead of his herd and selecting what seemed the most favorable route. He forded the Red River near the mouth of Mud Creek, followed that stream to its head, kept northwest to Wild Horse Creek, to the west of Signal Mountains, and crossed the Washita at Elm Spring. Due north took him to the Canadian River, after leaving which he soon struck the Kingfisher Creek Valley. This was followed to the Cimarron. Touching the head of Black Bear and Bluff Creeks, its next considerable stream was the Salt fork of the Arkansas, which was crossed at Sewell's Ranch. Sewell was a Government post-trader, who was a favorite with the Indians, and had two large ranches in the Territory. Coming into Kansas near Caldwell, the course was a little east of north, crossing the Arkansas near Wichita. Here was the famous "First and Last Chance" saloon, with its sign-board facing two ways to attract the cow-boys coming up across the territory and those returning from market. Thence the trail turned northeasterly, striking Newton, and so on over the divide between the Smoky Hill and the Arkansas to the prairies south of Abilene. Following Chisholm's track came thousands of herds, and the trail became a notable course.

From two hundred to four hundred yards wide, beaten into the bare earth, it reached over hill and through valley for over six hundred miles (including its southern extension) a chocolate band amid the green prairies, uniting the North and South. As the marching hoofs wore it down and the wind blew and the waters washed the earth away it became lower than the surrounding country and was flanked by little banks of sand, drifted there by the wind. Bleaching skulls and skeletons of weary brutes who had perished on the journey gleamed along its borders, and here and there was a low mound showing where some cow-boy had literally "died with his boots on." Occasionally a dilapidated wagon-frame told of a break-down, and spotting the emerald reaches on either side were the barren circle-like "bedding grounds," each a record that a great herd had there spent a night.

The wealth of an empire passed over the trail, leaving its mark for decades to come. The traveller of to-day sees the wide trough-like course, with ridges being washed down by the rains, and with fences and farms of the settlers and the more civilized red-men intercepting its track, and forgets the wild and arduous life of which it was the exponent. It was a life now outgrown, and which will never again be- possible.

The number of cattle reaching Abilene in 1870 bounded to three hundred thousand, and almost a continuous line of bovine travellers was pouring over the Chisholm Trail. In order to facilitate the herds' movements surveyors were sent out to straighten the trail from the point where it entered Kansas to the shipping-station. Fresh mounds of earth were thrown up to mark the route, and the drovers found considerable saving in distance. They spread the news of the efforts being made to accommodate the cattle-men, and the Texas ranch-owners, appreciating these advantages as well as the rapidly increasing prices of stock in the Eastern markets, prepared to send forward still greater supplies.

The ranches were, for the most part, in southern and southwestern Texas, and the hundreds of young men who at the close of the war had sought fortune in the far Southwest were just coming into a position to put some of their salable stock on the market. In 1871 nearly a million cattle were driven north. Six hundred thousand came to Abilene alone, while Baxter Springs and Junction City received half as many. For miles around the chief shipping points the stock was herded awaiting a chance to sell or ship. From any knoll could be seen thousands of sleek beeves, their branching horns glistening in the sunlight and their herders watchfully riding in the distance. Several counties of central Kansas were practically turned into cattle-yards, and it seemed that the industry would soon absorb the energies of the entire State.

But it was the height of the wave. Prices fell off; wet weather and cold winds injured the cattle's condition, and the so-called Spanish fever, always a terror to the Northerners, and which seemed ineradicable from the Texas cattle's blood, was causing more trouble than usual. The herds were held on the grazing grounds until fall, in the hope of better prices, but to no purpose. Finally, shipping was stopped entirely, and over three hundred thousand cattle were unsold. Every year there had been some carried over, either because of their being unsalable, or, as has been so general in late years, to fatten on the Northern corn; but this number was unprecedented. The drovers took their stock westward to the buffalo grass region, it being impossible to procure hay and corn in central Kansas for the great throng.

At the beginning of winter (1871-72) came a storm of sleet, putting an icy coat over the sod; and multiplied thousands of cattle and hundreds of horses died of cold and starvation. Some of the carcasses were skinned, but the majority were left for food for the wolves. A hundred thousand hides were shipped from three stations after the storm. The winter was severe throughout, and it was estimated that less than fifty thousand cattle lived through it. From herds of sixty and seventy thousand, only a few hundred survived. Like other booms in which the West has overreached itself, this one had its collapse.

Document 8.3

Domestic Life with the Seventh Cavalry (1870s)

Elizabeth Bacon "Libby" Custer (1842-1933) outlived her husband, the noted cavalry officer George Armstrong Custer, by fifty-seven years. During their thirteen-year marriage, Libby followed her husband west during the Plains Indian campaigns, spending several years in various military outposts. Following her husband's death at the Battle of the Little Big Horn, she devoted the remainder of her life to preserving and defending her husband's reputation with a series of books and lecture tours. The following passages describe domestic garrison life and offer insights into the close relationship shared by the Custer's.*

* Elizabeth B. Custer, *"Boots and Saddles" Or Life in Dakota with General Custer,* (New York: Harper and Brothers Publishers, reprint 1913), 126-130, 143-145.

A woman on the frontier is so cherished and appreciated, because she has the courage to live out there, that there is nothing that is not done for her if she be gracious and courteous. In twenty little ways the officers spoiled us: they never allowed us to wait on ourselves, to open or shut a door, draw up our own chair, or to do any little service that they could perform for us. If we ran to the next house for a chat, with a shawl thrown over our heads, we rarely got a chance to return alone, but with this undignified head-covering were formally brought back to our door! I wonder if it will seem that we were foolishly petted if I reveal that our husbands buttoned our shoes, wrapped us up if we went out, warmed our clothes before the fire, poured the water for our bath out of the heavy pitcher, and studied to do innumerable little services that a maid would have done for us in the States.

I don't think it made us helpless, however. In our turn we watched every chance we could to anticipate their wants. We did a hundred things we would not have remembered to do had not the quickly passing time brought nearer each day those hours of separation when we would have no one to do for. I am sure I never saw more tender men than the officers. One learned to conceal the fact that one was ailing or fatigued, for it made them so anxious. The eyes of sister Margaret's husband come to me now, full of intense suffering for his wife, as she silently read her home letters telling of our mother Custer's failing strength. She suppressed her weeping until they had retired and she believed him asleep. She found her mistake when his gentle hands stole softly to her cheeks to feel if they were moistened with tears.

So seldom did we hear of an officer's unkindness to his wife, that a very old legend used to be revived if a reference to anything of the kind was needed. Before the war some officer wished to measure the distance of a day's march, and having no odometer elected his wife to that office. The length of the revolution of a wheel was taken, a white handkerchief tied to a spoke, and the madam was made to count the rotations all day long. The story seldom failed to fire the blood of the officers when it was told. They agreed that nothing but a long life among Indians, and having the treatment of the squaw before him, would cause a man to act with such brutality.

Domestic care sat very lightly on me. Nothing seemed to annoy my husband more than to find me in the kitchen. He determinedly opposed it for years, and begged me to make a promise that I would never go there for more than a moment. We had such excellent servants that my presence was unnecessary most of the time, but even in the intervals when our fare was wretched he submitted uncomplainingly rather than that I should be wearied. A great portion of the time my life was so rough that he knew it taxed me to the utmost, and I never forgot to be grateful that I was spared domestic care in garrison. We had so much company that, though I enjoyed it, I sometimes grew weary. When the winter came and there was little to do officially, my husband made every preparation for our receptions: ordered the supplies, planned the refreshment, and directed the servants. The consequence was that I sometimes had as enjoyable a time as if I had been entertained at some one else's house. To prove how much pleasure I had, I recall a speech that the family kept among a collection of my *faux pas*. They overheard me saying to some of our guests, "Don't go home, we are having such a good time." Afterwards the tormenting home circle asked me if it would not have been in a little better taste to let the guests say that!

We had such a number of my husband's family in garrison that it required an effort occasionally to prevent our being absorbed in one another. A younger brother came on from Michigan to visit us, and our sister Margaret's husband had a sister and brother at the post. Sometimes we found that nine of us were on one side of the room deeply interested in conversation. Something would rouse us to a sense of our selfishness, and I was the one sent off to look out the quiet ones at the hop who needed entertaining. If I chanced to be struggling to teach new steps in dancing to feet unaccustomed to anything but march or drill or strove to animate the one whom all pronounced a bore, the family never failed to note it. They played every sly trick they could to disconcert and tease me. I did not submit tamely. As soon as I could, I made my way to them, and by threats and intimidations scattered them to their duty!

At the hops the officers waited long and patiently for the women to dance with them; sometimes the first waltz they could get during the evening would not come before midnight. I think it would have been very hard for me to have kept a level head with all the attention and delightful flattery which the ordinary manners of officers convey, if I had not remembered how we ladies were always in the minority. The question whether one was old or young, pretty or plain, never seemed to arise with them. I have seen them solicit the honor of taking a grandmamma to drive, and even to ride as gallantly as if she were young and fair. No men discover beauty and youth more quickly, but the deference they feel for all women is always apparent.

It seemed very strange to me that with all the value that is set on the presence of the women of an officer's family at the frontier posts, the book of army regulations makes no provision for them, but in fact ignores them entirely! It enters into such minute detail in its instructions, even giving the number of hours that beansoup should boil, that it would be natural to suppose that a paragraph or two might be wasted on an officer's wife! The servants and the company laundresses are mentioned as being entitled to quarters and rations and to the services of the surgeon. If an officer's wife falls ill she cannot *claim* the attention of the doctor, though it is almost unnecessary to say that she has it through his most urgent courtesy. I have even known a surgeon, who from some official difficulty was not on friendly terms with an officer, go personally and solicit the privilege of prescribing through the illness of his wife, whom he knew but slightly.

The officers used sportively to look up the rules in the army regulations for camp followers, and read them out to us as they would the riot act! In the event of any question being raised regarding our privileges, we women really came under no other head in the book which is the sole authority for our army. If we put down an emphatic foot, declaring that we were going to take some decisive step to which they were justly opposed as involving our safety, perhaps, we would be at once reminded, in a laughingly exultant manner, of the provision of the law. The regulations provide that the commanding officer has complete control over all *camp followers,* with power to put them off the reservation or detain them as he chooses. Nevertheless, though army women have no visible thrones or sceptres, nor any acknowledged rights according to military law, never knew such queens as they, or saw more willing subjects than they govern.

It was a surprise to me that after the life of excitement my husband had led, he should grow more and more domestic in his tastes. His daily life was very simple. He rarely left home except to hunt, and was scarcely once a year in the sutler's store, where the officers congregated to play billiards and cards. If the days were too stormy or too cold for hunting, as they often were for a week or more at a time, he wrote and studied for hours every day. We had the good-fortune to have a billiard-table loaned us by the sutler, and in the upper room where it was placed, my husband and I had many a game when he was weary with writing.

The general sometimes sketched the outline of my pictures, which I was preparing to paint, for he drew better than I did, and gladly availed himself of a chance to secure variety of occupation.

The relatives of the two young housemaids whom we had in our service regretted that they were missing school, so the general had the patience to teach them. The day rarely passed that Col. Tom, my husband, and I did not have a game of romps. The grave orderly who sat by the hall-door used to be shocked to see the commanding officer in hot pursuit of us up the steps. The quick transformation which took place when he was called from the frolic to receive the report of the officer of the day was something very ridiculous.

Occasionally he joined those who gathered in our parlor every evening. He had a very keen sense of his social responsibilities as post-commander, and believed that our house should be open at all hours to the garrison. His own studious habits made it a deprivation if he gave up much of his time to entertaining. I learned that in no way could I relieve him so much as by being always ready to receive. He grew to expect that I would be in the parlor at night, and plan whatever diversions we had. I managed to slip away several times in the evening, and go to him for a little visit, or possibly a waltz, while the rest danced in the other room. If I delayed going to him while absorbed in the general amusement, a knock at the door announced the orderly carrying a note for me. Those missives always reminded me of my forgetfulness in some ingenious arrangement of words. When I laughed outright over one of these little scraps, our friends begged me to share the fun with them. It was only a line, and read, "Do you think I am a confirmed monk?" Of course they insisted laughingly upon my going at once to the self-appointed hermit.

We spent the days together almost uninterruptedly during the winter. The garrison gave me those hours and left us alone. My husband had arranged my sewing-chair and work-basket next to his desk, and he read to me constantly. At one time we had read five authorities on Napoleon, whose military career was a never-ending source of interest to him. He studied so carefully that he kept the atlas before him, and marked the course of the two armies of the French and English with pencils of different color. One of his favorite books was a life of Daniel Webster, given him in the States by a dear friend. Anything sad moved him so that his voice choked with emotion, and I have known him lay down the book and tell me he could not go on.

Document 8.4

Building a Sod House (1888)

As settlers moved onto the treeless prairies, they faced a shortage in the construction materials required to build their traditional log houses. In response, pioneers constructed homes from sod. There was no typical design; some contained one room while others had several. Some were built into the side of a hill or ravine, while others were constructed on the barren flat terrain. Building a sod hut or "soddie" required great ingenuity. Settlers generally would plow the ground first and then cut bricks from the creases. It took roughly a half-acre of ground for one sod house. Interiors and roofs varied according to the financial status of the pioneers. The bane of most sod houses was heavy rain. Compared to log houses, however, "soddies" proved to be better insulated, offering cooler summers and warmer winters.*

To begin with, the habitation of the homesteader is either a dugout or a house built of squares of sod taken from the prairie—Nebraska or Kansas brick, as they are facetiously termed. The dugent consists of a hole dug in the side of a cañon or any sort of depression on the prairie which will serve as a wind-break. This hole is roofed across about on a level with the prairie, with inch boards, and these are covered with sod. A foot or so of stove-pipe protruding from the roof is the sole indication of a human habitation. One room generally serves all the purposes of the homesteader and his family. If he prospers for a season, he adds to the front of his abode by erecting walls of sod on the sides and putting in a new front, the old one serving as a partition between the two rooms. This is considered a commodious dwelling. After riding over the quarter section looking for an owner, espying such an abode, and guiding your team carefully down a breakneck descent to the front door, would it surprise you, upon entering this hole in the ground, to find, for instance, a very modern organ with an imposing cathedral back towering high in one corner of the room? But this is no cause for astonishment very frequently organs and ornate designs in furniture are to be found in the dugouts. Or, if the lady of the house should invite you to remain for the meeting of the literary club there in the evening, would you stare at that? Not at all. Literary clubs, which the members ride all the way from five to twenty miles to attend, and where they discuss with great earnestness everything from the latest political problem to the most abstruse point in metaphysics, are quite the regular thing with our homesteaders. But to behold this life so full of paradoxes in the height of its incongruousness you should be a spectator in the dugout when a neighborhood dance is in full blast. The earthen walls have been skilfully

---

* Frank H. Spearman, "The Great American Desert," *Harper's New Monthly Magazine*, (July 1888), pp. 235-236.

tapestried for the occasion with calico, and when the fun begins, the clay floor speedily responds to the capering of the many twinkling feet, and there arises a cloud of dust that would stifle an Indian. But, bless you! they don't mind a bit of dust. A polished floor and the most perfect system of ventilation attainable could add nothing to their enjoyment.

The homesteaders are very honest. You can leave a house unlocked at all times and your stores are perfectly safe with the exception of what liquor you may have on hand for medicinal purposes. In other words, the homesteader will steal whiskey every time. As a class they are neighborly, kind to one in distress, and exceedingly hospitable.

But it must not be supposed that all homesteaders live in dugouts or sleep six or seven in a room; such experiences attach to the first year or two of frontier life more than to any later period. Many sightly, commodious, and comfortable sod houses have been built, of which our illustrations will afford examples. The walls are usually two feet in thickness, the roof shingled, doors and windows set into the walls, and the house plastered inside, sometimes outside, altogether making a very neat and desirable residence. These structures, too, are free from the annoyances of dugouts, in which are found all manner of insects and rodents. Occasionally a rattlesnake will burrow through the earthen sides, and coil himself snugly in the bedclothes, where you will find him on a cold morning. Such intruders are rare, but there are some people who strenuously object to even rare visits of this sort; such are usually energetic enough to get out of the old house and into a new one before spending many months in an abode so uncomfortably near to nature's heart.

It is very common to find a lone and unprotected female "holding down a claim," as the Western phrase runs. The women of the East would look aghast at the prospect of living alone in a sod house for six months, miles from the nearest neighbor. Yet experience proves that the "unprotected" is much safer out on the lonely prairie than she would be in New York city. I never heard or read of a woman on a homestead receiving an insult at the hands of anybody. To be sure, they are always armed, and know how to handle a pistol, but they rarely have a more deadly use for it than the killing of a jack-rabbit or a prairie dog. Such women complain more of loneliness than of fear. For whatever charms solitude may have for the sage, it certainly has none for the fair sex, not even for our hardy Western representatives of it. Here is one of their ingenious ways of avoiding it. Two of them will locate on adjoining "quarters," and build their houses on the dividing line; so that while each house is on its occupant's claim, the two structures are practically one, affording frequent opportunities for the ladies to call on each other and discuss social topics. They are all provided with ponies, and think nothing of a horseback ride of fifteen or twenty miles, either for business or pleasure.

Documents 8.5

Army Letters From an Officer's Wife (1871)

The American frontier was certainly not just the domain of white men. From the very beginning of the westward movement, women participated in every dimension of frontier life. The following two documents illustrate their presence. Francis M. A. Roe was the wife of a United States army officer, a lieutenant in the cavalry whose orders took him and his wife out to the Colorado Territory in 1871. Ms. Roe described her experiences in hundreds of vivid letters to friends and family members back east. In 1909, selections of her letters were published as a book-*Army Letters From An Officer's Wife 1871-1888* (1909). The following are excerpts from some of these I letters.*

Fort Lyon, Colorado Territory, October, 1871.

After months of anticipation and days of weary travel we have at last got to our army home! As you know, Fort Lyon is fifty miles from Kit Carson, and we came all that distance in a funny looking stage coach called a "jerkey," and a good name for it, too, for at times it seesawed back and forth and then sideways, in an awful breakneck way. The day was glorious, and the atmosphere so clear, we could see miles and miles in every direction. But there was not one object to be seen on the vast rolling plains—not a tree nor a house, except the wretched ranch and stockade where we got fresh horses and a perfectly uneatable dinner.

It was dark when we reached the post, so of course we could see nothing that night. General and Mrs. Phillips gave us a most cordial welcome—just as though they had known us always. Dinner was served soon after we arrived, and the cheerful dining room, and the table with its dainty china and bright silver, was such a surprise-so much nicer than anything we had expected to find here, and all so different from the terrible places we had seen since reaching the plains. It was apparent at once that this was not a place for spooks! General Phillips is not a real general-only so by brevet, for gallant service during the war. I was so disappointed when I was told this, but Faye says that he is very much afraid that I will have cause, sooner or later, to think that the grade of captain is quite high enough. He thinks this way because, having graduated at West Point this year, he is only a second lieutenant just now, and General Phillips is his captain and company commander...

These soldiers are not nearly as nice as one would suppose them to be, when one sees them dressed up in their blue uniforms with bright brass buttons. And they can make

---

* Francis M. A. Roe, *Army Letters From An Officer's Wife 1871-1888* (New York: D. Appleton and Company, 1909), pp. 1-10, 51-65.

mistakes, too, for yesterday, when I asked that same man a question, he answered, "Yes, sorr!" Then I smiled, of course, but he did not seem to have enough sense to see why. When I told Faye about it, he looked vexed and said I must never laugh at an enlisted man—that it was not dignified in the wife of an officer to do so. And then I told him that an officer should teach an enlisted man not to snicker at his wife, and not to call her "Sorr," which was disrespectful. I wanted to say more, but Faye suddenly left the room.

The post is not at all as you and I had imagined it to be. There is no high wall around it as there is at Fort Trumbull. It reminds one of a prim little village built around a square, in the center of which is a high flagstaff and a big cannon. The buildings are very low and broad and are made of adobe—a kind of clay and mud mixed together-and the walls are very thick. At every window are heavy wooden shutters, that can be closed during severe sand and wind storms. A little ditch—they call it *acéquia*—runs all around the post, and brings water to the trees and lawns, but water for use in the houses is brought up in wagons from the Arkansas River, and is kept in barrels...

We saw our house yesterday—quarters I must learn to say—and it is ever so much nicer than we had expected it to be. All of the officers' quarters are new, and this set has never been occupied. It has a hall with a pretty stairway, three rooms and a large shed downstairs, and two rooms and a very large hall closet on the second floor. A soldier is cleaning the windows and floors, and making things tidy generally. Many of the men like to cook, and do things for officers of their company, thereby adding to their pay, and these men are called strikers...

Camp Supply, Indian Territory,
May, 1872.

This place is quite as dreadful as it has been represented to us. There are more troops here than at Fort Lyon, and of course the post is very much larger. There are two troops of colored cavalry, one of white cavalry, and three companies of infantry. The infantry companies that have been stationed here, and which our three companies have come to relieve, will start in the morning for their new station, and will use the transportation that brought us down. Consequently, it was necessary to unload all the things from our wagons early this morning, so they could be turned over to the outgoing troops. I am a little curious to know if there is a second lieutenant who will be so unfortunate as to be allowed only one half of a wagon in which to carry his household goods.

Their going will leave vacant a number of officers' quarters, therefore there will be no selection of quarters by our officers until to-morrow. Faye is next to the junior, so there will be very little left to select from by the time his turn comes. The quarters are really nothing more than huts built of vertical logs plastered in between with mud, and the roofs are of poles and mud! Many of the rooms have only sand floors. We dined last evening with Captain and Mrs. Vincent, of the cavalry, and were amazed to find that such wretched buildings could be made so attractive inside. But of course they have one of the very best houses on the line, and as company commander, Captain Vincent can have done about what he wants. And then, again, they are but recently married, and all their furnishings are new and handsome. There is one advantage in being with colored troops—one can always have good servants. Mrs. Vincent has an excellent colored soldier cook, and her butler was thoroughly trained as such before he enlisted. It did look so funny, however, to see such a black man in a blue uniform.

The march down from Fort Dodge was most uncomfortable the first two days. It poured and poured rain, and then poured more rain, until finally everybody and everything was soaked through. I felt so sorry for the men who had to march in the sticky mud. Their shoes filled fast with water, and they were compelled constantly to stop, take them off, and pour out the water. It cleared at last and the sun shone warm and bright, and then there was another exhibition in camp one afternoon, of clothing and bedding drying on guy ropes.

All the way down I was on the lookout for Indians, and was laughed at many a time for doing so, too. Every time something unusual was seen in the distance some bright person would immediately exclaim, "Oh, that is only one of Mrs. Rae's Indians!" I said very little about what I saw during the last day or two, for I felt that the constant teasing must have become as wearisome to the others as it had to me. But I am still positive that I saw the black heads of Indians on the top of ever so many hills we passed. When they wish to see and not be seen they crawl up a hill on the side farthest from you, but only far enough up to enable them to look over, and in this position they will remain for hours, perfectly motionless, watching your every movement. Unless you notice the hill very carefully you will never see the black dot on top, for only the eyes and upper part of the head are exposed. I had been told all this many times; also, that when in an Indian country to be most watchful when Indians are not to be seen...

Camp Supply is certainly in an Indian country, for it is surrounded by Comanches, Apaches, Kiowas, Cheyennes, and Arapahoes—each a hostile tribe, except the last. No one can go a rod from the garrison without an escort, and our weekly mail is brought down in a wagon and guarded by a corporal and several privates. Only last week two couriers—soldiers—who had been sent down with dispatches from Fort Dodge, were found dead on the road, both shot in the back, probably without having been given one chance to defend themselves.

We are in camp on low land just outside the post, and last night we were almost washed away again by the down-pouring rain, and this morning there is mud everywhere. And this is the country that is supposed never to have rain! Mrs. Vincent invited me most cordially to come to her house until we at least knew what quarters we were to have, and Captain Vincent came early to-day to insist upon my going up at once, but I really could not go. We have been in rain and mud so long I feel that I am in no way fit to go to anyone's house. Besides, it would seem selfish in me to desert Faye, and he, of course, would not leave the company as long as it is in tents. We are delighted at finding such charming people as the Vincents at this horrid place.

Camp Supply, Indian Territory,
June, 1872.

We are in our own house now and almost settled. When one has only a few pieces of furniture it does not take long to get them in place. It is impossible to make the rooms look homelike, and I often find myself wondering where in this world I have wandered to! The house is of logs, of course, and has a pole and dirt roof, and was built originally for an officers' mess. The dining room is large and very long, a part of which we have partitioned off with a piece of canvas and converted into a storeroom. We had almost to get down on our knees to the quartermaster before he would give us the canvas. He is in the quartermaster's department and is most arrogant; seems to think that every nail and tack is his own personal property and for his exclusive use.

Our dining room has a sand floor, and almost every night little white toadstools grow up all along the base of the log walls. All of the logs are of cottonwood and have the bark on, and the army of bugs that hide underneath the bark during the day and march upon us at night is to be dreaded about as much as a whole tribe of Indians!

I wrote you how everyone laughed at me on the march down because I was positive I saw heads of Indians on the sand hills so many times. Well, all that has ceased, and the mention of "Mrs. Rae's Indians" is carefully avoided! There has been sad proof that the Indians were there, also that they were watching us closely and kept near us all the way down from Fort Dodge, hoping for a favorable opportunity to steal the animals. The battalion of the—th Infantry had made only two days' march from here, and the herders had just turned the horses and mules out to graze, when a band of Cheyenne Indians swooped down upon them and stampeded every animal, leaving the companies without even one mule! The poor things are still in camp on the prairie, waiting for something, anything, to move them on. General Phillips is mightily pleased that the Indians did not succeed in getting the animals from his command, and I am pleased that they cannot tease me any more.

Document 8.6

Isabella Bird's Life in the Rocky Mountains (1882)

Isabella Lucy Bird (1831-1904) bucked tradition as a woman travel writer in the nineteenth century. She captures some of the worst aspects and attitudes of the late nineteenth-century West in her popular book, *A Lady's Life in the Rocky Mountains.* Her impressions of the Indian question and environmental destruction resulting from hardrock mining are couched in the sensibilities of a social conscience.*

The Americans will never solve the Indian problem till the Indian is extinct. They have treated them after a fashion which has intensified their treachery and "devilry" as enemies, and as friends reduces them to a degraded pauperism, devoid of the very first elements of civilisation. The only difference between the savage and the civilised Indian is that the latter carries firearms and gets drunk on whisky. The Indian Agency has been a

* Isabella L. Bird, *A Lady's Life in the Rocky Mountains,* (New York: G. P. Putnam's Sons, 1882), pp. 215-216; 224-226.

sink of fraud and corruption; it is said that barely thirty per cent of the allowance ever reaches those for whom it is voted; and the complaints of shoddy blankets, damaged flour, and worthless firearms are universal. "To get rid of the Injuns" is the phrase used everywhere. Even their "reservations" do not escape seizure practically; for if gold "breaks out" on them they are "rushed," and their possessors are either compelled to accept land farther west or are shot off and driven off. One of the surest agents in their destruction is vitriolised whisky. An attempt has recently been made to cleanse the Augean stable of the Indian Department, but it has met with signal failure, the usual result in America of every effort to purify the official atmosphere. Americans specially love superlatives. The phrases "biggest in the world," "finest in the world," are on all lips. Unless President Hayes is a strong man they will soon come to boast that their government is composed of the "biggest scoundrels" in the world.

I shall forget many things, but never the awfulness and hugeness of that scenery. I went up a steep track by Clear Creek, then a succession of frozen waterfalls in a widened and then narrowed valley, whose frozen sides looked 5000 feet high. That is the region of enormous mineral wealth in silver. There are the "Terrible" and other mines, whose shares you can see quoted daily in the share lists in the *Times,* sometimes at cent per cent premium, and then down to 25 discount. These mines, with their prolonged subterranean workings, their stamping and crushing mills, and the smelting works which have been established near them, fill the district with noise, hubbub, and smoke by night and day; but I had turned altogether aside from them into a still region, where each miner in solitude was grubbing for himself, and confiding to none his finds or disappointments. Agriculture restores and beautifies, mining destroys and devastates; turning the earth inside out, making it hideous, and blighting every green thing, as it usually blights man's heart and soul. There was mining everywhere along that grand road, with all its destruction and devastation, its digging, burrowing, gulching, and sluicing; and up all along the seemingly inaccessible heights were holes with their roofs log-supported, in which solitary and patient men were selling their lives for treasure. Down by the stream, all among the icicles, men were sluicing and washing, and everywhere along the heights were the scars of hardly-passable trails, too steep even for pack-jacks, leading to the holes, and down which the miner packs the ore on his back. Many a heart has been broken for the few finds which have been made along those hill-sides. All the ledges are covered with charred stumps, a picture of desolation, where nature had made everything grand and fair.

Document 8.7

Cowboy Vernacular (1895)

The Mexican cowboy, or vaquero, provided the prototypical American cowboys with much of the techniques and jargon of their trade. Texan cowboys borrowed many of their distinctive traditions from Mexican vaqueros, including the roundup, the western saddle, roping, and cowboy clothing. In the process, such words as cinch, chaps, and lariat entered the lexicon of nineteenth-century America. The following passage was written by Owen Wister, creator of *The Virginian* and an amateur cowboy in his own right.*

As with his get-up, so it went with his vocabulary; for any manner of life with a rule and flavor of its own strong enough to put a new kind of dress on a man's body will put new speech in his mouth, and an idiom derived from the exigencies of his days and nights was soon spoken by the cow-puncher. Like all creators, he not only built, but borrowed his own wherever he found it. *Chaps,* from *chapparajos,* is only one of many transfers from the Mexican, one out of (I should suppose) several hundred; and in *lover-wolf* is a singular instance of half-backed translation. *Lobo,* pronounced *lovo,* being the Spanish for wolf, and the coyote being a sort of wolf, the dialect of the southern border has slid into this name for a wolf that is larger, and a worse enemy to steers than the small coward coyote. Lover-wolf is a word anchored to its district. In the Northwest, though the same animal roams there as dangerously, his Texas name would be as unknown as the North west's word for Indian, *siwash,* from *sauvage,* would be along the Rio Grande. Thus at the top and bottom of our map do French and Spanish trickle across the frontier, and with English melt into two separate amalgams which are wholly distinct, and which remain near the spot where they were moulded; while other compounds, having the same Northern and Southern starting-point, drift far and wide, and become established in the cowpuncher's dialect over his whole country. No better French specimen can be instanced than *cache,* verb and noun, from the verb *cacher,* to conceal. In our Eastern life words such as these are of no pertinent avail; and as it is only universal pertinence which can lift a fragment of dialect into the dictionary's good society, most of them must pass with the transient generation that spoke them. Certain ones there are deserving to survive; *cinch,* for instance, from *cincha,* the Mexican girth. From its narrow office under the horse's belly it has come to perform in metaphor a hundred services. In cinching somebody or something you may mean that you hold four aces, or the key of a political crisis; and when a man is very much indeed upper-dog, then he is said to have an air-tight cinch; and this phrase is to me so pleasantly eloquent that I

---

* Owen Wister, "The Evolution of the Cow-Puncher," *Harper's New Monthly Magazine,* (September, 1895), 612-614.

am withheld from using it in polite gatherings only by that prudery which we carry as a burden along with the benefits of academic training. Besides the foreign importations, such as *arroyo* and *riata,* that stand unchanged, and those others which under the action of our own speech have sloughed their native shape and come out something new, like quirt-once *cuerta,* Mexican for rawhide-is the third large class of words which the cowboy has taken from our sober old dictionary stock and made over for himself. Pie-biter refers not to those hailing from our pie belt, but to a cow-pony who secretly forages in a camp kitchen to indulge his acquired tastes. Western whiskey, besides being known as tonsil varnish and a hundred different things, goes as benzine, not unjustly. The same knack of imagery that upon our Eastern slope gave visitors from the country the brief, sure name of hayseed, calls their Western equivalents junipers. Hay grows scant upon the Rocky Mountains, but those seclusions are filled with evergreens...

The cow-puncher's talent for making a useful verb out of anything shows his individuality...Here the cowboy made ordinary words suffice for showing the way he went, but his goings can be of many sorts besides in front of and behind something, and his rich choice of synonyms embodies a latent chapter of life and habits. To the several phases of going known to the pioneer as vamose, skip, light out, dust, and git, the cowboy adds, burn the earth, hit, hit the breeze, pull your freight, jog. amble, move, pack, rattle your hocks, brindle, and more, very likely, if I knew or could recall them; I think that the observer who caught the shifting flicker of a race or a pursuit, and said brindle first, had a mind of liveliness and art...

With a speech and dress of his own, then, the cow-puncher drove his herds to Abilene or Westport Landing in the Texas times, and the easy abundant dollars came, and left him for spurs and bridles of barbaric decoration. Let it be remembered that the Mexican was the original cowboy, and that the American improved on him.

Document 8.8

Homesteaders (1910)

In 1910 the Flathead Reservation in northwestern Montana was thrown open for settlement. Following a land drawing and advertisement campaign sponsored by the federal government, almost 450,000 acres of rangeland became available for settlers hungering for cheap lands. But almost one quarter of the land would require irrigation. Families moved on to the upland range and the valleys expecting the Reclamation Service to build canals and reservoirs. However, twelve years later many still waited on their parched plots of land, barely scratching out an existence using dry farming methods. Others pulled up stakes and abandoned the territory altogether. Even in the twentieth century, the arid West proved a barrier to homesteading.*

The government made no definite promise as to when it would deliver water, but the settlers assumed, naturally, that it would be soon. People were just beginning to be enthusiastic, moreover, about "dry farming." They had a notion that here was a magic for all dry-country troubles, and that even if irrigation didn't come at once, they might get along well enough without it. Land that had been "sheeped" over or used for cattle range-stony flats and bare hills, beautiful to look upon when burned a tawny brown in summer, but about as easy to farm as an ash heap-was divided into homesteads and labeled "agricultural land." Families flocked in here, put up their little pine boxes of one-room houses, got a plow and team of horses, and started in to fight a living from the desert.

The water did not come. The building of reservoirs and canals was simply "wished" on the Reclamation Service, while the matter of appropriations for the work was left in the hands of the Indian Commissioner. His annual estimates were based largely on what could be spend on Indian reservations as a whole, and not on what the Reclamation Service needed to complete the work properly. For twelve years construction has dribbled along in this fashion, the inadequate appropriations scattered over the whole project instead of concentrated to finish up each section as they went along.

And the settlers waited. Where the water came little towns have sprouted and farms are in good shape, although even now only about 50,000 of the 100,000 irrigable acres are actually in use. Where the water did not come a few, with especially good land, succeeded by dry farming in getting a crop once in every three or four years, perhaps. Those who had taken up the stony claims could not do even this. The father plowed the unwilling earth; mother and children picked up stones and piled them in little pyramids over the bare fields. They scratched and waited; threw together a shelter for the horses and themselves; handled in timber from the distant foothills and built fences; harvested their handful of grain and hay; dug in for the winter, and with the spring went at it again. But it was a losing fight, and most of these little family plants shriveled up and died, like pots of flowers forgotten and left behind when people go away for the summer....

One after another we passed them-the empty pine shack with broken windows, the hit of tumble-down fence, the rusty, abandoned hay rake, the row of tiny trees, stunted or dead-pitiful ruins of hopes and homes...

---

* Arthur Ruhl, "Fast and Loose with the Homesteader," *Harper's Magazine,* (August, 1922), pp. 378-380.

9

Promoting the West: Western Icons

Soon after Europeans arrived in the New World the mythmaking process was at work, creating heroic figures out of ordinary human beings. The prototype of the frontier hero can be traced back to Captain John Smith of the seventeenth-century Jamestown colony. According to contemporary narratives, Smith, who was cast as both a romantic lover and man of action, dealt firmly with the Indians and saved the fledgling settlement from extinction. His numerous hand-to-hand battles with Indians and the saving of his life by Pocahantas were instrumental in making him into America's first folk hero.

While other heroes followed in the tradition of Smith during the Colonial era, none gained such a widespread and enduring audience as Daniel Boone, one of the earliest heroes to emerge from America's pioneering experience. Like many of the Western icons who would be created over the next century, Boone's heroic image was promoted through the printed word. When a Pennsylvania schoolteacher named John Filson published a short sketch portraying Daniel Boone as a prototypical Western hero in 1784 the legend was born. Filson depicted Boone as a simple man, in the mold of Rousseau's "natural man." Although Boone was often described as a large physical specimen, almost bigger than life, in reality he was five feet, eight inches tall. Ironically, Boone would live long enough to criticize the creation of his own myth.

From the mid-eighteenth-century New York state of James Fenimore Cooper's *Leatherstocking Tales,* which freely adapted the Boone legend, to the dime novels of the late-nineteenth century, the frontier has provided American popular culture with a seemingly endless procession of Western heroes. But for every Daniel Boone or Wild Bill Hickock there were a dozen less celebrated but no less heroic Western citizens who are not forgotten. When dime novels first appeared on the literary scene in the 1860s, Americans could purchase ten-cent books starring their favorite heroes, some based on reality and others probably not. Counting an audience in the millions, dime novels were remarkably successful. Thanks in part to the dime novels, Western figures such as Buffalo Bill Cody were transformed from Western scout to legendary status. Today television and film have replaced the dime novels in the dreammaking business and the business of creating icons for popular consumption.

The outlaw gunman remains one of the most popular Western icons. There was little to distinguish one criminal from another, it just mattered who had the best press agent. When considering the cast of Western badmen, Billy the Kid wins hands down on this account. Scores of plays, movies, poems, and biographies written since his death have enshrined a rather ordinary thug, who lived only twenty-one years, in the pantheon of

Western heroes. Although little is known about his early life, recent scholarship suggests that he was born in New York, rather than the West. Initially, his death at the hands of Sheriff Pat Garrett in 1881 inspired a series of dime novels in which the Kid was cast as a cold-blooded killer. Over the next several decades his image would be softened and recast into the "Robin Hood of the Southwest," a social outlaw in the antihero tradition.

The lawman gunfighter is an icon closely associated with the outlaw tradition. Many gunfighters worked both sides of the law, so it is here that the dividing line between lawman and outlaw gunfighters becomes murky. While there is little argument that Hickok was a heroic figure whose legend stands up to scrutiny, he contributed in its creation by disseminating fictional accounts about an early gunfight he participated in against a gang of well-armed adversaries. In this encounter at the Rock Creek Stage Station Hickok actually shot three men, but in less than heroic fashion. With the help of a generation of dime novels the number of victims multiplied to almost thirty victims. During his last years the famous lawman traveled the West and spent a stint with Buffalo Bill's Wild West Show as his reputation as a gunfighter grew with each retelling of his exploits.

The cowboy is probably the most recognizable icon of the West. Few men spent a lifetime as a cowboy or participated in more than one cattle drive and rarely did one see an old cowboy. While the traditional image of the cowboy is more in keeping with the noble Virginian character from Owen Wister's classic novel, recent scholarship points to the fact that like Nat Love, close to one-third of the Western cowboys were of either Mexican or African-American extraction.

Few women icons on a par with Calamity Jane or Belle Starr emerged from the nineteenth-century West. As the best-known female bandit until the emergence of Bonnie Parker in the 1930s, Belle Starr was probably the most romanticized woman to step foot in the West. However, despite an unpleasant appearance, Starr's place in history was assured by a fabricated biography published soon after her death.

Sitting Bull and the Sioux symbolized the Native American to generations of Americans. In virtually every film ever made on the American West, Native Americans are portrayed in prototypical Plains Indian fashion, wearing a headdress and mounted on a fine stallion. Since few films depict agricultural, coastal, or root gathering Indian cultures, Americans remain almost innocent to the fact that many Native American peoples never integrated the horse into their cultures. Perhaps the newspaper editor in *The Man Who Shot Liberty Valance* said it best when he commented, "when the legend becomes fact, print the legend."

Suggestions for Further Reading

John Mack Faragher, *Daniel Boone: The Life and Legend of an American Pioneer* (New York: Holt, 1992).

Frank R. Prassel, *The Western Peace Officer: A Legacy of Law and Order* (Norman: University of Oklahoma Press, 1972)

Joseph Rosa, *The Gunfighter: Man or Myth* (Norman: University of Oklahoma Press, 1969)

Kent Ladd Steckmesser, *The Western Hero in History and Legend* (Norman: University of Oklahoma Press, 1965).

Stephen Tatum, *Inventing Billy the Kid: Visions of the Outlaw in America, 1881-1981* (Albuquerque: University of New Mexico Press, 1982).

Critical Thinking

1. Why is the "cowboy" considered the most enduring image of the American West?

2. Contrast the evolving image of the "Western hero" from Daniel Boone to the late nineteenth-century cowboy.

3. Compare the mythical Wild Bill Hickock and Billy the Kid to actual observations by their contemporaries.

4. What stereotypical western experience contributed to Teddy Roosevelt's reputation as a "cowboy?"

5. Depict the "typical" cowboy and pony express rider. Be sure and describe their physical attributes and requisite equipment.

Document 9.1

Daniel Boone (1814)

One of America's most famous frontiersmen, Daniel Boone (1734-1820) was born near Reading, Pennsylvania, and moved south with his family several years later. In 1755, he served as a blacksmith with the ill-fated Braddock expedition, narrowly escaping with his life. Boone explored parts of Kentucky and trailblazed the Cumberland Gap in the 1760s. In 1778, he was captured by Shawnees before escaping in time to warn the settlers at Boonesborough of an impending attack. Over the next thirty years, Boone served as a legislator, sheriff, surveyor, frontier scout, and was involved in various unsuccessful land development ventures. In 1814, Congress awarded him 850 acres in Missouri, where he died in 1820. Larger than life, his story has been chronicled by numerous writers. However, who was the real Daniel Boone? He was not the first to explore Kentucky and was probably not any different from other frontiersmen of his era. The physical portrait that emerges in this passage contrasts with the popular conception of one of the frontier's most enduring legends.*

If we endeavor to see Daniel Boone, the man, as he actually was, we find ourselves at the outset dealing with a character already approaching the mythical in quality. Thus, in regard to his personality, certain folk imagine him as tall, thin, angular, uncouth. Others will portray to you a man with voice like thunder in the hills, with gore ever in his eye, in his voice perpetually the breathings of insatiate hate and rage. They will insist that Boone was bloody minded, overbearing, a man delighting in slaughters and riotings. Such pictures are utterly wrong; so much we may discover to be absolutely sure from the scant record of Boone's real life...

He was learned in the knowledge useful at his time, although of books he wist not at all. Deeply religious in the true sense of religion, a worshiper of the Great Maker as evidenced in His works, he was not a church member. There was no vaunting in his soul of his own righteousness; yet never was he irritable even in old age, when the blood grows cold, and the thwarted ambitions come trooping home to roost in the lives of most of us. "God gave me a work to perform," said he, "and I have done my best." With this feeling he lived and died content.

Regarding the Boone of early years, we find it difficult to frame a clear picture, but there is more information obtainable regarding his later life, and we can see him then clearly. A man reaching the ripe age of eighty-six, with five generations of his family living at the same time; a man snowy haired, yet still of ruddy complexion, of frame still unbent, with kindly and gentle personal habits-this is the real Daniel Boone; no swearer of oaths, no swash-buckler, no roisterer, but a self-respecting, fearless gentleman, steadfast, immovable from his fixed purpose, inalienable from the mission which he conceived to be his own.

A writer who knew him late in life says that on his introduction to Colonel Boone his impressions were those of "surprise, admiration and delight." In boyhood he had read of Daniel Boone, the pioneer of Kentucky, the celebrated hunter and Indian fighter, and in imagination he portrayed a "rough, uncouth looking specimen of humanity, and, of course, at this period of life, an irritable and intractable old man. But in every respect," says this biographer, "the reverse appeared. His high bold forehead was slightly bald, and his silver locks were combed smooth. His countenance was ruddy and fair, and exhibited the simplicity of a child. His voice was soft and melodious, and a smile frequently played over his face in conversation. His clothing was of the plain, coarse manufacture of the family. Everything about him indicated that kind of comfort that was congenial to his habits and feelings, and he evinced a happy old age. Boone was a fair specimen of the better class of Western pioneers, honest of heart and liberal-in short, one of nature's noblemen. He abhorred a mean action and delighted in honesty and truth. He never delighted in the shedding of human blood, even that of his enemies in war. His remarkable quality was an unwavering and invincible fortitude."

As to personal description, Boone was neither a tall nor a thin man. He was not angular nor bony. His frame was covered not with cloying fat but with firm and easily

---

* Emerson Hough, *The Way to the West* (New York: Grosset and Dunlap, 1903), 88-94.

playing muscles, and he carried none of the useless tissue of the man of civilization. His weight was "about one hundred and seventy-five pounds." Audubon, who met him late in his life, says: "He approached the gigantic in stature. His chest was broad and prominent, and his muscular powers were visible in every limb. His countenance gave indication of his great courage, enterprise and perseverance."

Yet in person Boone did not quite reach the six-foot mark, but was just below five feet and ten inches in stature, some say five feet eight inches, being therefore of exactly that build which good judges of men esteem to be most desirable for combined strength, activity and endurance. He was rather broad shouldered: that is to say, his shoulders nicely overhung his hips. All agree that he was of "robust and powerful proportions." One historian speaks of his "piercing hazel eye"; yet this is but romancing.

Most portraits of Daniel Boone are the products of imagination. The most authentic, perhaps the only authentic portrait of him, is that painted in 1820 by Chester Harding, "who," says an early writer, "of American artists is the one most celebrated for his likenesses." When Harding made his portrait of Boone, the latter was very feeble, and had to be supported during the sittings. This portrait shows a face thin and pale, with hair of snowy whiteness and eye "bright blue, mild and pleasant." This blue eye is of the best color in all the world for keenness of vision, for quickness and accuracy with the rifle. The Harding portrait does not show the square chin that some writers give to Boone; and certainly it portrays no ferocious looking ruffian, but a man mild, gentle and contemplative, "not frivolous, thoughtless or agitated."

As to Boone's appearance early in life, we must to some extent join the others who imagine or presume. It is fair to suppose that in complexion he was florid, with the clear skin, sometimes marked with freckles, that you may see to-day in the mountains of the Cumberland, in parts of Tennessee, Kentucky, sometimes in North Carolina and Mississippi. The color of his hair was never that of "raven blackness." Perhaps it was brown, but not a finely filamented brown. It was more likely blood, and perhaps indeed carried a shade of red. Certainly the ends of his hair were bleached a tawny yellow, that splendid yellow that you may see even to-day in the hair and beard and mustaches of the outdoor men of the American West.

In this younger days he often wore the half savage garb of the early American hunters-the buckskin or linsey hunting shirt, the fringed leggings of the same material, with moccasins made of the skin of the deer or buffalo. His hat was as chance would have it. Perhaps sometimes he wore a cap of fur.

His weaponry we may know exactly, for his rifle can be seen to-day, preserved by his descendants. It is the typical long-barreled, crooked-stocked, small-bore American rifle, with the wooden stock or fore end extending along the full length of the barrel. There are a few rude attempts at ornamentation on this historic arm. The sights lie close to the barrel, after the fashion of those deadly ancient weapons. The wood is rotting a little bit where the oil of long-ago cleaning operations has touched it. Perhaps the spring of the lock is a trifle weak. Yet we may not doubt that, were Daniel Boone alive to-day, he could teach the old piece to voice its music and could show again its ancient deadly art.

Document 9.2

Pony Express Rider (1860)

On April 3, 1860, the Pony Express began service between St. Joseph, Missouri and Sacramento, California. Under the sponsorship of the well-known freighting firm of Russell, Majors, and Waddell, the Pony Express waged an intense competition with the Overland Mail Company. The Pony Express advertised that it would deliver letters between Missouri and the Pacific Coast within ten days, or twice as fast as its competition. Close to two hundred way stations were established between ten and fifteen miles apart. While the public was under the impression that the riders delivered the mail by horseback the entire distance, in reality most of the pony trips were between Fort Kearny, Nebraska, and Fort Churchill, Nevada, where telegraph lines were under construction. More a dramatic success than a financial one, the Pony Express was only in existence for eighteen months. Facing mounting losses and indebtedness, as well as the government support of its competition and completion of the overland telegraph, this experiment in mail delivery came to an end in October 1861.*

Of the eighty daring riders employed on the line, at times forty were in the saddle going west and forty east. With some of them it mattered little whether it was night or day. Their business was to keep a going, rain or shine; for every twenty-four hours an average distance of about 200 miles must be covered. To make the long ride, it was necessary to cross many ravines, gullies, creeks and rivers on the prairies and plains; ford a number of mountain torrents; go over parched stretches of sand and alkali, often facing clouds of dust; pass through weird and rugged canons and gorges; and wind their way along high and difficult passes of the snow-capped Rockies and Sierras. Some of the places encountered on the western slope were at first pronounced to be next to impassable, and then only in the late summer and autumn months.

The weight of the letters was limited to twenty pounds, though usually not to exceed fifteen pounds were carried; and these were, as nearly as possible, distributed into four equal parts. While it cost five dollars for each half-ounce letter when the pony enterprise went into operation, it was not long until the post-office department ordered that the rates be reduced to one dollar per half-ounce, and these were the charges which continued until the line was driven out by the Pacific telegraph.

While crossing the mighty western range of mountains, the daring riders demonstrated that there were passes over which they could go at a good speed. As a

---

* Frank A. Root and William Elsey Connelley, *The Overland Stage to California*, (Topeka, Kansas, 1901), pp. 115-124

result, the route selected by them was afterward agreed upon as one of the most feasible by which a railroad might be built and operated through Utah and Nevada, connecting with bands of steel the Atlantic and Pacific oceans.

A considerable part of the distance, it should be remembered, was through a country inhabited by various tribes of hostile Indians. Other portions of the vast region were often swept by terrific hail, sleet, wind and rain storms, and occasionally by furious blizzards and blinding snows. The route across the country embraced a wide stretch of rolling prairie, through which coursed a number of beautiful streams at intervals fringed with belts of timber and willow; thence over the plains and across the back-bone of the continent; over the Wasatch range into the Salt Lake valley through vast expanses of sage-brush; across a long stretch of desolate alkali plains; through the parched region known as the "Sink of the Carson"; thence across the rugged Sierra Nevadas, down the Pacific slope into Placerville; and, lastly, on to the Sacramento valley and into the capital city of California.

The daring riders were sometimes obliged to grapple with sudden dangers, such as snow slides, roaring mountain torrents, and almost irresistible wind-storms, frequently facing clouds of dust and sand; but, in spite of the numerous difficulties, and while occasionally some hours were lost on the trail, there was seldom a trip that was not made on time. The schedule was ten days for eight months in the year, and twelve days for the other four months.

The most lonesome and worst part of the long route lay between Salt Lake City and Sacramento. For several hundred miles the trail extended through a parched, desolate region-virtually a desert waste-much of it a section of alkali dust, where it would appear neither man nor beast could subsist. Along the eastern foot-hills of the Sierras and in the mountain canons it is said hostile bands of Indians were numerous, and there the relay stations were farther apart.

The first was a highly interesting but somewhat novel and exciting trip. In making the journey the riders were obliged to go day and night, in all kinds of weather, rain or shine, never stopping except to change ponies, until the end of their stretch was reached, often from 75 to 100 miles. Two minutes were allowed for a change at the various relays; but so expert had the "pony" boys become in the business of changing animals that it was usually made in about fifteen seconds.

The time occupied in making the first trip from St. Joseph to Sacramento was nine days and twenty-three hours, while it took eleven days and twelve hours to make the initial trip eastward. But this was little more than one-half the time consumed in making the fastest trip to San Francisco that had ever been made by the Butterfield overland mail coach from St. Louis through southwestern Missouri, the Indian Territory, Texas, New Mexico, and Arizona.

During the last six or seven weeks before the enterprise was abandoned, there were on an average 700 letters a week brought by the "pony" through from the Pacific coast. The telegraph having been finished from the Missouri river to Fort Kearney, the letter pouches were brought from there to Atchison by the overland stage. The pony line was operated semiweekly, and each trip brought about 350 letters. In those last few weeks every pony express letter was mailed at the Atchison post-office, and I thus became quite familiar with them from handling and postmarking each letter-in all, over 4500-while at time employed in that office in the capacity of assistant postmaster and chief clerk, while the great overland mail stages every morning left that city.

The letters, many of which were written on tissue paper, were very light; for it cost something in those days, even after the "pony" rates were reduced to one dollar per half-ounce, to indulge in California correspondence. It was necessary that each letter and message transmitted by the "pony" route should be enclosed in a ten-cent (Government) stamped envelope. Some of the letters were rather bulky, and I have postmarked those that had affixed to them as many as twenty-five one dollar "pony" stamps. In addition to these, there were affixed the regular Government stamps, which were ten cents for each half-ounce. These heavy letters thus cost, in the early '60's, $27.50 each for transit by the pony conveyance. Such correspondence looked like an expensive luxury to an outsider; but time, then as now, to the wide-awake business man, was money, and many of those patronizing the pony express seemed not to care for expense. But this was in the early days of the civil war.

The San Francisco newspaper men were considerably interested in the result of the remarkable run that conveyed to the Pacific President Lincoln's inaugural speech. They contributed a handsome gold watch, which was presented to the fearless rider on the California division who made the best record in annihilating distance on the journey in the Sierra Nevada mountains.

Most of the letters that were brought by the "pony" from California were from merchants, miners, business and professional men in San Francisco, Sacramento, Oakland, Portland, and other prominent points near the coast. A large majority of them were addressed to merchants and business men in New York, Boston, Philadelphia, Baltimore, Chicago, St. Louis, and other cities in the East, while there was an occasional one addressed to the chief magistrate of the nation. Quite a number were for senators and representatives from California, and the delegates from Oregon and other Western territories.

It is useless to disguise the fact that the enthusiastic projector of the "pony" sunk at least $100,000, and that his partners who lent aid to the enterprise also lost their fortunes. Whether its operation for several years would have brought better results can only be surmised.

It cost an enormous sum of money to organize and equip the pony line, and it was a matter of continual expense to keep the line in shape. Nearly 500 of the best saddle-horses were used; 190 stations had to be kept up, and nearly 200 men were employed as station keepers, in addition to the riders. Most of the grain used by the animals between St. Joseph and Salt Lake had to be transported from Missouri and Iowa across the plains and over the Rocky Mountains at a freight cost of ten to twenty-five cents a pound. On the western division, much of the feed was purchased in Salt Lake City from the Mormons, and distributed over the route beyond as far as the Sierra Nevadas.

While the express proved to be a costly undertaking, it soon demonstrated-but at an enormous loss-what could be done by Western men of energy and determination.

Really the pony express was the original "fast mail" over the plains and Rockies-across the so-called "Great American Desert" to the golden shore of the Pacific. In its day it was a blessing to the country; but after it was fairly in operation, annihilating space between the Missouri river and the Golden Gate beating the fastest time that had ever been made across the continent, it was not long until it was distanced itself by the magnetic telegraph. While the pony line was very useful in its day, the period of its life was comparatively brief. It could not stand the race with electricity, and, when the telegraph line was finished, its usefulness was ended; the enterprise was wiped out almost instantly.

While the pony express lasted, it was of incalculable benefit on the Pacific coast, particularly while there was a rupture between the North and the South, for copies of Eastern metropolitan newspapers, printed to order on tissue paper, and placed in letter envelopes, were carried across the continent by the fleet pony to the leading San Francisco dailies, which could furnish the news to their readers at least two weeks ahead of the Concord overland mail coach, and nearly three weeks in advance of the Pacific Mail Company's ocean steamers.

The pay of pony express riders was fixed at from $50 to $150 a month and board. William F. Cody ("Buffalo Bill") and a few others, who had extra risks from riding through regions infested by the Cheyennes and Comanches-among the most-feared savages roaming the plains of Nebraska and Colorado in those days-were paid $150 for their services. To make the ride they were often obliged to take their lives in their own hands. Along the 2000 mile trail, stretching from the "Big Muddy" to the great ocean, relay stations were established at regular intervals, and bronchos and a number of men equipped with rifles and revolvers were stationed at each.

It was not unexpected that mishaps should occur while making the long journey across the continent. Now and then a rider would lose the road, and, bewildered, wander around for hours in search of the lost trail. Once in a while a rider would be caught in a blinding snow-storm; another would be impeded in his ride by a swollen stream on the plains or in the mountains; and thus considerable valuable time would be lost. Occasionally a horse would drown and the rider, knowing it was a case of life or death with him, would be obliged to swim ashore and, with the mail-pouch of valuable letters on his back, walk to the next station and secure a fresh pony to complete his ride.

The letters in care of the pony express were wrapped in oil-silk as a protection against the weather, being then placed in the four pockets of the leather pouch specially prepared for them. The reason for so many pockets was that the weight might be, as near as possible, evenly distributed, and that there be little inconvenience to both pony and rider. The pouch was provided with locks, and keys to it were distributed at the various forts along the route and also at Salt Lake City and Carson. Even with the packages of letters wrapped in oil-silk, they were sometimes injured by water when it became necessary for the riders to swim their horses across swollen streams. In at least one instance it is recorded that the horse was drowned, but the rider, with the letters, was saved. At times there would be a lively chase for the rider by Indians, but only once has there been mention made when he was overtaken. On this occasion the rider was scalped, but the pony escaped with the letter pouch, which was subsequently recovered out on the plains and the letters promptly forwarded to their destination.

At first the idea of a pony express that would do what was promised early in 1800 was hooted at by the enemies of the novel enterprise. But, in spite of this, the originators of the scheme were so firm in their belief that it would finally win that they did not hesitate to invest $100,000 in it. They equipped the line and established stations at frequent intervals for a distance of about 2000 miles. Russell's partners in the freighting business, Messrs. Majors and Waddell, did not have great faith in its success, but they sunk a vast fortune in it, believing that it would be as "bread cast on the waters."

The pony express lasted less than eighteen months. Two months before it stopped it was followed by the daily overland stage-coach, in July, 1861; four months later came the Pacific telegraph, in competition with which it was as an ox train compared to the lightning express; and finally the completion of the first railway across the continent, in May, 1869, forced the Concord stage-coach, as the telegraph had the pony, to the rear.

Document 9.3

Wild Bill Hickock (1869)

James Butler "Wild Bill" Hickock (1837-1878) was one of the few Western icons whose legendary exploits were rooted in reality. Born on the Illinois frontier, Hickock worked as a civilian scout for the Union Army during the Civil War, engaged in numerous face-down gunfights, and scouted for Custer's 7th Cavalry before becoming a lawman in Kansas in 1869. He served as marshal and sheriff in several Kansas cowtowns before joining Buffalo Bill's Wild West Show in 1873. By then his eyes were beginning to fail, and in 1878 he was gunned down from behind in a Deadwood, South Dakota, saloon while playing poker. His last poker hand consisted of aces and eights, which became part of the poker vernacular as a "dead man's hand." The following is a first-person account that captures the essence of the vaunted gunfighter.*

During the construction of the road I was afterwards at Hays City (near old Fort Hays) when it was the end of passenger traffic, in the fall of 1867. The track was laid some distance west of there, but only trains loaded with construction material were passing beyond. It was a town like those which preceded it farther east-made up largely of rough board shanties and tents. I don't believe there was a painted house in the "city." It was here that I first met James B. Hickock ("Wild Bill"), who was there, and had for some time previous been in the service of the Government as a scout on the frontier. I talked perhaps half an hour with him, and found him a very pleasant and affable gentleman, thoroughly familiar with the geography of that part of the West, and in conversing with him obtained much valuable information relating to that section of Kansas, as I also had gathered from Dr. W. E. Webb, stationed there for some time as agent for the Kansas Pacific railroad lands.

* Frank A. Root and William Elsey Connelley, *The Overland Stage to California* (Topeka, Kansas, 1901), 143-47.

In the spring of 1869 the first municipal election took place in Hays, and from that time the place boasted of a city government and began to put on metropolitan airs. Hickock was chosen city marshal. He had an important task to perform. His principal duties were to stop the lawless acts that had so long been of frequent occurrence, to the detriment of the growth and standing of the place. While gamblers, highwaymen and other law-breaking persons had for some time been running things to suit themselves, they soon found that they could not ride with impunity over the orders of the newly installed brave and fearless marshal. He was selected to keep law and order and was determined to do it. Nothing of the kind had existed since the town was started. While Hickock was a quiet sort of a man, it was claimed that he had killed more than a dozen bad men on the frontier, but of all those whom he had shot, it is believed that he never killed a man except in self-defense. In the old cemetery a little west of Hays all the dead were buried until 1880. Among the various graves on the hillside of that last resting-place, it is said, upwards of eighty of them were filled by tragedies of some sort.

There was no better marksman on the frontier than Wild Bill. Every one acquainted him knew he was a dead shot. On assuming his duties he buckled on two huge revolvers and started out. It was not his desire to bring on trouble or kill any one. One of his favorite ways in bringing a fellow to terms was clubbing with his guns. When occasion required, he could pound with ease an unruly cowboy or lawless thug until his face resembled a raw beefsteak. It was not long after he took hold until there was a decided improvement in the affairs of the town. Quiet began to reign almost from the start. Naturally many of the saloonkeepers and cowboys who had so long been running the town their own way soon became his enemies. Because they could not override his authority they secretly resolved on taking his life. In his strolls around town he steered clear of the sidewalk as far as possible, knowing he was liable at any moment to be shot down by an armed foe, who, secreted between buildings, could easily get the drop on him.

Wild Bill was one of the early characters in Hays City. "In physique," according to a writer in the St. Louis *Republic,* "he was as perfect a specimen of manhood as ever walked in moccasins or wore a pair of cavalry boots-and Bill was a dandy at times in attire, a regular frontier dude. He stood about six feet two inches tall, had a lithe waist and loins, broad shoulders, small feet, bony and supple hands with tapering fingers, quick to feel the cards or pull the trigger of a revolver. His hair was auburn in hue, of the tint brightened but not reddened by the sunlight. He had a clean, clear-cut face, clean shaven, except a thin, drooping, sandy-brown mustache, which he wore and twirled with no success even in getting an upward twist at either end. Brown haired as he was, he had clear, gray eyes. He had a splendid countenance, amiable in look, but firm withal. His luxuriant growth of hair fell in ringlets over his shoulders. There was nothing in his appearance to betoken the dead shot and frequent murderer, except his tread. He walked like a tiger, and, aroused, he was as ferocious and pitiless as one.

It was not long after his arrival until he had put himself on record as one in every way built to protect himself. He had already achieved a reputation, having followed the Kansas Pacific and seen almost every mile of the road built west from Manhattan. He had won considerable notoriety for "killing a man," having been a Government scout in the Arkansas valley during the war, while along the line of railroad he was known as "the Slade of western Kansas." His first exploit at Hays witnessed by the *Republic* correspondent was "a double shot-a right-and-left fusilade," concerning which the writer said:

"Two men came out of a saloon and walked toward the newly built depot surrounded by a raised platform. Each man had a pistol drawn, when suddenly from a group of four or five 'crack! crack!' went two pistol shots, and Wild Bill stood on the edge of the platform with smoking, bone-handled revolvers in each hand, and the two men who had been approaching the platform were seen to totter, stumble forward, and fall. Death was instantaneous in each case, as if Jove had hurled a bolt at the men. A row over cards the night before caused the double death, and a double funeral as soon as the corpses could be prepared for interment.

"It was only a few months after the obsequies following the demise of the two gentlemen whose taking off has just been re-recorded that Wild Bill came near furnishing, in his own person, the subject for a 'first-class funeral.' He was sauntering west on Front street (traversed by the railroad) when, near the corner of Fort street (the avenue leading toward Fort Hays), a small man, an Irishman, of the name of Sullivan, jumped out in front of Bill with a cocked revolver, exclaiming: 'I have got you! Hold up your hands. I am going to kill you, you – –.' Up went Bill's hands, Sullivan having 'the drop' on him. Sullivan then started into a gloating dissertation about killing him, while Bill stood before him as rigid as the Apollo Belvedere. Opening his eyes wide and frowning, Bill in a few moments uttered in an expostulatory tone, looking over Sullivan's head: 'For God's sake, don't stab the man in the back. Give him a chance for his life.' Sullivan turned to see his enemy in the rear-and his funeral came off the next day. Strange to say, several years after the death of Sullivan. Wild Bill 'died with his boots on,' in Wyoming, while at a game of cards."

Document 9.4

Billy the Kid (1870s)

Despite a lifespan of only twenty-one years, William H. Bonney, alias Billy the Kid, was perhaps the most chronicled gunman in Western lore. Plays, ballets, poems, movies, and countless books and articles have been written about the young killer. Contrary to most inaccurate accounts of his life, "the Kid" was born in New York City, was not left-handed, and did not kill one man for each year of his life. By most accounts, he was well liked and affable, with a good sense of humor, and was popular with the ladies. Wanted for murder, Billy the Kid was hunted down and killed by Sheriff Pat Garrett on July 14, 1881, at Fort

Sumner, New Mexico. The following excerpt is an early portrait of Billy the Kid.*

The true name of Billy the Kid was William H. Bonney, and he was born in New York City, November 23, 1859. His father removed to Coffeyville, on the border of the Indian Nations, in 1862, where soon after he died, leaving a widow and two sons. Mrs. Bonney again moved, this time to Colorado, where she married again, her second husband being named Antrim. All the time clinging to what was the wild border, these two now moved down to Santa Fé New Mexico, where they remained until Billy was eight years of age. In 1868, the family made their home at Silver City, New Mexico, where they lived until 1871, when Billy was twelve years of age. His life until then had been one of shifting about, in poverty or at best rude comfort. His mother seems to have been a wholesome Irishwoman, of no great education, but of good instincts. Of the boy's father nothing is known; and of his stepfather little more, except that he was abusive to the stepchildren. Antrim survived his wife, who died about 1870. The Kid always said that his stepfather was the cause of his "getting off wrong."

The Kid was only twelve years old when, in a saloon row in which a friend of his was being beaten, he killed with a pocket-knife a man who had previously insulted him. Some say that this was an insult offered to his mother; others deny it and say that the man had attempted to horsewhip Billy. The boy turned up with a companion at Fort Bowie, Pima county, Arizona, and was around the reservation for a while. At last he and his associate, who appears to have been as well saturated with border doctrine as himself at tender years, stole some horses from a band of Apaches, and incidentally killed three of the latter in a night attack. They made their first step at easy living in this enterprise, and, young as they were, got means in this way to travel about over Arizona. They presently turned up at Tucson, where Billy began to employ his precocious skill at cards; and where, presently, in the inevitable gambler's quarrel, he killed another man. He fled across the line now into old Mexico, where, in the state of Sonora, he set up as a youthful gambler. Here he killed a gambler, Jose Martinez, over a monte game, on an "even break," being the fraction of a second the quicker on the draw. He was already beginning to show his natural fitness as a handler of weapons. He kept up his record by appearing next at Chihuahua and robbing a few monte dealers there, killing one whom he waylaid with a new companion by the name of Segura.

The Kid was now old enough to be dangerous, and his life had been one of irresponsibility and lawlessness. He was nearly at his physical growth at this time, possibly five feet even and a half inches in height, and weighing hundred and thirty-five pounds. He was always slight and lean, a hard rider all his life, and never old enough to begin to take on flesh. His hair was light or light brown, and his eyes blue or blue-gray, with curious red hazel spots on them. His face was rather long, his chin narrow but long, and his front teeth were a trifle prominent. He was always a pleasant mannered youth, hopeful and buoyant, never glum or grim, and he nearly always smiled when talking.

---

* Emerson Hough, *The Story of the Outlaw: A Study of the Western Desperado* (New York: The Outing Publishing Company, 1907), pp. 257-261.

The Southwestern border at this time offered but few opportunities for making an honest living. There were the mines and there were the cow ranches. It was natural that the half-wild life of the cow punchers would sooner or later appeal to the Kid.

That the Kid worked for a time for John Chisum, on his ranch near Roswell, is well known, as is the fact that he cherished a grudge against Chisum for years, and was more than once upon the point of killing him for a real or fancied grievance. He left Chisum and took service with J. H. Tunstall on his Feliz ranch late in the winter of 1877, animated by what reason we may not know. In doing this, he may have acted from pique or spite or hatred. There was some quarrel between him and his late associates. Tunstall was killed by the Murphy faction on February 18, 1878. From that time, the path of the Kid is very plain and his acts well known and authenticated. He had by this time killed several men, certainly at least two white men; and how many Mexicans and Indians he had killed by fair means or foul will never be really known. His reputation as a gun fighter was well established.

Document 9.5

Interview with Sitting Bull (1881)

Born Tatanka Iyotake, Sitting Bull (c. 1831-1890) was one of the most famous Native American leaders. A chief and holy man of the Teton Sioux, he is perhaps best remembered as the architect of Custer's defeat at the Little Big Horn in 1876. After this battle, Sitting Bull and his followers retreated to Canada. Without the support of the Canadian government, his band was forced to return to the United States, surrendering at Fort Buford in July 1881. The following is a rare interview with a newspaper reporter only one month after his return.*

Interpreter—Where were you born, and when?

Sitting Bull—I don't know where I was born and cannot remember. I know that I was born, though, or would not be here. I was born of a woman; I know this is a fact, because I exist.

Sitting Bull here held a long conversation with his uncle, Chief Four Horns, and after pointing at different fingers for some time, said:

"I was born near old Fort George, on Willow Creek, below the mouth of the Cheyenne River. I am 44 years old, as near as I can tell; we count our years from the moons between great events. The event from which I date my birth is the year in which

---

* "A Talk With Sitting Bull," *St. Paul Pioneer-Press,* August 7, 1881.

Thunder Hawks was born. I am as old as he. I have always been running around. Indians that remain on the same hunting-grounds all the time can remember years better."

Reporter—How many wives and children have you?

Sitting Bull (running over his fingers and then with thumb and forefinger of one hand pinching and holding together two fingers of his other hand) —I have nine children and two living wives, and one wife that has gone to the great spirit. I have two pairs of twins.

Lieut. Dowdy—Tell Sitting Bull he is more fortunate than I am. I can't get one wife.

At this interruption Sitting Bull laughed.

Reporter—Which is your favorite wife?

Sitting Bull—I think as much of one as the other. If I did not I would not keep them. I think if I had a white wife I would think more of her than the other two.

Reporter—What are the names of your wives?

Sitting Bull (raising the side of the tent and calling a squaw to him; evidently he asked her) —Was-Seen-By-The-Nation is the name of the old one. The One-That-Had-Four-Robes is the name of the other.

Reporter—Are you a chief by inheritance, and if not, what deeds of bravery gave you the title?

Sitting Bull—My father and two uncles were chiefs. My father's name was The Jumping Bull. My uncle that is in the teepee is called Four-Horns and my other uncle was called Hunting-His-Lodge. My father was a very rich man, and owned a great many good ponies in four colors. In ponies he took much pride. They were roan, white, and gray. He had great numbers, and I never wanted for a horse to ride. When I was 10 years old I was famous as a hunter. My specialty was buffalo calves. [Here Bull indicated with his arms how he killed the buffalo.] I gave the calves I killed to the poor that had no horses. I was considered a good man. [Here Bull again counted on his fingers and joints.] My father died 21 years ago. For four years after I was 10 years old I killed buffalo and fed his people, and thus became one of the fathers of the tribe. At the age of 14 I killed an enemy, and began to make myself great in battle, and became a chief. Before this, from 10 to 14, my people had named me The Sacred Standshoty. After killing an enemy they called me Ta-Tan-Ka I-You-Tan-Ka, or Sitting Bull. An Indian may be an inherited chief, but he has to make himself a chief by his bravery. [Although several efforts were made and much tact used, Sitting Bull would not speak of his life beyond the age of 14.]

Reporter—Besides yourself, whom do you think the greatest and bravest chief of the Sioux nation?

Before answering this question Sitting Bull took a long smoke, then handed his pipe around, and played with a knife in his sheath. Withdrawing it, he said: "When I came in Buford I gave up everything. I even gave up all my knives but this. This is the only weapon I have. It is not sharp. I keep it to fix pipes. [Meditatively again be recalled the last question and said:] There are five great chiefs of the Sioux nation before me. They were: He-to, (meaning Four Horns,) Ce-su-ho-tan-ka, (meaning Loud Voiced Hawk,) Helo-ta, (meaning Scarlet Horn,) Can-te-tanka, (meaning Big Heart,) and Ta-to-ka-en-yan-ka, (meaning Running Antelope.) All are dead but Running Antelope and Four Horns. Ho is the bravest chief besides myself. Antelope is witko, (meaning a Fool.) He has been among the whites, and asked all of us to surrender.

At the conclusion of this sentence the interpreters turned to the reporter and told him that this statement of Sitting Bull was made from a spirit of hatred and jealousy, and that Running Antelope was a great chief, and had done more than any other to get the Indians to surrender. Sitting Bull, it was ascertained, had in some manner interpreted or understood this conversation, for he shortly interfered, and said he had no hatred or jealousy is his heart when speaking of other chiefs.

"What induced you to surrender and what wrongs have you suffered at the hands of the Government?" These and other questions were put in all sorts of ways, and at first the chief refused to answer them, saying this was an ordinary talk, and these were questions of great importance to him. After hesitating a long time, and being assured by the interpreter that it was best to speak, he finally spoke in an excited and rambling way as follows: "Already have I told my reasons.' I was not raised to be an enemy of the white. These five chiefs that I have named were not enemies of the white man. The pale faces had things that we needed in order to hunt. We needed ammunition. Our interests were in peace. I never sold that much land. [Here Sitting Bull picked up with his thumb and forefinger a little of the pulverized dirt in the tent, and holding it up let it fall and blow away.] I never made or sold a treaty with the United States. I came in to claim my rights and the rights of my people. I was driven in force from my land and I now come hack to claim it for my people. I never made war on the United States Government. I never stood in the white man's country, I never committed any depredations in the white man's country. I never made the white man's heart bleed. The white man came on to my land and followed me. The white man made me fight for my hunting grounds. The white man made me kill him or he would kill my friends, my woman, and my children."

Reporter—The white man admires your conduct in a battle. You showed yourself to be a great chief in the Custer fight.

Sitting Bull—There was a Great Spirit who guided and controlled that battle. I could do nothing. I was sustained by the great mysterious One. [Here Sitting Bull pointed upward with his forefinger.]

Reporter—You conducted the battle well; so well that many thought that you were not an Indian, but that you were a white man and knew the white man's ways.

Sitting Bull, (pointing to his wrist) —I was not a white man, for the Great Spirit did not make me a white skin. I did not fight the white man's back. I came out and met him on the grass. When I say Running Antelope is a fool I mean he made treaties and allowed the white man to come in and occupy our land. Ever since that time there has been trouble. I do not want aid or assistance from the whites or any one else. I want them to stay from my country and allow me to hunt on my own land. I want no blood spilled in my land except the blood of the buffalo. I want to hunt and trace for many moons. You have asked me to come in. I wanted the white man to provide for me for several years if I came in. You have never offered me any inducements to come in. I did not want to come. My friends that come got soap and axe-handles, but not enough to eat. I have come in, and want the white man to allow me to hunt in my own country. That is the way I live. I want to keep my ponies. I can't hunt without ponies. The buffalo runs fast. The white man wanted me to give up everything.

Reporter—What treatment do you expect from the Government ? If not satisfied, what shall you do?

Sitting Bull—I expected to stay but a few days at Buford. When I came in I did not surrender. I want the Government to let me occupy the Little Missouri country. There is plenty of game there. I have damages against the Government for holding my land and game. I want the Great Father to pay me for it.

The reporter here asked the interpreter to get an idea of what Sitting Bull meant by the Little Missouri country?

Sitting Bull—My hunting ground is from the bad lands to the end of the Little Missouri and I want it extended down here where some of my people are, so that I can trade.

Reporter—What do Chiefs Gall and Running Antelope say about their treatment here?

Sitting Bull—Antelope is a fool. I have seen Gall. He can't tell me anything. He is not a chief of my people.

Reporter—Don't you think the Indians here are treated well?

Sitting Bull—I have not had a chance to talk with them. They are waiting for me to speak. They want to give me a feast and hold a council. I am not jealous of them. I don't know whether we will hold a council or not.

Reporter—Tell us all about the Custer battle. How did it happen? Did you direct the main forces?

Sitting Bull (after a long silence) —I am not afraid to talk about that. It all happened; it is passed and gone. I do not lie, but do not want to talk about it. Low Dog says I can't fight until someone lends me a heart. Gall says my heart is no bigger than that, [placing one forefinger at the base of the nail of another finger.] We have all fought hard. We did not know Custer. When we saw him we threw up our hands and I cried: "Follow me and do as I do." We whipped each other's horses, and it was all over.

Reporter—Custer's men were all killed. There is no one to tell us about the battle but you. We keep a record of our battles and study them. We write histories of brave men. We will never fight the Sioux again. Tell us more about it.

Sitting Bull—There was not as many Indians as the white man says, They are all warriors. There was not more than 2,000.

Reporter—Crow King says, on the second day, when you were fighting Reno's men, that you asked your warriors not to kill any more, that you had already killed enough.

Sitting Bull—Crow King speaks the truth: I did not want to kill any more men. I did not like that kind of work. I only defended my camp. When we had killed enough, that was all that was necessary.

All further efforts by a series of a dozen questions failed to induce Sitting Bull to say anything further about this matter.

Reporter—Do you understand what this is all for? Do you know how a great newspaper like the *Pioneer Press* goes out to thousands of people every morning?

Sitting Bull (making a mark on the ground and placing his finger on one side of it) —Yes, I have seen the great newspaper over there, [Meaning across the British lines.].

Reporter—Have you ever been interviewed before by a newspaper man upon these subjects?

Sitting Bull—I have never talked about these things to a reporter before. None of them ever before paid me money. My words are worth dollars, If the Great Father gives me a reservation I do not want to be confined to any part of it. I want no restraint, I will keep on the reservation, but want to go where I please. I don't want a white man over me. I don't want an Agent. I want to have the white man with me, but not to be my chief. I ask this because I want to do right by my people and can't trust any one else to trade with them or talk to them. I want interpreters to talk to the white man for me and transact my business, but I want it to be seen and known that I have my rights. I want my people to have light wagons to work with. They do not know how to handle heavy wagons with cattle. We want light wagons and ponies. I don't want to give up game as long as there is any game. I will be half civilized till the game is gone. Then I will be all civilized. I want peace and no trouble. I want to raise my children that they may have peace and prosperity. I like the way the white brother keeps his children. Miss Fanny Culbertson, of Poplar River, was the first person I shook hands with when I came over the line. My daughter came to see me last night. We both cried. I was happy to see her. The soldiers would not let her come into my camp at first. She came here before I did, and I listened a long time to hear word from her, and for the winds to tell me how she was treated. I did not hear. I came down to see her. She seems to be doing well, but I saw she had no respect from the whites. The soldiers would not spread down a blanket for her to walk into my camp. She is well dressed, but she says her relatives at the Agency gave her her clothes.

Reporter (to the interpreter) —Explain to Sitting Bull how President Garfield has been shot by a coward, and ask him what he thinks about the act; also, what the Indians would do if a coward would shoot their chief.

Sitting Bull—It was a cowardly act. If the warrior had been there he would have gone to the Great Father's face and looked him in the eyes, and then shot him. I heard when way up there about the Great Father being shot, but had no one to tell me all about it. I don't know whether the warrior was wise in doing it or not. He might have shot the Great Father because he was not treating the Indians right. If that was so it was not a bad thing to do. If a coward should shoot one of our chiefs or warriors without looking him in the eyes our friends would go and kill him. If he was a very rich coward he could pay the damages in many ponies and we would let him leave.

Reporter—How many scalps have you taken, not counting those taken by your people, which are always credited to the chiefs?

Sitting Bull (spreading out both hands and putting his two thumbs together, and pointing to his joints, and thinking for fully five minutes) —I have killed is 16 enemies. I never killed a white man. I have made raids upon the Crees, Gros Ventres, and Northern Blackfeet, and stolen horses 22 times. I never stole horses from the whites.

Reporter—The President takes the *Pioneer Press*. He will read your words. What message do you wish to send to him?

Sitting Bull—I have told you all I want. I would like to have the Great Father listen to what I have said and help me accomplish what I ask.

Document 9.6

Teddy Roosevelt, Cowboy (1884)

Following the deaths of his wife and mother in February 1884, the historian, conservationist, and politician Theodore Roosevelt (1858-1919) exiled himself to two ranches in the Dakota Badlands. His experience in the West was short-lived. Two years later he left the West to run for Mayor of New York City. However, his interlude on the frontier transformed him in many ways, giving him the self-confidence that would later lead him up San Juan Hill during the Spanish American War and then to the presidency. When President McKinley was assassinated in 1901 and Vice-President Roosevelt ascended to the oval office, one official reportedly said that "now that damn cowboy is president." In the following passages from Roosevelt's autobiography we see the tenderfoot transformed into a tougher western specimen.*

The only time I ever had serious trouble was at an even more primitive little hotel than the one in question. It was also on an occasion when I was out after lost horses. Below the hotel had merely a bar-room, a dining-room, and a lean- to kitchen; above was a loft with fifteen or twenty beds in it. It was late in the evening when I reached the place. I heard one or two shots in the bar-room as I came up, and I disliked going in. But there was nowhere else to go, and it was a cold night. Inside the room were several men, who, including the bartender, were wearing the kind of smile worn by men who are making believe to like what they don't like. A shabby individual in a broad hat with a cocked gun in each hand was walking up and down the floor talking with strident profanity. He had evidently been shooting at the clock, which had two or three holes in its face.

He was not a "bad man" of the really dangerous type, the true man-killer type, but he was an objectionable creature, a would-be bad man, a bully who for the moment was having things all his own way. As soon as he saw me he hailed me as "Four eyes," in reference to my spectacles, and said, "Four eyes is going to treat." I joined in the laugh and got behind the stove and sat down, thinking to escape notice. He followed me, however, and though I tried to pass it off as a jest this merely made him more offensive, and he stood leaning over me, a gun in each hand, using very foul language. He was foolish to stand so near, and, moreover, his heels were close together, so that his position was unstable. Accordingly, in response to his reiterated command that I should set up the drinks, I said, "Well, if I've got to, I've got to," and rose, looking past him.

As I rose, I struck quick and hard with my right just to one side of the point of his jaw, hitting with my left as I straightened out, and then again with my right. He fired the guns, but I do not know whether this was merely a convulsive action of his hands or

---

* Theodore Roosevelt, *An Autobiography*, (New York: The Macmillan Company, 1919), pp. 135-136.

whether he was trying to shoot at me. When he went down he struck the corner of the bar with his head. It was not a case in which one could afford to take chances, and if he had moved I was about to drop on his ribs with my knees; but he was senseless. I took away his guns, and the other people in the room, who were now loud in their denunciation of him, hustled him out and put him in a shed. I got dinner as soon as possible, sitting in a corner of the dining-room away from the windows, and then went upstairs to bed where it was dark so that there would be no chance of any one shooting at me from the outside. However, nothing happened. When my assailant came to, he went down to the station and left on a freight.

Document 9.7

The American Cowboy Today (1886)

By the 1880s, the impersonal world of big business had made its mark on cattle country. Eastern and European capitalists replaced the individualist cattle kings of the post-Civil War era, and the cattle trade became an industry, rapidly transformed by outside investment and the introduction of refrigeration in 1881.*

The cow-boy of to-day, especially on the northern ranges, is of entirely different type from the original cow-boy of Texas. New conditions have produced the change. The range cattle business of Kansas, Nebraska, Colorado, Wyoming, Montana, and Dakota is, as already stated, a new business. Those engaged in it as proprietors are chiefly from the States situated east of the Missouri River and north of the Indian Territory. Among them are also many Englishmen, Scotchmen, Frenchmen, and Germans of large means, embracing titled men who have embarked in the business quite extensively. Many of these came to America originally as tourists or for the purpose of hunting buffaloes, but the attractiveness of the cattle business arrested them, and they have become virtually, if not through the act of naturalization, American herds-men. Some of this class have, from the force of romantic temperament and the exhilaration of range life, themselves participated actively in the duties of the cow-boy.

Organization, discipline, and order characterize the new undertakings on the northern ranges. In a word, the cattle business of that section is now and has from the beginning been carried on upon strictly business principles. Under such proprietorships, and guided by such methods, a new class of cow-boys has been introduced and developed. Some have come from Texas, and have brought with them a knowledge of the arts of their calling, but the number from the other States and the Territories

* Joseph Nimmo, Jr., "The American Cow-Boy," *Harper's New Monthly Magazine,* (November, 1886), 883

constitutes a large majority of the whole. Some are graduates of American colleges, and others of collegiate institutions in Europe. Many have resorted to the occupation of cowboy temporarily and for the purpose of learning the range cattle business, with the view of eventually engaging in it on their own account, or in the interest of friends desirous of investing money in the enterprise.

Document 9.8

The Death of Belle Starr, the Bandit Queen (1889)

The outlaw Belle Starr (1848-1889) was born Myra Belle Shirley near Carthage, Missouri. One of the most remarkable women in western lore, Starr rose to prominence as the "bandit queen," leading a gang of cattle and horse thieves. Starr cut quite a figure in the Indian Territory in the 1880s, dressed in velvet skirts and plumed skirts astride her mare, Venus. In 1883 she became one of the first women to be convicted in the court of the "Hanging Judge" Isaac Parker at Fort Smith, Arkansas. The following passage is from a dime novel, purporting to be an account of Starr's murder in 1889. In reality, she was indeed ambushed from behind while on her way home, but no one was ever convicted for the crime. Some blamed her neighbor Watson, others pointed the finger at her own son.*

The Bandit Queen had gone to McAlister, in the Choctaw Nation, to spend Christmas and New Years, and it was only four days after her return to the Bend when the news of her death reached Eufaula. Her murder was one of the most dastardly acts ever committed. There are various versions of the tragedy, but the following, furnished to the papers by her husband, Bill July, is probably correct:

"Last Saturday I started from home to Fort Smith, and Bella accompanied me as far as San Bois. Here we remained over night, and on Saturday morning Bella started back home, while I came on to Fort Smith. About 3 o'clock Sunday afternoon Bella took dinner at the house of Jack Rose, two miles from her home. When she rode up to the house several men were sitting around in the yard, among them E. A. Watson, whose home was about 150 yards away. A few minutes after Bella arrived Watson left the crowd and went home. About half an hour after he left Bella mounted her horse and started, the road leading around the field of Watson. As she turned the corner at the back of the field her assassin was inside of the fence, where she must have seen him, as there

---

* *Bella Starr, the Bandit Queen, or the Female Jesse James,* (New York: Richard K. Fox, Publisher, 1889), pp. 62-64.

were no bushes or trees to conceal his person. After she had passed by he shot her in the back with a load of buckshot, knocking her from her horse. He then jumped over the fence, and as she lay prostrate in the mud he fired a load of buckshot into her side, neck and face, and the frightened animal she was riding dashed off home, where he was caught by Bella's daughter, Pearl, who immediately mounted him and set out to see what had befallen her mother, and soon arrived at the spot where she lay in the throes of death. She spoke two or three words to the girl and expired. I arrived home Tuesday afternoon, and learning the above facts, caused the arrest of Watson. We tracked him from his house to the spot where he murdered Bella, saw where he jumped over the fence and shot her the second time, and then tracked him by a circuitous route to his house. He is now wearing the same shoes he had on when he murdered my wife."

Being asked what motive Watson had for committing the dastardly act, he said:

"I don't know further than the fact that they had a falling out sometime previous about Watson getting her mail from the office, and I believe Bella knew more about him than he cared to be divulged. He had been living there fourteen months, and came from Florida. I think he was a fugitive from justice, and knowing her reputation for friendship to outlaws, he had divulged to her his true character, and having incurred her dislike, he murdered her. This is my theory of the cause."

Watson is confined in the jail at Fort Smith awaiting trial, and will undoubtedly undergo a rigorous sentence should he be found guilty.

Mrs. Sherley, mother of the Bandit Queen, who resides in Dallas, Texas, is now in the Younger Bend looking after her granddaughter, Pearl, whom, it is to be hoped, will not follow in the footsteps of her unfortunate mother.

Document 9.9

Nat Love, Alias Deadwood Dick (1907)

Recent evidence suggests that one in seven cowboys was African-American during the years following the Civil War. Other estimates indicate that perhaps one-third of the cowboys were either African-American or Hispanic. Many of them were ex-slaves from Texas ranches, while others had come west to escape the Black Codes and oppressive local Southern governments.One of the best-known African-American cowboys was Nat Love (1854-1907?). Love was born in a Tennessee slave cabin, and following the Civil War headed west, where he apparently found race to be no barrier. For more than a generation he worked on Texas cattle drives to Kansas. In 1907 he published his autobiography chronicling his frontier exploits. According to one authority, Love wanted to be accepted as the prototype of the famous dime novel hero "Deadwood Dick," hence the subtitle of his book. In his book he claimed to be scarred by fourteen bullet wounds and to have met most of the western folk heroes of the nineteenth century. In fact his autobiography often reads like a dime novel, with little insight into the black West, leading the noted authority Ramon Adams to suggest that Love "either has a bad memory or a good imagination." By 1890 Love had traded in his horse and saddle for a position as a Pullman car porter, one of the few opportunities available for an African-American man in the West. In the following passage "Deadwood Dick," visits Dodge City and meets up with the noted western lawman Bat Masterson, before introducing the reader to his acquaintances Buffalo Bill and Jesse James.*

In the spring of 1877, now fully recovered from the effects of the very serious wounds I had received at the hands of the Indians and feeling my old self again, I joined the boys in their first trip of the season, with a herd of cattle for Dodge City. The trip was uneventful until we reached our destination. This was the first time I had been in Dodge City since I had won the name of "DEADWOOD DICK", and many of the boys, who knew me when I first joined the cow boys there in 1869, were there to greet me now. After our herd had been delivered to their new owners, we started out to properly celebrate the event, and for a space of several days we kept the old town on the jump.

And so when we finally started for home all of us had more or less of the bad whiskey of Dodge City under our belts and were feeling rather spirited and ready for anything.

I probably had more of the bad whiskey of Dodge City than any one and was in consequence feeling very reckless, but we had about exhausted our resources of amusement in the town, and so were looking for trouble on the trail home.

On our way back to Texas, our way led past old Fort Dodge. Seeing the soldiers and the cannon in the fort, a bright idea struck me, but a fool one just the same. It was no less than a desire to rope one of the cannons. It seemed to me that it would be a good thing to rope a cannon and take it back to Texas with us to fight Indians with.

The bad whiskey which I carried under my belt was responsible for the fool idea, and gave me the nerve to attempt to execute the idea. Getting my lariat rope ready I rode to a position just opposite the gate of the fort, which was standing open. Before the gate paced a sentry with his gun on his shoulder and his white gloves showing up clean and white against the dusty grey surroundings. I waited until the sentry had passed the gate, then putting spurs to my horse I dashed straight for and through the gate into the yard. The surprised sentry called halt, but I paid no attention to him. Making for the cannon at full speed my rope left my hand and settled square over the cannon, then turning and putting spurs to my horse I tried to drag the cannon after me, but strain as he might my horse was unable to budge it an inch. In the meantime the surprised sentry at the gate had given the alarm and now I heard the bugle sound, boots and saddles, and glancing around I saw the soldiers mounting to come after me, and finding I could not move the cannon, I

---

* Nat Love, *The Life and Adventures of Nat Love, Better Known in the Cattle Country as "Deadwood Dick"*, (Los Angeles, 1907), pp. 106-109; 156-157.

rode close up to it and got my lariat off then made for the gate again at full speed. The guard jumped in front of me with his gun up, calling halt, but I went by him like a shot, expecting to hear the crack of his musket, but for some reason he failed to fire on me, and I made for the open prairie with the cavalry in hot pursuit.

My horse could run like a wild deer, but he was no match for the big, strong, fresh horses of the soldiers and they soon had me. Relieving me of my arms they placed me in the guard house where the commanding officer came to see me. He asked me who I was and what I was after at the fort. I told him and then he asked me if I knew anyone in the city. I told him I knew Bat Masterson. He ordered two guards to take me to the city to see Masterson. As soon as Masterson saw me he asked me what the trouble was, and before I could answer, the guards told him I rode into the fort and roped one of the cannons and tried to pull it out. Bat asked me what I wanted with a cannon and what I intended doing with it. I told him I wanted to take it back to Texas with me to fight the Indians with; then they all laughed. Then Bat told them that I was all right, the only trouble being that I had too much bad whiskey under my shirt. They said I would have to set the drinks for the house. They came to $15.00, and when I started to pay for them, Bat said for me to keep my money that he would pay for them himself, which he did. Bat said that I was the only cowboy that he liked, and that his brother Jim also thought very much of me. I was then let go and I joined the boys and we continued on our way home, where we arrived safely on the 1st of June, 1877.

Some men I met in the cattle country are now known to the world as the baddest of bad men, yet I have seen these men perform deeds of valor, self sacrifice and kindness that would cause the deeds recorded as performed by gentlemen in "ye olden time when knighthood was in flower" to look insignificant in comparison, and yet these men lay no claim to the title of gentlemen. They were just plain men.

It was my pleasure to meet often during the early seventies the man who is now famous in the old world and the new world, Buffalo Bill (William F. Cody), cowboy, ranger, hunter, scout and showman, a man who carried his life in his hands day and night in the wild country where duty called, and has often bluffed the grim reaper Death to a standstill, and is living now, hale, hearty and famous.

Others who are equally famous but in another way are the James brothers, Jesse and Frank. I met them often in the old days on the range, and became very well acquainted with them and many others of their band. Their names are recorded in history as the most famous robbers of the new world, but to us cowboys of the cattle country who knew them well, they were true men, brave, kind, generous and considerate, and while they were robbers and bandits, yet what they took from the rich they gave to the poor. The James brothers band stole thousands of dollars; yet Jesse was a poor man when he fell a victim to the bullet of a cowardly, traitorous assassin, and Frank James is a poor man today. What then did they do with the thousands they stole? The answer is simple, they gave it away to those who were in need. That is why they had so many friends and the officers of the law found it so hard to capture them.

And if they were robbers, by what name are we to call some of the great trusts, corporations and brokers, who have for years been robbing the people of this country, some of them, I am glad to say, are now behind prison bars, still others are even now piling up the dollars that they have been and are still stealing from the American people, and who on account of these same dollars are looked up to, respected and are honored members of society, and the only difference between them and the James brothers is that the James brothers stole from the rich and gave to the poor, while these respected members of society steal from the poor to make the rich richer, and which of them think you reader, will get the benefit of the judgment when the final day arrives and all men appear before the great white throne in final judgment?

Jessie James was a true man, a loving son and husband, true to his word, true to his principles and true to his comrads and his friends. I had the pleasure of meeting Frank James quite recently on the road while he was en route to the coast with his theatrical company and enjoyed a pleasant chat with him. He knew me and recalled many incidents of the old days and happenings in "no man's land."

10

New Western Politics

The late nineteenth century was a volatile era in American politics. The 1890s was a transitional era as the nation was transformed into the leading industrial power in the world. This transformation was accompanied by labor and agrarian unrest, and the woman suffrage and temperance movements. Racial and ethnic discrimination found its most reprehensible expression in the Chinese Exclusion Act passed in 1882. By the turn of the new century the eccentric poet Joaquin Miller, and James D. Phelan, the mayor of San Francisco, had reopened the very public debate over the question of Chinese immigration.

The campaign for woman suffrage was several decades old in the East by the time its first Western proponents hit the lecture circuit. In 1868 Laura Deforce Gordon delivered a speech on the issue in San Francisco, and the following year Anna Dickinson and Redelia Bates embarked on lecture tours from Colorado and Wyoming to California on behalf of extending the franchise to women. Much to the surprise of their Eastern counterparts, the first significant legislation granting voting rights to women was passed in the West when in 1869 the Wyoming Territory granted suffrage to women.

By 1896 four Western mountain states—Utah, Wyoming, Idaho, and Colorado, were the only woman suffrage states in the nation. A variety of explanations have been offered to explain this phenomenon. Some authorities have argued that Western men were more chivalrous and egalitarian than other men or that Western men were rewarding their female partners for their sacrifices and endurance. Others contended that extending woman suffrage was an attempt to attract more women to the West or even an attempt by Mormons in Utah to demonstrate to their critics in Congress that their women were not mere slaves but were capable of free will. There is no easy explanation for the success of woman suffrage, with motivations varying widely in these four Western states as well as the states and territories that did not pass suffrage legislation.

A series of farming booms came to a crashing halt in a region extending from the Dakotas down through Nebraska, Kansas, and Texas. The collapse triggered the creation of the People's Party, a designation that would lead to the derivation "Populism." During the 1890s the Populist Party grew into the most significant third-party movement of its time. Primarily rooted in the agricultural regions of the South and the West, many historians saw it as the culmination of several decades of agrarian unrest resulting from what Frederick Jackson Turner described as the closing of the frontier.

Politically, Populism was more successful on the state level in the South, however it still remained a force to be reckoned with in the West, sending two Western senators to Congress. In 1892 a national meeting of the party faithful convened at Omaha, Nebraska, which culminated in the Populist platform calling for changes that would benefit the nation's afflicted farmers. Crucial to the Populist cause was the notion that it was the duty of the government "to protect the weak from the oppression of the strong," in this case the railroads and big business. In the end the Populists saw few victories, but many of the planks in their platform would come to fruition during the Progressive era.

Labor union organizing came early to the mining camps of the American West, with the first miners' union appearing in Virginia City, Nevada, in 1863. By the 1890s, relations between organized labor and management had disintegrated into a protracted struggle that resulted in numerous incidents involving lethal violence. Years of bombings, shootings, and anti-union oppression caused rancor to run deep on both sides. In one of the more notorious examples of labor violence, and as a measure of how deep animosity toward the mine owners ran on the union side, former Idaho governor Frank Steunenberg, whose involvement in the clash between between the Western Federation of Miners and the miners had been deeply resented while he was governor, was assassinated in 1905, despite the fact that he was years removed from office.

With the dawning of the twentieth century, the West was undergoing growing pains along with the rest of the nation. One of the West's greatest strengths and sources of vitality has always been its multicultural population. With Chinese, Japanese, and African-American newcomers joining the hundreds of different native cultures, including Mexicans, and Mexican Americans, the West seemed as much a melting pot as the East. Always a source of artistic inspiration, the poets confronted the racial problems better than the politicians. Walt Whitman suggested that Hispanic culture would exert an enormous impact on America in the future, while Joaquin Miller noted that San Francisco's rise to prominence was in part due to the Chinese, who were now legally barred from entering the United States. These authors recognized, in the face of great opposition, that the heterogeneous nature of American society was its greatest strength.

Suggestions for Further Reading

Sucheng Chan, et al., eds. *Peoples of Color in the American West* (Lexington, Mass.: D.C. Heath and Company, 1994).

Ruth Barnes Moynihan, *Rebel for Rights: Abigail Scott Duniway* (New Haven: Yale University Press, 1983).

Walter K. Nugent, *The Tolerant Populists: Kansas Populism and Nativism* (Chicago: University of Chicago Press, 1963).

Ronald Takaki, *Strangers from a Different Shore: A History of Asian Americans* (Boston: Little, Brown and Company, 1989).

Mark Wyman, *Hard Rock Epic: Western Miners and the Industrial Revolution, 1860-1910* (Berkeley: University of California Press).

Critical Thinking

1. According to the Omaha Platform, what did western Populists hope to gain?

2. How did Carry Nation justify her crusade against alcohol consumption?

3. What rights did women enjoy in Wyoming that were off limits to them in the rest of the country?

4. Discuss both sides of the Chinese exclusion issue.

5. How did sentiments vary among westerners in regard to Chinese and Japanese immigration? Were they more favorably disposed toward one group over the other? If so, why?

Document 10.1

The Omaha Platform of the Populist Party (1892)

During the 1880s and 1890s, farmers in the Great Plains, the South, and the Far West faced desperate economic circumstances. Farm production often outpaced demand, which led to steadily falling crop prices. Millions of farmers had a difficult, if not impossible, time making ends meet. Income all too often was insufficient to cover expenses. In searching for culprits, they focused on eastern banks and railroads, which farmers felt exploited poor people. As a solution, many farmers joined the Populist Party, a third political party designed to compete with the Democrats and the Republicans. The following document provides a description of Populist demands in the presidential election of 1892.*

The Omaha Platform

Preamble

The conditions which surround us best justify our cooperation; we meet in the midst of a nation brought to the verge of moral, political, and material ruin. Corruption dominates the ballot-box, the Legislatures, the Congress, and touches even the ermine of the bench. The people are demoralized; most of the States have been compelled to isolate

---

* Edward Mcpherson, *A Handbook of Politics for 1892* (New York: Da Capo Press, 1894), pp. 183-185

the voters at the polling places to prevent universal intimidation and bribery. The newspapers are largely subsidized or muzzled, public opinion silenced, business prostrated, homes covered with mortgages, labor impoverished, and the land concentrating in the hands of capitalists. The urban workmen are denied the right to organize for self-protection, imported pauperized labor beats down their wages, a hireling standing army, unrecognized by our laws, is established to shoot them down, and they are rapidly degenerating into European conditions. The fruits of the toil of millions are boldly stolen to build up colossal fortunes for a few, unprecedented in the history of mankind and the possessors of these, in turn, despise the Republic and endanger liberty. From the same prolific womb of governmental injustice we breed the two great classes—tramps and millionaires...

Assembled on the anniversary of the birthday of the nation, and filled with the spirit of the grand general and chief who established our independence, we seek to restore the government of the Republic to the hands of the "plain people," with which class it originated. We assert our purposes to be identical with the purposes of the National Constitution; to form a more perfect union and establish justice, insure domestic tranquillity, provide for the common defense, promote the general welfare, and secure the blessings of liberty for ourselves and our posterity...

Platform

We declare, therefore—

First.—That the union of the labor forces of the United States this day consummated shall be permanent and perpetual; may its spirit enter into all hearts for the salvation of the Republic and the uplifting of mankind.

Second.—Wealth belongs to him who creates it, and every dollar taken from industry without an equivalent is robbery. "If any will not work, neither shall he eat." The interests of rural and civil labor are the same; their enemies are identical.

Third.—We believe that the time has come when the railroad corporations will either own the people or the people must own the railroads...

FINANCE.—We demand a national currency, safe, sound, and flexible issued by the general government only, a full legal tender for all debts, public and private...

1. We demand free and unlimited coinage of silver and gold at the present legal ratio of 16 to 1.
2. We demand that the amount of circulating medium be speedily increased to not less than $50 per capita.
3. We demand a graduated income tax.
4. We believe that the money of the country should be kept as much as possible in the hands of the people, and hence we demand that all State and national revenues shall

be limited to the necessary expenses of the government, economically and honestly administered.

5. We demand that postal savings banks be established by the government for the safe deposit of the earnings of the people and to facilitate exchange.

TRANSPORTATION.—Transportation being a means of exchange and a public necessity, the government should own and operate the railroads in the interest of the people. The telegraph and telephone, like the post-office system, being a necessity for the transmission of news, should be owned and operated by the government in the interest of the people.

LAND.—The land, including all the natural sources of wealth, is the heritage of the people, and should not be monopolized for speculative purposes, and alien ownership of land should be prohibited. All land now held by railroads and other corporations in excess of their actual needs. and all lands now owned by aliens should be reclaimed by the government and held for actual settlers only.

Expressions of Sentiments

1. RESOLVED, That we demand a free ballot, and a fair count of all elections, and pledge ourselves to secure it to every legal voter without Federal intervention. through the adoption by the States of the unperverted Australian or secret ballot system.

2. RESOLVED, That the revenue derived from a graduated income tax should be applied to the reduction of the burden of taxation now levied upon the domestic industries of this country.

3. RESOLVED, That we pledge our support to fair and liberal pensions to ex-Union soldiers and sailors.

4. RESOLVED, That we condemn the fallacy of protecting American labor under the present system, which opens our ports to the pauper and criminal classes of the world and crowds out our wage-earners; and we denounce the present ineffective laws against contract labor, and demand the further restriction of undesirable emigration.

5. RESOLVED, That we cordially sympathize with the efforts of organized workingmen to shorten the hours of labor, and demand a rigid enforcement of the existing eight-hour law on Government work, and ask that a penalty clause be added to the said law.

6. RESOLVED, That we regard the maintenance of a large standing army of mercenaries, known as the Pinkerton system, as a menace to our liberties, and we demand its abolition…

7. RESOLVED, That we commend to the favorable consideration of the people and the reform press the legislative system known as the initiative and referendum.

8. RESOLVED, That we favor a constitutional provision limiting the office of President and Vice-President to one term, and providing for the election of Senators of the United States by a direct vote of the people.

9. RESOLVED, That we oppose any subsidy or national aid to any private corporation for any purpose.

Document 10.2

William Jennings Bryan's Cross of Gold Speech (1896)

Known as "The Boy Orator of the Platte," William Jennings Bryan (1860-1925) was the Democratic party candidate for President in 1896. Beginning in 1890, he represented Nebraska for two terms in the House of Representatives. It was during this time that he became a spokesman for western views on the silver issue. Western residents, particularly in the mining states, wanted the federal government to purchase silver without limitations. Vying for the presidency in 1896 as a delegate from Nebraska to the Democratic Convention at Chicago, Bryan delivered his "Cross of Gold" speech, eloquently conveying the injured feelings of the populist West, and heralding the rhetoric of the Sagebrush rebels of the 1980s. This speech led to his nomination on the fifth ballot.

Unfortunately, Bryan's presidential bid ended with his decisive loss to William McKinley, due in no small part to Bryan's single-issue campaign and his inability to reach rural voters outside the West and the South. Bryan continued to harbor presidential aspirations, running again in 1900 and 1908, but to no avail.*

When this debate is concluded, a motion will be made° to lay upon the table the resolution offered in commendation of the Administration, and also, the resolution offered in condemnation of the Administration. We object to bringing this question down to the level of persons. The individual is but an atom; he is born, he acts, he dies; but principles are eternal; and this has been a contest over a principle.

Never before in the history of this country has there been witnessed such a contest as that through which we have just passed. Never before in the history of American politics has a great issue been fought out as this issue has been, by the voters of a great party. On the fourth of March 1893, a few Democrats, most of them members of Congress, issued an address to the Democrats of the nation, asserting that the money question was the paramount issue of the hour; declaring that a majority of the Democratic party had the right to control the action of the party on this paramount issue; and concluding with the request that the believers in the free coinage of silver in the Democratic party should organize, take charge of, and control the policy of the Democratic party. Three months later, at Memphis, an organization was perfected, and the silver Democrats went forth openly and courageously proclaiming their belief, and declaring that, if successful, they would crystallize into a platform the declaration which they had made. Then began the

---

* William Jennings Bryan, *The First Battle*, pp. 199; also *Documents of American History; The Memoirs of William Jennings Bryan*, ch. vi., P. Hibben, *The Peerles Leader: WJB*, ch. 15, 16.

struggle. With a zeal approaching the zeal which inspired the Crusaders who followed Peter the Hermit, our silver Democrats went forth from victory unto victory until they are now assembled, to discuss, not to debate, but to enter up the judgement already rendered by the plain people of this country. In this contest brother has been arrayed against brother, father against son. The warmest ties of love, acquaintance, and association have been disregarded; old leaders have been cast aside when they have refused to give expression to the sentiments of those whom they would lead, and new leaders have sprung up to give direction to this cause of truth. Thus has the contest been waged, and we have assembled here under as binding and solemn instructions as were ever imposed upon representatives the people.

We do not come as individuals. As individuals we might have been glad to compliment the gentleman from New York [Senator Hill], but we know that the people for whom we speak would never be willing to put him in a position where he could thwart the will of the Democratic party. I saw it was not a question of persons; it was a question of principle, and it is not with gladness, my friends, that we find ourselves brought into conflict with those who are now arrayed on the other side...

When you [turning to the gold delegates] come before us and tell us that we are about to disturb your business interests, we reply that you have disturbed our business interests by your course.

We say to you that you have made the definition of a business man too limited in its application. The man who is employed for wages is as much a business man as his employer; the attorney in a country town is as much a business man as the corporation counsel in a great metropolis; the merchant at the cross-roads store is as much a business man as the merchant of New York; the farmer who goes forth in the morning and toils all day, who begins in the spring and toils all summer, and who by the application of brain and muscle to the natural resources of the country creates wealth, is as much a business man as the man who goes upon the Board of Trade and bets upon the price of grain; the miners who go down a thousand feet into the earth, or climb two thousand feet upon the cliffs, and bring forth from their hiding places the precious metals to be poured into the channels of trade are as much business men as the few financial magnates who, in a back room, corner the money of the world. We come to speak of this broader class of business men.

Ah, my friends, we say not one word against those who live upon the Atlantic Coast, but the hardy pioneers who have braved all the dangers of the wilderness, who have made the desert to bloom as the rose—the pioneers away out there [pointing to the West] who rear their children near to Nature's heart, where they can mingle their voices with the voices of the birds-out there where they have erected schoolhouses for the education of their young, churches where they praise their Creator, and cemeteries where rest the ashes of their dead—these people, we say, are as deserving of the consideration of our party as any people in this country. It is for these that we speak. We do not come as aggressors. Our war is not a war of conquest; we are fighting in the defense of our homes, our families, and posterity. We have petitioned, and our petitions have been scorned; we have entreated, and our entreaties have been disregarded; we have begged, and they have mocked when our calamity came. We beg no longer; we entreat no more; we petition no more. We defy them!

The gentleman from Wisconsin [Vilas] has said that he fears a Robespierre. My friends, in this land of the free you need not fear that a tyrant will spring up from among the people. What we need is an Andrew Jackson to stand, as Jackson stood, against the encroachments of organized wealth.

They tell us that this platform was made to catch votes. We reply to them that changing conditions make new issues; that the principles upon which Democracy rests are as everlasting as the hills, but they must be applied to new conditions as they arise. Conditions have arisen, and we are here to meet those conditions. They tell us that the income tax ought not to be brought in here; that it is a new idea. They criticize us for our criticism of the Supreme Court of the United States. My friends, we have not criticized; we have simply called attention to what you already know. If you want criticisms read the dissenting opinions of the court. There you will find criticisms. They say that we passed an unconstitutional law; we deny it. The income tax was not unconstitutional when it was passed; it was not unconstitutional when it went before the Supreme Court for the first time; it did not become unconstitutional until one of the judges changed his mind, and we cannot be expected to know when a judge will change his mind. The income tax is just. It simply intends to put the burden of government justly upon the backs of the people. I am in favor of an income tax. When I find a man who is not willing to bear his share of the burdens of the government which protects him, I find a man who is unworthy to enjoy the blessings of a government like ours.

They say that we are opposing national bank currency; it is true. If you will read what Thomas Benton said, you will find he said that, in searching history, he could find but one parallel to Andrew Jackson; that was Cicero, he destroyed the conspiracy of Cataline and saved Rome. Benton said that Cicero only did for Rome what Jackson did for us when he destroyed the bank conspiracy and saved America. We say in our platform we believe that the right to coin and issue money is a function of government. We believe it. We believe that it is a part of sovereignty, and can no more with safety be delegated to private individuals than we could afford to delegate to private individuals the power to make penal statutes or levy taxes. Mr. Jefferson, who was once regarded as good Democratic authority, seems to have differed in opinion from the gentleman who has addressed us on the part of the minority. Those who are opposed to this proposition tell us that the issue of paper money is a function of the banks, and that the government ought to go out of the banking business. I stand with Jefferson rather than with them, and tell them, as he did, that the issue of money is a function of government, and that the banks ought to go out of the governing business.

They complain about the plank which declares against life tenure in office. They have tried to strain it to mean that which it does not mean. What we oppose by that plank is the life tenure which is being built up in Washington, and which excludes from participation in official benefits the humbler members of society...

And now, my friends, let me come to the paramount issue. If they ask us why it is that we say more on the money question than we say upon the tariff question, I reply that, if protection has slain its thousands, the gold standard has slain its tens of thousands. If they ask us why we do not embody in our platforms all the things that we believe in, we reply that when we have restored the money of the Constitution, all other necessary reform will be possible; but that until this is done, there is no other reform that can be accomplished.

Why is it that within three months such a change has come over the country? Three months ago when it was confidently asserted that those who believed in the gold standard would frame our platform and nominate our candidates, even the advocates of the gold standard did not think that we could elect a President. And they had good reason for their doubt, because there is scarcely a State here today asking for the gold standard which is not in the absolute control of the Republican Party. But note the change Mr. McKinley was nominated at St. Louis upon a platform which declared for the maintenance of the gold standard until it can be changed into bimetallism by international agreement. Mr. McKinley was the most popular man among the Republicans, and three months ago everybody in the Republican Party prophesied his election. How is it today? Why, the man who was once pleased to think that he looked like Napoleon—that man shudders today when he remembers that he was nominated on the anniversary of the battle of Waterloo.

Not only that, but as he listens, he can hear with ever-increasing distinctness the sound of the waves as they beat upon the lonely shores of St. Helena.

Why this change? Ah, my friends, is not the reason for the change evident to any one who will look at the matter? No private character, however pure, no personal popularity, however great, can protect from the avenging wrath of an indignant people a man who will declare that he is in favor of fastening the gold standard upon this country, or who is willing to surrender the right of self-government and place the legislative control of our affairs in the hands of foreign potentates and powers.

We go forth confident that we shall win. Why? Because upon the paramount issue of this campaign there is not a spot of ground upon which the enemy will dare to challenge battle. If they tell us that the gold standard is a good thing, we shall point to their platform and tell them that their platform pledges the party to get rid of the standard and substitute bimetallism. If old standard is a good thing why try to get rid of it? I call your attention to the fact that some of the very people who are in this Convention today and who tell us that we ought to declare in favor of international bimetallism-thereby declaring that the gold standard is wrong and that the principle of bimetallism is better-these very people four months ago were open and avowed advocates of the gold standard, and were then telling us that we could not legislate metals together, even with the aid of all the world. If the gold standard is a good thing, we ought to declare in favor of its retention and not in favor of abandoning it; and if the gold standard is a bad thing why should we wait until other nations are willing to help us to let go? Here is the line of battle, and we care not upon which issue they force the fight; we are prepared to meet them on either issue or on both. If they tell us that the gold standard is the standard of civilization, we reply to them that this, the most enlightened of all the nations of the earth, has never declared for a gold standard and that both the great parties this year are declaring against it. If the gold standard is the standard of civilization, why, my friends, should we not have it? If they come to meet us on that issue we can present the history of our nation. More than that; we can tell them that they will search the pages of history in vain to find a single instance where the common people of any land have ever declared themselves in favor of the gold standard. They can find where the holders of fixed investments have declared for a gold standard, but not where the masses have. Mr. Carlisle said in 1878 that this was a struggle between the "idle holders of idle capital" and "the struggling masses, who produce the wealth and pay the taxes of the country," and, my friends, the question we are to decide is: Upon which side will the Democratic party fight; upon the side of "the idle holders of idle capital" or upon the side of "the struggling masses"? That is the question which the party must answer first, and then it must be answered by each individual hereafter. The sympathies of the Democratic party, as shown by the platform, are on the side of the struggling masses who have ever been the foundation of the Democratic party. There are two ideas of government. There are those who believe that if you will only legislate to make the well-to-do prosperous, their prosperity will leak through on those below. The Democratic idea, however, has been that if you make the masses prosperous, their prosperity will find its way up through every class which rests upon them.

You come to us and tell us that the great cities are in favor of the gold standard; we reply that the great cities rest upon our broad and fertile prairies. Burn down your cities and leave our farms, and your cities will spring up again as if by magic; but destroy our farms and the grass will grow in the streets of every city in the country.

My friends, we declare that this nation is able to legislate for its own people on every question, without waiting for the aid or consent of any other nation on earth; and upon that issue we expect to carry every state in the Union. I shall not slander the inhabitants of the fair state of Massachusetts nor the inhabitants of the state of New York by saying that, when they are confronted with the proposition, they will declare that this nation is not able to attend to its own business. It is the issue of 1776 over again. Our ancestors, when but three million in number, had the courage to declare their political independence of every other nation; shall we, their descendants, when we have grown to seventy millions, declare that we are less independent than our forefathers?

No, my friends, that will never be the verdict of our people. Therefore, we care not upon what lines the battle is fought. If they say bimetallism is good, but that we cannot have it until other nations help us, we reply, that instead of having a gold standard because England has, we will restore bimetallism, and then let England have bimetallism because the United States has it. If they dare to come out in the open field and defend the gold standard as a good thing, we will fight them to the uttermost. Having behind us the producing masses of this nation and the world, supported by the commercial interests, the laboring interests and the toilers everywhere, we will answer their demand for a gold standard by saying to them: You shall not press down upon the brow of labor this crown of thorns, you shall not crucify mankind upon a cross of gold.

Document 10.3

Carry Nation (1889)

With her trademark axe in hand, the temperance leader Carry A. Nation (1846-1911) made national headlines as she busted up bars from

Kansas to Montana. After reaching an epiphany in which she decided that demon rum was responsible for most of the sin in Kansas, Nation embarked on her campaign against the liquor trade. In 1889 she broke up her first saloon in Kiowa, Kansas. Discovering the utility of the hatchet, she conducted what she called her first "hatchetation" in Topeka before heading East, where she achieved even greater notoriety. More an embarrassment than a boon to the temperance movement, there is no question that the six foot, 175-pound Nation instilled fear in saloon owners wherever she went. Jailed and beaten on several occasions, she never wavered from her moral crusade. Several years before her death she published a rambling account of her life. In the following passage she describes her destructive modus operandi.*

The next morning I was awakened by a voice which seemed to be speaking in my heart, these words, "Go to Kiowa," and my hands were lifted and thrown down and the words, "I'll stand by you." The words, "Go to Kiowa," were spoken in a murmuring, musical tone, low and soft, but, "I'll stand by you," was very clear, positive and emphatic. I was impressed with a great inspiration, the interpretation was very plain, it was this: "Take something in your hands, and throw at these places in Kiowa and smash them." I was very much relieved and overjoyed and was determined to be, "obedient to the heavenly vision." Acts 26:19.) I told no one what I heard or what I intended to do.

I was a busy home keeper, did all my house work, was superintendent of two Sunday schools, one in the country, was jail evangelist, and president of the W. C. T. U. and kept open house for all of God's people, where all the Christian workers were welcome to abide at my house.

When no one was looking I would walk out in the yard and pick up brick bats and rocks, would hide them under my kitchen apron, would take them in my room, would wrap them up in newspapers one by one. I did this until I got quite a pile. A very sneaking degenerate druggist in Medicine Lodge named Southworth had for years been selling intoxicating liquors on the sly. I had gotten in his drug store four bottles of Schlitz Malt. I was going to use them as evidence to convict this wiley dive keeper.

One of the bottles I took to a W. C. T. U. meeting and in the presence of the ladies I opened it and drank the contents. Then I had two of them to take me down to a Doctor's office. I fell limp on the sofa and said: "Doctor, what is the matter with me?"

He looked at my eyes, felt my heart and pulse, shook his head and looked grave.

I said: "Am I poisoned?" "Yes, said the Doctor."

I said: "What poisoned me is that beer you recommended Bro. — to take as a tonic." I resorted to this stratagem, to show the effect that beer has upon the system. This Doctor was a kind man and meant well, but it must have been ignorance that made him say beer could ever be used as a medicine.

There was another, Dr. Kocile, in Medicine Lodge who used to sell all the whiskey he could. He made a drunkard of a very prominent woman of the town, who took the Keeley cure. She told the W. C. T. U. of the villainy of this doctor and she could not have

---

* Carry A. Nation, *The Use and Need of the Life of Carry A. Nation*, (Topeka: F.M. Steves & Sons, 1909), pp. 130-135

hated any one more. Oh! the drunkards the doctors are making! No physician, who is worthy of the name will prescribe it as a medicine, for there is not one medical quality in alcohol. It kills the living and preserves the dead. Never preserves anything but death. It is made by a rotting process and it rots the brain, body and soul; it paralyzes the vascular circulation and increases the action of the heart. This is friction and friction in any machinery is dangerous, and the cure is not hastened but delayed.

Any physician that will prescribe whiskey or alcohol as a medicine is either a fool or a knave. A fool because he does not understand his business, for even saying that alcohol does arouse the action of the heart, there are medicines that will do that and will not produce the fatal results of alcoholism, which is the worst of all diseases. He is a knave because his practice is a matter of getting a case, and a fee at the same time, like a machine agent who breaks the machine to get the job of mending it. Alcohol destroys the normal condition of all the functions of the body. The stomach is thrown out of fix, and the patient goes to the doctor for a stomach pill, the heart, liver, kidneys, and in fact, the whole body is in a deranged condition, and the doctor has a perpetual patient. I sincerely believe this to be the reason why many physicians prescribe it.

At half past three that day I was ready to start, hitched up the buggy myself, drove out of the stable, rode down a hill and over a bridge that was just outside the limits of Medicine Lodge. I saw in the middle of the road perhaps a dozen or so creatures in the forms of men leaning towards the buggy as if against a rope which prevented them from coming nearer. Their faces were those of demons and the gestures of their hands as if they would tear me up. I did not know what to do, but I lifted my hands, and my eyes to God, saying: "Oh! Lord, help me, help me." When I looked down these diabolical creatures were not in front of the buggy, but they were off to the right fleeing as if they were terrified. I did not know or think what this meant. My life was so full of strange, peculiar things at that time that I could not understand the meaning. Not for years did I interpret the meaning of this vision. I know now what those creatures were. They were real devils that knew more of what I was going to do than I did. The devil is a prophet, he reads scripture, he knew Jesus when He was here, and he knew that I came to fulfill prophecy, and that this was a death blow to his kingdom.

The peoples' consciences were asleep while these dreadful burglars of saloons were robbing the homes and God had to shock them to rouse them up. God cannot work with a people whose conscience is dead. The devil cannot continue with an awakened conscience. I expected to stay all night with a dear friend, Sister Springer, who lived about half way to Kiowa. When I arrived near her home the sun was almost down, but I was very eager to go to Kiowa and I said: "Oh, Lord, if it is Thy will for me to go to Kiowa tonight, have Price, (my horse,) pass this open gate," which I knew he would never do unless God ordered it. I gave him the reins and when I got opposite the open gate my horse jumped forward as if some one had struck him a blow. I got to Kiowa at half past eight, stayed all night. Next morning I had my horse hitched and drove to the first dive kept by a Mr. Dobson, whose brother was then sheriff of the county. I stacked up these smashers on my left arm, all I could hold. They looked like packages wrapped in paper. I stood before the counter and said: "Mr. Dobson, I told you last spring to close this place, you did not do it, now I have come down with another remonstrance, get out of the way, I do not want to strike you, but I am going to break this place up." I threw as hard, and as fast as I could, smashing mirrors and bottles and glasses and it was astonishing how quickly this was done. These men seemed terrified, threw up their hands and backed up in the corner. My strength was that of a giant. I felt invincible. God was certainly standing by me.

I will tell you of a very strange thing. As the stones were flying against this "wonderful and horrible" thing, I saw Mr. McKinley, the President, sitting in an old fashion arm chair and as the stones would strike I saw them hit the chair and the chair fell to pieces, and I saw Mr. McKinley fall over. I did not understand this until very recently, now I know that the smashing in Kansas was intended to strike the head of this nation the hardest blow, for every saloon I smashed in Kansas had a license from the head of this government which made the head of the government more responsible than the dive-keeper. I broke up three of these dives that day, broke the windows on the outside to prove that the man who rents his house is a partner also with the man who sells. The party who licenses and the paper that advertises, all have a hand in this and are *particeps criminis*. I smashed five saloons with rocks, before I ever took a hatchet.

In the last place, kept by Lewis, there was quite a young man behind the bar. I said to him: "Young man, come from behind that bar, your mother did not raise you for such a place." I threw a brick at the mirror, which was a very heavy one, and it did not break, but the brick fell and broke everything in its way. I began to look around for something that would break it. I was standing by a billiard table on which there was one ball. I said: "Thank God," and picked it up, threw it, and it made a hole in the mirror.

By this time, the streets were crowded with people; most of them seemed to look puzzled. There was one boy about fifteen years old who seemed perfectly wild with joy, and he jumped, skipped and yelled with delight. I have since thought of that as being a significant sign. For to smash saloons will save the boy.

I stood in the middle of the street and spoke in this way: "I have destroyed three of your places of business, and if I have broken a statute of Kansas, put me in jail; if I am not a law-breaker your mayor and councilmen are. You must arrest one of us, for if I am not a criminal, they are."

Document 10.4

Woman Suffrage, Wyoming (1889)

Between 1869 and 1871, almost every legislature in the United States took up the subject of woman suffrage. However, out of all the states and legislatures considering the question during this era, only the Wyoming and Utah territories actually passed suffrage legislation. This can be partially explained by the disparity between state and territory voting regulations. Compared to a territory, where women could be granted suffrage merely by a simple majority vote of the legislature with the approval of the governor, in a state, a constitutional amendment was first required, which involved a two-thirds vote of the legislature and a majority vote of the electors. The successful campaign for woman's suffrage in Wyoming culminated in a suffrage victory on December 10, 1869. The following passage suggests that the fewer than two thousand women in this sparsely populated territory enjoyed political rights and practiced them responsibly.*

For a number of years women served on grand and petit juries. In compiling the first volume of the Laws of Wyoming, Secretary and Acting Governor Edward M. Lee said:

In the provisions of the woman suffrage clause, enacted in 1869, we placed this youngest Territory on earth in the van of civilization and progress. That this statement has been verified by practical experience the testimony is unanimous, continuous and conclusive. Not a link is wanting in the chain of evidence and, as a Governor of the Territory once said: "The only dissenting voices against woman suffrage have been those of convicts who have been tried and found guilty by women jurors." Women exercised the right of jurors and contributed to the speedy release of the Territory from the régime of the pistol and bowie-knife. They not only performed their new duties without losing any of the womanly virtues, and with dignity and decorum, but good results were immediately seen. Chief Justice J. H. Howe, of the Supreme Court, under whose direction women were first drawn on juries, wrote in 1872: "After the grand jury had been in session two days the dance-house keepers, gamblers and *demi-monde* fled out of the State in dismay to escape the indictment of women jurors. In short, I have never, in twenty-five years' experience in the courts of the country, seen a more faithful and resolutely honest grand and petit jury than these."

The best women in the Territory served as jurors, and they were treated with the most profound respect and highly complimented for their efficiency. The successor of Chief Justice Howe was opposed to their serving and none were summoned by him. Jury duty is not acceptable to men, as a rule, and the women themselves were not anxious for it, so the custom gradually fell into disuse. The juries are made up from the tax lists, which contain only a small proportion of women. There are no court decisions against women as jurors, and they are still summoned occasionally in special cases.

Women have not taken a conspicuous part in politics. The population is scattered, there are no large cities and necessarily no great associations of women for organized work. They are conscientious in voting for men who, in their opinion, have the best interests of the community at heart. More latitude must necessarily be permitted in new States, but in 1900 they decided that it was time to call a halt on the evil of gambling, and as the result of their efforts a law was passed by the present Legislature (1901) forbidding it. The Chicago *Tribune* gave a correct summing-up of this matter in the following editorial:

* Susan B. Anthony and Ida Husted Harper, eds., *The History of Woman Suffrage, Vol. IV.*, (Rochester, NY.: Susan B. Anthony, 1902), pp. 1008-1011.

The women of Wyoming are to be credited with securing one reform which is a sufficient answer, in that State at least, to the criticism that woman suffrage has no influence upon legislation and fails to elevate political action. There will be no legalized gambling in Wyoming after the first of January next, the Legislature having just passed a law which makes gambling of every kind punishable by fine and imprisonment after the above date.

This has been the work of the women. When they began their agitation about a year and a half ago, gambling was not only permitted but was licensed. The evil was so strongly entrenched and the revenue accruing to the State so large that there was little hope at first that anything would be accomplished. The leaders of the crusade, however, organized their forces skillfully in every town and village. Their petitions for the repeal of the gambling statute and for the passage of a prohibitory act were circulated everywhere, and were signed by thousands of male as well as female voters. When the Legislature met, the women were there in force, armed with their voluminous petitions. The gamblers also were there in force and sought to defeat the women by the use of large sums of money, but womanly tact and persuasion and direct personal appeals carried the day against strong opposition. The Legislature passed the bill, but it was the women who won the victory.

Document 10.5

Why the Chinese Should be Excluded (1901)

Following the passage of the Chinese Exclusion Act of 1901, Ho Yow, the Imperial Chinese Consul-General wrote to the influential *North American Review*, inquiring whether exclusion was a benefit or harm, reopening a debate on this issue. His inquiry provoked a response by James D. Phelan, the mayor of San Francisco. According to Phelan the question at hand was not wholly labor or race related. However, his polemic suggests that it had everything to do with these issues.*

I contend that this is not a mere labor question, nor a race question. It is an American question, affecting the perpetuity of our institutions and the standard of our civilization. But let us examine Ho Yow's allegations of fact.

For the most part the Chinese who have so far come to this country do menial work and manual labor; but they also extensively engage in skilled employments. They work on railroads, in mines, in fields and orchards and forests, crowding out the white laborer

* James D. Phelan, "Why the Chinese Should be Excluded," *The North American Review*, DXL (November 1901), pp. 667-669

everywhere on account of their willingness to work for a smaller wage. That is the experience of the West. As mere laborers, there is little to complain of in them; but for all purposes of citizenship their usefulness ends with their day's work; and whatever they are paid, they are paid too much, because they make no contribution by service or citizenship or family life to the permanent interests of the country.

The Chinese are to the last degree imitative. They have taken up the skilled work of our white population, and mechanically duplicate it. They are makers of cigars, shoes, shirts, clothing, women's underwear, overalls, children's clothes; they have acquired skill in dentistry and photography; they engage in journalism, commercial electricity, watchmaking, painting, brick-laying; they are carpenters, broom-makers, butchers, and in the culinary arts they particularly excel, supplanting white domestic servants.

In most of these trades and vocations they have unions which are well known in San Francisco. The Hong Tuck Tong, or Cigarmakers' Union, contains 1,500 members, who are employed throughout California. The Shoemakers' Union has 1,000 members. In Chinatown, San Francisco, evidences of their skilled labor are everywhere seen; and in the business streets of the city proper they have opened numerous stores in their own names, in which they sell their own products and especially women's and children's underwear. White sewing girls have been driven out of employment; and recently, on the advice of a large dealer in dry goods who promised support, a philanthropic gentleman assisted in the establishment of a factory for the employment of white girls exclusively, under the charge of a competent superintendent. After a few months' trial it failed, on account of the impossibility of meeting Chinese competition. The Chinese work day and night without cessation, subsisting on the most meagre food, and it is physically impossible for white women to turn out goods that will sell against Chinese prices in the open market. This is a very serious phase of the labor question on account of the small number of the fields in which women may profitably work.

Fruit canneries throughout California give employment to boys and young women; but next door to the Consulate occupied by Ho Yow in San Francisco there is an extensive cannery, which is owned and operated by Chinese. They run the steam engines, they handle the cans and boxes made by Chinese boxmakers and carpenters; they pack the fruit; their tinsmith solders the cans. It has been known that when they are short of Chinese labor they employ white boys and girls, who work under conditions and amidst surroundings which deprive labor of a great part of its dignity...

It is vain, therefore, to claim that Chinese are "mere laborers or agriculturists."

One thing certain is that when they come to this country they know little else than manual labor; but they soon acquire a skill which enables them to compete with the trained American workingman. The Chinese in any considerable numbers are, consequently, a great potential danger to skilled labor.

Document 10.6

The Chinese and the Exclusion Act (1901)

The eccentric poet Joaquin Miller (1839-1911) returned to San Francisco in 1886, following twenty years of wanderlust to find a city transformed since the heady days of the 1849 gold rush. His was a lone voice in the wilderness railing against the Chinese Exclusion Act. In the following excerpt, Miller implores California to reconsider its Chinese policy, arguing that the Chinese were in part responsible for the ascension of San Francisco to national prominence.*

Do the real proprietors of the Pacific coast, the owners of property and the taxpayers, want the Chinese with us? They do, almost without exception, and it would be strange if they did not; for, since the exclusion of the Chinese, property in our largest cities has, in the main, been at a standstill. And behold! our chiefest city, San Francisco, has slid back from its proud place as the seventh city in the Union to that of the ninth! Of course, if we had excluded all other foreigners along with the Chinese, we might have held our own, perhaps advanced as at the first; but these remaining foreigners have kept up such a turmoil that capital, always very sensitive, has been afraid to come and in many cases has moved out, and moved out to stay...

One word more about these "degraded" foreigners. They are, all their hundreds of millions of them, the best educated people in the world. They, as a rule, spend just about twice as much time at school as the Americans. They, perhaps, learn more than twice as much; but, unfortunately for them, their lessons are all of the past. They know little of the present and trust their future entirely to the just precepts of Confucius, however antique and impracticable these may be. A child is taken to school almost as soon as it is big enough to walk, and it stays there ten hours in the day, seven days in the week and ten months in the year.

* Joaquin Miller, "The Chinese and the Exclusion Act," *North American Review,* (December 1901), pp. 783-786

Document 10.7

Harry Orchard, Labor Union Assassin (1905)

In 1896 Frank Steunenberg (1861-1905) was elected governor of the state of Idaho. Labor trouble between the Western Federation of Miners and mine owners frustrated the last two years of his administration. Conflict in the mining region of Coeur d'Alene was especially violent. Responding to the striking miners, Steunenberg called for Federal troops and proclaimed martial law in 1899. Following his retirement, Steunenberg embarked on a successful business career before being targeted for assassination by the Western Federation of Miners. On December 30, 1905, the ex-governor opened a gate outside his home, detonating a bomb. He died several hours later. In the ensuing rush to judgement a hired killer and member of the Western Federation of Miners, Albert E. Horsley (1866-1954), working under the alias Harry Orchard, was captured by a Pinkerton detective. Orchard was sentenced to hang, a sentence later commuted to life imprisonment. He would die in prison in 1954 at the age of eighty-eight. The following excerpts detailing his exploits as a hired assassin and explosives expert are taken from his autobiography.*

I did not see Mr. Steunenberg again until the next Thursday. I did not know where he went when he was away, and I saw his son on the street one day, and I spoke to him and asked him if they had any sheep to sell. I thought I would find out this way where his father went. He told me that he knew nothing about it, as his father attended to that, but he said I could find out by telephoning to his father at the company ranch at Bliss. But he said he would be home the next day, and I could see him if I was there. I told him I just wanted to find out where some sheep could be bought, as a friend of mine wanted them to feed.

The next day, Friday, I went to Nampa and thought I might get a chance to put the bomb under Governor Steunenberg's seat, if I found him on the train, as the train usually stops fifteen to twenty minutes at Nampa. I had taken the powder out of the wooden box, and packed it in a little, light, sheet-iron box with a lock on, and I had a hole cut in the top of this and a little clock on one side. Both this and the bottle of acid were set in plaster [of] Paris on the other side of the hole from the clock, with a wire from the key which winds the alarm to the cork in the bottle. The giant-caps were put in the powder underneath this hole, and all I had to do was to wind up the alarm and set it and, when it went off, it would wind up the fine wire on the key, and pull out the cork, and spill the

---

* Albert E. Horsley, *The Confessions and Autobiography of Harry Orchard,* (New York: The McClure Company, 1907), pp. 129, 135-136, 197-198, 216-218.

acid on the caps. I had this fitted in a little grip and was going to set it, grip and all, under his seat in the coach, if I got a chance. I went through the train when it arrived at Nampa, but did not see Mr. Steunenberg, and the train was crowded, so I would not have had any chance, anyway. I saw Mr. Steunenberg get off the train at Caldwell, but missed him on the train.

I saw him again around Caldwell Saturday afternoon. I was playing cards in the saloon at the Saratoga, and came out in the hotel lobby at just dusk, and Mr. Steunenberg was sitting there talking. I went over to the post-office and came right back, and he was still there. I went up to my room and took this bomb out of my grip and wrapped it up in a newspaper and put it under my arm and went downstairs, and Mr. Steunenberg was still there. I hurried as fast as I could up to his residence, and laid this bomb close to the gate-post, and tied a cord into a screw-eye in the cork and around a picket of the gate, so when the gate was opened, it would jerk the cork out of the bottle and let the acid run out and set off the bomb. This was set in such a way, that if he did not open the gate wide enough to pull it out, he would strike the cord with his feet, as he went to pass in. I pulled some snow over the bomb after laying the paper over it, and hurried back as fast as I could.

I met Mr. Steunenberg about two and a half blocks from his residence. I then ran as fast as I could, to get back to the hotel if possible before he got to the gate. I was about a block and a half from the hotel on the foot-bridge when the explosion of the bomb occurred, and I hurried to the hotel as fast as I could. I went into the bar-room, and the bartender was alone, and asked me to help him tie up a little package, and I did, and then went up to my room, intending to come right down to dinner, as nearly everyone was in at dinner.

Document 10.8

Boley: A Negro Town in the West (1905)

After the Civil War and Reconstruction, large numbers of recently emancipated African Americans pulled up stakes in the South and headed West, where they hoped to achieve exactly what millions of white settlers wanted: the acquisition of land of their own. Out West, they would build their homes and reinvent themselves in a free society. Thousands of African Americans settled in the Indian territory of what is today Oklahoma. Boley was one of the African-American settlements there. In the following essay, the prominent African-American leader Booker T. Washington recounts his visit to the town of Boley.*

---

* Booker T. Washington, "Boley, A Negro Town in the West," *Outlook,* (January 4, 1908).

In 1905, when I visited Indian Territory, Boley was little more than a name. It was started in 1903. At the present time it is a thriving town of 2,500 inhabitants, with two banks, two cotton gins, a newspaper, a hotel, and a "college," the Creek-Seminole College and Agricultural Institute.

There is a story told in regard to the way in which the town of Boley was started, which, even if it is not wholly true as to the details, is at least characteristic, and illustrates the temper of the people in that region.

One spring day, four years ago, a number of gentlemen were discussing, at Wilitka, the race question. The point at issue was the capability of the negro for self-government. One of the gentlemen, who happened to be connected with the Fort Smith Railway, maintained that if the negroes were given a fair chance they would prove themselves as capable of self-government as any other people of the same degree of culture and education. He asserted that they had never had a fair chance. The other gentlemen naturally asserted the contrary. The result of the argument was Boley. Just at that time a number of other town sites were being laid out along the railway which connects Guthrie, Oklahoma, with Fort Smith, Arkansas. It was, it is said, to put the capability of the negro for self-government to the test that in August, 1903, seventy-two miles east of Guthrie, the site of the new negro town was established. It was called Boley, after the man who built that section of the railway. A negro town-site agent, T. M. Haynes, who is at present connected with the Farmers' and Merchants' Bank, was made Town-site Agent, and the purpose to establish a town which should be exclusively controlled by negroes was widely advertised all over the Southwest.

Boley, although built on the railway, is still on the edge of civilization. You can still hear on summer nights, I am told, the wild notes of the Indian drums and the shrill cries of the Indian dancers among the hills beyond the settlement. The outlaws that formerly infested the country have not wholly disappeared. Dick Shafer, the first town marshal of Boley, was killed in a duel with a horse thief, whom he in turn shot and killed, after falling, mortally wounded, from his horse. The horse thief was a white man.

There is no liquor sold in Boley, or any part of the Territory, but the "natives" go down to Prague, across the Oklahoma border, ten miles away, and then come back and occasionally "shoot up" the town. That was a favorite pastime, a few years ago, among the "natives" around Boley. The first case that came up before the mayor for trial was that of a young "native" charged with "shooting up" a meeting in a church. But, on the whole, order in the community has been maintained. It is said that during the past two years not a single arrest has been made among the citizens. The reason is that the majority of these negro settlers have come there with the definite intention of getting a home and building up a community where they can, as they say, be "free." What this expression means is pretty well shown by the case of C. W. Perry, who came from Marshall, Texas. Perry had learned the trade of a machinist and had worked in the railway machine shops until the white machinists struck and made it so uncomfortable that the negro machinists went out. Then he went on the railway as brakeman, where he worked for fifteen years. He owned his own home and was well respected, so much so that when it became known that he intended to leave, several of the county commissioners called on him. "Why are you going away?" they asked; "you have your home here among us. We know you and you know us. We are behind you and will protect you."

"Well," he replied, "I have always had an ambition to do something for myself. I don't want always to be led. I want to do a little leading."

Other immigrants, like Mr. T. R. Ringe, the mayor, who was born a slave in Kentucky, and Mr. E. L. Lugrande, one of the principal stockholders in the new bank, came out in the new country, like so many of the white settlers, merely to get land. Mr. Lugrande came from Denton County, Texas, where he had 418 acres of land. He had purchased this land some years ago for four and five dollars the acre. He sold it for fifty dollars an acre, and, coming to Boley, he purchased a tract of land just outside of town and began selling town lots. Now a large part of his acreage is in the center of the town.

Mr. D. J. Turner, who owns a drugstore and has an interest in the Farmers' and Merchants' Bank, came to Indian Territory as a boy, and has grown up among the Indians, to whom he is in a certain way related, since he married an Indian girl and in that way got a section of land. Mr. Turner remembers the days when everyone in this section of the Territory lived a half-savage life, cultivating a little corn and killing a wild hog or a beef when they wanted meat. And he has seen the rapid change, not only in the country, but in the people, since the tide of immigration turned this way. The negro immigration from the South, he says, has been a particularly helpful influence upon the "native" negroes, who are beginning now to cultivate their lands in a way which they never thought of doing a few years ago.

A large proportion of the settlers of Boley are farmers from Texas, Arkansas, and Mississippi. But the desire for western lands has drawn into the community not only farmers, but doctors, lawyers, and craftsmen of all kinds. The fame of the town has also brought, no doubt, a certain proportion of the drifting population. But behind all other attractions of the new colony is the belief that here negroes would find greater opportunities and more freedom of action than they have been able to find in the older communities North or South.

Boley, like the other negro towns that have sprung up in other parts of the country, represents a dawning race consciousness, a wholesome desire to do something to make the race respected; something which shall demonstrate the right of the negro, not merely as an individual, but as a race, to have a worthy and permanent place in the civilization that the American people are creating.

In short, Boley is another chapter in the long struggle of the negro for moral, industrial, and political freedom.

Document 10.9

The Japanese in California (1920)

During the mid-nineteenth century, hundreds of thousands of Chinese immigrants settled in the western states, where they worked building railroads, picking crops, and digging mines. American workers came to resent Chinese competition, and in 1882 Congress passed the Chinese Exclusion Act, outlawing future Immigration from China. Japanese workers soon filled the labor vacuum, and just as quickly, anti-Japanese prejudice began to develop in certain circles. In the following article, Edward Hungerford comments on the Japanese presence in the United States.*

One does not ordinarily regard California as an industrial state any more than one would ordinarily so regard Kansas. An Easterner, in particular with memories of Manchester or Lawrence or Bridgeport, would not regard her attempts to manufacture woolens at Oakland or locomotives at Sacramento as considerable additions to the nation's annual manufactured output. Yet, if he were willing to believe that agriculture is really America's one greatest industry—with 12,000,000 workers engaged in filling the larders of 24,000,000 workers in all the other industries of the United States—he might be prepared to say that the Golden State was fairly entitled to a considerable "say" in the industrial situation. She may not rank quite as Iowa—first in agricultural output, with from $1,000,000,000 to $1,500,000,000 a year—but she stands third or fourth among her sister states. Her workaday problems are distinctly agricultural. It is indeed germane to her that the workers in her melon fields are to-day paid $7 and $8 and $9 a day. It is most germane to her sensitive nature that her most successful agriculturists are Japanese.

On certain side lines of her railroads one may see from time to time signs opposite the local stations saying briefly, but definitely, "Japs Not Wanted," "No Japs Here," or other phrasings to the same effect. No signs say that the industrious little brown men from the Mikado's empire are the ones who advanced the melon production of the Imperial Valley a full thirty days by the patient but simple process of covering the vines in early season; that they accomplished similar horticultural marvels in the rich Santa Clara Valley among the berry patches.

If you ask the typical Californian about these things he will, with his typical frankness, tell you that they are quite true, but he will almost certainly add in the next instant:

"Would you, Mr. New-Yorker, want in your lovely small fruit farms of the valleys of the Hudson or the Genesee, a stolid race that, no matter how industrious and efficient

* Edward Hungerford, "America Goes Back to Work," *Harper's Magazine, 141* (September 1920), pp. 507-510.

they might be, remains aloof, unmoral, unreachable, and unassimilable; a people who repeatedly have shown themselves worthy of no trust whatsoever, but, on the contrary, as justifying almost any amount of suspicion?"

I can understand this typical Californian quite clearly. The Jap is an enigma to him, as to every other white man. He is baffling and perplexing to the nth degree. The Californian proceeds to give him up as entirely hopeless.

"We once ranted at the Chinese, our fathers and ourselves," he continues, "but with the Jap boy upon our heels, we have come to appreciate our China boy of other days, willing to do housework at $3 a week and to feed himself and sleep out in the wash house. The Jap servant of to-day—when we can get him—is not nearly so efficient, demands $125 a month and must eat and sleep in the house exactly as we eat and sleep. Moreover, he is not long content to remain a servant. He wants to be an employer, himself. If he is a farmer, he must soon become a leaser. From that his ambition vaults to being the town shopkeeper or the town banker and upon driving all Caucasian competitors out of the community. With his ability to live life an animal and his willingness to work unheard-of hours—in his own interest—he generally succeeds in doing this very thing.... It is this colonizing instinct of his that we hate and will no longer tolerate."

The Californian's indictment against the Japanese runs to great lengths. He divides it clearly into separate counts and recites with great unction and a sense of most definite injury the episodes of the "picture-brides," the thin-skinned device by which the Japanese have so rapidly advanced their plans for multiplying and colonizing upon American soil. It must be remembered in this connection that California has ruled that only native-born Japanese may hold title to land within her limits-a statute lay that is quite easily being evaded by the working of a natural one...

"How many Japanese are there out here upon the western rim of the United States?" you ask one of these typical Californians, who knows exactly what he is talking about.

He is immediate in his answer:

"Between 150,000 and 200,000. No one knows exactly except the Japanese consuls here—and they are not telling. But we are all remembering. We are recalling how when a dozen years ago we prepared to move legally against Japan—and in the fullness of our rights—she protested that it would hurt her national pride if we treated her with the humiliation with which we had treated the Chinese. She would recognize our rights and our wishes and adjust the thing herself. So she did, taking nearly two years in which to perform the adjustment. In the meantime Tokio—even though the agreement was verbally agreed to if not formally signed—sent 45,000 fresh Japanese into this country; 30,000 in 1907 and 15,000 more in 1908."

That California—probably Oregon, too—will take definite legal action against the little brown men this fall is hardly to be doubted. She feels that the moral obligation which bound her not to offend Japan, the Allied nation, during the last months of the Great War, and which sent the Secretary of State hurrying out from Washington to Sacramento and to Salem, no longer exists, while the Japanese "menace" grows and grows greatly. "What is Los Angeles going to do about it? There are two hundred more Japanese grocers in this city today than in 1915," read the advertising cards in the racks of the trolley-cars of that city.

What is California going to do about it is an even larger question. Here is an issue of vital importance to that great commonwealth of our Far West; in her opinion it far outrides in importance even that other great problem, the injustice which national prohibition did to her vineyard industry. Concretely it takes the form of the submission this fall to her electorate of measures limiting the present rights of the Japanese to lease her land, of tightening greatly the present rather loosely construed guardianship regulations of the state, and of preventing the Japs from acquiring land or other realty through the organization of "dummy corporations." "All of these are clearly within the provisions of our treaty with Nippon," adds our typical Californian.

It is hard for a New-Yorker to thrust himself quickly into a situation such as this and appreciate the importance of it; just as he must find it difficult to acquire the Southerner's real understanding of the black brother without having lived any considerable time in the South. If he is at all broad-minded he quickly gains a fair idea at least of the Californian's perplexity in regard to the Jap, and he does not credit it all either to inborn race antagonism or jealousy or the interference of the labor-union element. Yet he discounts this last by asking if the regulations that are desired against the Japanese could not be modified, in part at least, in regard to the Chinese who do not proselyte or colonize or follow high ambitions, but who are very honest and very faithful laborers, particularly in agriculture. And how our agriculture does need labor of that very sort, this day and hour!

It is a long time since Dennis Kearney and the Sand Lots Riots of San Francisco which led to the Chinese Exclusion Act of 1884. California has forgotten much since then—and remembered much. She has forgotten the bitterness and the prejudices of that day and remembered the serenity, the cheerfulness, the faithfulness, and the desire and ability to work of the China boy. Yet when we ask our typical Californian if the would permit the entrance of 50,000 or 100,000 of these—males only—and under rigid requirements and restrictions, he shakes his head sadly and replies:

"It would neither be fair nor would it be consistent toward the Japanese."

A funny people these big-hearted Californians, and with passing strange ideas of what constitutes consistency. How about our national consistency for all these years in excluding one nation of Orientals—which was weak—and admitting another nation—which was strong? Are we the people to be too critical in the question of Shantung? What was once said about the folk who dwell in glass houses?

I think that our typical Californian represents what would still be a majority sentiment in his state—even though today there is a growing sentiment there for the admission of Chinese, always under strict limitations and restrictions, so as to relieve the very critical farm-labor situation upon the West Coast. But the old prejudice against Orientals of any sort still thrives there. Traditions do not die easily. The Californian keeps reverting to his own peculiar problem of the Japanese.

11

Settlement and Environmental Change

The story of the American West has traditionally been a chronicle of human settlement with little consideration given to the natural environment. From the beginning, the North American continent seemed to possess an inexhaustible supply of natural resources. The eagle, the wolf, the buffalo, and the grizzly bear have become national symbols, yet they were among the multitudes of flora and fauna pushed to the brink of extinction over the past four centuries.

While few western animal species have gone the way of the passenger pigeon, the buffalo narrowly escaped the same fate. Congress responded to the wanton slaughter of the buffalo by proposing a bill to save the species, but President Grant ultimately voided it. It has been estimated that between 1872 and 1874 hide hunters killed more than four million buffalo on the southern plains. An additional 1.2 million were probably killed by Indians. Within a decade, the northern herd would be decimated as well. Recent scholarship suggests that the buffalo were already in trouble by the time of the final slaughter. Drought, habitat destruction, disease, and competition from other species for food and water had begun to make inroads on the bison population. By 1883 only a few herds persisted and in less than two decades only a few remnants of the once great herds survived, protected by Western ranchers. The decline of the great buffalo herds assisted the government's efforts to confine native peoples to reservations.

The term "mining" conjures up a variety of images, most indelibly the grizzled prospector with a pick, shovel, and prospecting pan. By the 1850s, placer or surface mining lost its appeal when the exhaustion of accessible surface deposits led to cooperative efforts such as hydraulic mining. In this ecologically-destructive innovation, water was shot out of high-pressure hoses deep into the side of hills in order to expose ancient gold deposits hidden beneath layers of accumulated debris. Ultimately, rivers became clogged with gravel and rock that had been moved down out of the mountains, threatening orchards and towns alike with floods.

Early explorers of the lands between the 100th meridian and the Rocky Mountains described this region as the Great American Desert. Maps from the early 1800s until the post-Civil War era used this appellation to mark the area that we know today as the Great Plains. For years this misnomer proved a barrier to western expansion and settlers traveling overland to California viewed the region as unfit for white settlement and traditional farming techniques. The explorer John C. Fremont's expeditions in the 1830s and 1840s challenged the prevailing attitudes toward the region by suggesting that livestock could subsist on native grasses and subsistence agricultural was possible.

By the time the Homestead Act was passed in 1862 most of the arable lands had already been claimed by speculators or granted to railroads. The quarter-section units provided by the Homestead Act proved too small for the extensive type of farming required for farming in the drier portions of the West. The only way to successfully cultivate the land in the arid regions was through irrigation. With the completion of the transcontinental railroad in 1869, land speculators and railroad builders convinced ranchers and farmers to journey west to take advantage of the Homestead Act. Boosters and pseudo-scientists promoted the adage that "rains follow the plow," a theory that would be discredited in the Dust Bowl years of the 1930s. Another theory heralded the notion that planting trees would increase rainfall and alter the climate, thus the passage of the Timber Culture Act in 1873.

The publication of John Wesley Powell's *Report on the Lands of the Arid Region of the United States* contended that agriculture would prove destructive to the semiarid lands and that the 160-acre homestead was too small. His recommendations went unheeded, and when the region experienced a series of droughts, blizzards, and dust storms in the 1880s, Powell seemed like a sage. By the end of the twentieth century the Great Plains environment would be settled and transformed thanks to science and new technologies such as new farming equipment, barbed wire, windmills, dry farming techniques, and extensive irrigation.

Beginning in the early 1900s, federal reclamation programs led to the construction of high level dams and reclamation projects that became a significant factor in the development of the West. These dams would not only alter the landscape, but provide the growing urban populations in the West with water supplies, hydroelectric power, flood control, and recreation facilities.

Suggestions for Further Reading

Stephen Fox, *John Muir and His Legacy: the American Conservation Movement* (Boston: Little, Brown, and Co., 1981).

Roderick Nash, *Wilderness and the American Mind* (New Haven: Yale University Press, 1982)

Marc Reisner, *Cadillac Desert: The American West and its Disappearing Water* (New York: Viking, 1986).

Susan R. Schrepfer, *The Fight to Save the Redwoods: A History of Environmental Reform, 1917-1978* (Madison: University of Wisconsin Press, 1983).

Wallace Stegner, *Beyond the Hundredth Meridian* (Boston: Houghton Mifflin, 1954).

Critical Thinking

1. Contrast the methods of hydraulic and placer mining. Which was more destructive to the environment?

2. Discuss the various ways settlers could gain title to public lands.

3. How would you describe the western lands still available for homesteading after 1890? What obstacles did settlers have to contend with on these lands?

4. How had the natural habitat of the Great Plains changed between 1823 and 1900? Which animals were most impacted by the onslaught of settlers?

5. What impact did John Wesley Powell's Report on the Lands of the Arid Region have on the reclamation program of the early twentieth century?

Document 11.1

Extinction of the Passenger Pigeon (1823)

In recent years, the issue of endangered species has become a political football in the United States. Environmentalists often want to stop any economic development that threatens a species with extinction, while economic interest groups make the claim of higher priorities, that the welfare of human beings is more important than the survival of any particular insect, fish, bird, or mammal. One of the earliest expressions of concern about a species came from the pen of James Fenimore Cooper, the famous frontier novelist. In his novel *Pioneers* (1823), he describes a pigeon hunt and expresses concern about the survival of the species.*

If the heavens were alive with pigeons, the whole village seemed equally in motion with men, women, and children. Every species of fire-arms, from the French ducking-gun with a barrel near six feet in length, to the common horseman's pistol, was to be seen in the hands of the men and boys; while bows and arrows, some made of the simple stick of a walnut sapling, and others in a rude imitation of the ancient cross-bows, were carried by many of the latter.

The houses and the signs of life apparent in the village drove the alarmed birds from the direct line of their flight, toward the mountains, along the sides and near the bases of

* James Fenimore Cooper, *Pioneers* (New York: Waldham & Parker, 1923), pp. 48-49.

which they were glancing in dense masses, equally wonderful by the rapidity of their motion, and their incredible numbers...

Across the inclined plane which fell from the steep ascent of the mountain to the banks of the Susquehanna, ran the highway, on either side of which a clearing of many acres had been made at a very early day. Over those clearings, and up the eastern mountain, and along the dangerous path that was cut into its side, the different individuals posted themselves, and in a few moments that attack commenced.

Among the sportsmen was the tall, gaunt form of Leather-stocking, walking over the field, with his rifle hanging on his arm, his dogs at his heels; the latter now scenting the dead or wounded birds, that were beginning to tumble from the flocks, and then crouching under the legs of their master, as if they participated in his feelings at this wasteful and unsportsmanlike execution.

The reports of the fire-arms became rapid, whole volleys rising from the plain, as flocks of more than ordinary numbers darted over the opening, shadowing the field like a cloud; and then the light smoke of a single piece would issue from among the leafless bushes on the mountain, as death was hurled on the retreat of the affrighted birds, who were rising from a volley, in a vain effort to escape. Arrows, and missiles of every kind, were in the midst of the flocks; and so numerous were the birds, and so low did they take their flight, that even long poles, in the hands of those on the sides of the mountain, were used to strike them to the earth...

Among the relics of the old military excursions that occasionally are discovered throughout the different districts of the western part of New-York, there had been found a small swivel, which would carry a ball of a pound weight... This miniature cannon had been released from the rust, and being mounted on little wheels, was now in a state for actual service. For several years it was the sole organ for extraordinary rejoicings used in those mountains. On the mornings of the Fourths of July, it would be heard ringing among the hills...

"An't the woods his work as well as the pigeons? Use, but don't waste Wasn't the woods made for the beasts and birds to harbor in? And when man wanted their flesh, their skins, or their feathers, there's the place to seek them. But I'll go to the hut with my own game, for I wouldn't touch one of the harmless things that cover the ground here, looking up with their eyes on me, as if they only wanted tongues to say their thoughts."

With this sentiment in his mouth, Leather-stocking threw his rifle over his arm, and followed by his dogs, stepped across the clearing with great caution, taking care not to tread on one of the wounded birds in his path. He soon entered the bushes on the margin of the lake, and was hid from view.

Document 11.2

Placer Mining (1859)

With the discovery of gold at Sutter's Mill in 1848, thousands of gold-seekers were drawn to California to make their "pile." The majority of the so-called argonauts had no mining experience. However, the process of mining initially had few requirements. Placer mining required only a pick and shovel, prospecting pan, a rocker, "long tom," and a sluice. Miners used quicksilver, which would amalgamate with the gold to differentiate it from worthless minerals. The gold would then be separated from the quicksilver by heating in a retort. By the mid-1850s, most accessible deposits had been played out, and placer mining in California had given way to hydraulic mining and other more sophisticated methods.*

Placer mining first enlists the attention of gold-seekers, because it is easiest, most accessible, and makes prompt returns. It consists in washing the surface dirt. We saw that the thousands who invaded California in 1848-49 engaged at once in this sort of mining. When the process of washing the gold from the dirt is remunerative, the miner says "it *pans out* well." His pan furnishes the figure.

As compared with lode mining, there is no outlay to be made in the outset, and no risk to run. At the close of each day the miner knows just the amount he has earned. He may be entirely ignorant of practical and scientific mining, but he knows enough to separate gold from the surface dirt. He may be as poor as Job's long-eared companion, but his muscle and perseverance give him as good a chance as his more well-to-do co-worker enjoys. Poverty stands abreast with competency in this kind of work; or poverty may sift dirt as fast, and perhaps faster, than competency.

We have seen, also, that gold-seekers in Colorado, in 1858-59, devoted themselves to placer mining in Boulder, Gilpin, Park, Summit, Lake, and other counties. Here they could work but five or six months of the year on account of the severity of the weather; but *one million* a season was the average amount of gold secured for several years. Indeed, California Gulch alone, where three or four mouths of labor covered the working season, turned out *one million* each season for a series of years.

The gold gathered by placer mining has been washed down from the mountains, through past ages, into the creeks, rivers, and gulches. Much of it works through the loose gravel down to the bed of rivers, where miners find the richest deposits.

The rocker, sometimes called "cradle," is about as primitive as the *pan* in placer mining. A good illustration of it is found below, showing also the method of working it.

---

* William M. Thayer, *Marvels of the West,* (Norwich, CT.: The Henry Bill Publishing Company, 1890), 446-448.

It is simply a box about four feet long, mounted on rockers and furnished with graded sieves. The gold dirt is placed in the hopper, where the water is also poured, and, by the use of amalgamated plates and blankets, the gold is separated from the dirt as it is washed down from the hopper into the box. It is still in use in certain localities, as on river-bars, where other methods are not practicable.

Of course there is a limit to placer mining. The gold is exhausted in time; and miners who are not prepared to engage in lode mining pack their traps and start for other placers. The word "placer" is from the Spanish, and means "content," "satisfaction"; and this class appeared to be "content" with placers only.

Document 11.3

The Federal Mining Act of 1872 (1872)

As placer mining was eclipsed by deep rock mining in the 1850s and 1860s, conflict often arose over lode claims. According to British and Spanish mining law, lode claim boundaries were determined by the downward extension of the surface boundaries. Californians ignored these precedents and adopted a principle that allowed a claimant to follow a vein wherever it might lead, which could possibly infringe on surrounding mining claims. The resultant confusion led to countless legal disputes. In 1872, Congress passed the General Mining Act or Apex Law of 1872, supporting the California rule. This law established the methods for determining the boundaries of lode claims. One of the major drawbacks of this legislation was the stipulation requiring a claimant to identify the "apex" or top of a vein, a requirement that two authorities could rarely agree on. If a claimant misjudged the apex when he set his boundary claims, he could lose the right to follow the vein under the surface. The uncertainty and imprecision of locating mining claims led to endless litigation.*

An act to promote the development of the mining resources of the United States.

Be it enacted by the senate and house of representatives of the United States of America, in congress assembled, § 1. That all valuable mineral deposits in land belonging to the United States, both surveyed and unsurveyed, are hereby declared to be free and open to exploration and purchase, and the lands in which they are found to occupation and purchase, by citizens of the United States, and those who have declared

---

* "General Mining Act of 1872," in *A Treatise on the American Law Relating to Mines and Mineral Lands Within the Public Land States and Territories,* (1914), pp. 1634-1638.

their intention to become such, under regulations prescribed by law, and according to the local customs or rules of miners, in the several mining districts so far as the same are applicable and not inconsistent with the laws of the United States.

·§ 5. That the miners of each mining district may make rules and regulations not in conflict with the laws of the United States, or with the laws of the state or territory in which the district is situated, governing the location, manner of recording, amount of work necessary to hold possession of a mining claim, subject to the following requirements: The location must be distinctly marked on the ground so that its boundaries can be readily traced. All records of mining claims hereafter made shall contain the name or names of the locators, the date of the location, and such a description of the claim or claims located by reference to some natural object or permanent monument as will identify the claim. On each claim located after the passage of this act, and until a patent shall have been issued therefor, not less than one hundred dollars' worth of labor shall be performed or improvements made during each year. On all claims located prior to the passage of this act, ten dollars' worth of labor shall be performed or improvements made each year for each one hundred feet in length along the vein until a patent shall have been issued therefor; but where such claims are held in common, such expenditure may be made upon any one claim; and upon a failure to comply with these conditions, the claim or mine upon which such failure occurred shall be opened to relocation in the same manner as if no location of the same had ever been made; provided, that the original locators, their heirs, assigns, or legal representatives, have not resumed work upon the claim after such failure and before such location. Upon the failure of any one of several co-owners to contribute his proportion of the expenditures required by this act, the co-owners who have performed the labor or made the improvements may, at the expiration of the year, give such delinquent co-owner personal notice in writing or notice by publication in the newspaper published nearest the claim, for at least once a week for ninety days, and if, at the expiration of ninety days after such notice in writing or by publication, such delinquent should fail or refuse to contribute his proportion to comply with this act, his interest in the claim shall become the property of his co-owners who have made the required expenditures.

Document 11.4

Hydraulic Mining (1873)

By the 1850s, placer mining in California became less profitable as easily accessible mineral deposits were depleted. In California, the technique of hydraulic mining was devised. Environmentally devastating, the process required washing down deep gravels in order to expose gold-bearing deposits with quantities of water shot out of cannon-like high pressure hoses. Over time the debris created by this innovation began to clog rivers, which periodically overflowed their banks, covering surrounding farmland with rocks and gravel. After long legal battles by farmers to cease this calamitous process, an 1884 legal ruling issued a permanent injunction leading to the phasing out of hydraulic mining in California.*

Hydraulic Mining.-All along the road now, for miles, we see little ditches filled with running water. These are dug around the sides of the hills, tapping the river near its source, where perpetual snows furnish a constant supply, and are carried on and on to the various mining 'claims' below in the valleys. These claims are located upon what is known as the Blue Lead, which extends from Gold Run, a few miles beyond, through Nevada County, into and through a part of Sierra County, and constitute the best large 'placer-mining' district in the State. The whole tract was, without doubt, the bed of a once large mountain stream, which has piled up these great beds, within which are the fine particles of gold, worn away from the great quartz mountains by the action of the water upon them. Petrified trees are now found like those growing upon the hills around-pines, oaks, the manzanita, the mahogany, and others-in this peculiar formation, which is from one to five or six miles in width. From these ditches the water is taken in a 'telegraph,' which is a long, narrow flume of wood, extending out over the claim; to this hose with a nozzle is attached, from which the water spouts in a constant stream, and is by the miners directed against the hillside. By this action the soft dirt is washed away from the gravel, and, forming one liquid mass, is carried through a 'tail-race' into long flumes, often miles in length. Within these flumes are placed 'riffles'-little slats attached to the bottom of the flume, for arresting the gold, which by its own gravity seeks the bottom. Along the flumes, at intervals, are stationed men, who throw out the large stones and pieces of rock from which the dirt has been washed. When the 'riffles' are supposed to be full, the water is turned off, and the dirt, which contains the particles of gold, is taken out.

The next process is the use of the 'long tom,' which is a sheet-iron box with a duplicate bottom extending diagonally over a little more than half the box. This secondary iron plate is perforated with holes; and under it, in pockets made by two cross-slats upon the bottom, is placed the quicksilver. This 'long tom' is now attached to a sluice-way, and the water turned through it. The dirt which has been taken from the riffles is shovelled upon this perforated plate; the particles of gold fall through, and unite their atoms with the quicksilver. This process of throwing the dirt upon the plate, washing away the sand and rock by the flowing water, and the taking up of the gold by the quicksilver, is continued until the 'quicksilver is full,' as they term it. Then the amalgam is removed, placed in a retort, heated to some 480° Fahrenheit; when the quicksilver is sublimed, and passes away in a vapour, leaving the gold.

Of course such mining is very expensive (vast sums having been laid out in building the ditches and flumes), and can never be an economical mode; for, with every precaution, much of the gold is carried away. After the last riffle is passed, the 'slum,' as

* John Erastus Lester, *The Atlantic to the Pacific: What to See and How to See It,* (London: Longmans, Green, and Co., 1873), 63-65.

it is called, is carried into the streams which empty into the great Sacramento, the waters of which are now muddy and dirty from the vast amount of sand, clay, and loam washed into it, as each miner, by his ceaseless labour, wears away the hills and the mountains, and carries them by his flumes into the rivers. It is a strange sight to look around and see what this constant flow of water has done in so short a time; and then we are enabled to understand some of those great changes which Nature has wrought by her rivers flowing on for ages and ages.

Since the miners began their work in California in 1849, they have levelled hills, often 300 feet in height and hundreds of acres in extent, and carried them into the valleys; they have denuded whole counties, and now only the waterworn surface and jaggy sides of the bed-rock are to be seen; they have turned the course of great rivers and dug their beds over and over; they have thrown the surface of the plains into ridges; and all this for the gold which they held.

Document 11.5

Timber Act (1873)

The original Timber Culture Act of 1873 was an attempt to forest the prairies where a lack of timber proved a barrier to settlement. Intended "to encourage the growth of timber on the western Prairies," it was hoped that the resulting growth of trees would change the climate and increase the rainfall. According to this legislation, a homesteader could apply for an extra 160 acres, which would become his property if he planted trees on at least forty acres of it within four years. Over the next several years the tree planting requirement was trimmed down to ten acres. More than sixty thousand settlers acquired ten million acres under this act. However, there was apparently little conservation value in this process, and some homesteaders only grew one or several trees for this requirement. In addition, area ranchers had their cowboys file false claims near rivers and streams, preventing farmers from settling in the vicinity. An overwhelming failure, in 1891 Congress repealed the act.*

Be it enacted by the Senate and House of Representatives of the United States of America, in Congress assembled, That any person who shall plant, proctect and keep in a healthy growing condition for ten years, forty acres of timber, the trees thereon not being

---

* "Timber Culture Act of 1873," Forty-Second Congress, Sess. III., CH. 277, (March 3, 1873), pp. 605-606; "Amendment of Timber Act of 1873," Forty-Third Congress, Sess. I., CH. 55, (March 13, 1874), pp. 21-22.

more than twelve feet apart each way on any quarter-section of any of the public lands of the United States shall be entitled to a patent for the whole of said quarter-section at the expiration of said ten years, on making proof of such fact by not less than two credible witnesses; *Provided,* That only one quarter in any section shall be thus granted.

SECTION 2. That the person applying for the benefit of this act shall, upon application to the register of the land-office in which he or she is about to make such entry, make affidavit before said register or receiver that said entry is made for the cultivation of timber, and upon filing said affidavit with said register and receiver, and on payment of ten dollars, he or she shall thereupon be permitted to enter the quantity of land specified: *Provided however,* That no certificate shall be given or patent issue therefor until the expiration of at least ten years from the date of such entry; and if at the expiration of such time, or at any time within three years thereafter, the person making such entry, or if he or she be dead, his or her heirs or legal representatives, shall prove by two credible witnesses that he, she, or they have planted, and for not less than ten years have cultivated and protected such quantity and character of timber as aforesaid, they shall receive the patent for such quarter-section of land.

Document 11.6

John Wesley Powell Reports on the Arid West (1879)

John Wesley Powell (1834-1902) overcame the loss of his right arm at the Battle of Shiloh to carve out a career as a soldier, teacher, scientist, explorer, anthropologist, and geologist. But his greatest achievements were his contributions to the conservationist movement. Powell advocated a program of land reform that would make settlement possible in the arid regions of the West, and through his work for the U.S. Geological Survey, he revealed the limits of western resources. His groundbreaking *Report on the Lands of the Arid Region of the United States* was the first realistic portrayal of the benefits of irrigation. However, his battle to reform land settlement laws would bring him into conflict with mining, cattle, and timber interests who feared that land laws would bring an end to an era of exploitation.*

The eastern portion of the United States is supplied with abundant rainfall for agricultural purposes, receiving the necessary amount from the evaporation of the Atlantic Ocean and the Gulf of Mexico; but westward the amount of aqueous

* J. W. Powell, *Report of the Arid Region of the United States with a More Detailed Account of the Lands of Utah,* (Washington: Government Printing Office, 1879), 1-4, 10.

precipitation diminishes in a general way until at last a region is reached where the climate is so arid that agriculture is not successful without irrigation. This Arid Region begins about midway in the Great Plains and extends across the Rocky Mountains to the Pacific Ocean. But on the northwest coast there is a region of greater precipitation, embracing western Washington and Oregon and the northwest corner of California. The winds impinging on this region are freighted with moisture derived from the great Pacific currents; and where this water-laden atmosphere strikes the western coast in full force, the precipitation is excessive, reaching a maximum north of the Columbia River of 80 inches annually. But the rainfall rapidly decreases from the Pacific Ocean eastward to the summit of the Cascade Mountains. It will be convenient to designate this humid area as the Lower Columbia Region. Rain gauge records have not been made to such an extent as to enable us to define its eastern and southern boundaries, but as they are chiefly along high mountains, definite boundary lines are unimportant in the consideration of agricultural resources and the questions relating thereto. In like manner on the east the rain gauge records, though more full, do not give all the facts necessary to a thorough discussion of the subject; yet the records are such as to indicate approximately the boundary between the Arid Region, where irrigation is necessary to agriculture, and the Humid Region, where the lands receive enough moisture from the clouds for the maturing of crops. Experience teaches that it is not wise to depend upon rainfall where the amount is less than 20 inches annually, if this amount is somewhat evenly distributed throughout the year; but if the rainfall is unevenly distributed, so that "rainy seasons" are produced, the question whether agriculture is possible without irrigation depends upon the time of the "rainy season" and the amount of its rainfall. Any unequal distribution of rain through the year, though the inequality be so slight as not to produce "rainy seasons", affects agriculture either favorably or unfavorably. If the spring and summer precipitation exceeds that of the fall and winter, a smaller amount of annual rain may be sufficient; but if the rainfall during the season of growing crops is less than the average of the same length of time during the remainder of the year, a greater amount of annual precipitation is necessary. In some localities in the western portion of the United States this unequal distribution of rainfall through the seasons affects agriculture favorably, and this is true immediately west of the northern portion of the line of 20 inches of rainfall, which extends along the plains from our northern to our southern boundary...

In fact, a broad belt separates the Arid Region of the west from the Humid Region of the east. Extending from the one hundredth meridian eastward to about the isohyetal line of 28 inches, the district of country thus embraced will be subject more or less to disastrous droughts, the frequency of which will diminish from west to east. For convenience let this be called the Sub-humid Region. Its western boundary is the line already defined as running irregularly along the one hundredth meridian. Its eastern boundary passes west of the isohyetal line of 28 inches of rainfall in Minnesota, running approximately parallel to the western boundary line above described. Nearly one-tenth of the whole area of the United States, exclusive of Alaska, is embraced in this Sub-humid Region. In the western portion disastrous droughts will be frequent; in the eastern portion infrequent. In the western portion agriculturists will early resort to irrigation to secure immunity from such disasters, and this event will be hastened because irrigation when properly conducted is a perennial source of fertilization, and is even remunerative for this purpose alone; and for the same reason the inhabitants of the eastern part will gradually develop irrigating methods. It may be confidently expected that at a time not far distant irrigation will be practiced to a greater or less extent throughout this Sub-humid Region. Its settlement presents problems differing materially from those pertaining to the region to the westward. Irrigation is not immediately necessary, and hence agriculture does not immediately depend upon capital. The region may be settled and its agricultural capacities more or less developed, and the question of the construction of irrigating canals may be a matter of time and convenience. For many reasons, much of the sub-humid belt is attractive to settlers: it is almost destitute of forests, and for this reason is more readily subdued, as the land is ready for the plow. But because of the lack of forests the country is more dependent upon railroads for the transportation of building and fencing materials and for fuel. To a large extent it is a region where timber may be successfully cultivated. As the rainfall is on a general average nearly sufficient for continuous successful agriculture, the amount of water to be supplied by irrigating canals will be comparatively small, so that its streams can serve proportionally larger areas than the streams of the Arid Region. In its first settlement the people will be favored by having lands easily subdued, but they will have to contend against a lack of timber. Eventually this will be a region of great agricultural wealth as in general the soils are good. From our northern to our southern boundary no swamp lands are found, except to some slight extent in the northeastern portion, and it has no excessively hilly or mountainous districts. It is a beautiful prairie country throughout, lacking somewhat in rainfall; but this want can be easily supplied by utilizing the living streams; and, further, these streams will afford fertilizing materials of great value...

There are two considerations that make irrigation attractive to the agriculturist. Crops thus cultivated are not subject to the vicissitudes of rainfall; the farmer fears no droughts; his labors are seldom interrupted and his crops rarely injured by storms. This immunity from drought and storm renders agricultural operations much more certain than in regions of greater humidity. Again, the water comes down from the mountains and plateaus freighted with fertilizing materials derived from the decaying vegetation and soils of the upper regions, which are spread by the flowing water over the cultivated lands. It is probable that the benefits derived from this source alone will be full compensation for the cost of the process. Hitherto these benefits have not been fully realized, from the fact that the methods employed have been more or less crude. When the flow of water over the land is too great or too rapid the fertilizing elements borne in the waters are carried past the fields, and a washing is produced which deprives the lands irrigated of their most valuable elements, and little streams cut the fields with channels injurious in diverse ways. Experience corrects these errors, and the irrigator soon learns to flood his lands gently, evenly, and economically. It may be anticipated that all the lands redeemed by irrigation in the Arid Region will be highly cultivated and abundantly productive, and agriculture will be but slightly subject to the vicissitudes of scant and excessive rainfall.

Document 11.7

Shooting Prairie Dogs (1901)

Mass migration disrupted the ecological balance throughout the West because the presence of so many human beings altered the environment in fundamental ways. Traditional habitats were disrupted, and in order to survive, animals had to adapt or leave. If they could do neither, they disappeared. In the following document, a frequent frontier traveller recalls the impact of settlement on the prairie dog population.*

The steady advance of civilization long years ago drove the prairie-dog, like the shaggy bison, westward beyond the Mississippi and Missouri rivers. For many years the home of the little animal was almost exclusively on the plains and prairies between the "Big Muddy" and the Rockies. Much of that region having become partially settled, and the dogs naturally increasing in numbers, some of the animals seem to have emigrated. Their villages are now visible west of the Snowy Range-the dogs, apparently, having climbed over the mountains, and thousands are at this time making their homes on the western slope of the continental divide.

During the later '60's I saw the prairie-dog villages along both the Atlantic and Pacific slopes of the Rocky Mountains. In the early '80's I noticed them on the western slope, in some places at an elevation of near 9000 feet above sea-level. Along the railroads stretching from the Missouri to the Rockies, their towns and cities can still be seen at intervals, where vast numbers of the little animals continue to make their homes.

It is popularly supposed that of all burrowing animals the prairie-dog is the most worthless. That this supposition is erroneous may be guessed from the fact that a western Kansas man is said to be making a great success in buying and tanning prairie-dog hides. He has been operating in a local way for some time, but not long since an order came to him from a New York house for hides, and now he expects to go into the business quite extensively.

In the early '60's the little dogs were to be found in their abiding-places by the thousands, and their presence even at this date shows that they still hold forth at the old location. Along the Platte, in overland staging days, we would go through occasional "towns"-in fact, "cities"-some of them many miles long. Often, when the dogs appeared, they would be the first animals of the kind the passengers ever set eyes on. If the passengers were of a sporting nature there would at once be fun ahead. The "towns" extended some distance to the north and south of the road. One after another of the passengers would yank out his six-shooter and forthwith begin peppering away from either side of the stage at the little dogs, that would sit up on their haunches by the side of

---

* Frank A. Root and William Elsey Connelley, *The Overland Stage to California* (Topeka, Kansas: Published by the Authors, 1901), pp. 503-06.

their houses for a few seconds and, wagging their tails briskly, would keep up a lively barking at the passers-by, and, as the stage would be getting pretty close, then dodge quickly into their holes.

It was not unusual at those times for half a dozen passengers to be engaged at the same time in the exciting pastime of blazing away at prairie-dogs only a few rods distant. If any were so fortunate as to kill one of the little animals, nine chances out of ten he would be unable to get it, for, if shot, a prairie-dog instantly rolls over into his hole and that is usually the last seen of him. Underneath their towns, it is said, the earth is completely honeycombed; that their paths run in all directions, to every hole in their "town." To drown them out by pouring water in their abiding-places is an impossibility.

At Valley Station, on the South Platte, in the summer of 1863, the keeper had a pet prairie-dog-the first domesticated one I had ever seen. While playing with it one afternoon on my way east from Denver, as the stage teams were being changed, the little animal caught hold of the first joint of one of my fingers and bit through it to the nail. With all the tenacity of a genuine bulldog, the "pet" hung on and wouldn't let go. I tried to shake him off and couldn't. The harder I shook him the tighter he clung; so I raised my arm and swung him once or twice around my head, and, with a sudden jerk, threw him at least ten feet high and fully three rods away. In swinging the animal round his weight tore the flesh from my finger, badly lacerating it, and he fell heavily to the ground, remaining insensible for a few seconds, but recovered and ran into the station.

The stage boys saw me going through some unusually queer antics-dancing around like a chicken with its head out off and yelling like a wild Comanche-trying to shake off the "pet." They all looked at me and laughed at the fun; they thought it a splendid show, but I couldn't see anything especially funny to laugh at. On the contrary, I never before felt so much like swearing; but on this occasion I was like the fellow who thought he was unable to do the subject justice. The station keeper was a looker-on, and witnessed all the fun; so he joined in with the drivers and laughed just as heartily as they. After it was all over, he tried to console me by saying that the dog was merely "playing with me"; but all this I felt was little consolation. In consequence of the bite I suffered intense pain for hours; but I have something to show for the "fun." It is a scar that I shall carry as long as life lasts, which will make me remember until the end that "pet" prairie-dog.

Speaking of prairie-dogs, we are reminded that a pair of the animals, in the '80's, by some means got to Lawrence, Kan., and, according to a paper, "located in the Union Pacific park. They were not disturbed, and they multiplied rapidly, until now they hold possession of about ten square rods in the park, and number several hundred. They have not disturbed the gardens in the vicinity, and they are very tame. The citizens feed them with cabbages during the winter. The 'town' is increasing its limits rapidly, and it may not be long before Lawrence will have to take up arms against the little animals."

Document 11.8

The Disappearance of the Buffalo (1893)

Millions of head of buffalo once roamed the Great Plains of America, from southern Canada in the north to Central Texas in the South. The Plains Indians built their lifestyles around the animal. But the arrival of Europeans decimated the herds. A fashion craze for coats made of buffalo hides and sporting hunters gone wild all but destroyed the herds, reducing the buffalo from approximately ten million head in 1800 to less than 10,000 head in 1900. The decimation of the buffalo also spelled the end of plains Indian culture. In the following document a Picurí Indian wonders about the disappearance of the buffalo.*

The Picurí Indians used to go buffalo hunting among the plains of Mora, as the buffaloes were then plentiful there. As late as the time when my uncle was a young man, the buffaloes existed in great abundance. I still remember him saying that he once saw them on the plains of Mora as thick as the pinyon trees that grow in the mountains. It seems strange that these animals should disappear so quickly. I suppose after guns were introduced they were all killed off.

The Indians say that the buffaloes never lived in the mountains, but they used to live on the plains, eating the grass there like cows. I believe that this is the reason that the buffaloes never lived near the Rio Grande.

Nowadays the buffalo hides are very scarce, and also the horns of the buffalo and anything else pertaining to the buffalo. These, also, are beginning to be forgotten. The hides which the Indians used in former times to put over them when they danced the buffalo dance, and those that they used in their ceremonial dances, and those that they used to spread as mats on their floors, are nowadays very rarely seen.

---

* *Forty-Third Annual Report of the Bureau of American Ethnology, 1925-1926* (Washington, D.C.: Government Printing Office, 1928), p. 397.

Document 11.9

Irrigation and the Carey Act of 1894 (1896)

The one feature that most distinguishes the Western United States from the rest of the nation is the lack of water. For most of this region, life and livelihood is dependent on irrigation and water control. The passage of the Carey Act on August 18, 1894, was intended to grant federal public lands to the arid states and territories, with the caveat that the land be reclaimed by the state through irrigation and sold to settlers in sections not exceeding 160 acres. In addition, a ten-year time limit was required for land reclamation. This was later extended to twenty years. Close to one million acres of desert lands were granted to arid states in this manner. However, ten years after the passage of the act, much of this land had yet to be reclaimed due to a lack of funding. In this 1895 report, the Secretary of the Interior notes some of the defects of the act and the struggle between states and the federal government over public lands.*

I can not too urgently impress upon Congress the necessity for legislation upon the subject of the reclamation and disposal of lands within the arid region. When it is considered that five-sixths of the vacant public lands lie within a region where the rainfall is not sufficient to produce agricultural crops without artificial irrigation, that a comparatively small per cent of this territory can be utilized by reason of the limited supply of the water subject to control, and that existing laws are ineffective to secure the reclamation of the lands susceptible of irrigation, the demand for Congressional action comes to us with irresistible force.

It is assumed by persons familiar with the subject that of the 500,000,000 acres of arid lands, about 100,000,000 acres might be reclaimed by the most conservative use of the water and by the judicious selection of the lands to be irrigated. But unless some plan is adopted "by which the waters of the perennial streams which are wasted during the winter months could be stored and reservoirs constructed upon appropriate sites to impound the storm waters," the percentage would be very much reduced.

It is impossible, under the laws now in operation, to control the reclamation of lands in the arid region so as to prevent the improvident use of water over which the General Government has no control. This can only be accomplished by a system which contemplates the reclamation of the entire territories from a common source of supply and the utilization of that supply.

In his report for the fiscal year ending June 30, 1895, my predecessor suggested that in view of the fact that the States control the water which is more valuable chiefly in the

---

"eport of the Secretary of the Interior," (1896), Vol. I, pp. XVII-XIX.

reclamation of the arid lands, that the practical solution of this question would be to place the lands under the direct control of the States in which they lie, under such restrictions and limitations as will insure their reclamation to the benefit of the actual settlers, to the end that the States may control both elements necessary to their development.

The act of August 18, 1894, known as the Carey Act, authorized the Secretary of the Interior, with the approval of the President, and upon proper application of each of the States in which there may be situated desert lands, to agree to donate and patent to the State free of cost such desert lands, not exceeding 100,000,000 acres to each State, conditioned upon the reclamation and settlement of the land, before title shall pass from the United States. The Carey Act, if properly amended so as to give to the State the power to pledge the lands for their reclamation, might accomplish the work of reclamation to the extent of the donation as effectually as if the lands were granted to the States unconditionally; but unless the bill could be so amended it would, in my judgment, be better to place the lands under the direct control of the States, only so far as may be necessary to secure their reclamation for the benefit of actual settlers.

But the Carey Act, using the language of Secretary Smith in the report above referred to, "fails to give to the State sufficient control over the lands to enable it to contract for their reclamation on the most favorable terms, because it is apparent that the lands to be reclaimed must in every instance form the basis of security for repayment of the money expended in their reclamation, and with such certificate of donation as is provided by the bill capital will not easily be induced to assume such risks."

Document 11.10

Reclamation Act (1902)

The National Reclamation Act, or Newlands Act of 1902, inaugurated a national program of land reclamation in the arid West. Named after its principle author, Nevada Congressman Francis G. Newlands, the act introduced a plan to place the proceeds from the sale of western public lands into a special "reclamation fund" for the construction of irrigation projects. With the passage of this legislation, the Bureau of Reclamation began construction on numerous dams and irrigation projects. The existence of the great urban centers of the Southwest, created by adequate water supplies, hydroelectric power, and flood control, stand today as a testament to the success of this program.*

---

* "The National Reclamation Act," (June 17, 1902), Fifty-Seventh Congress, Session I, CH. 1093, pp. 388-390.

Be it enacted by the South and House of Representations of the United States of America in Congress assembled. That all moneys received from the sale and disposal of public lands in Arizona, California, Colorado, Idaho, Kansas, Montana, Nebraska, Nevada, New Mexico, North Dakota, Oklahoma, Oregon, South Dakota, Utah, Washington, and Wyoming, beginning with the fiscal year ending June thirtieth, nineteen hundred and one, including the surplus of fees and commissions in excess of allowances to registers and receivers, and excepting the five per centum of the proceeds of the sales of public lands in the above States set aside by law for educational and other purposes, shall be, and the same are hereby, reserved, set aside, and appropriated as a special fund in the Treasury to be known as the "reclamation fund," to be used in the examination and survey for and the construction and maintenance of irrigation works for the storage, diversion, and development of waters for the reclamation of arid and semiarid lands in the said States and Territories, and for the payment of all other expenditures provided for in this Act: *Provided,* That in case the receipts from the sale and disposal of public lands other than those realized from the sale and disposal of lands referred to in this section are insufficient to meet the requirements for the support of agricultural colleges in the several States and Territories, under the Act of August thirtieth, eighteen hundred and ninety, entitled "An Act to apply a portion of the proceeds of the public lands to the more complete endowment and support of the colleges for the benefit of agriculture and the mechanic arts, established under the provisions of an Act of Congress approved July second, eighteen hundred and sixty-two." the deficiency, if any, in the sum necessary for the support of the said colleges shall be provided for from any moneys in the Treasury not otherwise appropriated.

SEC. 2. That the Secretary of the Interior is hereby authorized and directed to make examinations and surveys for, and to locate and construct, as herein provided, irrigation works for the storage, diversion, and development of waters, including artesian wells, and to report to Congress at the beginning of each regular session as to the results of such examinations and surveys, giving estimates of cost of all contemplated works, the quantity and location of the lands which can be irrigated therefrom, and all facts relative to the practicability of each irrigation project: also the cost of works in process of construction as well as of those which have been completed.

SEC. 3. That the Secretary of the Interior shall, before giving the public notice provided for in section four of this Act, withdraw from public entry the lands required for any irrigation works contemplated under the provisions of this Act, and shall restore to public entry any of the lands so withdrawn when, in his judgment, such lands are not required for the purposes of this Act: and the Secretary of the Interior is hereby authorized, at or immediately prior to the time of beginning the surveys for any contemplated irrigation works, to withdraw from entry, except under the homestead laws, any public lands believed to be susceptible of irrigation from said works, *Provided,* That all lands entered and entries made under the homestead laws within areas so withdrawn during such withdrawal shall be subject to all the provisions, limitations, charges, terms, and conditions of this Act: that said surveys shall be prosecuted diligently to completion, and upon the completion thereof, and of the necessary maps, plans, and estimates of cost, the Secretary of the Interior shall determine whether or not said project is practicable and advisable, and if determined to be impracticable or unadvisable he shall thereupon restore said lands to entry: that public lands which it is proposed to irrigate by means of any contemplated works shall be subject to entry only under the provisions of the homestead laws in tracts of not less than forty nor more than one hundred and sixty acres, and shall be subject to the limitations, charges, terms, and conditions herein provided: *Provided,* That the commutation provisions of the homestead laws shall not apply to entries made under this Act.

SEC. 4. That upon the determination by the Secretary of the Interior that any irrigation project is practicable, he may cause to be let contracts for the construction of the same, in such portions or sections its it may be practicable to construct and complete as parts of the whole project, providing the necessary fund for such portions or sections are available in the reclamation fund, and thereupon he shall give public notice of the lands irrigable under such project, and limit of area per entry, which limit shall represent the acreage which, in the opinion of the Secretary, may be reasonably required for the support of a family upon the lands in question: also of the charges which shall be made per acre upon the said entries, and upon lands in private ownership which may be irrigated by the waters of the said irrigation project, and the number of annual installments, not exceeding ten, in which such charges shall be paid and the time when such payments shall commence. The said charges shall be determined with a view of returning to the reclamation fund the estimated cost of construction of the project, and shall be apportioned equitably: *Provided,* That in all construction work eight hours shall constitute a day's work, and no Mongolian labor shall be employed thereon.

SEC. 5. That the entryman upon lands to be irrigated by such works shall, in addition to compliance with the homestead laws, reclaim at least one-half of the total irrigable area of his entry for agricultural purposes, and before receiving patent for the lands covered by his entry shall pay to the Government the charges apportioned against such tract, as provided in section four. No right to the use of water for land in private ownership shall be sold for a tract exceeding one hundred and sixty acres to any one landowner, and no such sale shall be made to any landowner unless he be an actual bona fide resident on such land, or occupant thereof residing in the neighborhood of said land, and no such right shall permanently attach until all payments therefore are made. The annual installments shall be paid to the receiver of the local land office of the district in which the land is situated, and a failure to make any two payments when due shall render the entry subject to cancellation, with the forfeiture of all rights under this Act, as well as of any moneys already paid thereon. All moneys received from the above sources shall be paid into the reclamation fund. Registers and receivers shall be allowed the usual commissions on all moneys paid for lands entered under this Act.

SEC. 6. That the Secretary of the Interior is hereby authorized and directed to use the reclamation fund for the operation and maintenance of all reservoirs and irrigation works constructed under the provisions of this Act: *Provided,* That when the payments required by this Act are made for the major portion of the lands irrigated from the waters of any of the works herein provided for, then the management and operation of such irrigation works shall pass to the owners of the lands irrigated thereby, to be maintained at their expense under such form of organization and under such rules and regulations as may be acceptable to the Secretary of the Interior: *Provided,* That the title to and the management and operation of the reservoirs and the works necessary for their protection and operation shall remain in the Government until otherwise provided by Congress.

SEC. 7. That where in carrying out the provisions of this Act it becomes necessary to acquire any rights or property, the Secretary of the Interior is hereby authorized to acquire the same for the United States by purchase or by condemnation under judicial process, and to pay from the reclamation fund the sums which may be needed for that purpose, and it shall be the duty of the Attorney-General of the United States upon every application of the Secretary of the Interior, under this Act, to cause proceedings to be commenced for condemnation within thirty days from the receipt of the application at the Department of Justice.

SEC. 8. That nothing in this Act shall be construed as affecting or intended to affect or to in any way interfere with the laws of any State or Territory relating to the control, appropriation, use, or distribution of water used in irrigation, or any vested right acquired thereunder, and the Secretary of the Interior, in carrying out the provisions of this Act, shall proceed in conformity with such laws, and nothing herein shall in any way affect any right of any State or of the Federal Government or of any landowner, appropriator, or user of water in, to or from any interstate stream or the waters thereof: *Provided.* That the right to the use of water acquired under the provisions of this Act shall be appurtenant to the land irrigated, and beneficial use shall be the basis, the measure, and the limit of the right.

SEC. 9. That it is hereby declared to be the duty of the Secretary of the Interior in carrying out the provisions of this Act, so far as the same may be practicable and subject to the existence of feasible irrigation projects, to expend the major portion of the funds arising from the sale of public lands within each State and Territory hereinbefore named for the benefit of arid and semiarid lands within the limits of such State or Territory: *Provided,* That the Secretary may temporarily use such portion of said funds for the benefit of arid or semiarid lands in any particular State or Territory hereinbefore named as he may deem advisable, but when so used the excess shall be restored to the fund as soon as practicable, to the end that ultimately, and in any event, within each ten-year period after the passage of this Act, the expenditures for the benefit of the said States and Territories shall be equalized according to the proportions and subject to the conditions as to practicability and feasibility aforesaid.

SEC. 10. That the Secretary of the Interior is hereby authorized to perform any and all acts and to make such rules and regulations as may be necessary and proper for the purpose of carrying the provisions of this Act into full force and effect.

Approved, June 17, 1902.

Document 11.11

Last Stand of the Redwoods (1915)

One of the most spectacular sights of the American West was, and remains today, the breathtaking redwood forests of the Pacific Coast. Huge in circumfrance and hundreds of feet tall, the redwoods are among the oldest living species in the world. In the following essay, Henry Canby describes his first encounter with a redwood stand, and with the loggers who harvested wood there.*

I suppose that I shall be accused of sentimentality, but yet I confess that after weeks in the most beautiful forest in the world the sight of that torn hillside was as painful as human misery. The dying were everywhere: broken trees, broken ferns, withering flowers, shrinking streams. But far worse was the scene of their death: the desert of plowed-up sand and littered branches where the work was complete. Ponderous logs, snorting and tearing across, above, below, had annihilated the forest, as cavalry in panic tear through and annihilate the infantry behind them. For years that valley will be an arid waste-if fire reaches it, perhaps for a half-century. The first crop of timber has been gathered, the second and the third wantonly destroyed.

No other kind of lumbering is profitable, say the apologists. In the first place, I doubt it, having many expert opinions to the contrary. In the second, profitable for whom?-surely not for those who hope to live for the twenty-odd years in which a second crop of timber might have ripened in that and many another now worthless valley, and been ready for a more honest plucking. Immediately profitable it may be for a few; in the long run it can be profitable neither for producer nor consumer, neither for the individual nor the state, I left that valley in pain and disgust, and followed our friends the trees, who had sheltered beauty and been beautiful themselves for so many centuries, down to their final change, feeling as I went as might a fifth-century Greek trudging after the sledge which bore some marble Apollo from its niche in the ruined Roman baths to the ignominy of the lime-kiln. At No. 4 we joined the funeral procession, the cornucopia chimney of our little engine blew up a puff of wood smoke, the whistle screamed, and we chugged down the mountain. Rotting logs, broken trees littered the earth everywhere. We passed over bridges made of six-foot trunks of solid timber piled crisscross to the proper height, and ran over trestles with planking enough in them to build a village. Surely it cost two trees to get a dozen boards in these mountains! On through three miles of ruin we went, then hugged a steep incline and slid down to Hume and the lake.

Our flat-cars were coupled in pairs, and each pair held from six to eight of the big logs, securely chained. Running out upon a scaffolding over the clear take water, we stopped by a hoisting-engine, which promptly hooked a claw beneath a carful of logs,

---

* Henry Seidel Canby, "The Last Stand of the Redwoods," *Harper's Magazine, 131* (June 1915), 52-58.

gave one mighty puff and swayed them, another mightier and tumbled them, until they rolled with majestic splashings deep into the lake, whence they wallowed up like angry sea monsters, shaking the foam from their moss, and sailing angrily off toward the outer waters. For a day or so they toll there quietly and shelter the trout. Then the sharp books of the lumber-jacks catch them, they are lifted slowly into the dark and screaming interior of the mill, and spurt out in slabs and planks. Quick hands bind the boards into new unities, each one a raft of fir or pine, and down they slide to join the lumber-train in the big chute.

The big chute is a fifty-mile aqueduct which follows the caᵖon, and later stalks across the flat lower valley to the planing-mills of Sanger on the railroad. It bears a five-foot stream of mountain water, which for the first rapid miles surges downward, then swirls onward calmly to its destination. Down the chute goes the lumber-train, package after package of planks, dashing boatwise between the narrow walls, reported as they fly downward by little bells which ring as the passing lumber swings them, and by telephones at the inspectors' stations on the way. Down the mountain-side they rush, and out across the plain, in a twelve-hour trip for the fifty miles. If you want excitement, nail together some boards into a rough boat, and follow the lumber-train, as may be done if the chute boss does not catch you. The ride down the foaming strip of water far above the edge of deep precipices is said to be-well, thrilling. Unless your boat jams at a corner and spills you into space, or is caught and bumped by a lumber-train behind, this is the cheapest, the quickest, and certainly the least dusty way to ride from Hume to the valley.

Our work at last called us out of the forest, past the lumber-camps, to the great basins of the outer ranges. There devastation had come and gone twenty years before, and many stumps of the decaying sequoias were available for our study of the relations between tree growth and the cycles of climate through many centuries.

Our way led us up from the low level of Hume and across a barrier of outlying crests. On the top of one of these is the Grant National Park, and it was beneath the little grove of redwoods for which this reservation was made that we passed a lazy noon awaiting the slow crawl of our mule-team up the circuitous mountain road.

The "tourist groves" of big trees are a little harrowing after weeks spent among the free sequoias in the deep forest. To be sure, it is not so bad here as in Tulare County, where, so I am told, the fathers of the woods have pinned upon their great trunks such names as "Blanche" and "Sally," as if a bow of pink baby-ribbon should be tied to a Great Dane's neck! Nevertheless, it was painful to see our noble giants fenced in, bepathed, stuck full of arrows in their lustrous bark, and initialed as high as their great buttresses would allow the vandal to climb. I felt shame for the indignities, the flippancies, which these ancients of days must suffer from the horde of curious insects discharged by stage and automobile in the shadow world far below them.

However, these necessary evils of popularity are slight in comparison with the benefits of preservation. In the Grant Park one regrets only that the redwoods are so few as to seem to be specimens merely, rather than an integral part of the Sierra forest. If we hope to get the greatest value from this wonderful mountain country, we must preserve not simply individual trees, or groups of trees, because they are very big or very accessible, but more especially whole ranges of this forest, where the plains-dweller may go "back to nature" for his vacation under conditions that can scarcely be found elsewhere. The potential value in pleasure, recreation, and inspiration of such a real forest as the great Sequoia National Park of Tulare County includes is measurable in dollars and cents. Regarded as capitalized enjoyment (and that is how we estimate the cash value of a novel, a summer resort, or a touring automobile), it will be worth far more in money than the sale of its timber would bring. There is a mountain near this National Park called Redwood Mountain, entirely covered with an unmixed sequoia forest, such a forest as nowhere else exists, as never again will exist when its private owners saw it away. If only California could see its duty, and, more especially, its profit there; or if Washington could turn a little rill of the flowing public moneys thither! But it is still difficult for this spendthrift nation to save. Redwood Mountain, I suppose, must go to serve as text for the economists and the nature-lovers of a wiser generation. Let us be thankful for such morsels as the Grant Park.

We dropped down a thousand feet or so, left our wagon by the roadside, and laboriously packed up another thousand, to get to the Comstock Basin. It lay, a great bowl, open and near the sky, views down from its southern rim to the great plain, an edge of forest cresting it to the north. All within was a vast and lonely cemetery. A stream wound among broken trunks, torn roots, and whitened slabs of lumber, through the midst of the grassy valley. Above the thin turf rose weathered pines or clumps of feathery sequoia, like Italian cypresses, and beneath and beside them, at decorous intervals, were the great tombs of the dead sequoia.

They were only stumps, but in that melancholy landscape stumps like these had power over the imagination. The bark had long since gone from them, but the wood held firm and fast. Ten feet, fifteen feet, twenty feet, they rose above the ground, and two of us could lie head to head upon the tops as we pored over their thousand years of rings.

Twenty years had brought back beauty to this wasted valley, though beauty of a strange and melancholy sort. Flowers were everywhere, most of all where the little stream at intervals drew over its ripples a canopy of pink azalea, now in fullest bloom. But the forest had gone. An indiscriminate slaughter had let in the sun, its enemy; had dried the springs, which were its life-blood; and such tearing and ripping as we had seen at Hume had rendered the soil, its mother, unfit except for barren grass. A few lonely redwoods, spared out of wantonness, had done their best to plant the spaces, but the younglings near them could only patch the ground; the pines and firs had well-nigh given up the struggle. Ranging cattle were more than a match for Nature and her seedling trees. In the great stumps themselves, in blocks and fragments scattered over the soil, in the logs which choked the streams, was more dead and wasted lumber than a forester could hope to grow on so many acres in a hundred years. The story of the Appalachians was being told again, and more loudly.

The Sierra world was full of associations as I looked back upon its tumbled, hazy masses from the orchards and the hot dust of the plains. The dim snowfields were rich with the memory of cliffs and the cool, green cañon floor beneath them; the faint peaks sharpened into gray towers as I remembered how they rose over us when our trail swung out to the edges of the woods; the dark and heavy mass rolling beneath them was the forest. The thought of its still grandeur came like a cool shadow through my mind. And nearer, above the bare foot-hills, the straggling, broken line as of an army on the march-it was the first and broken ranks of the pines, where the destroyers had been hewing. I thanked Heaven, as I looked north and south at the length and far depth of the great Sierra, that for a few decades at least they could not spoil it all. And in a decade or two, perhaps, we may have learned the value of natural beauty, we may even have attained to economic common sense.

12

The West in Transition

As the West made the transition into the new century it continued to encounter the same social, economic, and political problems that plagued other regions of the country. Racial and ethnic discrimination were facts of life from the agricultural centers near Sacramento, California, to the military outposts along the Mexican border. Smoldering tensions in Brownsville, Texas even led to gunfire one hot summer night resulting in several deaths and the destruction of 167 black military careers.

No Western state or territory characterized the inexorable links to the past as it moved into the twentieth century as the territory of Arizona. Once identified with Geronimo and the Apache wars and Wyatt Earp's Tombstone, their West was quickly receding into memory. By 1904 Geronimo was driving in an automobile at the St. Louis World's Fair and Wyatt Earp was on his way to the future motion picture capital of Los Angeles. The following year the Governor of the Arizona territory issued a report heralding the potential growth of his desert domain while downplaying the prevailing perception of his territory as a land brimming with outlaws and hostile Indians.

While the West continued to draw attention from European and Eastern capitalist speculators others began to recognize the West merely for its intrinsic natural beauty. Artists and writers, ranging from Georgia O'Keeffe and Rebecca Salsbury to D.H. Lawrence and Mabel Dodge Luhan were drawn to Taos and Santa Fe New Mexico, seeking inspiration from the Southwestern landscape and Spanish traditions.

In 1872 the West became home to the nation's first national park when Yellowstone National Park was created in an area encompassing parts of Wyoming, Montana, and Idaho. America finally had reversed course by introducing the concept of protecting unique natural environments from commercial exploitation through legislation after over two centuries of plundering the wilderness. In 1919 the National Park Service took over the administration of the park. One thing that has not changed, as the following reports from the Secretary of the Interior make clear, is the consistent wrangling by the Park Service to receive sufficient funding from the federal government.

The turn-of-the century West witnessed one of the most vigorous campaigns of railroad expansion in the nation's history. It had been less than fifty years since the completion of the transcontinental railroad at Promontory Point, Utah, yet between 1890 and 1917 railroad systems across America were already being re-engineered and rebuilt, especially in the West.

261

But, although prices and wages rose by almost fifty percent, and railroad rates rose only seven percent, the railroad business became a target of the labor movement, the Populist Party, and the federal government. Theodore Dreiser referred to the railroads as a "soul-less corporation" and despite improvement campaigns inaugurated by the railroads, the federal government sought to fix maximum rates with the Hepburn Act of 1906, while railroad labor unions embarked on a crusade for higher wages.

The campaign to assimilate the Native American population of America continued unabated into the twentieth century. Under the Dawes Act, passed in 1887, Indian land holdings plummeted from 138 million acres to forty seven million acres over the next four decades. According to the thirteenth census taken in 1910, the Indian population had increased seven percent, or 17,430, over the past twenty years to just over a quarter million people living mostly west of the Mississippi River. However, the experience of another group of westerners was painted on a much brighter canvas. Once threatened with annihilation, by the 1920s the membership of the Mormon church had grown to 250,000 people, almost equalling the entire Native American population.

With "civilization" and the modern age encroaching, the American West seemed to be changing so rapidly that social commentators such as Harrison Rhodes were led to ask themselves "Is there a West?," a lament that has been expressed by every generation of Americans since.

Suggestions for Further Reading

Samuel Hays, *Conservation and the Gospel of Efficiency: The Progressive Conservation Movement, 1890-1920* (Cambridge: Cambridge University Press, 1959).

Robert V. Haynes, *A Night of Violence: the Houston Riot of 1917* (Baton Rouge: Louisiana State University Press, 1976).

Roger Lotchin, Fortress California. *1910-1961: From Warfare to Welfare* (New York: Oxford University Press, 1992).

James S. Olson and Raymond Wilson, *Native Americans in the Twentieth Century* (Provo: Brigham Young University Press, 1984).

William H. Truettner, ed., *Art in New Mexico, 1900-1945: Paths to Taos and Santa Fe* (New York: Abbeville Press, 1986).

Critical Thinking

1. Why did some people consider the railroads to be a "soul-less corporation"?

2. Why would anyone want to move to Arizona during the early 1900s?

3. What conditions precipitated the events that led to the Brownsville Court Martial?

4. What did Geronimo learn at the World's Fair? What do you think he enjoyed most about the fair?

5. Which articles best describe the West in transition?

Document 12.1

Yellowstone National Park (1894, 1896)

Ever since the first European explorers travelled throughout North America, they had found the vistas of the West absolutely breathtaking. As more and more settlers moved out west in the nineteenth century, a number of conservationists began to feel that some regions were so spectacular that they should be set aside and left undeveloped so that future generations could enjoy their pristine beauty. Yellowstone National Park was the first region to receive such status. The following congressional reports demonstrate some of the early concerns and problems faced by administrators of the park.*

REPORT
OF THE
SUPERINTENDENT OF YELLOWSTONE NATIONAL PARK.

DEPARTMENT OF THE INTERIOR,
OFFICE OF THE SUPERINTENDENT
YELLOWSTONE NATIONAL PARK,
Mammoth Hot Springs, Wyo., August 13, 1894.

SIR: Complying with your request of the 14th ultimo, I submit the following report of operations and events in the Yellowstone National Park during the past year:

The tourist season of last year was the most peculiar of any in the history of the Park. My last report bears date of the 27th of July. From that time on, until the end, the falling off that I then noted continued and increased. The regular travel only amounted to 3,076, as against 3,645 for the year previous. Camping parties and irregular outfits suffered more from the depression than did the regular stage and hotel business. This was doubtless due to two causes-the Columbian Exhibition and the financial condition of the country. There was never a season when the hotel registers showed such a cosmopolitan list of names. Nearly every country in the world was represented, and it was no unusual thing to find in the arrivals of a single day people from ten or twelve different foreign nations. Had it not been for this foreign contingent, business in the Park would have

---

* "Report of the Superintendent of Yellowstone National Park," in *The Executive Documents of the House of Representatives for the Third Session of the Fifty-third Congress, 1894-95* (Washington: Government Printing Office, 1895), pp. 651-660.
Report of the Secretary of the Interior (Washington: Government Printing Office, 1896), Vol. I, pp. XCIX-CIV.

proved ruinous; I doubt if any of the companies having franchises here made any money, and it is probable that nearly all found the balance against them at the end of the season.

The travel during the month of June is mostly from the West. Extensive washouts on that part of the railroads, occasioned by the rapid melting of the very heavy snow of last winter, kept tourists out.

From June 26 until July 20 there were no trains running over the railroads, owing to the strikes; thus one-half of the season was passed with no profitable business. This is particularly to be regretted, as the hotel, stage, and boat companies were in better shape than ever before to care for tourists, and the Park was in many ways unusually attractive. There is now little prospect of a prosperous ending of the season, and 1894 will probably stand as the most disastrous to business interests of any in the history of the Park. People who had planned to make the tour at even later dates than this have become alarmed at the interference with travel and have abandoned their trip.

The road over the divide was opened on June 20, the same date as last year; but at the opening it was in much better condition than ever before at this period. With small expenditures for repairs the road will be one of the best, as it is one of the most interesting, in the whole circuit.

A more thorough and exact system of registry will enable me to report in future the number of tourists who go through in their own conveyances and in camping parties. There is no more satisfactory way of seeing the Park than on horseback and with camp equipment. To many who live near here, and to people of limited means, this affords a cheap and delightful excursion. Such parties are, however, the source of many annoyances in park management:

(1) They are often careless about leaving fires. (2) They leave their camping places unpoliced. (3) They are more inveterate specimen hunters than any other class. (4) They are more apt to disfigure the Park by inscribing their names on all available places.

The proposition made by some parties to establish semipermanent camping places has not received my approval, nor that of the Department, for the reason that they would soon degenerate into ill-kept, unsightly structures, fit breeding places for vermin of all kinds.

THE YELLOWSTONE NATIONAL PARK.

This is a tract of land near the head waters of the Yellowstone River, in the States of Montana and Wyoming. It is 62 miles in length from north to south, 54 miles in width from east to west, and contains about 3,348 square miles, or 2,142,720 acres; its area is greater than that of the States of Delaware and Rhode Island combined. The average altitude is about 8,000 feet.

Capt. George S. Anderson, U.S.A., the acting superintendent, reports that the past winter was not severe, though there were heavy falls of snow. The spring was stormy and backward, and snow fell every day from the 2d to the 21st of May. Owing to the great depth of snow a working party was sent out on May 15 to open the roads over the circuit and were so occupied up to June 16 in making the rounds. The road over the divide between the Lake and Upper basin could not be used by tourists until after June 20.

The season opened with promise of heavy travel, which, however, was not fulfilled, owing no doubt to the financial depression and disturbances of a political campaign. Two thousand eight hundred and sixty-six tourists made the regular tour, stopping at the hotels, and 2,588 went through the park in camping parties with their own or hired transportation. The increase in the volume of travel has been comparatively small. There have been no changes in the hotel accommodations in the park, expenditures having been confined to necessary repairs. Small hotels are needed, and should be constructed at Norris and at the Thumb of the Lake, and a good and substantial one should be erected at Upper Geyser Basin. There is a reasonable prospect that accommodations at the points indicated will be furnished in the near future by the Yellowstone Park Association...

Though last season was very dry, there was no serious destruction of the forests from fire, owing to the constant vigilance of the patrol. More than one hundred smoldering fires, many due to the carelessness of campers, were extinguished. A few parties were arrested for such neglect, tried, and sentenced, and a number of others were cautioned, resulting in a more careful observance in such respect of the park regulations...

Strenuous efforts have been made to arrest poachers within the park, but frequently without success, owing to various causes. One James Courteny was arrested for killing a buffalo in the southwest corner of he park; he was tried before the commissioner, but was acquitted or lack of satisfactory evidence. The trial, however, proved so expensive to the accused that its effect upon him and his marauding neighbors has been excellent. Four arrests were made for killing game in the 2-mile strip north of the Wyoming line, and the poachers were fined $50 each.

The game continues to increase, and all varieties except the bison are found in great numbers. There is a fair certainty of the existence of possibly fifty bison. During the spring months the elks are found in their several winter ranges in herds of thousands. Deer wander through the post, going within a few feet of the buildings and often as near to the men who are about their work. The usual herds of mountain sheep and antelope have wintered on Mount Evarts, and show great increase of number. The carnivora have also increased, and have proved objects of interest to tourists. Collections have been made during the year for the National Zoological Park in Washington, and there are now ready for shipment a number of birds, six elks, six antelopes, four beavers, and two black bear cubs. The corral built at the expense of the Smithsonian Institution for the purpose of inclosing a portion of the buffalo herd, which was visited in January and February by a small heard of about eight, and also by many elks. It was intended to shut the herd up and retain them, but this was not done, as it was hoped that more would eventually winter there. They did not do so, however, and in the course of time this small herd wandered away and was not captured. Reports indicate that the majority wintered in the extreme southwest corner of the park in Falls River Meadows, and that there are a number east of the Yellowstone River. Whether it will be practicable to save the few remaining bison seems a doubtful problem, as the forces of nature and the hand of man appear to be alike against them.

The claims of Mr. Baronett on account of a bridge built by him over the Yellowstone River and those of Messrs. McCartney and McGuirk, respectively, for improvements made within the park prior to the act of dedication are equitable and just, and payment of them should not be longer delayed. A recommendation was made in the last annual report that Congress make proper appropriation for the adjustment of their claims, which is renewed.

The acting superintendent of the park suggests that as it is not probable that he will remain in charge of the park long enough to receive the benefit of the next year's appropriation, that an extra allowance be made him for services as superintendent of the park. This principle, he states, was recognized many years ago in extra rations given to post commanders, and especially at certain posts where the burden of entertaining was great; and more recently it has been recognized by extra rank, pay, or allowances given to certain officers stationed at West Point, Military Prison, and at the Carlisle Indian School. He adds further, that there is no station in the Army where so much is expected of an officer; that letters of introduction are sent to him by the hundreds, and the smallest measure of hospitality requires the expenditure of his entire pay in very meager entertaining. The attention of Congress is directed to this matter, with the recommendation that suitable allowance be made Captain Anderson, in addition to his pay as an officer of the Army, for the valuable services rendered by him in superintending the matters relating to the Yellowstone National Park during the past six years. It is recommended that liberal appropriations for the completion of the road system be made and that the same be continued until the roads in the park are macadamized and put in a satisfactory condition; that the completion of the work of locating and marking the boundaries of the park be provided for, and that accommodations be furnished for another company to be stationed at the military post, Fort Yellowstone.

RECOMMENDATION.—The employment of an experienced landscape architect, whose taste and skill would enable him to design a comprehensive and harmonious plan for the improvement of the park, is at this stage of its development very desirable. The improvements hitherto made can not be unfavorably criticised in themselves, but every road constructed and every structure erected should be parts of one harmonious whole. I strongly recommend, therefore, that Congress authorize that department of the Government which is charged with the improvement and care of this wonderful natural park to secure the services of one or more architects whose judgment and talent can be utilized to this end. By this method the beauties of the park can be enhanced and exhibited to advantage, its unsightly scenes made picturesque, and the marvelous work of nature not only preserved but be made to serve as a monument to man's genius and the nation's liberality and foresight.

Document 12.2

Railroads: The "Soul-less Corporation." (1900)

The greatest technological innovation of the nineteenth century was the invention and development of the railroad. It dramatically changed the nature of American economic life, not only by creating a national market but also by giving rise to huge, powerful corporate entities. Among working-class people and farmers, the railroads came to epitomize capitalism at its worst and became targets of the labor movement and the Populist Party. In the following essay, Theodore Dreiser, who went on to become one of the country's most distinguished literary figures, captures the national suspicion toward railroads that existed at the turn of the century.*

When the term "soulless corporation" was first coined, it was used to describe the nature of those largest of the then existing commercial organizations, the railroads. They were declared to be all that the dictionary of iniquity involves-dark, sinister, dishonest associations which robbed the people "right and left," as the old phrase put it, and gave nothing in return. They were, as the public press continually averred, bribe-givers, land-grabbers, political corruptionists, hard-fisted extortionists, thieves-in short, everything that an offended and an outraged opposition could invent or devise in the way of descriptive phraseology. To-day the application of the term has broadened considerably, but the railroads are not by any means exempt. By the masses of the people they are still viewed with suspicion, and everything which they undertake to do is thought to be the evidence of a scheme whereby the people are to be worsted, and the railroad strengthened in its position of opulent despotism.

That so much accusation and opposition has some basis in fact we may well believe, and yet not injure the subject of the present discussion. If we were to assume that all that has ever been said concerning railroads is absolutely true, the fact that a new policy had been adopted by some roads, looking to a cordial and sympathetic relationship with their public, would be all the more remarkable. For if the public has had nothing save greed and rapacity to expect of its railroads, the sight of the latter adopting a reasonable business policy, whereby they seek to educate and make prosperous the public in order that they in turn may be prosperous, is one which, if not inspiring, is at least optimistic. No corporation is soulless, whatever else may be thought of it, which helps all others in helping itself. The philosophy involved in this statement is the enlivening breath of the latest and most successful railroad policy, now being generally adopted.

Like many another good idea, this policy originated in the West, and it is there that it is to be found in its most advanced practical form. There the general freight agent of a road is an official of educational importance. He has associated with him as many as a hundred assistants, who carry out the work of instructing and educating the people in the knowledge that makes for prosperity. He has under him a horticultural agent, who in turn has assistants. There is a poultry agent, a superintendent of dairies, a land inspector, a travelling commercial agent, buyers, salesmen, and so forth, all with assistants, and all working under the direction of the general freight agent.

Through this department the railroads are doing a remarkably broad educational work-not only of inspecting the land, but of educating the farmers and merchants, and helping them to become wiser and more successful. They give lectures on soil-nutrition and vegetable-growing, explain conditions and trade shipments, teach poultry-raising and cattle-feeding, organize creameries for the manufacture of cheese and butter, and explain new business methods to merchants who are slow and ignorant in the matter of conducting their affairs. On two roads there is a poultry department, which buys for cash

---

* Theodore Dreiser, "The Railroad and the People," in *Harper's New Monthly Magazine, 100* (February 1900), pp. 479-84.

of all farmers along the route, running poultry-cars, which are scheduled for certain stations on certain days, with cash buyers in charge. On three other roads there are travelling agents who go over the line three times a year, stop at every station, and visit every merchant in the town and every farmer of merchant proclivities in the country. These men make plain the attitude of the railroad toward the citizen, inquire after the state of his business, ask him what his difficulties are, and what, if anything, can be done to strengthen and improve his situation. Lastly, there is a department of sales agents under the general freight agent, which, by individuals, represents the road in the great cities. These latter study the markets, look after incoming shipments, and work for the interests of the merchants and farmers along the line of the road by finding a market for their product. The reward for the road for all this is nothing more than an increased freight and passenger traffic, which flows from and to a successful community.

It has been seven years since the first of the roads to adopt the new policy began to reach out and study the social condition of its public, but since then the idea has spread rapidly, until to-day there is scarcely a road west of Chicago and St. Louis that is not doing more or less educational work among its public. The original movement was dictated by the fact that along great stretches of the line of one road were vacant tracts of land which were excellent for farming purposes, but which were somehow generally ignored. The road decided to make this region profitable to itself by calling attention to its merits and inducing farmers and merchants to settle there. The aid of the United States Department of Agriculture was called in. The ground was tested, and its specific qualities advertised. After that educational pamphlets were prepared, and agents of the road sent into various populous sections of the country to induce individuals to come and take up residence there. At the same time it was decided that it would be of little use to induce settlement and then leave the settlers to get along as best they could, so a policy of instruction and assistance was inaugurated. The road undertook to organize enterprises which should utilize the natural resources and production of the country and put ready money into the hands of the farmers. As a result, it found that it would need to discover markets for the goods manufactured, or it would lose much of the advantage of its labor, and thus came about the present policy, which is nothing if not broad. Its success has stimulated imitation to such an extent that nearly all roads have some one of the many features of the first road in operation, and several have all of them. So general has the feeling among railroad men become that the new policy is the more natural and more profitable one, that a certain general manager felt called upon to apologize for the backwardness of his road by explaining that the general freight agent was of the old school of thought and not suited for the place.

Another understood the new policy so well that he readily formulated the attitude of his road toward its public, saying:

"To reach the man who is trying to do something is our object. The man with energy is our friend. I am not talking now about the man who has fifty or a hundred thousand dollars. He can take care of himself. I refer to the man who has little or nothing, but who wants to have something; the man who is ambitious and willing to work. Such men need encouragement, and they will get it if they are a part of our public. We have found that if we are to be prosperous our people must be prosperous, and so the welfare of every single individual in our territory becomes our welfare. That is business."

"But," I asked, "can a railroad deal with all of the individual members of its public?"

"Yes and no. It can deal with a great many individually. With more it deals collectively, but the result is the same. The individual is benefited. As, for instance, if a railroad gives a series of lectures on tomato-growing, it might be said to be dealing collectively with its public, and yet every farmer might have the benefit of personal counsel with the lecturer. Our aim is to reach the individuals, whether we do it collectively or not."

A railroad paying for lectures on tomato-growing! Shades of Mark Hopkins and Jay Gould!

"And why not?" said the general freight agent of another, a large Southwestern line which reaches Texas and New Mexico. "If the land is good for growing tomatoes, the farmers ought to be instructed. We have found that our road would be a great deal better if the farmers used their land for the purposes for which it is best fitted. If they do that, their crops are larger. It is our business to instruct them in the matter of soils and crops, and aid them in finding a market."

The instruction of farmers in the matter of soils and crops certainly has been anything but the function of a railroad in the past, and yet to-day we are told that it is good business. The agent for the inspection of land now makes it his business to discover just what the nature of the soil along the line of the railroad is, and what can be grown upon it. In this labor he has the co-operation not only of the national, but the State agricultural bureaus of the State through which his line travels. The government is only too anxious to spread information on this subject among the people, and gladly furnishes reports upon the nature of soils anywhere in the United States when requested. It also willingly analyzes specimens of soil and conducts agricultural experiments.

The knowledge thus gathered is used by the road in several ways. In the first place, in discovering what certain soils are good for, it picks out the thing which is least grown and is in greatest demand. The general freight agent will say to his horticultural agent:

"I see by this report here that the land around Denison, Texas, is good for tomato-raising. Tomatoes are in great demand now and bring good prices. Why couldn't we induce the farmers down there to go into the tomato business? It would be a great thing for that section."

The horticultural agent immediately takes the reports concerning the land about Denison and sends an agent into the country. Meetings of the farmers are called, and the nature of the land and the profit of tomato-growing explained.

"Now," says the horticultural agent, "you gentlemen are raising wheat on your land, and getting, say, sixty cents a bushel, if the market is fair. If not, you get less, or hold your wheat and wait for your money. Now this land about here has been tested, not only by the State, but by the United States Agricultural Department, and it is found that it is much better adapted to the growing of tomatoes. It will do a great deal better planted in tomatoes than it will in wheat. Besides, our agents in other places inform us that tomatoes, such as you can raise here early in the season, will command a dollar a crate. Allowing for the freightage and the cost of the packing-cases, which we will secure for you at the lowest possible rates, you still have forty cents on the crate. An acre of this ground will yield, say, a hundred and twenty crates at forty cents. Figure for yourselves, gentlemen. Only remember the railroad guarantees you your market. You are not, as in the case of wheat, competing with a million other growers in your own country. You have something out of which you should make fifteen per cent. more on the acre easily."

The result of such lectures and conferences is that, with the aid and advice of the agent, the whole region is turned to tomato-growing. The general freight department keeps track of the progress of the crop. Through its representatives in the large and medium-sized cities it finds out where a number of car-loads of tomatoes will command a high market-rate. The local agent confers with the wholesale produce merchants, and contracts with them to deliver so many crates at a given time. The result is that the crop of the section is readily marketed and the region about Denison improved. The farmers, having slightly more ready money, indulge in farm or personal improvements, with the result that the whole district about Denison is enlivened and trade increased. The railroad profits in every way, not only by the new supplies that are shipped in to meet an aroused demand, but by the travel of the man who has a few cents more to expend on car fare in looking after his interests or visiting his friends.

The above is no hypothetical case, but an actual recorded occurrence. The region affected was that which lies sixty miles east and west of Trinity, Texas. The general freight agent who engineered this successful local enterprise said:

"We study the market question before we go into any region with any such proposition. We want our farmers to succeed, not fail. They will avoid an uncertainty as quickly as you will. Those tomatoes are shipped to all the Northern markets. We move them in car-loads only. We have people in the cities who are practical commission men, who have not only knowledge of the commission business, but also have knowledge of the trade. After we have secured the information as to where the tomatoes will be available, our horticultural agent, on the ground with the farmers, helps them decide where they will ship."

Such a tale may not only be recorded of tomatoes. The same general freight agent remarked:

"In addition to that success, our horticultural department is encouraging some sections, where the soil is adapted to it, to plant early cabbage. We want the farmers to make the best use of their land. Half the time they don't know; the other half they can't do anything because they have no way of reaching a market. With our knowledge of markets we can easily encourage them. Why, just the other day one of my men was in here, and I said to him, 'I want you to stop at every single station in Missouri; go out and see the farmers, and see what you can do with the development of the potato business.' We find that the soil along the Missouri River is particularly adapted to raising potatoes. Now I warrant you that our farmers along the Missouri will make more money out of potatoes in a year or two than they ever have made out of their other crops. We will show them how."

In looking over the. Missouri Labor Commissioners' map, one finds that in 1898 there were 70,081,267 surplus pounds of poultry shipped out of the State, an increase of 18,267,743 over 1897. In the same year 4,081,833 pounds of butter were exported, an increase of 162,866 pounds over 1897; and in the matter of eggs, 33,935,325 dozen were shipped, showing a substantial increase over previous years. Those figures tell an interesting story of the new railroad policy now in force, and the growth can be directly traced to the policy in question.

The dairy or creamery business, which involves the production of butter and eggs, has been energetically promoted by two great roads leading out of St. Louis, and encouraged in a moderate way by several others. This fact is attested by the presence in the State of twoscore or more of flourishing creameries, scattered throughout the counties, which were organized and built by the railroads, though the latter do not hold a single share of stock in any of them. The original idea was suggested, the meetings called, the money raised, and the buildings erected under the supervision of one or the other agent of the several general freight departments of the roads. Even the machinery was purchased in every case for the farmers by the railroad agent, and the method of conducting a dairy taught by another representative of the road free of charge, and all to make the county prosperous, in order that the railroad might be prosperous.

Document 12.3

Report of the Governor of Arizona (1905)

Still seven years away from statehood, the governor clearly paints a rosy future for his territory. He notes the higher-than-usual rainfall, the booming copper mines, and progress in railroad construction. As the territory's biggest booster, the governor counters perceptions of a lawless inhospitable land. However, this portrait of Arizona is balanced with the less attractive aspects of the desert land as well, noting conditions of the soil and climate and the reliance on irrigation.*

REPORT OF THE GOVERNOR OF ARIZONA.

OFFICE OF THE GOVERNOR,
Phoenix, Ariz., August 26, 1905.
SIR: In compliance with your instructions, I have the honor to submit to you the following report of the affairs of Arizona for the fiscal year ended June 30, 1905:
INTRODUCTORY.

I am pleased to report the general prosperity of the Territory. Population is increasing at a rapid rate; all the various industrial interests are developing at an accelerated ratio, and a buoyant and hopeful feeling pervades our people.

Arizona presents so many unique features, so many difficulties that can not be appreciated by the inhabitants of the older communities of the country, that it is almost hopeless to attempt to present within the limits of an official report either the conditions to be met or the splendid developments that have been attained notwithstanding those difficulties. It is difficult for the resident of the Eastern States to realize that the products of the soil of the greater part of Arizona are only possible with the artificial application of water to the land; that the hay and the grain, and the fruits, are only obtained from irrigated lands.

---

* "Report of the Governor of Arizona," *Reports of the Department of the Interior,* (August 26, 1905), pp. 129-132.

The average eastern or middle western farmer would think it almost a prohibitive tax upon his industry to have to pay \$1, \$2, \$3, or even more, per acre per year merely to supply his land with the water sufficient to sustain and promote the growth of his crops; but on lands of the fertility of ours and with a climate like that of our valleys such an apparent imposition is trivial when compared with the results. The conditions of soil and climate of those countries inhabited by the Anglo-Saxon are generally such that the artificial application of water for the cultivation of crops seems to him anomalous. In a vague, indefinite way we may know that a very large proportion of the inhabitants of the globe obtain their food supply from irrigated lands, but it is only in the comparatively newly settled arid parts of the United States that the significance of the fact is brought home to our realization. The American, with his accustomed energy, genius, and audacity, is just entering upon the contest with the desert. The subject is a new one to him; yet the intricate problems are being solved with characteristic promptness and upon lines entirely consistent with his notions of justice and individual freedom and independence.

The National Government is engaged in an interesting experiment in the reclamation of the arid lands. It is an interesting experiment from many points of view-from the social, the political, and the economic, as well as from the engineering standpoint.

Briefly stated, the Government has appropriated the proceeds of the sales of public lands in certain of the States and Territories to be used for the construction of dams and other works for the storage and diversion of water for the reclamation of arid lands. In any given project the cost of the works is added to the Government price of the lands supplied with water by it and repaid in annual installments. In the event that lands already in private ownership are included within the area of service by the projected works, the Government may grant a water right to the owner upon terms to be fixed by the Secretary of the Interior. In either case the entire cost of the works is eventually returned to the Government and may be used by it in the construction of other works. The lands so reclaimed are worthless without the water. Eventually, when the Government has been reimbursed for the cost of construction, the works become the property and subject to the management of the associated landowners. This plan avoids the vice and evil tendencies of subsidy by the Government, for the relation between the Government and the owner of the reclaimed land is essentially that of creditor and debtor and not that of patron and pensioner. The Government simply takes the money it receives from the sales of certain of its lands to construct works to render other of its lands habitable and profitable, and consequently marketable, where it has been that individual or private corporate effort was inadequate. The Government gets back the money expended, and the settler retains his self-respect. It would be an unfortunate policy for the American Government to adopt that any of its citizens should become mere gratuitous beneficiaries of its bounty.

I advert specifically in later portions of my report to the projects now under way in this Territory under the provisions of the national irrigation act.

I am pleased, too, to note that there has been a perceptible growth in the civic pride of our people. It is so usual to associate the fact of Territorial government with crudity, lawlessness, laxity of morals, want of stability, and indifference to business faith and integrity that great injustice is often done us. It is true that in a new country there is at least a greater disregard of the conventionalities than in our older communities, but it does not necessarily follow that there is more real lawlessness, less of probity and integrity, or even a greater laxity of morals. Arizona has been made the subject of many careless criticisms by indifferent, incapable, and thoughtless observers. Many profess a profound shock of their moral sensibilities, while they are willfully or ignorantly blind to vices at home that would not be tolerated in "wide-open Arizona." I do not attempt in any degree to palliate any matter of just criticism, but the criticism should be just and the critic should know something of the conditions. That conditions are different here from those in the older communities is not evidence, as it is often assumed to be that they are therefore worse here. This would suggest itself to those not wholly provincial, and Arizona can not be charged with provincialism. I think I can safely assert that life and property are safer in Arizona than in many, if not in most, of the States. Nowhere, I am sure, can a man who respects himself and his neighbor and his neighbor's rights with reasonably strict attention to his own business go about with more freedom and with greater confidence of personal safety than be can in Arizona. Locked and barricaded doors are in most parts of Arizona a novelty. The professional thief, as he is known in the older and more thickly populated communities, is almost unknown in Arizona.

I have had occasion in my report to call attention to many things that may provoke instant criticism-the mere statement of some of them suggests it. But it is my opinion that fair criticism is not harmful, but on the contrary productive of good. It is a matter of common observation that most of the evils of the administration of public affairs arises from an indifference of the people. This indifference is chiefly because of a want of knowledge by the people of the evils, other than in a general way. As long as there is no publicity there is encouragement and opportunity for the growth of these evils. If the statement of these matters which are the subject of criticism shall call attention to them, it will also suggest the remedy.

The rainfall during the year has been far in excess of the normal. Its immediate effect was to renew the grasses on the ranges and to relieve the conditions threatening disaster to the live-stock interests. The streams relied upon to supply water for irrigation were replenished, and an abundance of water has been available for that purpose. Springs and streams in the mountains, which had for a long time, owing to the continued drought been dead, are again living. The indirect results are reflected in all industries, doing much to revive hope and promote confidence in the development of the resources of the Territory. The good effected by the copious rains was not wholly unmixed with injury, however. Floods in the various streams were numerous and inflicted considerable damage to property. Railroad bridges and embankments were washed away; dams for diverting water for irrigation were destroyed, and canals were to a greater or less extent seriously damaged. In Apache County the damage to irrigation works was, proportionately, particularly heavy, dams and reservoirs which were the sole dependence of large cultivated areas having been destroyed. The aggregate of good, however, greatly outbalanced the ill that was done. Arizona had experienced a series of droughts extending over a period of six years. Each seemed more serious than the one preceding.

In his report of last year the governor reported that, as noted at the station at Phoenix, there was a deficit for the year of rainfall below the normal of 3.97 inches. For the year ending June 30, 1905, there was an excess over the normal of 12.33 inches. This condition is one full of encouragement.

The mining industry is being prosecuted with more energy than ever. A persistent and sensible effort is being made to take mining in Arizona out of the category of the purely speculative-"gambling"-pursuits. Intelligence, ability, and special scientific training and processes are being applied to the business in a greater degree than ever before, with the effect, naturally to be expected, of making it a more certain and less hazardous one. In times past much misdirected energy and many wasted thousands of dollars have been expended in the business. Better methods now prevail, with consequently better and more certain results.

The copper product is increasing enormously. If the ratio now prevailing shall continue Arizona will easily be the first copper-producing country in the world, if she has not in fact already attained that distinction.

The production of gold and silver is also increasing, but naturally at not so great a ratio as the baser metal.

Railroad construction has been almost continuously in progress throughout the year, opening up to the markets new or hitherto difficult sources of our natural wealth. Some of the new lines constructed constitute real scenic routes, and the achievements of the engineer and the courage of the builder challenge the wonder and admiration even more than the rugged difficulties encountered and overcome.

Harvests have been abundant, the ranges prolific, the mines productive beyond any previous record, and the people of Arizona are full of hope and courage for the greater and accelerated development sure to follow.

Document 12.4

Brownsville Court Martial (1906)

On the night of August 13, 1906, one of the most controversial racial incidents of the twentieth-century West took place near Fort Brown, just outside of Brownsville, Texas. Black soldiers garrisoned there heard shots nearby and assumed, because of the tenuous race relations that then existed with the nearby town, that they were being attacked by a local mob. On the other hand, the local citizenry thought that they were being set upon. Ten minutes of gunfire led to the deaths of a young bartender and a police lieutenant. In one of its darker moments, the War Department discharged one hunded and sixty-seven soldiers without honor. The soldiers were not offered so much as a public hearing.

In September 1972, the victims of the "gross injustice" were granted honorable discharges by the Secretary of the Army. The following

February, Dorsie W. Willis personally received his honorable discharge papers on his eighty-seventh birthday. The first extract is part of the court-martial proceedings against Captains Edgar A. Macklin and Samuel P. Lyon, the white commanders of regiments. Their testimony captures the racial tension between the soldiers and the townspeople. The second piece offers testimony by several witnesses from the town who offer their account of the night's carnage.*

The Miller Hotel witnesses.

M. YGNACIO DOMINGUEZ was first duly sworn by Maj. A. P. Blocksom, and, upon being examined by Mr. Purdy, testified as follows:

Q. What is your full name?—A. M. Ygnacio Dominguez.

Q. How long have you resided in Brownsville?—A. I was born and raised in Brownsville.

Q. What is your age?—A. On the 16th day of this last October I was 58 years old.

Q. What is your official position?—A. I have been in different capacities most of the time on the police force for the last twenty or twenty-five years.

Q. What is your position now on the police force?—A. I am lieutenant of police of the city of Brownsville.

Q. You remember the 13th of August 1906?—A. Yes. On August 13, at about eight minutes of 12 o'clock, more or less, I heard some shots fired near the garrison.

Q. Where were you located at that time?—A. I was on the market, where the station is.

Q. Where is that located?—A. In the center of the town, between Eleventh and Twelfth streets. I was there waiting until the bell rang—you know the bell rings every night at 12 o'clock and about eight minutes before 12. As I said before, I heard some shots down near the garrison, on Washington street. When I got up by Mrs. Suder's I heard the shooting going on. When I got on Thirteenth street, on the corner, they had just got through shooting at Mr. Cowen's house, and I stopped there for a moment, and then the shooting stopped; and then they went across the alley—the alley that goes across Thirteenth street between Elizabeth street and Washington street—and fired a few shots. That is the same alley that leads down back of the Miller Hotel. At Fourteenth street I turned my horse and came back to Thirteenth to guard myself against the fence, and when I got to the corner I could hear them coming through the alley toward Miller's Hotel; they were walking, and every now and then you could hear them murmuring. When I crossed the alleyway I heard a voice once or twice that said: "Give them hell!"

Q. Did you see the men at that time?—A. No. I heard those words though, and then a volley fired. I paused a little and hollered out, "Halt, there!" and then I commenced talking louder, so as to wake up the people in the Miller Hotel, as I knew the downstairs doors were open, and as I knew there were lots of passengers—women and children—there. I thought the best plan was to try to wake them up and tell them that the colored

_____

* "Summary Discharge or Mustering Out of Regiments or Companies," *Senate Documents*, 59th Congress, 2nd Session, Vol. 11, (Washington: Government Printing Office, 1907), pp. 57-62.

soldiers were shooting at the people. I kept on to Elizabeth street, and while I was in my stirrup standing just so (indicating). I could see that one file took one side of the sidewalk and the other the side by Miller's Hotel.

Q. About how many men did you see?—A. I could tell that there were between fifteen and twenty of them.

Q. Could you see who they were?—A. I could recognize that they were soldiers.

Q. Were they white or black?—A. Black.

Q. Which way did they go?—A. They came out from the alley and one file went on one side of the walk and the other by Miller's Hotel. Just as I got to the corner of Elizabeth street, as I started to raise. I received this wound and my horse was shot, too. The horse stumbled and fell right across the street, opposite Mr. Wreford's office.

Q. That is the last you saw of the soldiers?—A. Yes. The horse fell on this leg (indicating), and while I was trying to pull my leg out from under him I turned around and saw the soldiers tiptoeing, going back toward the corner of the alley.

Q. Did you see them when they went into the alley?—A. I saw them when they got to the corner.

Q. You did not see whether they went down toward the fort or toward the Ruby Saloon?—A. No, sir. I went on Elizabeth street, away from the fort. When I got to the lamp on the corner I heard some shots on the opposite side by the alley where this man Frank Natus was killed.

Q. And you heard shots being fired in the rear of that saloon?—A. I heard some shots fired and after that I did not hear anymore.

Q. Where did you go then?—A. I kept on going and when I got to the corner of Mrs. Bolark's more I met two Mexicans. They said Lieutenant, you are badly full of bullets," I said "No. I only got my arm broke." I was getting weaker, and they brought me to the first drug store, and I had my arm bandaged after they had taken me upstairs.

Q. During the time of the shooting did you have your revolver out?—A. No. I never took it out; it was in my belt. I thought the best plan was to try to wake up the people. I knew very well that there was such a constant shooting that if I stopped a moment I would get riddled with bullets and I would not get a chance to tell anybody to get up.

Q. How far were you from these soldiers when you saw them there at the alley?—A. About 25 feet.

Q. Were they in the dark or in the shadows of the buildings at that time?—A. No; there was a lamp on the corner and one by Mr. Bolack's; I was between the two lamps; it was not very dark; there was no moon, but there wasn't any clouds.

Q. You could recognize that they were colored troops?—A. Yes.

Q. How far were they away from you at the time you received burn wound in the arm?—A. I think it must have been about 60 feet between me and them.

Q. Mr. Dominguez, were you looking toward the soldiers at the time you received the wound in your right arm?—A. I was standing the stirrup just in this position (stood up in the bed, indicating); I did not exactly have my back to them, but I was standing so as to make myself appear as thin as I could. I could see them, but I could not tell whether they were noncommissioned or not. The ball struck me on the inside of my arm—that is, the side next to my body—and then exploded.

Q. That is all that you know about the affair?—A. Yes, sir.

Q. Had you ever had any trouble with any of these soldiers stationed there at the fort?—A. Well. I can't say that I had trouble with them; I have had to arrest several of other troops, but I never had any trouble with these. I very seldom ever spoke to any of them.

Q. How long have you been lieutenant of police?—A. About fifteen years, twelve or fifteen.

M. Y. DOMINGUEZ.

GENABO PADRON was first duly sworn by Maj. A. P. Blocksom, and, upon being examined by Mr. Purdy, testified as follows:

(This testimony was given through Interpreter John J. Kleiber, Sq.)

Q. Mr. Padron, you are a police officer of the city of Brownsville?—A. Yes, sir.

Q. How long have you been on the police force of this city?—A. I have been a policeman for about two years past. Prior to that I was a constable of this precinct. I have been a police officer for the past two years; prior to that, a constable for four years, and prior to that, or four years, a deputy sheriff under Sheriff Forto.

Q. You were on duty on the night of the 13th of August, 1906?—A. Yes, sir.

Q. Where were you at the time that the shooting occurred in the Vicinity of Fort Brown?—A. I was at the corner of the Merchants' National Bank.

Q. At about what time was that?—A. About five to ten minutes before midnight.

Q. Was there anybody with you at that time?—A. There were several people. There were Florencio Briseño, Miguel Jagou, who has since died, Manuel Alpnzo, jr., and, I think, Mr. Schmidt. I am not sure whether he was present or not.

Q. When you heard the shooting, where did you go?—A. I came down this street (Elizabeth street) to the hotel (Miller Hotel) corner, and turned toward Washington street. I reached the corner of Washington street and went down one block on Washington street to the corner.

Q. Was there anyone with you at that time?—A. Briseño came down the street with me as far as the Miller Hotel. Briseño continuing down Elizabeth street.

Q. During this time did you hear any shots fired?—A. Yes, sir; when I got down to the corner of Washington street they came out of this alley firing.

Q. Where is that alley where you first saw them?—A. The alley just as you come out of Mr. Cowen's.

Q. How near were you to these men when you saw them firing at the entrance of the alley and Mr. Cowen's house?—A. About 150 feet, more or less.

Q. Were you then standing on Washington and Fourteenth street?—A. Yes, sir.

Q. How many men did you see near the Cowen residence?—A. Not less than ten or twelve.

Q. Who were they?—A. They were dressed in soldiers' uniforms—the Hash of the guns showed clearly the yellow uniform.

Q. How many shots were fired by these men at that time?—A. I can not tell you, sir. They fired quite a number.

Q. Could you tell from the position of their guns and the flash of the shot in which direction or into what building they were firing?—A. Over toward the Leaby Hotel.

Q. How long did they remain there at that time?—A. Just as they ran out into the alley they fired. Then I ran back and met Ygnacio Dominguez.

Q. Where did you meet Ygnacio Dominguez?—A. In the middle of the street, in front, almost, of the Pecina house.

Q. Is that near the corner of Washington and Fourteenth streets?—A. It is on Washington street and near Fourteenth street.

Q. In which direction did you then go with Dominguez?—A. When I met Dominguez. I told him to dismount, as he was too conspicuous a target for them, if they passed who were firing.

Q. Did he do so?—A. Dominguez dismounted and tightened the girdle of his saddle on his horse.

Q. Where did you and Dominguez go?—A. As soon as Dominguez tightened the girdle he remounted his horse and we went on up the street. I ahead of Dominguez on foot.

Q. Where did you go from there?—A. We got to the corner of Thirteenth street, and I turned then into Thirteenth toward the Miller Hotel. At this time the firing was going on by the alley toward the hotel. When I got about to the door of Mr. Bolack's house, I saw the lieutenant of police coming behind me. When he reached me, I said to him: "Lieutenant, don't go any further, because they will likely shoot you from where they are now firing." I told him this two or three times. He paid no attention to me. He proceeded on. Then I retreated, went back. As the lieutenant crossed the alley some one said: "There goes one;" and one replied: "Shoot him; hell." By that time I was nearly to the corner, and I saw three men throw their carbines down onto Dominguez and I fired and shot at them. They fired on him. As they fired, others came out of the alley, and said: "Here are others." By that time I was at the corner. I fired a shot and then hid myself behind the house at the corner.

Q. Was that at the corner of Washington and Thirteenth streets?—A. This was at the corner of Washington and Thirteenth streets.

Q. Then you were about a half a block, or 150 feet, away from these men who were doing the firing?—A. Yes, sir; I peeped out from behind the corner, and I saw a number of men, half a dozen or more, coming in my direction. I then retreated on up Washington street, hiding myself behind the trees as I came to them. As they reached the corner of Washington and Thirteenth streets they then fired a volley in my direction—that is, up the street. I then ran to the upper corner, they still firing. As I reached the upper corner there was a lighted lamp a street lamp. They evidently saw me as another shot was fired and the bullet struck the shed, went through and struck the wall. At that time I stumbled and fell, and then went forward on my hands and knees. Then I arose and went on to the next corner. They went on up Washington street to the store on the corner of Washington and Twelfth. Then they turned into Twelfth street, toward Elizabeth. When I got to the corner of Washington and Eleventh, a man from a second-story window inquired of me what was going on. I replied that soldiers had come out of the post. I then turned into Eleventh and went to the corner of Elizabeth street, at the First National Bank, came down on Elizabeth street to the corner of Elizabeth and Twelfth, at the Merchants' Bank, looking for the lieutenant of police, who had started toward Elizabeth street, not knowing what had happened to him. While I was standing there I heard some one striking on the uprights of the store about half a block away. I went in that direction, thinking some one was calling me, and I there met the mayor of the city and his brother, Dr. Joe Combe. They asked me what had happened, and I told them the soldiers had broken out of the post and were firing upon the town. I told them I was looking for the lieutenant of police, Dominguez, who ought to have been there on the street somewhere. We then turned and came on down Elizabeth street along the sidewalk. As we approached the Merchants' Bank we saw blood on the sidewalk. We then came on down the street toward the barroom. We found everything closed.

Q. When you saw there men come down the alley on to Thirteenth street and five or six of them go toward Washington street in your direction, will you state whether or not you could tell whether they were white men or colored men?—A. All I can tell you is that I can describe to you how they were dressed, and that they had carbines—guns.

Q. Describe how they were dressed.—A. They were dressed in yellow uniforms.

Q. What portion of the uniform was yellow?—A. All the uniform.

Q. Did you know whether or not they had on hat or caps?—A. I could not be sure, but it appeared to me as if they wore hats. One man was bareheaded.

Q. About how many men did you see come out of the alley at the time Dominguez went down toward Elizabeth street?—A. Not less than ten or twelve.

Q. Do you know where the men other than those who followed you went? A. I do not, sir.

Q. Did you hear any other firing than that which was directed to ward you over on Washington street?—A. Over in the direction of that same alley—I can not say that there was but there was firing in the direction of that same alley they were going up.

Q. Do you know where Tillman's saloon is located?—A. Yes, sir.

Q. Did you hear any firing in that direction of the saloon while you were in the vicinity of Washington and Thirteenth streets?—A. Yes. sir; I could hear the shots in that direction while I was going up Washington street.

Q. You did not see Dominguez when he was wounded and when his horse fell with him at the corner of Elizabeth and Thirteenth streets?—A. No, sir.

Q. At that time you were retreating up Washington street toward Twelfth street?—A. I only saw him when they fired the first shot at him, as his horse was running. I looked for him up in the other direction, thinking he had gone by.

Q. During the time of your retreat from near the alley on Thirteenth street over to Washington street and then up Washington street toward Twelfth street were you running or walking?—A. I was running.

Q. From the time that you heard the first shots down in the neighborhood of the garrison until the last shots were fired about how long a period of time elapsed?—A. From ten to fifteen minutes, more or less.

Q. When you saw these men over in the vicinity of the Cowen residence how were they dressed?—A. With this yellow uniform.

Q. About how many men did you see about the Cowen residence?—A. Ten to twelve, more or less.

Q. During the whole time of the firing you were east of the alley running between Elizabeth street and Washington street and parallel to said streets?—A. With the exception that when the first shots were fired I was up here on this street. After that I was east of this alley.

Q. Are you familiar with the reports of firearms generally?—A. Yes, sir; fairly so. There is a great difference between the detonation of pistols and the firearms such as we use and the class of firearms used by soldiers.

Q. What was the nature of the report of these shots?—A. Not a loud report, something like a firecracker, a quick, sharp report.

Q. Do you think of anything else concerning which you care to make a statement?—A. Only that I saw that dead man.

Q. You have told substantially all you know that took place on the night of the 13th of August?—A. At present I can think of nothing else.

GENARO PADRON.

Document 12.5

Geronimo at the World's Fair

The Chirichua Apache medicine man and leader Geronimo (1829?-1909) was the last American Indian to surrender formally to the United States. Between 1848 and 1886 he was constantly at war with Mexican and American forces. In 1886 he surrendered to General Nelson Miles unaware that he had agreed to "unconditional terms." His last years were spent in exile in Florida and then Fort Sill, Oklahoma. On occasion, the federal government viewed the Apache leader as an asset that could be displayed at prominent public affairs. In 1904 Geronimo visited the St. Louis World's Fair. In his autobiography, transcribed by S.M. Barrett, Superintendent of Education at Lawton, Oklahoma, Geronimo recounts his experience at the exhibition.*

When I was at first asked to attend the St. Louis World's Fair I did not wish to go. Later, when I was told that I would receive good attention and protection, and that the President of the United States said that it would be all right, I consented. I was kept by parties in charge of the Indian Department, who had obtained permission from the President. I stayed in this place for six months. I sold my photographs for twenty-five cents, and was allowed to keep ten cents of this for myself. I also wrote my name for ten, fifteen, or twenty-five cents, as the case might be, and kept all of that money. I often made as much as two dollars a day, and when I returned I had plenty of money-more than I had ever owned before.

---

* S.M. Barrett, ed., *Geronimo's Story of His Life*, (New York: Duffield and Company, 1906), pp. 197-205.

Many people in St. Louis invited me to come to their homes, but my keeper always refused.

Every Sunday the President of the Fair sent for me to go to a wild west show. I took part in the roping contests before the audience. There were many other Indian tribes there, and strange people of whom I had never heard.

When people first came to the World's Fair they did nothing but parade up and down the streets. When they got tired of this they would visit the shows. There were many strange things in these shows. The Government sent guards with me when I went, and I was not allowed to go anywhere without them.

In one of the shows some strange men with red caps had some peculiar swords, and they seemed to want to fight. Finally their manager told them they might fight each other. They tried to hit each other over the head with these swords, and I expected both to be wounded or perhaps killed, but neither one was harmed. They would be hard people to kill in a hand-to-hand fight.

In another show there was a strange-looking negro. The manager tied his hands fast, then tied him to a chair. He was securely tied, for I looked myself, and I did not think it was possible for him to get away. Then the manager told him to get loose.

He twisted in his chair for a moment, and then stood up; the ropes were still tied, but he was free. I do not understand how this was done. It was certainly a miraculous power, because no man could have released himself by his own efforts.

In another place a man was on a platform speaking to the audience; they set a basket by the side of the platform and covered it with red calico; then a woman came and got into the basket, and a man covered the basket again with the calico; then the man who was speaking to the audience took a long sword and ran it through the basket, each way, and then down through the cloth cover. I heard the sword cut through the woman's body, and the manager himself said she was dead; but when the cloth was lifted from the basket she stepped out, smiled, and walked off the stage. I would like to know how she was so quickly healed, and why the wounds did not kill her.

I have never considered bears very intelligent, except in their wild habits, but I had never before seen a white bear. In one of the shows a man had a white bear that was as intelligent as a man. He would do whatever he was told-carry a log on his shoulder, just as a man would; then, when he was told, would put it down again. He did many other things, and seemed to know exactly what his keeper said to him. I am sure that no grizzly bear could be trained to do these things.

One time the guards took me into a little house that had four windows. When we were seated the little house started to move along the ground. Then the guards called pay attention to some curious things they had in their pockets. Finally they told me to look out, and when I did so I was scared, for our little house had gone high up in the air, and the people down in the Fair grounds looked no larger than ants. The men laughed at me for being scared; then they gave me a glass to look through (I often had such glasses which I took from old officers after battles in Mexico and somewhere), and I could see rivers, lakes and mountains. But I had never been so high in the air, and I tried to look into the sky. There were no stars, and I could not look at the sun through this glass because the brightness hurt my eyes. Finally I put the glass down, and as they were all laughing at me, I too, began to laugh. Then they said, "Get out!" and when I looked we were on the street again. After we were safe on the land I watched many of these little houses going up and coming down, but I cannot understand how they travel. They are very curious little houses.

One day we went into another show, and as soon as we were in, it changed into night. It was real night, for I could feel the damp air; soon it began to thunder, and the lightnings flashed; it was real lightning, too, for it struck just above our heads. I dodged and wanted to run away, but I could not tell which way to go in order to get out. The guards motioned me to keep still, and so I stayed. In front of us were some strange little people who came out on the platform; then I looked up again and the clouds were all gone, and I could see the stars shining. The little people on the platform did not seem in earnest about anything they did; so I only laughed at them. All the people around where we sat seemed to be laughing at me.

We went into another place and the manager took us into a little room that was made like a cage; then everything around us seemed to be moving; soon the air looked blue, then there were black clouds moving with the wind. Pretty soon it was clear outside; then we saw a few thin white clouds; then the clouds grew thicker, and it rained and hailed with thunder and lightning. Then the thunder retreated and a rainbow appeared in the distance; then it became dark, the moon rose and thousands of stars came out. Soon the sun came up, and we got out of the little room. This was a good show, but it was so strange and unnatural that I was glad to be on the streets again.

We went into one place where they made glassware. I had always thought that these things were made by hand, but they are not. The man had a curious little instrument, and whenever he would blow through this into a little blaze the glass would take any shape he wanted it to. I am not sure, but I think that if I had this kind of an instrument I could make whatever I wished. There seems to be a charm about it. But I suppose it is very difficult to get these little instruments, or other people would have them. The people in this show were so anxious to buy the things the man made that they kept him so busy he could not sit down all day long. I bought many curious things in there and brought them home with me.

At the end of one of the streets some people were getting into a clumsy canoe, upon a kind of shelf, and sliding down into the water. They seemed to enjoy it, but it looked too fierce for me. If one of these canoes had gone out of its path the people would have been sure to get hurt or killed.

There were some little brown people at the Fair that United States troops captured recently on some islands far away from here.

They did not wear much clothing, and I think that they should not have been allowed to come to the Fair. But they themselves did not seem to know any better. They had some little brass plates, and they tried to lay music with these, but I did not think was music-it was only a rattle. However, they danced to this noise and seemed to think they were giving a fine show.

I do not know how true the report was, but I heard that the President sent them to the Fair so that they could learn some manners, and when they went home teach their people how to dress and how to behave.

I am glad I went to the Fair. I saw many interesting things and learned much of the white people. They are a very kind and peaceful people. During all the time I was at the Fair no one tried to harm me in any way.

Document 12.6

Japanese and Italian Truck Gardeners in Sacramento, California (1911)

The following is a comparison between Italian and Japanese truck gardeners in Sacramento, California. Truck gardeners are farmers who brought their produce to markets where they sold to peddler middlemen who in turn sold to produce stands and grocery stores. Included in this government report is comparative sociological and historical data covering the various immigrant groups of the Sacramento Valley.*

There are about 150 truck gardeners and berry growers who sell their products in the Sacramento market to be locally consumed. Eighty or more of these are Japanese, some 45 or 50 are Chinese, and between 20 and 25 are North Italians. Other races find practically no place in this small farming. These producers bring their produce to the free market and dispose of a good part of it to hucksters and peddlers. The peddlers in the city are largely Chinese; the hucksters, Japanese, Italians, and "white men." All told, they number about 70. Besides these there are three hucksters who serve the country communities and small villages near by. After these peddlers and hucksters obtain their supplies, the numerous growers sell to the many fruit stands and vegetable stalls and the large groceries of Sacramento.

A short distance south of Sacramento, along the Sacramento River, are two groups of gardeners. One is on the "Y street road," the other on the "Riverside road." The former group includes some 10 Japanese and 15 Chinese, the latter, 10 Japanese, 15 Chinese, and about 10 Italians. Between Sacramento and Brighton, 5 miles to the east, there are 8 Japanese, 3 Chinese, and several Italian gardeners. Among the latter, however, are three farmers who produce some truck along with grain and hay on large farms (100, 80, and 30 acres, respectively). Near Broderick, a village across the Sacramento River, there are some 15 Japanese and 10 Chinese gardeners. A few gardeners of these races are found also in other localities not specializing in the growing of truck. Finally, a large number of Japanese berry growers and gardeners come to the Sacramento market from Florin, a village some 10 miles south of the city.

The Chinese have long engaged in growing vegetables for the Sacramento market. Indeed for many years the vast majority of the gardeners were of that race. More recently, however, their numbers have diminished somewhat as an effect of the exclusion laws and with the growth of population and expansion of the market other races have

---

* *Report of the Immigration Commission: Immigrants in Industries, Part 25: V.II Japanese and Other Immigrant Races in the Pacific Coast and Rocky Mountain States,* (Washington: Government Printing Office, 1911), pp. 453-454; 457-458.

entered this branch of production, so that they have become a less and less important element in the total number.

A small number of Italians have migrated directly to Sacramento since shortly after 1870, while others in recent years have moved there from other places-chiefly along the lower Sacramento. Toward 1890 they began to grow vegetables, and from 1890-1900 occupied a place in this industry as important as that occupied by the Chinese.

The Chinese gardeners have always been tenants. So were most of the Italians to begin with. As a rule, after working for wages for a few years they have formed a partnership or purchased a share in one already organized. After gardening as a member of one of these groups of from two to nine partners for a few years the typical Italian has purchased land and become an independent grower. As a result of this evolution, which usually takes place, perhaps one-half of the Italian gardens are owned by the single grower and contain from 5 to 20 acres, and are worth from $1,500 to $5,000. The other gardeners are cash tenants who have little property, who usually form partnerships, and in this way hold larger tracts of land.

The first Japanese came to Sacramento about thirty years ago, but their numbers did not amount to 100 until shortly after 1890. From that time, however, Sacramento has served as a distributing point for laborers for the orchards, vineyards, and gardens along the Sacramento and its tributaries and for the orchards about Newcastle. In fact, it has been the most important distributing point in California for agricultural laborers. Beginning about 1895, a few of these Japanese leased land and engaged in truck gardening, and since 1903 the number of such gardeners has rapidly increased until they now are the most important race engaged in that branch of production. As a result of their influx, it is asserted by growers of other races, the amount of produce has been increased more rapidly than the needs of the market warrant, and the Italians, who are not technically so efficient, are being forced to give up gardening because of the losses they have sustained. However this may be, it is true that few Italians have taken up the growing of vegetables for this market in recent years.

Seventeen of the male members of the Japanese families investigated are married, 13 are single, and one is widowed. Thirteen were married previous to immigrating to the United States, 2 were married during subsequent visits to Japan, and 2 were married in this country. Three, including 1 who, with his wife, had been in Hawaii, brought their wives with them. Three other wives have joined their husbands more recently. Hence, of the 17 wives, 10 are in the United States, 7 in Japan. Of the 30 farmers, 7, for the most part married men with wives in the United States, expressed their intention of remaining permanently in this country. Fifteen, on the other hand, expected to return to their native land at a later time, while the remaining 8 were in doubt as to what they would eventually do. Four of these farmers are members of and attend the Buddhist Mission in Sacramento, 2 are members of the Japanese Methodist Mission, while the remaining 24 have no active membership in any religious organization.

A large percentage of these farmers came from the prefecture of Kochi, and 12 of them have membership in the club organized by the Japanese about Sacramento who have come from that prefecture. Aside from this the Japanese truck farmers are without organization. American fraternal organizations are closed to them.

All of the Japanese farmers save one, and all of their wives, were found to be literate. All of the men, but only 2 women, could speak English. However, only 7 men and 2 women could read and write our language. The slight command of English by the women is explained in part by the fact that 5 of them had been in the United States less than five years and none had been here more than nine. Most of the Japanese are living most economically. Nine of the individuals and groups, for example, subscribed for no newspaper; the other 8 subscribed for from one to three-all published by Japanese in Sacramento or San Francisco and printed in their native language. This fact is indicative of the degree of their assimilation, their interests, and the character of the information they receive from printed sources.

The housing is on the whole poor and the premises neglected. Some of the houses occupied are "bunk houses," others cottages erected for white families, while still others are rough "box houses" erected for or by the Japanese tenants. Most of them are small, but inasmuch as the extra "help" hired during the busy season are usually provided with lodging elsewhere, there is not much over-crowding. Most of the dwellings are scantily furnished. In a large percentage of the cases the housework is poorly done by the men, and even where the wife is in the United States it is usually neglected in order that she may work in the field. In 9 of the 17 cases the agent reported the care of the house as "bad," in the other 8 as "fair."

Data were also gathered with reference to the cost of food and drink. In making use of these data, however, it should be remembered that these Japanese are all gardeners and produce most of the vegetables they use. Their purchases are chiefly of tea and soft drinks, rice, canned fish and meats, and sauce-most of them at Japanese provision stores in Sacramento. The 17 farming groups reported the cost per month per person as varying from $5 to $10. The median figure was $7.50, the average $7.11 per month.

The social life of these truck farmers, their families, and employees centers in Sacramento, near by, where there are many forms of amusement conducted by Japanese. Their relations with the white population are almost entirely incidental to the transaction of business. There is a strong prejudice among the white people against the Japanese which practically precludes contact in other forms save in exceptional instances.

Document 12.7

Is there a West? (1920)

Frederick Jackson Turner heralded the closing of the Western frontier in 1890. By the 1920s, many Americans lamented the disappearance of the so-called "Old West." There has never been any real consensus on how to define "The West." Indeed, there have always been many Wests, but mostly imaginary ones. In the modern era, California has represented all of the possibilities engendered by the "Old West." The existence of the 1950s Beat Generation and the 1960s Counterculture, both centered in California, suggest that in the late twentieth century, California still remains a safety valve for people who need a frontier where they can go and re-invent themselves. In the following article, California is portrayed as a Shangri-la for the nature lover, capable of restoring both vigor and health as well as renewing the spirit. In a little more than a decade, however, the Joads of the *Grapes of Wrath* would find another California and another West. Note the description of California young women in this article, so redolent of 1960s Beach Boys melodies heralding California "girls" and the outdoors.*

The West, if it exists, has already been pushed beyond the High Sierras. It only remains to discover whether or not it has been shoved into the Pacific and safely out of American life.

The West, in the old sense of anything cruder, less civilized, rougher than the East, is unquestionably gone. There is a bathroom to each hotel bedroom, and the younger English poets lecture in all the smallest towns. It takes an eagle's eye to find the traditional lack of cultivation, and few Easterners, at any rate, have eagles' eyes. This question of "culture" may as well be disposed of now and flung out of our way; it impedes our westward progress. As you advance toward the Pacific, "culture," if anything, only takes on a more passionate, almost exacerbated quality, as though its possessors were determined to prove to the scoffing how brightly the piously guarded flame burns on the sunset altar to the muses. For decades, daughters of the Californian aristocracy have been educated in Paris at the Convent of the Sacred Heart. The French note is indeed firmly struck in the West. You find small children, who, reared by foreign governesses, are more at ease with the Latin languages than with their own. And, to choose but one very symptomatic example, nowhere did the temporary cessation lately in *L'Illustration* of the publication of the latest plays upon the Parisian stage cause greater discomfort and emptiness of life than in California. As for the volumes of our latest poets and *vers-libristes,* they lie even thicker upon library tables in California than in Kansas. Universities dot the plain, and one of the world's great libraries is soon to be among the orange-groves near Pasadena. Culture is certainly not treated rough near the Pacific's shore.

Bret Harte was, and Alfred Henry Lewis. Their West is gone. Yet there remains California, which, though certainly not Western as we once used the word, is most Californian. And Californianism is something as amazing and as different as Westernism can ever have been in that earlier day. It is a subject which would well repay years of loving and intent study, and demands, indeed, space and some epic gift of style, yet must be treated here as briefly and as best may be. The gospel of impressionism is in the end the only defense of any alien writer attempting to describe a social landscape, he sets the thing down *as it looks to him.*

The Californians, in spite of their comparative hauteur in the Pullman, are accessible enough. Many of them, even on the transcontinental trip, may be "met." Indeed, they

* Harrison Rhodes, "Is There A West?," *Harper's Magazine*, (June, 1920), pp. 70-75.

travel freely, constantly, and easily to and fro, making nothing of four nights out to Chicago, and training their infant progeny, as may richly be observed in the train, to the same happy facility of movement. (It should be said, parenthetically, that as far as that goes, all over the country motherhood seems merely to incite American women to travel, by preference in sleeping-cars.) These returning Californians have been East for various alleged purposes of business or pleasure. But it is really as missionaries that they have gone, to bring the bright gospel of Californianism to those benighted races which still persist in living east of the High Sierras.

The universal delusion of the Pacific slope is that California is heaven. And indeed there is so much to support the theory that it merits calm and judicial examination. The beauty of the Californian landscape is indisputable and heavenly. The combination of sea and mountains with the adorable valleys which diversity it beneath an almost perpetually cloudless sky, the great woodland regions, the majesty and wonder of the High Sierras-all these are unrivaled, unmatched by anything in our land. There is a curious Mediterranean quality in the country; one loses oneself inevitably in golden memories of Greece, of Italy, and of the sunburned coast of Spain...

The Californian dooryards everywhere are a riot of tropical and subtropical blooming plants; perhaps nowhere in the world is there anything like the lushness of their growth and the profusion of their blossoming. To any flower-lover these are gardens in paradise. Yet in no sense is California the tropics. Even when the days are hot the nights are most often crisp and cold. There is no languor in the air. The night breeze does not whisper of the dark magic of the South, of hot passions and unbridled pleasures. It is not, in short, the Californian zephyrs which fill the Californian divorce courts. Instead they seem clean, properly sterilized, even cold-storage airs.

The Pacific, too, a calm, cold ocean not much fretted by traffic, adds its curious note of aloofness. It sends forth fogs, but somehow they carry no hint of salt. And in days of sunshine when it sparkles sapphire blue it seems somehow to exhale no breath. You never "smell the sea" as by the Atlantic's verge, and, though you well know that rotting sea-weed gives forth that odor, you miss it on this western shore. The oceans you have known seem playful children, by turns gay and irritable, by comparison with this monstrous, lovely, inhuman sea. If you are by fate predestined to Californianism, you find in this eternal changeless quality a suggestion that happiness, too, may be everlasting, and that behind the mountains you have left forever change and whim and anxiety and all the responsibilities of the past.

The first impression of California must be for every one a sense of release, whether it be merely from the winter climate of Iowa or from the carking cares of the eastern seaboard. Every one is, as it were, under a new flag and a new name, ready to forget the past and keep clear eyes fixed only on the future. Here every earthly care may be sloughed off, except, perhaps, the pangs of love. And as for physical ills, these should easily be disposed of. On every hand there are faith healers of all varieties, divine healers, nature healers, and child healers, these last an agreeable novelty ranging from ten to fourteen years in age, but competent, no doubt, as only an American child can be.

The Californian population has been recruited from all parts of the country and, though happy in this new environment, still bears traces of its origin. A Boston lady, lately viewing a parade in honor of the sovereigns of Belgium, said it made her feel at home to "see all them silk hats"; yet she was doubtless a converted and ardent Californian, finding this in her old age a pleasant shelter from the east wind.

One of the pleasantest things about California (perhaps, after its natural beauty) is the simplicity of life so widely prevalent there. Of course there are plenty of enormously rich people, and quite enough extraordinarily gay and fashionable. Yet in the end it is the paradise of the common people and the small income. Even when the immigrant to California comes with work in his mind it is so often some sublimated and poetic industry like orange-growing which has lured; the culture of that golden fruit, with Mexicans or Japanese doing the manual labor, is an ideal, easy, and Arcadian occupation for any one...

Of course there are plenty of rich people in California-the sight-seeing automobiles take you past miles of "homes" of all the seats of lumber, paper, packing, chewing-gum, or sawdust "kings," as we so delightfully term all our successful business men in America. But the really exciting and significant thing is to go past the hundreds of miles of "homes" of those humble people who are not and never will be "kings," never, perhaps, be masters of anything but their own souls, but are leading a serene, neighborly, American existence. It is in this mood that the bungalow seems the solution of all the difficulties of even a revolutionized future. California seems somehow to offer every tired human creature from that humming, tormented East a refuge and a new chance...

Nature-loving is of course a cheap and simple pleasure anywhere, but it peculiarly fits into the scheme of Western frugality and soulfulness. Of course California has no monopoly; even in central Illinois bands of nature-lovers now go forth on Saturday afternoons to caress trees. But probably never before in the same area were so many almost professional devotees of the Great Mother as on the Pacific slope. There is, of course, a vast deal of rather windy talk upon the subject, and a strong disposition to dilute it with a vague religiosity...

But there is a side simpler and more engaging. There is an extraordinary proportion of the inhabitants of California which knows the wild places-they are always astonishingly near the centers of population-and has been near the mysteries. The coming of the good road and the bad car has facilitated this. The migration in the summer to the High Sierras of thousands of family camping-parties, in overloaded vehicles of the many kinds which may be generically grouped as tin cars, is an epic of democracy. They live long weeks really close to that so famous heart; a young lady was heard in the autumn complaining that she couldn't seem to cook at the sea-level-she had learned the art during a long summer twelve thousand feet up, where water boils at a lower temperature and is much less hot! Camping and all the pioneer crafts are still a real part of the life of a true Californian from childhood on.

Even week-ends and Sundays are used in pleasant outdoor expeditions. In spite of the automobile, the Californians can still walk. Of course they do not use such an old-fashioned expression; they "hike"; this new word, as Boy Scouts have already found, makes a thing that had grown dull a real pleasure. The railway and trolley stations late Saturday afternoon are an amazing sight. They swarm with boys and girls in "hiking" costumes of khaki. The young ladies are all in trim, tight knickers, to be distinguished from the young men only by their superior shape, by their beauty of countenance, and by the students' caps in bright colored velvet which surmount them. There are undoubtedly more young ladies in knickers in California than anywhere else in the world.

13

The New Deal West

No region of the United States escaped the Great Depression unscathed. The federal government responded to the crisis with a cornucopia of programs collectively known as the New Deal. During the 1930s and 40s the Western states became increasingly dependent on federal funding, a trend that has continued into the late twentieth century. The landscape was transformed with Washington dollars, creating new jobs and opening new lands to settlement in the process. New Deal programs financed the construction of the Hoover Dam (formerly Boulder Dam), irrigation projects, new roads, schools, and courthouses.

The Depression coincided with a persistent drought made worse by poor farming techniques and overgrazing. Thousands of farmers from the Texas and Oklahoma panhandles as well as parts of Kansas, Colorado, and New Mexico were drawn west to California like so many others have been over the years, bent on attempting to improve their economic prospects.

Prior to the 1930s, the federal government advocated the transfer of public lands to private ownership and development. However, with the passage of the conservation-oriented Taylor Grazing Act of 1934 the federal government effectively reversed course by removing 142 million acres of western lands from future speculation and placing them under federal control. Thus began a new era in which the public domain was placed under federal management instead of for sale to the highest bidder.

In the 1930s it became clear that western problems could not be solved through state or regional action alone. It would take the intervention of the federal government to lead the region back to prosperity. For a territory so identified with rugged individualism it came as a shock to many that the West had become reliant on the government dole, leading the nation in per capita payments for work relief and loans.

The New Deal and the Second World War profoundly affected race relations in the American West. With the passage of the Indian Reorganization Act in 1934, the federal government admitted, albeit forty seven years too late, that the Dawes Act and allotment policy in general was a colossal blunder. Under the aegis of John Collier, an attempt was made to organize tribal self-government and restore tribal government.

Although World War II brought new opportunities for Mexican Americans, African Americans, Asian Americans, and other minorities, racial unity was thwarted by simmering tensions and discrimination. The years following the Japanese bombing of Pearl Harbor on December 7, 1941, highlighted racial and ethnic divisions in the West. The most dramatic example of this occurred in 1942 when more than 112, 00 people of Japanese ancestry, the majority of which were American citizens, were relocated to ten relocation centers dispersed throughout the American West. Coming on the heels of a generation of anti-Japanese sentiment in the West, the *Japanese Relocation Order* and subsequent legislation also demonstrates the suspicion with which Americans of European descent viewed anyone of Japanese ancestry during the war years.

Mounting tension in Los Angeles between Mexican and Anglo Americans led to the "zoot suit" riots in 1943. In the 1930s and early 1940s the Mexican community of Los Angeles had increased to close to four hundred thousand, eliciting anti-Mexican editorials from local newspapers and increasing discrimination, leading to an attack on Hispanics, blacks, and other non-white inhabitants by mobs led by off-duty sailors and soldiers.

The years of the New Deal transformed the American West from a region not far removed from a pioneering ethos rooted in careless exploitation of natural resources to an economy that emphasized planning and conservation. The expansion of the federal government in the 1930s and 40s reverberated throughout America, but nowhere did it have more impact than in the West.

Suggestions for Further Reading

James N. Gregory, *American Exodus: The Dust Bowl Migration and Okie Culture in California* (New York: Oxford University Press, 1989).

Richard Lowitt, *The New Deal and the West* (Bloomington: Indiana University Press. 1984)

Mazon, Mauricio, *The Zoot Suit Riots: The Psychology of Symbolic Annihilation* (Austin: University of Texas Press, 1984).

Gerald D. Nash, *The American West Transformed: The Impact of the Second World War* (Bloomington: Indiana University Press, 1985).

Graham D. Taylor, *The New Deal and American Indian Tribalism: The Administration of the Indian Reorganization Act. 1934-45* (Lincoln: University of Nebraska Press, 1980).

Critical Thinking

1. How did the government justify the relocation of American citizens of Japanese heritage in the West during the 1940s?

2. What parallels can be detected in the treatment of Mexican Americans and Japanese Americans by whites during the 1940s?

3. Were relations between the ethnic and racial minorities and the Anglo population in the West representative of race relations in America in general or just a regional phenomenon?

4. What environmental conditions had changed for farmers on the Great Plains during the New Deal? Were the changes man-made, environmental or both?

5. When considered in environmental terms what correlation did the Taylor Grazing Act have with the Dust Bowl?

Document 13.1

Indian Reorganization Act (1934)

In 1887, Congress passed the Dawes Severalty Act, also known as the General Allotment Act, to solve the so-called "Indian problem." Assimilationists were convinced that as long as Indians remained on reservations, they would never mix in with American society. The Dawes Act provided for the breakup of reservation land and its distribution to individual Indian heads of families. Surplus lands left over were sold to white settlers. During the next half-century, the Dawes Act led to a dramatic loss of Indian land and an enormous increase in Indian poverty. In 1934, with passage of the Indian Reorganization Act, Congress tried to rectify the wrong done by restoring sovereignty and land to Indian tribes. The following document is a copy of the Indian Reorganization Act.*

INDIAN REORGANIZATION ACT

[June 18, 1034. [S. 3045.] Public, No. 383.]

AN ACT To conserve and develop Indian lands and resources; to extend to Indians the right to form business and other organizations; to establish a credit system for Indians; to grant certain rights of home rule to Indians; to provide for vocational education for Indians; and for other purposes.

---

* House Report No. 2503, 82nd Congress, 2nd Session, Report with Respect to the House Resolution Authorizing the Committee of Interior and Insular Affairs to Conduct an Investigation of the Bureau of Indian Affairs (Washington, D.C., 1953), pp. 1035-1039.

Be it enacted by the Senate and House of Representatives of the United States of America in Congress assembled, That hereafter no land of any Indian reservation, created or set apart by treaty or agreement with the Indians, Act of Congress, Executive order, purchase, or otherwise, shall be allotted in severalty to any Indian.

SEC. 2. The existing periods of trust placed upon any Indian lands and any restriction on alienation thereof are hereby extended and continued until otherwise directed by Congress.

SEC. 3. The Secretary of the Interior, if he shall find it to be in the public interest, is hereby authorized to restore to tribal ownership the remaining surplus lands of any Indian reservation heretofore opened, or authorized to be opened, to sale, or any other form of disposal by Presidential proclamation, or by any of the public-land laws of the United States: *Provided, however,* That valid rights or claims of any persons to any lands so withdrawn existing on the date of the withdrawal shall not be affected by this Act: *Provided further,* That this section shall not apply to lands within any reclamation project heretofore authorized in any Indian reservation: *Provided further,* That the order of the Department of the Interior signed, dated, and approved by Honorable Ray Lyman Wilbur, as Secretary of the Interior, on October 28, 1932, temporarily withdrawing lands of the Papago Indian Reservation in Arizona from all forms of mineral entry or claim under the public land mining laws, is hereby revoked and rescinded, and the lands of the said Papago Indian Reservation are hereby restored to exploration and location, under the existing mining laws of the United States, in accordance with the express terms and provisions declared and set forth in the Executive orders establishing said Papago Indian Reservation: *Provided further,* That damages shall be paid to the Papago Tribe for loss of any improvements on any land located for mining in such a sum as may be determined by the Secretary of the Interior but not to exceed the cost of said improvements: *Provided further,* That a yearly rental not to exceed five cents per acre shall be paid to the Papago Tribe for loss of the use or occupancy of any land withdrawn by the requirements of mining operations, and payments derived from damages or rentals shall be deposited in the Treasury of the United States to the credit of the Papago Tribe: *Provided further,* That in the event any person or persons, partnership, corporation, or association, desires a mineral patent, according to the mining laws of the United States, he or they shall first deposit in the Treasury of the United States to the credit of the Papago Tribe the sum of $1.00 per acre in lieu of annual rental, as hereinbefore provided, to compensate for the loss or occupancy of the lands withdrawn by the requirements of mining operations: *Provided further,* That patentee shall also pay into the Treasury of the United States to the credit of the Papago Tribe damages for the loss of improvements not heretofore paid in such a sum as may be determined by the Secretary of the Interior, but not to exceed the cost thereof; the payment of $1.00 per acre for surface use to be refunded to patentee in the event that patent is not acquired.

Nothing herein contained shall restrict the granting or use of permits for easements or rights-of-way; or ingress or egress over the lands for all proper and lawful purposes; and nothing contained herein, except as expressly provided, shall be construed as authority for the Secretary of the Interior, or any other person, to issue or promulgate a rule or regulation in conflict with the Executive order of February 1, 1917, creating the Papago Indian Reservation in Arizona or the Act of February 21, 1931 (46 Stat. 1202).

SEC. 19. The term "Indian" as used in this Act shall include all persons of Indian descent who are members of any recognized Indian tribe now under Federal jurisdiction, and all persons who are descendants of such members who were, on June 1, 1934, residing within the present boundaries of any Indian reservation, and shall further include all other persons of one-half or more Indian blood. For the purposes of this Act, Eskimos and other aboriginal peoples of Alaska shall be considered Indians. The term "tribe" wherever used in this Act shall be construed to refer to any Indian tribe, organized band, pueblo, or the Indians residing on one reservation. The words "adult Indians" wherever used in this Act shall be construed to refer to Indians who have attained the age of twenty-one years.

Approved, June 18, 1934.

Document 13.2

John Collier Defends the Indian Reorganization Act (1934)

In 1932, social reformer John Collier (1884-1968) was appointed commissioner of Indian affairs, a position he would hold until 1945. A formidable critic of federal Indian policy, Collier opposed the allotment of Indian tribal lands while championing the preservation of Indian traditions and rights of limited self-government on the reservations. In what was considered the most important achievement of his administration, the Indian Reorganization Act, or Wheeler-Howard Act, was passed in June 1934. In the following passage, Collier defends the rights of Indians to organize "for the purposes of local self-government and economic enterprise." In abolishing the allotment policy, Collier promised federal aid in developing "a constructive program of Indian land use and economic development."[*]

The Wheeler-Howard Act, the most important piece of Indian legislation since the eighties, not only ends the long, painful, futile effort to speed up the normal rate of Indian assimilation by individualizing tribal land and other capital assets, but it also endeavors to provide the means, statutory and financial, to repair as far as possible, the incalculable damage done by the allotment policy and its corollaries....

The repair work authorized by Congress... aims at both the economic and the spiritual rehabilitation of the Indian race. Congress and the President recognized that the cumulative loss of land brought about by the allotment system, a loss reaching

---

[*] *Annual Report of the Secretary of the Interior,* 1934, 78-83.

90,000,000 acres-two-thirds of the land heritage of the Indian race in 1887-had robbed the Indians in large part of the necessary basis for self-support. They clearly saw that this loss and the companion effort to break up all Indian tribal relations had condemned large numbers of Indians to become chronic recipients of charity; that the system of leasing individualized holdings had created many thousands of petty landlords unfitted to support themselves when their rental income vanished; that a major proportion of the red race was, therefore, ruined economically and pauperized spiritually....

Through 50 years of "individualization", coupled with an ever-increasing amount of arbitrary supervision over the affairs of individuals and tribes so long as these individuals and tribes had any assets left, the Indians have been robbed of initiative, their spirit has been broken, their health undermined, and their native pride ground into the dust. The efforts at economic rehabilitation cannot and will not be more than partially successful unless they are accompanied by a determined simultaneous effort to rebuild the shattered morale of a subjugated people that has been taught to believe in its racial inferiority.

The Wheeler-Howard Act provides the means of destroying this inferiority complex, through those features which authorize and legalize tribal organization and incorporation, which give these tribal organizations and corporations limited but real power, and authority over their own affairs, which broaden the educational opportunities for Indians, and which give Indians a better chance to enter the Indian Service.

Document 13.3

Taylor Grazing Act (1934)

As the grazing capacity of the open rangelands continued to diminish because of overgrazing and poor management, Congress stepped in and ordered these lands withdrawn from public domain status. With the passage of the Taylor Grazing Act in 1934, the Division of Grazing was established to manage and regulate 142 million acres of range land on the public domain, effectively ending land sales and homesteading and placing this land, like the national forests, under bureaucratic stewardship. With this act, stock-raising on the public domain came under federal management. Although in spirit the legislation implied federal dictation of grazing policy, in reality the act gave significant power to livestock owners.*

AN ACT

---

* "Taylor Grazing Act," 73rd Congress, Sess. II, CH. 865, (June 28, 1934), pp. 1269-1275.

To stop injury to the public grazing lands by preventing overgrazing and soil deterioration, to provide for their orderly use, improvement, and development, to stabilize the livestock industry dependent upon the public range, and for other purposes.

Be it enacted by the Senate and House of Representatives of the United States of America in Congress assembled, That in order to promote the highest use of the public lands pending its final disposal, the Secretary of the Interior is authorized, in his discretion, by order to establish grazing districts or additions thereto and/or to modify the boundaries thereof, not exceeding in the aggregate an area of eighty million acres of vacant, unappropriated, and unreserved lands from any part of the public domain of the United States (exclusive of Alaska), which are not in national forests, national parks and monuments, Indian reservations, revested Oregon and California Railroad grant lands, or revested Coos Bay Wagon Road grant lands, and which in his opinion are chiefly valuable for grazing and raising forage crops: *Provided,* That no lands withdrawn or reserved for any other purpose shall be included in any such district except with the approval of the head of the department having jurisdiction thereof. Nothing in this Act shall be construed in any way to diminish, restrict, or impair any right which has been heretofore or may be hereafter initiated under existing law validly affecting the public lands, and which is maintained pursuant to such law except as otherwise expressly provided in this Act, nor to affect any land heretofore or hereafter surveyed which, except for the provisions of this Act, would be a part of any grant to any State, nor as limiting or restricting the power or authority of any State as to matters within its jurisdiction. Whenever any grazing district is established pursuant to this Act, the Secretary shall grant to owners of land adjacent to such district, upon application of any such owner, such rights-of-way over the lands included in such district for stock-driving purposes as may be necessary for the convenient access by any such owner to marketing facilities or to lands not within such district owned by such person or upon which such person has stock-grazing rights, Neither this Act nor the Act of December 29, 1916 (39 Stat. 862; U.S.C., title 43, secs, 291 and following), commonly known as the "Stock Raising Homestead Act", shall be construed as limiting the authority or policy of Congress or the President to include in national forests public lands of the character described in section 24 of the Act of March 3, 1891 (26 Stat. 1103; U.S.C., title 16, sec. 471), as amended, for the purposes set forth in the Act of June 4. 1897 (30 Stat. 35; U.S.C., title 16, sec. 475), or such other purposes as Congress may specify. Before grazing districts are created in any State as herein provided, a hearing shall be held in the State, after public notice thereof shall have been given, at such location convenient for the attendance of State officials, and the settlers, residents, and livestock owners of the vicinity, as may be determined by the Secretary of the Interior. No such district shall be established until the expiration of ninety days after such notice shall have been given, nor until twenty days after such hearing shall be held: *Provided, however,* That the publication of such notice shall have the effect of withdrawing all public lands within the exterior boundary of such proposed grazing districts from all forms of entry of settlement. Nothing in this Act shall be construed as in any way altering or restricting the right to hunt or fish within a grazing district in accordance with the laws of the United States or of any State, or as vesting in any permittee any right whatsoever to interfere with hunting or fishing within a grazing district.

Document 13.4

The Dust Bowl (1934)

The Dust Bowl of the 1930s is one the most enduring images of the Great Depression. The dust bowl region encompassed parts of Oklahoma, Texas, Kansas, Colorado, and New Mexico. The combination of drought and poor farming techniques resulted in huge dust storms. In the following passage, Ann Marie Low copes with chores and mundane affairs against a backdrop of extraordinary conditions.*

April 25, 1934, Wednesday

Last weekend was the worst dust storm we ever had. We've been having quite a bit of blowing dirt every year since the drought started, not only here, but all over the Great Plains. Many days this spring the air is just full of dirt coming, literally, for hundreds of miles. It sifts into everything. After we wash the dishes and put them away, so much dust sifts into the cupboards we must wash them again before the next meal. Clothes in the closets are covered with dust.

Last weekend no one was taking an automobile out for fear of ruining the motor. I rode Roany to Frank's place to return a gear. To find my way I had to ride right beside the fence, scarcely able to see from one fence post to the next.

Newspapers say the deaths of many babies and old people are attributed to breathing in so much dirt.

May 7, 1934, Monday

The dirt is still blowing. Last weekend Bud [her brother] and I helped with the cattle and had fun gathering weeds. Weeds give us greens for salad before anything in the garden is ready. We use dandelions, lamb's quarter, and sheep sorrel. I like sheep sorrel best. Also, the leaves of sheep sorrel, pounded and boiled down to a paste, make a good salve.

Still no job. I'm trying to persuade Dad I should apply for rural school #3 out here where we went to school. I don't see a chance of getting a job in a high school when so many experienced teachers are out of work.

He argues that the pay is only $60.00 a month out here, while even in a grade school in town I might get $75.00. Extra expenses in town would probably eat up that extra $15.00. Miss Eston, the practice teaching supervisor, told me her salary has been cut to $75.00 after all the years she has been teaching in Jamestown. She wants to get married. School boards will not hire married women teachers in these hard time because they have

---

* Ann Marie Low, *Dust Bowl Diary,* (Lincoln: University of Nebraska Press, 95-96.

husbands to support them. Her fianc, is the sole support of his widowed mother and can't support a wife, too. So she is stuck in her job, hoping she won't get another salary cut because she can scarcely live on what she makes and dress the way she is expected to.

Dad argues the patrons always stir up so much trouble for a teacher at #3; some teachers have quit in mid-term. The teacher is also the janitor, so the hours are long.

I figure I can handle the work, kids, and patrons. My argument is that by teaching here I can work for my room and board at home, would not need new clothes, and so could send most of my pay to Ethel [her sister] and Bud.

Document 13.5

Down and Out in the Great Depression (1930s)

Legions of Americans were so desperate for relief during the Great Depression that they resorted to writing to President Franklin Roosevelt and his wife Eleanor, as well as other agencies and administrators. Mail so engulfed the White House staff that fifty secretaries were hired to answer letters from the public; this compared to only one employed by the previous administration under Hoover. The following letters demonstate the impact of this era on westerners.*

Eureka, Calif.
June 14, 1934

Mrs. F. D. Roosevelt
Washington, D. C.
Dear Mrs. Roosevelt:

I know you are overburdened with requests for help and if my plea cannot be recognized, I'll understand it is because you have so many others, all of them worthy.

But I am not asking for myself alone. It is as a potential mother and as one woman to another.

My husband and I are a young couple of very simple, almost poor families. We married eight years ago on the proverbial shoe-string but with a wealth of love. We both wanted more than anything else to establish a home and maintain that home in a charming, quiet manner. I had a job in the County Court House before I married and my husband was, and is, a surveyor. I kept my job as it seemed the best and only way for us to pay for a home as quickly as we could. His work was not always permanent, as surveyors jobs seldom are, but we managed to build our home and furnish it comfortably.

* Robert S. McElvaine, *Down and Out in the Great Depression: Letters from the Forgotten Man*, (Chapel Hill: University of North Carolina Press, 1983), pp. 54-55; 72; 179-180.

Perhaps we were foolish to put all our money into it but we felt it was not only a pleasure but a saving for the future.

Then came the depression. My work has continued and my salary alone has just been sufficient to make our monthly payments on the house and keep our bills paid. But with the exception of two and one-half months work with the U.S. Coast and Geodetic Survey under the C.W.A., my husband has not had work since August, 1932.

My salary could continue to keep us going, but-I am to have a baby. We wanted one before but felt we should have more assurance for the future before we deliberately took such a responsibility. But now that it has happened, I won't give it up! I'm willing to undergo any hardship for myself and I can get a leave of absence from my job for a year. But can't you, won't you do something so my husband can have a job, at least during that year? I realize there is going to be a lot of expense and we have absolutely nothing but our home which still carries a mortgage of $2000. We can't lose that because our baby will need it. And I can't wait until the depression is over to have a baby. I will be 31 in October and I'll soon be too old.

We had such high hopes in the early spring that the Coast and Geodetic work would continue. Tommy, my husband, had a good position there, and we were so happy. We thought surely our dreams of a family could come true. Then the work ended and like "The best laid plans of mice and men" our hopes were crushed again. But now Fate has taken it into her own hands and left us to work it out somehow. I'm happy, of course, but Tommy is nearly out of his head. He has tried every conceivable prospect but you must know how even pick and shovel jobs do not exist.

If the Coast and Geodetic work could continue or if he could get a job with the Bureau of Public Roads,-anything in the surveying line. A year is all I ask and after that I can go back to work and we can work out our own salvation. But to have this baby come to a home full of worry and despair, with no money for things it needs, is not fair. It needs and deserves a happy start in life.

As I said before, if it were only ourselves, or if there were something we could do about it, we would never ask for help. We have always stood on our own feet and been proud and happy. But you are a mother and you'll understand this crisis.

Tommy is competent and dependable. He has a surveyor's license and was level man for the U.S. Coast and Geodetic work in this (Humboldt) county. He will go away from home for work, if necessary, but, dear Mrs. Roosevelt, will you see if you can arrange for a job for him? It sounds impossible, I know, but I am at a point where I *ask* the impossible. I have to be selfish now.

I shall hope and pray for a reply and tell myself that you are the busiest woman in America, if I don't receive it. I am going to continue to work as long as I can and then-an interval of waiting. God grant it will be serene and untroubled for my baby's sake.

Very sincerely yours,
Mrs. M. H. A.
Eureka,
Humboldt County,
California

I hate to see Xmas come this time

Sulphur Springs, Texas
December 11, 1934.

President Roosevelt
Washington, D. C.
Dear President:

I am in debt needing help the worst in the world. I own my own little home and a few live stock. Nine (9) head of red white face cattle and a span of mules. I have them all mortgaged to a man and he is fixing to foreclose me.

I have done all I could to pay the note and have failed on everything I've tried. I fell short on my crop this time and he didn't allow me even one nickle out of it to feed myself while I was gathering it and now winter is here and I have a wife and three (3) little children, haven't got clothes enough to hardly keep them from freezing. My house got burned up three years ago and I'm living in just a hole of a house and we are in a suffering condition. My little children talking about Santa Claus and I hate to see Xmas come this time because I know it will be one of the dullest Xmas they ever witnessed.

I have tried to compromise with the man that I am in debt to and he wont except nothing but the money or my stock and I can't borrow the money and I need my stock so I am asking you for help of some kind please.

So I remain,

Your humble servant,
N. S. [male]
Sulphur Springs, Texas.

P.S. That man won't even agree for me to have my stock fed.

[Los Angeles, Calif.]
January 9-1936

Mr Harry Hopkins
Washington, D. C.

Are you in favor of the Townsand Plan? You are certainly playing right into their hands by this continued unemployment in Los Angeles County and this continual cut of relief checks, one last week and another this week and the promise of others until we single women will be trying to exist on $17.50 per month. Try living on that, Mr. Hopkins, but you won't as long as you are in politics. How come that when the treasury is low for are relief money, the higher ups never take a cut in salary but hold meetings at the Biltmore Hotel and fill their bellies to deside to reduce our budgets to empty our bellies, some system and it is the worst thing can happen for the New Deal and Pres. Roosevelt also for you fellows dealing it out to the President's forgotten men and women for without this part of the administration you fellows would have no jobs and wouldn't be pulling out the plumbs from the pie. Also, why don't you get yourself informed as to how these local relief adminestrators are handling the funds and the the work program.

Why are the Mexicans and niggers being given white colar jobs and white Americans still are on the lousy dole or doing work entirely foreign to their calling. If our local distributors have no sense of justice, as the head of the whole lousy concern you should do your part to reajust this condition. Los Angeles County has more dishonest and paracitic officials than exists elsewhere in the whole world and I guess you all at Washington have found that out. If I have to continue much longer being unemployed and trying to exist on this low down dole which gets lower down each check, then I am off of the New Deal and will not vote for Roosevelt I hope your undersecretary permits you to read this as you should know these facts.

Yours truly-
A Los Angeles County Victim

Document 13.6

The Zoot Suit Riots (1943)

Tension resulting from the assault of several sailors by a group of Mexican youths resulted in violence between Mexicans and whites on the streets of Los Angeles in 1943. Between June 3 and June 13, mobs attacked Mexican and black youths in Los Angeles. Those attired in "zoot suit" garb were most often singled out. On June 7 alone, over one thousand soldiers, sailors, and civilians dragged mostly Mexican youths from movie theaters, streetcars, and homes and into the streets where they were stripped and beaten. Police stood by, either helpless or reluctant to intervene, depending on your perspective. What was probably most remarkable about these riots was that no one was killed or seriously injured and there was little property damage.

Following the 1943 Zoot Suit Riots, Governor Warren ordered an investigation into its causes. The resulting Citizen's Committee Report was a classic in understatement, concluding that racial prejudice was a factor in the outbreak. The term zoot suit, referring to the elaborate clothing preferred by some youths, entered the American lexicon. But the term took on a perjorative meaning and became synonomous for all Mexicans. Eventually the Los Angeles City Council made this form of sartorial elegance a misdemeanor, foreshadowing the uproar over gang paraphanelia in schools today.*

THE COMMITTEE HAS FOUND...

There are approximately 250,000 persons of Mexican descent in Los Angeles County. Living conditions among the majority of these people are far below the general level of the community. Housing is inadequate; sanitation is bad and is made worse by congestion. Recreational facilities for children are very poor; and there is insufficient supervision of the playgrounds, swimming pools and other youth centers. Such conditions are breeding places for juvenile delinquency....

Mass arrests, dragnet raids, and other wholesale classifications of groups of people are based on false premises and tend merely to aggravate the situation. Any American citizen suspected of crime is entitled to be treated as an individual, to be indicted as such, and to be tried, both at law and in the forum of public opinion, on his merits or errors, regardless of race, color, creed, or the kind of clothes he wears.

Group accusations foster race prejudice; the entire group accused want revenge and vindication. The public is led to believe that every person in the accused group is guilty of crime.

It is significant that most of the persons mistreated during the recent incidents in Los Angeles were either persons of Mexican descent or Negroes. In undertaking to deal with the cause of these outbreaks, the existence of race prejudice cannot be ignored....

On Monday evening, June seventh, thousands of *Angelenos,* in response to twelve hours' advance notice in the press, turned out for a mass lynching. Marching through the streets of downtown Los Angeles, a mob of several thousand soldiers, sailors, and civilians, proceeded to beat up every zoot-suiter they could find. Pushing its way into the important motion picture theaters, the mob ordered the management to turn on the house lights and then ranged up and down the aisles dragging Mexicans out of their seats. Street cars were halted while Mexicans, and some Filipinos and Negroes, were jerked out of their seats, pushed into the streets, and beaten with sadistic frenzy. If the victims wore zoot-suits, they were stripped of their clothing and left naked or half-naked on the streets, bleeding and bruised. Proceeding down Main Street from First to Twelfth, the mob stopped on the edge of the Negro district. Learning that the Negroes planned a warm reception for them, the mobsters turned back and marched through the Mexican east side spreading panic and terror.

Throughout the night the Mexican communities were in the wildest possible turmoil. Scores of Mexican mothers were trying to locate their youngsters and several hundred Mexicans milled around each of the police substations and the Central Jail trying to get word of missing members of their families. Boys came into the police stations saying: "Charge me with vagrancy or anything, but don't send me out there!" pointing to the streets where other boys, as young as twelve and thirteen years of age, were being beaten and stripped of their clothes... not more than half of the victims were actually wearing zoot-suits. A Negro defense worker, wearing a defense-plant identification badge on his workclothes, was taken from a street car and one of his eyes was gouged out with a knife.

* *Governor's Citizens Committee Report on Los Angeles Riots,* 1943; Carey McWilliams, *North From Mexico,* (Philadelphia: J.B. Lippincott, 1949), pp. 248-252; 256.

Huge half-page photographs, showing Mexican boys stripped of their clothes, cowering on the pavements, often bleeding profusely, surrounded by jeering mobs of men and women, appeared in all the Los Angeles newspapers...

At midnight on June seventh, the military authorities decided that the local police were completely unable or unwilling to handle the situation, despite the fact that a thousand reserve officers had been called up. The entire downtown area of Los Angeles was then declared "out of bounds" for military personnel. This order immediately slowed down the pace of the rioting. The moment the Military Police and Shore Patrol went into action, the rioting quieted down.

Document 13.7

Japanese Relocation Order (1942)

One of the more shameful acts in American history occurred on February 19, 1942 when President Franklin D. Roosevelt signed Executive Order 9066. Under this order more than 120,000 Japanese-American citizens and legal aliens were prohibited from living and working on the West Coast. Most were sent to bleak barracks surrounded by barbed wire and military guards in isolated locations of the West, where they would remain in relocation centers for two and a half years.

Japanese Americans were interned because of their Japanese ancestry, a clear violation of their constitutional rights. No program of mass detention was implemented for German or Italian aliens. Nor were American citizens of Italian and German descent excluded from participation in American society. The decision to exclude Japanese Americans from the west coast is not reducible to any one simple cause, but was the culmination of a long history of discrimination against ethnic Japanese in the western United States. It is worth noting that Hawaii, despite a substantial Japanese-American population, refrained from any mass exclusion or detention.

It is estimated that as a result of detention and exclusion, Japanese Americans lost between $108 and $164 million in income and between $41 and $206 million in property in 1945 dollars, for which no compensation was paid after the war. Adjusting these figures to account for inflation alone, these losses would be in the hundreds of millions of dollars.*

JAPANESE RELOCATION ORDER

February 19, 1942

EXECUTIVE ORDER

AUTHORIZING THE SECRETARY OF WAR
Prescribe Military Areas

Whereas the successful prosecution of the war requires every possible protection against espionage and against sabotage to national-defense materials, national-defense premises, and national-defense utilities...

Now, therefore, by virtue of the authority vested in me as President of the United States, and Commander in Chief of the Army and Navy, I hereby authorize and direct the Secretary of War, and the Military Commanders whom he may from time to time designate, whenever he or any designated Commander deems such action necessary or desirable, to prescribe military areas in such places and of such extent as he or the appropriate Military Commander may determine, from which any or all persons may be excluded, and with respect to which, the right of any person to enter, remain in, or leave shall be subject to whatever restrictions the Secretary of War or the appropriate Military Commander may impose in his discretion. The Secretary of War is hereby authorized to provide for residents of any such area who are excluded therefrom, such transportation, food, shelter, and other accommodations as may be necessary, in the judgment of the Secretary of War or the said Military Commander, and until other arrangements are made, to accomplish the purpose of this order. The designation of military areas in any region or locality shall supersede designations of prohibited and restricted areas by the Attorney General under the Proclamations of December 7 and 8, 1941,[1] and shall supersede the responsibility and authority of the Attorney General under the said Proclamations in respect of such prohibited and restricted areas.

I hereby further authorize and direct the Secretary of War and the said Military Commanders to take such other steps as he or the appropriate Military Commander may deem advisable to enforce compliance with the restrictions applicable to each Military area hereinabove authorized to be designated, including the use of Federal troops and other Federal Agencies, with authority to accept assistance of state and local agencies.

I hereby further authorize and direct all Executive Departments, independent establishments and other Federal Agencies, to assist the Secretary of War or the said

---

* *Federal Register*, Vol. II, No. 38.

Military Commanders in carrying out this Executive Order, including the furnishing of medical aid, hospitalization, food, clothing, transportation, use of land, shelter, and other supplies, equipment, utilities, facilities, and services....

Franklin D. Roosevelt

14

The Post-War West: New Realities

The years following World War Two were times of change as well as continuity in the American West. Technology and immigration would transform the environment like never before. The invention and mass marketing of air conditioning would enable large population centers like Phoenix to flourish in inhospitable climates. Wartime industries subsidized by the federal government launched western state economies into an era of unprecedented growth that continued undiminished into the late twentieth century.

In the nineteenth century, gold and silver rushes in the Far West were followed by town building and settlement in some of the most inhospitable places in America. Demand for uranium in the twentieth century led to renewed activity reminiscent of the Forty-niners as prospectors filed 309,380 uranium claims between 1946 and 1959 in four Utah counties. The radioactive substance, uranium, was first mined commercially in the western United States in the early years of the twentieth century. Initially used for radioactive research in scientific laboratories, until the development of an arms race in the 1940s and 1950s, uranium mining was small scale. But, following the birth of the atomic age, new uranium discoveries in the Four-Corners area of Utah, Colorado, New Mexico, and Arizona reinvigorated interest in the mining of radioactive materials in the West.

The 1960s clearly demonstrated that some of the new realities of the Modern West were very familiar components of the traditional western experience. Racial and ethnic conflict was nothing new to the West. A legacy of violence between Anglo culture and Indian, Black, Chinese, and Mexican inhabitants preceded African- American migration to California in response to the opportunities presented by wartime industry in the 1940s. By 1960 almost 500,000 blacks lived in Los Angeles alone. Five years later simmering racial tensions fueled by a tradition of police brutality led to the Watts riot in which thirty-five mostly black residents lost their lives. This outbreak presaged the 1990s Los Angeles riots, which would become the modern West's most violent racial outbreak.

Although there was a tradition of unrest in the agricultural regions of the Southwest, in earlier decades it was usually the Okies and Arkies fleeing the Dust Bowl conditions of the Great Plains who came into conflict with farm management. By the 1960s, a farm labor movement led by Cesar Chavez was on the national stage registering voters, organizing strikes and boycotts, and testifying in Washington before Senate subcommittees about migrant labor conditions. By the late 1960s, the image of the mythic Texas Rangers was tarnished after government hearings documented cases of ranger repression of Mexican Americans and suppression of union organizing efforts.

Throughout most of their history, Native Americans were the least urban of all Americans. By 1940, only seven percent lived in cities. However, between World War II and 1980, tens of thousands of Native Americans would be drawn by federal government programs, better jobs, and better housing to metropolitan areas. By 1980, more than half of the Native American population would live in urbanized areas.

In the late 1960s, Native Americans found a new voice with the birth of various activist organizations and the emerging activism of young urban Native Americans. The reservations were the scene of a resurgent nationalism as well. Native American militancy captured the attention of the American public during the occupation of Alcatraz and later the conflict at Wounded Knee II when members of the American Indian Movement took control of a trading post at Wounded Knee village, site of the 1890 massacre.

Many of the technological advances that allowed life in the West to prosper contained seeds for discord and destruction. Uranium prospecting and nuclear testing brought the threat of cancer to communities surrounding atomic test zones. Pesticides that helped agriculture flourish often led to higher child mortality rates and increased health risks for farm workers.

By the 1990s, the war against the American environment by farmers, ranchers, and miners showed few signs of abatement. The Mining Law Reform Act of 1991 and the Grazing and Public Lands Acts several years later did little to stop the ravaging of the western landscape. And Western communities played a willing partner with the federal government in their willingness to accept government compensation to store hazardous wastes in the wilderness.

In contrast to the new realities of the post-war West, despite his death in 1979, John Wayne continued his unsurpassed position as a symbol of the American West, exemplified by his standing as America's favorite movie star according to a Harris poll conducted sixteen years after his death.

Suggestions for Further Reading

Robert Athearn, *The Mythic West in Twentieth Century America* (Lawrence: University Press of Kansas, 1986).

Robert Gottlieb and Peter Wiley, *Empires in the Sun: The Rise of the New American West* (Tucson: University of Arizona Press, 1985).

William L. Graf, *Wilderness Preservation and the Sagebrush Rebellions* (Savage, Md.: Rowan and Littlefield, 1990).

Gerald Nash, *The American West in the Twentieth Century: A Short History of an Urban Oasis* Englewood Cliffs, N.J.: Prentice Hall, 1973).

Richard Slotkin, *Gunfighter Nation: The Myth of the Frontier in Twentieth-Century America* (New York: Atheneum Press, 1992).

Critical Thinking

1. Contrast the Texas Rangers of the 1960s with their mythic image.

2. What was life like for migrant farm workers in the Southwest?

3. Discuss the politicization of African Americans, Hispanics, and the Native Americans in the modern West using examples from the readings.

4. How did the children of Los Alamos remember New Mexico during the 1940s and 50s? What negative consequences of atomic testing are detailed in the readings?

5. What impact did technology have on the settlement of the Southwest? Could this region have been urbanized without modern technology?

Document 14.1

The Children of Los Alamos (1940s)

Beginning in 1943, strangers began descending on Santa Fe in preparation for the top secret Manhattan Project that would soon begin in the sleepy town of Los Alamos. Little did this community realize it at the time, but their lives would parallel the birth of the nuclear age. From 1943 through the late 1950s, scientists secretly built the atomic bomb in Los Alamos. The following stories offer three different perspectives on these years.*

Tilano

Edith Warner had not been in her house long when an Indian in his fifties, with long black braids came to build her a new fireplace and help with the chickens and gardening. His name was Tilano. After walking over daily from the San Ildefonso pueblo for a time, he eventually came to live at the little house. In his youth Tilano had traveled with friends from the pueblo to New York to perform Indian dances. From there he had gone on to perform dances in London, Berlin, and Paris, coming home by way of Edith's hometown, Philadelphia. This travel had given him a broad outlook but it also made it hard for him to return to the communal life of the pueblo.

---

* Katrina R. Mason, *Children of Los Alamos: An Oral History of the Town Where the Atomic Age Began*, (New York: Twayne Publishers, 1995), pp. 42-44; 57-59; 113.

As Peggy Pond Church has written, "In his own way [Tilano] was as much alone as Edith. His wife had died in childbirth, in the second year of their marriage. Because of his long absence as a young man from the pueblo he was in danger of becoming ... She must have given him the peace and security he needed... She found in him the masculine strength and wisdom that kept her own life in balance and a spirit of playfulness that had been lacking in her own serious upbringing."

Lidian King, daughter of physicist L. D. P. King and artist Edie King, remembers, "My first memories are when [I was about four and] my family was one of four or five families who went and helped Edith Warner and Tilano build [a new] house [across the road from the old one]. [My] memories begin . . . [with] Edith, her personality and Tilano-[a] sense of respect. . . . We would ride his horse, help him shuck corn. There was a... sense of closeness to the land... There was something very deep about that connection."

Tilano liked sharing his world with children. He was always giving them small gifts and pointing out natural wonders like a beautiful feather or a newly laid egg. He presented them with arrowheads he had found, miniature moccasins he made, and a postcard-size picture of himself that he mailed to children all over the country in the late 1940s. Both Robert Oppenheimer's son Peter, and Edward Teller's son Paul grew up with this picture of Tilano. Joan Bainbridge Safford, daughter of physicist Kenneth Bainbridge, says her younger sister Margaret's only "memory" of Los Alamos is the small black pottery bowl with a red tomato on it that Tilano gave her shortly before the Bainbridges left Los Alamos in 1945. Going to Edith Warner's was how Martha Bacher Eaton got to know Tilano: "At first I was kind of scared of him because he was a big man. But he was so gentle and so present. This made my Indian connection a lot stronger." She received a going-away present of two arrowheads and a little pair of moccasins.

Kim Manley, daughter of physicist John Manley, remembers Tilano as a gentle man who "had wonderful stories": "I just loved Tilano. . . . He was so quiet and gentle. He would take us for walks . . . and give us feathers from the turkeys. He made a pair of moccasins for one of my dolls. He made a feather headdress for me to wear. I have a picture of him on my wall in a ceremonial costume and he carved the frame himself." Catherine Allison Marshall remembers "sort of hanging out with Tilano, as they would say now." She also recalls that "Tilano loved comics books. Was it Superman? There was some particular comic book. Whenever we drove into Santa Fe . . . we would stop off, and my mother would visit with Miss Warner and Tilano, and we would always make sure we had the right comic book to give to him." Joan Mark Neary recalls that "Tilano had a horse called Chicko. He told me I could have the horse, that he would give it to me but keep it there. We could ride it when he was there. I was always convinced it was mine."

Remembered by the children of Los Alamos as gentle, patient, and giving, Tilano served as a bridge between cultures. From the time he came to stay with Edith Warner and help her with the heavy work of hauling water and wood and coaxing a garden to flourish, he lived somewhere between the worlds of the Native Americans and the newcomers. Edith Warner's house was well away from the pueblo proper, but still on the edge of San Ildefonso. Through his actions as much as his words, Tilano conveyed to the children of the scientists the sacredness of the natural world, the joys of living in harmony with nature and the peace to be found in sharing these joys.

Among his own people, Tilano bridged generations, passing along the traditions of his generation to the those growing up during World War II and going off to fight in Europe and the Pacific. "I used to help Tilano work in the garden at Miss Warner's and help him with the horses, the cows, chickens and geese," says his nephew Julian Martinez. "I learned a lot from my uncle. He had big responsibilities at the pueblo. After he started aging a bit, he came to take part in those responsibilities.... He was a good horseman and a great hunter, too. He showed me how to make traps to trap rabbits, quails and birds." Almost four decades after Tilano's death, Julian speaks of his uncle as if he were still alive. "Uncle Tilano is like a storyteller," he recalls. "He gets along with kids, is very giving in what he has taught me-how to hunt, how to track, how to survive."

Polly Richardson Boyles

Polly Richardson Boyles came to Los Alamos from Wisconsin by way of Santa Fe for the same reason that people had come to New Mexico in the early part of the century-for the healing qualities of the climate. Polly's sister had been diagnosed with a lung abscess, and the doctors back in Wisconsin did not think she would live. Polly's mother had read the Willa Cather novel *Death Comes to the Archbishop*, set in Lamy, New Mexico, and decided the climate might cure her daughter. While Polly's father stayed in Wisconsin, where he worked as an accountant for the state, the females set off for New Mexico, where Polly's mother got a job teaching high school in Santa Fe during the war.

The family moved to Los Alamos in 1948 when Polly's father got a job with the AEC doing accounting for the Lab: "My mother, sister, grandmother and I came to Santa Fe in 1943. Our first trip to Los Alamos, at least part of the way, was that year. We were on an excursion [from Santa Fe] to Bandelier... We wound up on the wrong road-on the narrow winding road to Los Alamos. Guards with machine guns met us and made us turn around in the middle of the steep part, with no guard rails. I remember my mother was not thrilled about that.

"I don't think anybody spent any time inside to speak of. I lived on horseback and roamed every square foot of the mountains. One game we liked was to ride out [of the fence] avoiding the gate, then ride up to the gate and say, "I can't get in. I don't have my pass." Horses, camping out, fishing in the river-that was our life. I'd be away all day, and nobody panicked. It wasn't that they didn't care: they figured you had enough sense to know what you were doing. You hitchhiked everywhere and never gave it a thought. It was very secure.

"We were all nonconformists-each going our own way and not feeling we had to do what everyone else was doing. We didn't divide people into groups [but saw each other as individuals]... We were taught to think for ourselves."

Severo Gonzales

Severo Gonzales, who graduated from Los Alamos High School in 1948, is one of a relatively few teenagers during the war years who had not come to Los Alamos from somewhere else. His grandparents and great grandparents are among the earliest homesteaders of the Pajarito Plateau. In 1891, his paternal grandfather began farming an area of Los Alamos that is now one of the Lab sites. Six years earlier, his great-grandfather on his mother's side, Antonio Sanchez, had begun a summer homestead on the Pajarito Mesa. Severo's father, Bences Gonzales, was a bean farmer hired to staff the Los Alamos Ranch School.

Bences knew not only how to survive in this rugged terrain, but how to thrive on it. He was a specialist at outdoor cooking. On the long pack trips that were a regular part of life at the school and especially the summer camp it ran, Bences served up dishes ranging from fresh meat baked in stone ovens to *sopaipillas* (similar to doughnuts), boiled in kettles of fat. At the school he also took care of the trading post, handled the mail, and ordered the groceries that had to be shipped in. When the army took over the school, Bences Gonzales signed up with the Manhattan Project, working in the commissary and later at the Lab until his retirement in 1959. Then he moved to the valley, and lived in Espanola into his ninety-seventh year.

His son Severo, now retired from a state government job in Santa Fe, was a teenager when the army took over the ranch. He recalls, "Dad was born in San Ildefonso [on the pueblo]. There were a few Spanish on the outskirts. [The Indians] didn't want anybody to live too close. They had secret ceremonies that they didn't want anybody to see or watch... My dad knew Tilano very well. He was friendly with all the Indians in San Ildefonso, especially Maria and Julian Martinez, the famous pottery makers. Dad bought a lot of their pottery and sold it to the boys at the Ranch School. They, in turn would mail it to their families around the world.

"My general impression of people coming in the early parts of the Manhattan Project is that [they thought] they were going [to a place] where everything was wild, [where] you might be shot with a bow and arrow by an Indian. [In fact], there's been people visiting Los Alamos from all over the country [since before the Manhattan Project]. Rich people from all over came to see their sons graduate. No airplanes then but all kinds of limousines... We were surprised in the old days [that] there weren't any kidnappings because there were some pretty famous kids in Los Alamos whose parents had money.

"We were poor, but we always had everything we wanted. A lot of the students, [when] they were graduating, they'd give us their tennis rackets, balls, skates, hockey clubs, pucks... I had a complete set of shin guards for playing hockey. Boys that were going back East, they had money-real nice jackets these boys would give us.

"You'd see the boys out there at six o'clock in the morning exercising. You'd see them every Saturday morning riding. Exercising, good living, good eating. When they'd leave, some of those kids really put on that weight and height. This fresh mountain air-I won't say that for Los Alamos now. You read in the papers about "Acid Canyon" and all that stuff that's going on up there-but then that was wild country...

"It was very peaceful, very quiet [in the days of the school]. The Manhattan Project brought in a lot of things... When the army first started going up there, and Mr. Oppenheimer and those people were looking for a site, the first person they had contact with was my dad... In the evenings when we were having supper, he would tell us that the general had come... My dad was one of the first persons Mr. Connell told what they were up there for... He was trying to figure out how he could block them or discourage them... Then he told my dad, "They're only going to be here for the duration. They'll give it back after the war is over. They need it for some special project for the war.... Then all of a sudden they had this gate...

"When the army took over, since he had all that experience in the store, [dad] immediately went to work for what they called the commissary [for] the GIs. . . . [In the beginning, before the individual passes] . . . they issued one letter and that was a pass to get in and out of Los Alamos. My dad had this one letter with all his family listed in there, just one letter. I can remember borrowing the letter to leave Los Alamos with some friends. I've often wondered what would have happened if [my parents] would have had to leave Los Alamos. Seems kind of funny and awkward that they would only type out one big letter...

"My mother became a professional babysitter. She babysat for some of the big shots of Los Alamos. These ladies loved my mother. They liked an older person to take care of their kids... She was bilingual and had six children of her own... I wish I'd kept the names of everybody she babysat for...

"My brother took care of the Oppenheimer horse... I can still see Oppenheimer most of the time walking, with his hat and walking with different people. With Fermi. From the Tech Area to where they lived they had to go almost in front of our house. Some of the biggest people are the nicest. They go about their business and treat you nice...

"They used to do a lot of blasting, up there. They would fire away, fire away. Everybody knew they were testing explosives, but nobody knew what was going to come of it... If Los Alamos wasn't what Los Alamos is, this whole valley would be about a fourth of what it is. Santa Fe would be half of what it is. It would be selfish to say I wish I was still homesteading."

Document 14.2

Air Conditioning in the Southwest (1950s)

Following World War Two, Phoenix, Arizona, emerged as the leading city of the Southwest. The arid West had lured health seekers since the nineteenth century and the climate continued to be a major draw into the current century. However, the oppressive summer heat remained a barrier to the city's growth until the advent of affordable air conditioning systems in the 1950s. The following excerpt illustrates the impetus air conditioning gave to the settlement of the Southwest.*

During the 1950s Phoenix emerged as the dominant metropolis in the Southwest. A post-World War II boom fueled by government expenditures, expanding private enterprise, and an extraordinary booster spirit transformed the city into a mecca. Thousands of people were attracted by economic opportunities in the Phoenix area. Scientists, engineers, and technicians were drawn to the city's burgeoning technological industry, healthful climate, and natural beauty. At the same time, however, Phoenix's rapid expansion created problems that threatened its distinctive Southwestern character. As the decade ended, the city was squarely in the mainstream of modern American life.

At the outbreak of World War II, Senator Carl Hayden of Arizona helped spark Phoenix's explosive growth when he persuaded the War Department to locate four air training centers on the flatlands west, north, and east of the city. Stirred to action by the war, the army in 1941 built Luke Field and the smaller Thunderbird Field near Glendale, Williams Field near Chandler, and Falcon Field near Mesa. In 1944, the Navy opened its own training base at Litchfield Park. The establishment of these facilities demonstrated the importance of the Phoenix area in the government's decentralization of the war industries program.

Large-scale manufacturing followed in the path of the air bases. In 1941 Goodyear Aircraft began producing airplane parts and balloons at Litchfield Park, and the following year the Garrett Corporation built an AiResearch plant at Phoenix Sky Harbor Airport. In 1943 the Aluminum Company of America (Alcoa) opened an aluminum extrusion plant. The Allison Steel Company, which had been operating in Phoenix since the 1920s, commenced wartime production of portable bridges. Laborers, flocking to the city to work in these plants, created a demand for housing that far surpassed existing housing facilities. As a result, auto trailer parks became a common form of company housing for war plant workers.

Although the end of hostilities in August of 1945 caused the termination of government defense contracts and the closing of war plants, Phoenix's growth continued. Many servicemen who had trained at local air bases returned with their families to make permanent homes amid the sunshine and relaxed living of the area. Some war plants only closed temporarily and were reopened by private industry, which leased the unoccupied government buildings at cheap rates. In 1946, for example, Reynolds Aluminum took over the Alcoa plant. AiResearch closed its doors in 1946 but reopened in 1951. Motorola Research, a major manufacturer of radio and electronic parts, established its first plant in Phoenix about this time. In their wake came Cold War defense contractors. Aircraft electronic component industries predominated, but they were soon followed by missile component manufacturers. In both instances, the value of the product justified shipping costs to distant markets. These defense industries produced a multiplier effect, for they, in turn, attracted a host of other manufacturing enterprises.

Postwar Phoenix presented some interesting paradoxes. By 1947 the city—already the largest center of trade, transportation, and government between Dallas and the Pacific

---

* Michael Konig, "Phoenix in the 1950s: Urban Growth in the Sunbelt," *Arizona and the West*, 24:1 (Spring 1982), pp. 19-23.

Coast—began developing into a financial center. Bank loans that year exceeded two billion dollars, and permits for new construction soared to $9,885,030. Air traffic in this desert community boomed in 1947. Sky Harbor Airport ranked first nationally in civilian traffic handled and fourth in total traffic. The population of Phoenix rose to 106,818, up sixty-three percent from 1940. The population of metropolitan Maricopa County represented forty-four percent of the entire population of the state.

Phoenix began expanding in every direction, but because of modest city planning the incorporated municipality in the early fifties occupied less than ten square miles. The city faced the possibility of geographical stagnation, if outlying sections were incorporated as independent villages or towns. A writer for the *Saturday Evening Post* toured the area and commented on the contrast in living conditions. Around the perimeter of the valley, ten to twenty miles from downtown, the estates of such gentry as the Wrigleys of Chicago and the Fowler McCormicks, founder of the International Harvester Company, stood in regal splendor. In sharp contrast, on the outskirts of Phoenix and south of the railroad tracks inside the city, there were unpaved streets lined with shacks which matched "misery for misery and squalor for squalor with slums anywhere."

Yet neither the wealthy nor the poor were truly representative of postwar Phoenix. The city was primarily an energetic, middle-class community whose businessmen and citizens were proud of their growth and confident of their destiny, the *Post* writer concluded. These attitudes-reflected in the improvement and reorganization of city government, expansion and modernization of educational and hospital facilities, and the increasing sophistication of financial operations-provided the framework for Phoenix's continued growth.

A major factor in this expansion during the 1950s was the salubrious climate. The sun flooded the 1,083-foot-high valley during eighty-five percent of the daylight hours, enabling the city to boast of more sunny days than any other major city in the Southern "sunbelt." Situated in one of the driest regions of North America, Phoenix enjoyed an average annual temperature of above seventy degrees Fahrenheit, while the normal precipitation rate was seven to eight inches per year. In addition, the average relative humidity varied monthly between nineteen and forty-seven percent-one of the lowest levels for any major metropolitan area in the United States. Winters in Phoenix were beautiful, with temperatures ranging between fifty and eighty degrees, but summer temperatures climbed as high as 118 degrees.

Prior to World War II, the heat discouraged many from settling in Phoenix. Businesses also hesitated to locate in the Valley of the Sun because of the summer exodus of the labor supply to the mountains or seashore. In the postwar years, however, air conditioning made summers tolerable. Introduced in 1930, the first evaporative coolers were little more than packing boxes containing pads, fan, and water supply, all held in place by chicken wire. Manufactured in the Phoenix area, these devices were widely used during World War II to cool barracks and shops at air bases and housing at armored training units in the desert. After the war the cooler became an established product. By 1951, more than ninety percent of Arizona homes had water coolers of some type, most of them manufactured in Phoenix. The five largest suppliers were Palmer Manufacturing, International Metal Products Company, Polaire Cooler Company, Wright Manufacturing Company, and Mountainaire Manufacturing Company. Altogether these manufacturers grossed $15 million annually, and accounted for fifty percent of the evaporative cooler production in the entire nation. More than three-quarters of these coolers were exported, principally to other Southwestern states.

In the 1950s, evaporative coolers gave way to sophisticated refrigeration units that met the needs of large office buildings, department stores, and spacious homes. The emergence of the local air conditioning industry played a significant role in city growth. By providing summer comfort, home air refrigeration contributed to Phoenix's unprecedented housing boom and urban development.

Document 14.3

The Texas Rangers (1968)

In 1968, the Director of the Texas Department of Public Safety, Colonel Wilson E. Speir, testified before the Hearings of the U.S. Civil Rights Commission in San Antonio, Texas. As the nominal head of the Texas Rangers, a division of the Department of Public Safety, Speir was answering charges that the Texas Rangers had traditionally been a force for the repression of Mexican Americans and that this organization was responsible for physically intimidating union organizing efforts in Starr County in 1966-1967.*

MR. RUBIN. Colonel Speir, we will start with you.

Could you give us your full name please, and your address and your current occupation?

COLONEL SPEIR. Yes, sir. I am Wilson E. Speir and I live in Austin, Texas and I am the director of the Texas Department of Public Safety.

MR. RUBIN. Can you tell us how long you have been associated with the department of public safety and in what capacities?

COLONEL SPEIR. I have been associated with the department of public safety since November 1, 1941, except for approximately 3 years during World War II when I was on military leave, thus making a total of a little over 27 years.

MR. RUBIN. And how long have you served as the director of the department?

COLONEL SPEIR. I have actually been director of this department since September of this year.

MR. RUBIN. And your previous capacity with the department was what?

COLONEL SPEIR. I came into the department as a highway patrolman and I advanced through the ranks of the uniform services as a sergeant, as captain, as a major or regional

---

* *Hearing Before the United States Commission on Civil Rights,* San Antonio, Texas, December 9-14, 1968, (Washington: U.S. Government Printing Office, 1968), pp. 715-723.

commander, and then for the last 6 years, approximately, preceding my elevation to the directorship I was the assistant director of the department.

MR. RUBIN. On the stage there is a chart which sets forth the employment statistics for your department as of the end of the month of October 1968. According to the figures which your department furnished to the Commission there are 1,640 uniform and 109 plainclothes law enforcement personnel employed by your department as of the time that you furnished the information. Of these 1,749 personnel, 28 or approximately 1½ percent are Mexican Americans.

Could you tell us why in your opinion the number of Mexican Americans employed by your department is so low?

COLONEL SPEIR. Well, of course, there may be many reasons. But those figures are not exactly right. I believe at this time in the uniform service of our department there are some 40 commissioned officers with maybe six or eight at this time training in addition to that in the academy.

MR. RUBIN. But that would still leave a relatively low number of Mexican American employees, is that correct?

COLONEL SPEIR. These are commissioned officers. Of course, we have many Mexican Americans in various categories of employment, in other areas of employment. We have made a concentrated effort to recruit people of all ethnic groups during the last 3 years. And, I to the best of my knowledge, every Mexican American that has qualified for employment that was an applicant and qualified during the last 3 years has been employed.

Now, why we don't receive more applicants, of course could be a matter of conjecture, the same thing could be true also, it would be true of Anglos. We don't get near as many applicants from Anglos or Negroes as we would like to get.

MR. RUBIN. Is there any particular reason why this should be so in your opinion, as to why Mexican Americans or Negroes should be reluctant to apply for jobs with the department of public safety?

COLONEL SPEIR. Well, I really don't know as to why more have not applied. I suppose one reason, employment in our State requires that you go anywhere in the State and I think, I have been told at least by many Mexican Americans that they are reluctant to leave their particular area of the State. Some tell us that they feel like they would like to have more money. I don't know why, really. Neither do I know why we don't get more Anglos.

MR. RUBIN. How many civilian employees are there who are located at your headquarters in Austin?

COLONEL SPEIR. Would you repeat that question?

MR. RUBIN. About how many civilian employees are there who are located at your headquarters in Austin?

COLONEL SPEIR. I don't know exactly but somewhere in the vicinity of 850, maybe 900.

MR. RUBIN. According to the chart there are a total of 1,803 civilian employees working for the department of public safety. And you indicate that about 800 or so are headquartered in Austin. Now, of the total number, 1,803, only 76, or approximately 4 percent are Mexican American. I take it the civilian employees are stationary. Is that right? They live in the area where they work?

COLONEL SPEIR. Yes, most of them do.

MR. RUBIN. To what do you attribute the fact that such a small number of your civilian employees are Mexican American?

COLONEL SPEIR. Well, actually we haven't had very much interest shown on the part of Mexican Americans for employment with us. Again, I think that the same statement that I made probably would apply.

Again, let me say that I don't know why we have not had more interest. Of course, it is difficult to employ, I think, a lot of times on account of salaries. Our salaries have been very low except up until last September when we got a material raise from the last regular session of the legislature and it has been very difficult to employ real qualified people of any race of the qualifications that you would desire up until this time. Since this time our recruiting has been very good.

MR. RUBIN. Could you tell us what type of jobs the Mexican American civilian employees hold in the department?

COLONEL SPEIR. Well, we have Mexican Americans in just about every section of the department. We have some in our intelligence section, we have many in the uniformed services, we have some that are mechanics, we have many ladies that are secretaries, many who work in various categories in the offices, some as clerks. We have-my administrative assistant is right here by my side, is Mr. Norman Suarez, with a surname.

Of course, I have never just gone around and asked my employees if they were Mexican Americans or, by name.

VOICES FROM COURTROOM. Boo!

We are proud of our Mexican American employees. We have many dedicated employees. And we would like to have more.

Speaking of recruiting, we have written to the various members of the legislature and sought their help. We have worked with the news media and I might add the news media has been very, very good in carrying our request and needs for employment throughout the State, all phases of the news media.

As I say, we have written to the legislature and we even sent individuals, recruiting officers like the military service does, into many of the cities. And we moved our recruiting to head-quarters, but we've made every regional office and every district office and every subdistrict office, so to speak, a headquarters area for recruiting. We tried to move recruiting to the field to make it just as available to everyone that might be qualified and interested as we could. This we have done.

We are real proud of the progress that we are making. Let me repeat again that we have employed every Mexican American that has sought employment with this department and qualified to my knowledge in the last 3 years in the uniformed service.

MR. RUBIN. Have you made any special efforts particularly directed toward recruiting Mexican Americans as distinguished from other groups?

COLONEL SPEIR. Yes, we have. We have-of course, many of our legislators are Mexican Americans and I have talked to many of them and sought their help, asked them to visit with people that they knew that were in positions of leadership. And I think this has resulted in us recruiting a number of good Mexican Americans.

MR. RUBIN. Our information indicates that there are no Mexican Americans in law enforcement who are employed in a supervisory capacity in your department. How would you account for that?

COLONEL SPEIR. Well, of course most of the Mexican Americans that we have in law enforcement have been employed in recent years. Competition is very keen in our department for promotion. It is based on competitive examination and the rules require that a person be in grade 2 years before he is eligible for a promotion. And, as I said, most of our Mexican Americans have not been in our employment for many years. And we have advanced two or three from the uniformed services into the intelligence services.

We have had in past years a captain of the Texas Rangers that was a Mexican American, Captain Gonzaulles, one of the most famous of all Ranger captains, who is now retired after 30 years of service. We just haven't had any that qualified at this particular time for advancement in the uniformed service.

MR. RUBIN. Are there presently any Mexican Americans who are members of the Texas Rangers?

COLONEL SPEIR. At this time?

MR. RUBIN. At this time.

COLONEL SPEIR. At this time I believe that there is not.

MR. RUBIN. How many men are employed as Texas Rangers?

COLONEL SPEIR. There are 62 Rangers in the State. This includes six captains and six sergeants and 50 Rangers, a grand total of 62, whose average tenure is 30, 35 years. And as you can see there will be very little turnover, very little opportunity for the employment of people because these are positions that are set by the legislature and it is not within our scope to employ more.

The legislature determines the number of Rangers that we have. So oftentimes I say that on the average we only have a turnover of maybe two or three positions a year, on an average. And therefore there is just not much opportunity for employment of anyone.

I suppose that I have some 300 applications for the Ranger service on file in our department. I would say that there are a few if any applications from Mexican Americans for the Ranger service among the applicants that I have on file.

MR. RUBIN. You mentioned two or three Mexican Americans who had been members of the Texas Rangers. Have there been any others in the past?

COLONEL SPEIR. I know of only two or three-actually Captain Gonzales, Mr. Trejo, several years ago. At the moment I don't recall another by name.

MR. RUBIN. Did the department of public safety receive any reports criticizing the actions of the Texas Rangers in the Starr County labor dispute?

COLONEL SPEIR. At that time I was not director of the department of public safety. I will say this, that it is my belief and to the very best of my knowledge, none of the people who were so widely quoted in the news media, by the news media ever came to my office to make any type of complaint whatsoever.

MR. RUBIN. But did the department receive any reports in connection with this?

COLONEL SPEIR. We received reports from our own people. And I was contacted by members of the Bureau of Investigation, the FBI, who conducted an investigation. And certainly we made any information that we had available to the Bureau, as we always do if there is a question on civil rights, it is always our pleasure to cooperate with any group that is trying to do what is right.

We cooperated with the Bureau in this instance, as you know. I am sure that the Commission knows that they did investigate this matter. Certainly we cooperated with them.

MR. RUBIN. Did the department of public safety make its own investigation?

COLONEL SPEIR. Yes, sir, we did.

MR. RUBIN. We have heard testimony to the effect that the Texas Rangers are feared and despised by Mexican Americans in south Texas.

In your opinion-in your opinion, what is the attitude of the Mexican American community of southern Texas toward the Texas Rangers?

COLONEL SPEIR. Would you repeat that?

MR. RUBIN. I wanted your opinion of the attitude of the Mexican American community in south Texas toward the Texas Rangers. How do you feel that the Mexican American community views the Rangers?

MR. SEAMAAN. Well, so long as the Committee understands that this is an opinion and a conclusion, and that is all, I have no objection to his answering it. But now, how correct or incorrect it may be is another question. But if all you want is an opinion?

MR. RUBIN. All I want is an opinion.

MR. SEAMAAN. All right.

COLONEL SPEIR. Now your question is as to what my opinion is as to how the Mexican Americans feel toward the department of public safety?

MR. RUBIN. Yes, and the Texas Rangers?

COLONEL SPEIR. Of course, the Texas Rangers is one service of the department of public safety.

MR. SEAMAAN. May we first ascertain from him if he feels that he is qualified to give such an opinion and what it is based on.

VOICES FROM AUDIENCE. Hiss!

COLONEL SPEIR. Well, I have no objection to giving you my opinion. I think that-I don't know how-who might agree with my opinion. I don't know how accurate the opinion is. But since you have asked I think that there are some Mexican Americans that feel that we have perhaps abused someone somewhere along the line. But I do think this, I think this, that most Mexican Americans have tremendous respect for the department of public safety and the Texas Rangers.

Document 14.4

Bulloch v. United States (1956)

In this 1956 case before the Federal District Court, ranchers from southern Utah brought suit under the provisions of the Federal Tort Claims Act against the federal government for damages because thousands of sheep were allegedly killed as a result of radioactive fallout from nearby atomic bomb tests which contaminated the sheep pastures. The government contended that the sheep deaths were not caused by fallout but by cold weather, inadequate feeding, infectious diseases, and unfavorable range conditions. The judge in this case ruled in favor of the government, concluding the deaths were not caused by atomic radiation.*

During the Spring of 1953, the United States Atomic Energy Commission conducted as "Operations Upshot Knothole" a series of nuclear tests at the Nevada Proving Ground, northwest of Las Vegas, Nevada. At the time of the first shot, plaintiffs' herd of sheep some fifty miles northeast of the test site was moving from the winter range in an easterly direction toward shearing and lambing grounds in the vicinity of Cedar City, Utah. During the trip, this herd was within, or near, areas of radioactive fallout resulting from some of these detonations. Following the first, and continuing more or less until after the last shot of the series, abnormal losses of sheep and lambs from the Bulloch herd were noted. Other herds in the same general vicinity suffered similar difficulties which are the subjects of companion suits.

Preliminary observations of the animals disclosed gross signs simulating the effects of beta radiation. There were other evidences which suggested damage from gamma rays. An extensive study was thereupon undertaken by cooperating governmental agencies concerning possible effects of radiation upon these animals. The conclusion reached by the investigating agencies, with dissents on the part of three of the veterinaries participating, was that certain lesions observed on the sheep and the losses and damages suffered by them were neither caused nor substantially contributed to by radiation. A denial of liability on the part of the Government resulted in this and similar suits.

Voluminous testimony and numerous exhibits have been received in evidence. It was thought that the nature of the issues commended the most liberal exploration of the facts consistent with the substantial rights of the parties. The case was presented with high ability and diligence by counsel, and an array of distinguished and informed witnesses appeared. The Government contends that the losses suffered by the Bullochs were the natural result of unprecedented cold weather during the lambing and shearing of sheep, inadequate feeding, unfavorable winter range conditions, and infectious diseases of

* Bulloch v. United States, *145 Federal Supplement 824*, October 26, 1956, pp. 824-828.

various types, the combined effects of which were improperly thought by some during the preliminary investigation to comprise irradiation syndromes. The plaintiffs contend that the coincidence of damage and location of the sheep in fallout areas, not only as regards the Bulloch herd but as to sheep similarly located and similarly affected, the inability of preliminary investigators to definitely rule out irradiation or to identify any other cause, the views of the three veterinaries which initially supported plaintiffs' theory in one respect or another, the measured radioactivity in samples from some of the sheep, the failure of subsequent experiments to take into account the peculiar conditions under which the sheep in question were operated, together with other claimed indications of a relationship, all established by preponderate evidence that plaintiffs' abnormal losses were proximately caused, or substantially contributed to, by radiation.

On the law phases of the case, plaintiffs assert that the damage was caused through the negligence of employees of the Government, acting within the scope of their authority and not in the exercise of any discretionary function; and that thus the Government is liable by virtue of the provisions of the Federal Tort Claims Act of August 2, 1946, Title 4, Public Law 601, 79th Congress, as amended, 28 U.S.C.A. §§1346, 2671 et seq. The Government contends that there was no negligence of any employee of the Government proximately causing damage to the Bulloch sheep, and that if there were any damages suffered as a result of governmental action, there could be no recovery in any event as they would be in consequence of the exercise of a discretionary function of Government. 28 U.S.C.A. § 2680(a).

Document 14.5

The Watts Riot (1965)

On August 11, 1965 rumors of an alleged incident of police brutality circulated through the hot streets of the Watts district of Los Angeles. Residents responded by looting white-owned businesses and hurling projectiles at police officers and white passersby. The particulars of the incident that set off this firestorm varied. According to one resident, a drunken driving arrest of a black driver had escalated to a brutal pummeling with police batons, foreshadowing the 1990s Rodney King case and the Los Angeles Riot. Another rumor had it that a pregnant woman had been clubbed by overzealous Los Angeles policemen. Despite the questionable reliability of these rumors, the inescapable reality that day was that poor housing conditions and rampant police brutality would no longer be tolerated, heralding a decade of racial strife in America's urban ghettos.

Over the following six days the Watts Riot would claim the lives of 34 individuals and injure 1,032. It was estimated that between seven and ten thousand residents took part in an "uprising" that destroyed hundreds of buildings resulting in forty million dollars in property losses. Governor Pat Brown appointed John McCone to head a commission to study the riot. The following passage is taken from the chronology of events published in the commission's findings.*

By 12:20 A.M. approximately 50 to 75 youths were on either side of Avalon Blvd. at Imperial Highway, throwing missiles at passing cars and the police used vehicles with red lights and sirens within the riot area perimeter in an effort to disperse the crowd. As they did so, the rock throwing crowd dispersed, only to return as the police left the scene. Some of the older citizens in the area were inquiring, "What are those crazy kids doing?" A number of adult Negroes expressed the opinion that the police should open fire on the rock throwers to stop their activities. The police did not discharge firearms at rioters. It was estimated that by 12:30 A.M. 70% of the rioters were children and the remainder were young adults and adults. Their major activity was throwing missiles at passing vehicles driven by Caucasians. One rioter stationed himself a block from the intersection of Avalon Blvd. and Imperial Highway, where the major group of rioters were centered, and signaled to this group, whenever a vehicle driven by a Caucasian approached the intersection, so that it could be stoned...

Witnesses stated at this time, young Negro rioters said: "I'm throwing rocks because I'm tired of a white man misusing me." "Man this is the part of town they have given us, and if they don't want to be killed they had better keep their -- out of here." "The cops think we are scared of them because they got guns, but you can only die once; if I get a few of them I don't mind dying."

... Sunrise disclosed five burned automobiles, amidst a large amount of rubble, broken bricks, stones, and shattered glass, in the vicinity of the intersection of Imperial Highway and Avalon Blvd.

As an indication of the mood of the crowd of approximately 400 persons who had gathered... on Thursday morning, the following comments of the youths in the crowd are quoted:

"Like why, man, should I go home? These-- cops have been pushin' me 'round all my life. Kickin' my -- and things like that. Whitey ain't no good. He talked 'bout law and order, its his law and his order it ain't mine..."

"--, if I've got to die, I ain't dyin' in Vietnam, I'm going to die... "

"I don't have no job. I ain't worked for two years. —He, the white man, got everything, I ain't got nothin. What you expect me to do? I get my kicks when I see Whitey running-If they come in here tonight going to kill me one."

They always—with the Blood—beatin' them with stocks, hand-cuffing women, I saw one of them -- go up side a cat's head and split it wide open. They treat the Blood

---

* California Governor's Commission on the Los Angeles Riots, *Transcripts, Depositions, Consultants' Reports, and Selected Documents*, II, pp. 28; 32-33; 43-44; 86; 173-174; 188-189.

like dirt-They've been doing it for years. Look how they treated us when we were slaves—We still slaves..."

"Whitey use his cops to keep us here. We are like hogs in a pen-then they come in with those silly helmets sticks and guns and things-Who the -- Parker [i.e., Police Chief Parker] think he is, God?"

AUGUST 13

At 1:57 A.M. the Los Angeles Sheriff's deputies on perimeter control refused entry into the riot area to fire department units for the safety of the firemen.

Three cars were on fire as well as a building, in the 1200 block of Imperial Highway, and when fire department vehicles appeared in the area they were struck by thrown projectiles.

By 2:00 A.M. the perimeter established around the riot area was dissolved according to Deputy Chief Murdock, because of outbreaks of rioting beyond the original perimeter lines.

The owner of a liquor store in the 2000 block at East 103rd Street was reported to have barricaded himself in his store and to have shot persons attempting to break in.

At 2:16 A.M. a group of rioters proceding north on Central Avenue, on 120 St. overturned and burned automobiles in the street.

At 2:00 P.M. District Attorney investigators at Broadway and Manchester Avenue observed cars containing young men between the ages of 18 and 20 years. The youths were not stopped nor detained and it appeared that these youth had some type of communication system, because teen-agers and adults could be spotted using telephone booths. After making phone calls, the youngsters would get in their cars and head for other locations.

Business buildings on 103rd St. in Watts were burned completely for two blocks and firemen were driven off by uncontrolled rioters. Rioters completely overran law enforcement personnel and the number of fire alarms became so numerous that fire control was mainly by visual patrol.

At 2:08 P.M. a police officer was injured at 108th St. and Central Avenue as a result of the heavy stoning of police vehicles. The intersection became impassable.

... Between 6:00 P.M. and 6:15 P.M. police were requested at 49th St. and Avalon Blvd. as two hundred rioters were looting and overturning vehicles. Numerous shots were fired in the vicinity of Broadway and 88th St. Two vehicles were on fire at 51st St. and Avalon Blvd. and 200 rioters were throwing rocks and bottles in that area. Looters had completely taken over the Safeway market...

The LAPD officers swept 103rd St., posting fixed positions. The area was in flames. The fire department had been driven from the area by rioters but was now able to return under police protection. Police swept Broadway and also established fixed posts on that thoroughfare. At 89th St. and Broadway the police formed a skirmish line in order to break up rioters. Warning shots were fired by police over the heads of rioters and Leon Posey Jr., who was standing on the sidewalk was struck in the head by a 38 caliber bullet. (A coroner's inquest subsequently held the death of Posey was accidental.)

AUGUST 14

At 5:15 A.M. Paul E. Harbin was shot and killed by police... as a looter. (Coroner's inquest held this a justifiable homicide.) At 5:15 A.M. George Fentroy was killed by police at 62nd St. and South Broadway, as a looter. Police had observed two looters leaving the buildings with their arms full of clothing and ordered them to halt. The persons refused to heed the command. One suspect escaped. (Coroner's inquest held the killing of Fentroy was justifiable homicide.) At 5:30 A.M. Miller C. Burroughs was shot and killed by police ... as a looter. (Coroner's inquest held this a justifiable homicide.) At 5:30 A.M. Leon Cauley was shot and killed... by police, as a looter. (Coroner's inquest held this a justifiable homicide.)

Document 14.6

Cesar Chavez to the United Farm Workers of America (1979)

On the day before Thanksgiving 1960, journalist Edward R. Murrow moderated the CBS television broadcast of *Harvest of Shame,* one of the most moving documentaries ever produced on the condition of farm workers in America. Since the 1960s, the conditions of farmworkers have improved, but still pale in comparison to the conditions enjoyed by organized industrial workers.
In the 1960s, Cesar Chavez (1927-1993) became a household name, a Martin Luther King to the mostly Hispanic migrant workers. The child of Mexican immigrants, his family followed the migrant laborer's calling from Arizona to California. Chavez joined the a farm labor organization at the age of nineteen and through the 1950s became increasingly involved with the farm labor movement. In the following testimony Chavez addresses the hearings on Farmworker Collective Bargaining in 1979.*

Mr. CHAVEZ. Mr. Chairman, many of the workers who do not speak the English language we have provided for translations. I would like to inquire if that equipment is working.
The CHAIRMAN. Where are they? Oh, I see, everybody has them.

* *Hearings Before the Committee on Labor and Human Resources*, U.S. Senate, 96th Cong., 1st Session, (Washington: U.S. Government Printing Office, 1979), pp. 4-7.

Mr. CHAVEZ. Some are, some aren't.

Mr. Chairman, we are pleased to be here today before your committee. I have with me Union General Counsel Jerry Cohen who will be here to assist me and advise me of any legal questions which may arise. I understand Mr. Cohen will be testifying later on.

I want to make some general remarks and then we have a number of farmworkers who will come up and testify, eyewitnesses to events I will allude to in my general remarks. They will bring to this committee specific testimony from their own eyewitness experience.

We are again grateful to have the committee here, to have a forum to which we can point out injustices we feel are committed against us daily in this struggle.

After 3 months of striking in 1979 we have come to the conclusion very little progress has been made in the last 40 years.

In the 1930's when the farmworkers tried to organize a strike, they were looked upon and treated by the local power structures in the rural communities as un-American, as subversive, and as some sort of criminal element. We today are looked upon pretty much the same way.

Just as in the 1930s, when a union strike occurred, they were called criminal whether they be in Salinas, Calexico, Monterey County, Imperial County, or in Delano and Bakersfield, Calif. When a union strikes, it becomes then not simply a labor-management dispute as you see in other cases, but in our experience it becomes then on one side the workers, on the other side agribusiness and all of the local institutions, political and social, organize then to break the strike—the police, the sheriffs, the courts, the schools, the boards of supervisors, city councils. Not only that, but the State or Federal agencies that reside within those rural areas, are also greatly influenced by this overwhelming political power. The agribusiness industry wields this political power and uses it to break our strikes and destroy the union.

They have two standards of conduct against Mexicans and against unions. As long as we, Mexican farmworkers, keep our place and do our work we are tolerated, but if the Mexican worker joins a union, if he stands up for justice and if he dares to strike, then all the local institutions feel dutybound to defend what they consider to be their ideal of the American way of life. These communities, then, do not know what to do with us and they don't know what to do without us.

We have here a few examples that will be expanded upon by eyewitnesses a little later on. For so many years we have been involved in agricultural strikes; organizing almost 30 years as a worker, as an organizer, and as president of the union—and for all these almost 30 years it is apparent that when the farm workers strike and their strike is successful, the employers go the Mexico and have unlimited, unrestricted use of illegal alien strikebreakers to break the strike. And for over 30 years, the Immigration and Naturalization Service has looked the other way and assisted in the strikebreaking.

I do not remember one single instance in 30 years where the Immigration service has removed strikebreakers to the extent the workers were helped and the illegal alien workers were removed. The employers use professional smugglers to recruit and transport human contraband across the Mexican border for the specific act of strikebreaking, rampant in the strikes of the last 30 years.

Lawbreaking begets more lawbreaking, and when these illegal aliens come in to break a strike they have to be harbored; they have to be transported; and labor contractors have to be used to direct them and supervise them.

What about the other laws? What about the contributions the employers have to make to social security and unemployment insurance? How are those contributions made? These men do not have social security numbers. They do not live here; they are just here for a little while to break the strike.

The Immigration and Naturalization Service steadfastly refuses to enforce the law; not only that, but then they get into a dispute with us because we call their shortcomings to their attention. We accuse them of looking the other way while the strike is being broken and then they have a way of taking punitive action against us and our people.

We have supplied the Commissioner of the Immigration and Naturalization Service and his agents with details, specific information of where and how and in some cases who are the illegal aliens breaking the strike, who transports them, who feeds them, where they live, where they work—enough information, more than enough information, to have them deported. We see by the comments of the Immigration Service that they make to the press, that they are also very good at turning around the truth. Mr. Castillo, in the Washington Post of April 18, told that paper that he was sympathetic to our frustrations but that the complaints we had given were vague or unproductive when checked out, that searches had been made, but when they got there the information that we gave them was not what it was supposed to be.

In the Salinas, Calif., newspaper of April 25—the newspaper contacted them. A statement was made in a telephone interview. Officials of INS in San Pedro said that they would maintain a neutral stance, including a policy of paying little attention to tips called in by the UFW strikers.

We gave the Immigration and Naturalization Service—and we will make this a part of the record—some information. We called them and told them that at this moment as we sit in this hearing here in Salinas there is a camp of illegal aliens housed there by Sun Harvest to break the strike. They have at least five other locations where they keep illegal aliens. We gave this information to the INS last week in Washington and we told how California Coastal Farms has a camp on Westfall Road just outside, south of Salinas, with 60 or 70 illegal aliens there, and they are breaking the strike right this moment, and the Immigration Service knows specifically they are there.

We also told Mr. Castillo that around 85 or so illegal alien strikebreakers are picked up every morning in Salinas at Rosita's cafe on North Main Street by labor contractor Paul Nava, who transports the illegal aliens into the fields to break the strike, which is illegal.

We also told them about the 50 or so illegal aliens here to break the strike in the Huron area are transported and housed by Jimmy Garza, a labor contractor working there for Growers Exchange.

In Phoenix, Sun Harvest had over 60 illegal strike breakers at their camp on Sosamean Road. To be more specific with just one sample-and we have many more-Sun Harvest, Growers Exchange at the Olmost Motel on Date Street and Highway 1 in Oxnard in rooms 27, 29, 32, and 53, there are housed more than 30 illegal aliens who are used exclusively for purposes of breaking the strike. And the Immigration Service comes back and says information is vague and unproductive.

We have observed all these years the Immigration Service has a policy as it has been related to us, that they will not take sides in any agricultural labor dispute and they have been telling unions and farmworkers that same policy problem for 30 years. That they have not taken sides means permitting the growers to have unrestricted use of illegal aliens as strikebreakers, and if that isn't taking sides, I don't know what taking sides means.

The growers have armed their foremen. They have looked to professional agencies to provide them unlimited numbers of armed guards recruited from the streets, young men who are not trained, many of them members of Ku-Klux Klan and the Nazi Party in California and other such groups, who are given a gun and a club and a badge and a canister of tear gas and the authority and permission to go and beat our people up, frighten them, maim them, and try to break the strike by using this unchecked raw power against our people.

Not only that, but when one of our strikers is killed, and this is the fourth one now, Judge William Lenhardt in El Centro found insufficient evidence and last Monday dropped the charges against the murderers, thereby encouraging other such men to come and continue killing our people. A stop has to be put to that.

The sheriff's deputies, the sheriff's departments in Salinas, Imperial Valley become nothing more than private armies for the growers. The question of human rights, the issue President Carter raises all over the world, doesn't apply, I suppose, to this country specifically. Where is the issue of human rights with the law administration in Salinas County, Calif.; where is the issue of human rights? Why is it not being raised in this area when people are being murdered and maimed and beaten?

The only neutral agency, and I say neutral now, is the Agricultural Labor Relations Board, but you will see in the course of this testimony that the slick management attorneys will come here whining, crying, and complaining to try and destroy that Board, the only hope we have, because they as yet do not control it. They will try to do a job on the Board because they know this is the only hope we have here.

For too long now our people, farmworkers, union members, striking workers, have suffered at the hands of the law enforcement people; the administration of justice is never going to work as long as it continues to be controlled by the employers, as long as it continues to be used against the best interest of its citizens.

Things have deteriorated so much that the public defender in one case is trying to subpoena the union's membership records. I know of no local agency in this area that remains neutral or, in fact, that will carry out the law when a strike takes place. I think it is a very serious state of affairs, not only because of the way that the local authorities take it upon themselves to say what they consider to be the American way of life, but even more so that their lawlessness, their breaking of the law, their police state activities and the attitude they develop in this area will continue long after the strike ends. And we need to have relief because what they are doing; they are engendering for a long time to come disaffection on the part of the men and women who work here for residents and citizens. The local sheriffs and others who are here to protect the rights of all citizens, the power structure, loses sight of that responsibility when the strike takes place and they do more damage to the future of this country than anybody can do outside this country.

Mr. Chairman, that concludes my remarks.

Document 14.7

Red Power (1969)

In the 1960s, taking their cue from the African-American civil rights movement, many Native Americans decided to pursue their own rights militantly. In general, they wanted an end to discrimination against Native Americans, the restoration of lands stolen from them, and protection of the natural environment. In 1969, a group of Native Americans known as the Native Alliance for Red Power summarized the demands of many Indian militants.*

1. We will not be free until we are able to determine our destiny. Therefore, we want power to determine the destiny of our reservations and communities. Gaining power in our reservations and communities and power over our lives will entail the abolishment of the "Indian Act" and the destruction of the colonial office (Indian Affairs Branch).

2. This racist government has robbed, cheated, and brutalized us, and is responsible for the deaths of untold numbers of our people. We feel under no obligation to support this government in the form of taxation. Therefore, we want an end to the collection of money from us in the form of taxes....

5. When brought before the courts of this country, the red man cannot hope to get a fair hearing from white judges, jurors, and court officials. Therefore, we want natives to be tried by a jury of people chosen from native communities or people of their racial heritage. Also, we want freedom for those of our brothers and sisters now being unjustly held in the prisons of this country.

6. The treaties pertaining to fishing, hunting, trapping, and property rights and special privileges have been broken by this government. In some cases, our people did not engage in treaties with the government and have not been compensated for their loss of land. Therefore, for those of our people who have not made treaties, we want fair compensation. Also, we want the government to honour the statutes, as laid down in these treaties, as being supreme and not to be infringed upon by any legislation whatsoever.

7. The large industrial companies and corporations that have raped the natural resources of this country are responsible, along with their government, for the extermination of the resources upon which we depend for food, clothing and shelter. Therefore, we want an immediate end to this exploitation and compensation from these thieves. We want the government to give foreign aid to the areas comprising the Indian Nation, so that we can start desperately-needed programs concerning housing, agricultural, and industrial cooperatives. We want to develop our remaining resources in the interests of the red man, not in the interests of the white corporate-elite.

---

* "Red Power: An Eight Point Program," *Akwesasne Notes*, 1 (May 1969), p. 4

8. The white power structure has used every possible method to destroy our spirit and the will to resist.

RED POWER IS THE SPIRIT TO RESIST!
RED POWER IS PRIDE IN WHAT WE ARE!
RED POWER IS LOVE FOR OUR PEOPLE!
RED POWER IS OUR COMING-TOGETHER TO FIGHT FOR LIBERATION!
RED POWER IS NOW!

Document 14.8

Alcatraz (1970)

In the early morning hours of November 20, 1969, eighty-nine American Indians landed on Alcatraz Island in San Francisco Bay. Identifying themselves as "Indians of All Tribes," this group of young urban Indian college students claimed the island by "right of discovery" and by the terms of the 1868 Sioux Treaty of Fort Laramie, which they interpreted as giving Indians the right to claim unused federal property that had been Indian land previously. The occupiers demanded clear title to Alcatraz Island and the establishment of an American Indian University, an American Indian Cultural Center, and an American Indian Museum on Alcatraz Island. They remained on the island until June 11, 1971. The following document is a statement of their demands.*

Indians of All Tribes greet our brothers and sisters of all races and tongues upon our Earth Mother. We here on Indian land, Alcatraz, represent many tribes of Indians.

We are still holding the island of Alcatraz in the true names of freedom, justice, and equality, because our brothers and sisters of this earth have lent support to our just cause. We reach out our hands and hearts and send spirit messages to all Indians.

Our anger at the many injustices forced upon us since the first white men landed on these sacred shores has been transformed into a hope that we be allowed the long suppressed right of all men to plan and to live their own lives in harmony and cooperation with all fellow creatures and with nature. We have learned that violence breeds only more violence and we therefore have carried on our occupation of Alcatraz in a peaceful manner, hoping that the government will act accordingly.

Be it known, however, that we are quite serious in our demand to be given ownership of this island in the name of Indians of All Tribes. We are here to stay, men, women, and children. We feel that this request is but little to ask from a government

---

* *Congressional Record*, 91st Congress, 1970.

which has systematically stolen our lands, destroyed a once beautiful landscape, killed off the creatures of nature, polluted air and water, ripped open the very bowels of our earth in senseless greed, and instituted a program to annihilate the many Indian tribes of this land by theft, suppression, prejudice, termination, and so-called relocation and assimilation.

We are a proud people! We are Indians! We have observed and rejected much of what so-called civilization offers. We are Indians! We will preserve our traditions and ways of life by educating our own children. We are Indians! We will join hands in a unity never before put into practice. Our Earth Mother awaits our voices. We are Indians of All Tribes!!!

We came to Alcatraz because we were sick and tired of being pushed around, exploited, and degraded everywhere we turned in our own country. We selected Alcatraz for many reasons but most importantly, we came to Alcatraz because it is a place of our own. Somewhere that is geographically unfeasible for everybody to come and interfere with what we would like to do with our lives. We can beat our drums all night long if we want to and not be bothered or harassed by non-Indians and police. We can worship, we can sing, and we can make plans for our lives and the future of our Indian people and Alcatraz.

After we landed on Alcatraz, we got a lot of attention and publicity. Support came in from the local areas and the nation, and even worldwide. People wanted to give us benefits, have us speak at schools, be in programs on television and radio, and even have movie premieres on the island. We were flooded with everything and everybody, from opportunists and vultures to sincere and dedicated people. Somehow, we survived all the glory and confusion even though we have never been the victims of attention before and the symbol of the American Indian shined out before the nation and the whole world.

Indians of All Tribes united on the Alcatraz issue and for the first time in the Bay area, Indian organizations representing over 40,000 Indian people, united and formed the Bay Area Native American Council, in order to push the government to deal with Alcatraz as the priority issue.

The Bay Area Native American Council is a support group for Alcatraz. They do not speak for Indians on Alcatraz, although we consult with them, and support them in their work to help Indians in the Bay area.

Our work on Alcatraz is different from BANAC. We are maintaining the island during the occupation, as a way of promoting the general welfare of all Indian people, which means that our occupation is not strictly Alcatraz but rather for all Indian people. We hope to concern and involve ourselves with national Indian problems as well as planning and building our own Indian university and cultural center.

We on Alcatraz formed a nonprofit corporation called Indians of All Tribes, Inc. We represent who we are, and we are Indians of All Tribes.

We don't speak for Indians all over the country. The Indians all over the country speak for themselves.

When Indian people come to see what Alcatraz is all about and to see what they can do for the Alcatraz movement, then they speak for themselves. We have a radio station that broadcasts live from the island where they speak about their reservations and it draws attention to their particular problems. We have a newsletter as well. Anyone is welcome to write what they have to say.

Before we took Alcatraz, people in San Francisco didn't even know that Indians were alive, and if that's a sample of what the local people knew, considering that this is the main relocation point for Indians through the Bureau of Indian Affairs, then there are people across the nation who never even knew that Indians were alive or ever even knew our problems. They never knew anything about our suicide rate that is ten times the national average, or our education level that is to the fifth grade. Alcatraz focused on the Indian people. Now the Indian people have a chance for the first time to say what they have to say and to make decisions about themselves, which has never happened before.

The decision we want to make is in governing ourselves and our own people, without interference from non-Indians. Naturally we don't have all the tools that we need in order to make decisions on the engineering or structural engineering on Alcatraz or the planning of the island, so we would need non-Indian advice as well. We need everyone's advice who has something to contribute.

Our main concern is with Indian people everywhere. One of the reasons we took Alcatraz was because the students were having problems in the universities and colleges they were attending. This was the first time that Indian people had ever had the chance to get into a university or college because relocation was all vocation-oriented and it was not until 1968 and 1969 that Indians started getting into the universities and colleges. So, when this happened, we all realized that we didn't want to go through the university machinery coming out white-orientated like the few Indian people before us, or like the non-Indian people who were running our government, our Indian government, or our Indian Affairs. We didn't want to alienate ourselves from the non-Indian people because we were learning from everyone else as well, but we also wished to retain our own identity, with the whole conglomeration of everybody. We didn't want to melt with the melting pot, which was the object of federal relocation programs. We wanted to remain Indians. That's why native American studies became a prime issue, and when we had a big confrontation with the administration, we could see that we weren't going to fool ourselves about the university; we could see that we could never get everything through it. They would make small concessions, but still didn't give us what we needed. It was just a token of what we actually wanted and we didn't want to be used like that.

This was one of the reasons why we wanted our own Indian university, so that they would stop whitewashing Indians, which was happening, not only on the university level, but in the Indian boarding schools and summer home programs for Indians and just everything that the government had to do with Indians.

We were also concerned about our own lives and our children and what was happening on the reservations as well, because while we were physically away, we still had our families and people in our hearts and on our minds, the problems that they were facing, and the frustration of not being able to help them because we were trying to get the necessary tools so we could return to our reservations some day. In the meantime, there were all types of roadblocks. We needed attention brought to our people, and we needed a place to get together in the city so that we didn't become victims of assimilation. It finally all came to a point and we decided we would just go liberate our own land since all of our other lands had been taken away and the cities were so crowded and we had no where to go together for Indian dances or powwows or anything, or even to have our own religious ceremonies. We'd get arrested if we practised our own religion and had peyote in our home. In 1964 a Sioux landing party had taken Alcatraz which was federal surplus land that, according to the Sioux treaty, should revert back to the Indians after use. The Sioux wanted the government to live up to their treaty and they landed on Alcatraz and staked their claim. They were rejected and turned away, so we followed it through, when all of the proposals came out from Hunt, Treshman, and other millionaires.

What we want to do in the long range view is to get some type of help for our people all across the nation. We must look at the problem back on the reservation, where it all begins, with the Bureau of Indian Affairs. There's going to have to be some changes made within our own government structure. We often thought of ourselves as a sovereign nation within a nation, but through the years, this has fallen apart, because the state has beaten us on jurisdiction rights on different reservations, and the termination of the Indian people is close in sight. We all can see those things that are coming on and we want to avoid having our life taken away from us. What few lands we do have left on the reservations, we want to keep. We have no government for our own people and we live under what is really a colonial system because we do not select the people who govern us, like the commissioner of Indian Affairs, who is appointed by the secretary of the interior, who is appointed by the President, and the superintendent on every reservation, who is appointed by the commissioner. We must somehow make up our own plan of government for ourselves and for our people, rather than have someone else decide or plan what is ahead for us. We must make up those plans and decisions for ourselves.

Alcatraz is a beginning, because we are doing that on Alcatraz now. We are making up our own plans...

We'd like to change laws, which are not made for us. Even the Constitution of the United States, which says that all men are created equal, was made for white men at the time it was written, and didn't include any Third World people. The Constitution has not included us, as history will bear out. It's hard for us to look around and see all the destruction that has happened to our country and feel good about it. Every day that we go over on the boat, we can see all that garbage and junk that's in the water, and it makes us sad. The air that is being polluted around us covers the sun and the sun is our giver of life and without the sun there will be no life on this earth. Part of us is being taken away by this destruction of nature. If you destroy everything around us, then you are destroying us. Maybe other people who are living in this country will have more respect and pride for the home that they are living in if we bring this to their attention.

We want to establish a center on ecology, as part of our cultural complex. The cultural complex also involves the tradition of our religion. The base of anything we do is our religion. We must have a place for our spiritual leaders and our medicine men to come. We also plan to have our own library and archives to help us document the wrongs which have been done in this country and the wisdom that has been lost. Also, we plan to have a place where we can practise our dances and songs and music and drums, where we can teach our children and not let this die, as it's dying on the reservation today.

Our parents were forbidden to speak their own language, or dance their own dances, and they were pushed into government boarding schools that were trying to teach them how to be "civilized," which meant losing their own identity. We have been forced to fit into a pattern which had been thought out a long time ago, not by us, but by the government that was over us. When there's no employment on the reservation, the only jobs that you would get were with the Bureau of Indian Affairs or the government and in this way, they can continue to indoctrinate the Indian people on the reservation by holding money in front of their faces. Because the non-Indians live in another world where they have cars and clothes and food to eat, they can always use that as a lure to get our people to want the same things, and by doing this, then they can brainwash our people the way they want them to be so that they would eventually work against their own Indian people. This is what has been happening when the Bureau of Indian Affairs set up the mock tribal governments on reservations. Since the Civil Rights law has passed, it hasn't affected the Indian that much because they've only taken down the signs that say "No Dogs and Indians Allowed." The feeling is still there.

We feel that the island is the only bargaining power that we have with the federal government. It is the only way we have to get them to notice us or even want to deal with us. We are going to maintain our occupation, until the island which is rightfully ours is formally granted to us. Otherwise, they will forget us, the way they always have, but we will not be forgotten.

Document 14.9

Employment Division, Department of Human Resources of Oregon, et. al., v. Alfred L. Smith (1990)

The following Supreme Court case offers a classic example of how the diverse religious traditions of Native Americans have often resulted in perplexing legal and constitutional questions. It was thought that following the passage of the American Indian Religious Freedom Act in 1978 that Native Americans would be granted full protection under the First Amendment. However, the ceremonial use of the hallucinogenic drug peyote by various Indian tribes has once again posed the difficult issue of tribal sovereignty versus individual rights. In this court case, a Native American was fired from his state job for peyote use. The Supreme Court ruled that it would not make any exceptions to existing state drug laws for Indian religious beliefs. In addition, the court upheld the right of the state to terminate and withhold unemployment benefits of Indians who used peyote during religious ceremonies.*

Respondents Smith and Black were fired by a private drug rehabilitation organization because they ingested peyote, a hallucinogenic drug, for sacramental purposes at a ceremony of their Native American Church. Their applications for unemployment compensation were

---

* *Employment Division, Department of Human Resources of Oregon, et al. v. Alfred L. Smith et al.,* 110 Supreme Court 1595 (1990), pp. 1595-1596.

denied by the State of Oregon under a state law disqualifying employees discharged for work-related "misconduct." Holding that the denials violated respondents' First Amendment free exercise rights, the State Court of Appeals reversed. The State Supreme Court affirmed, but this Court vacated the judgment and remanded for a determination whether sacramental peyote use is proscribed by the State's controlled substance law, which makes it a felony to knowingly or intentionally possess the drug. Pending that determination, the Court refused to decide whether such use is protected by the Constitution. On remand, the State Supreme Court held that sacramental peyote use violated, and was not excepted from, the state-law prohibition, but concluded that that prohibition was invalid under the Free Exercise Clause.

Held: The Free Exercise Clause permits the State to prohibit sacramental peyote use and thus to deny unemployment benefits to persons discharged for such use. Pp. 1598-1606.

Document 14.10

Mining Law Reform Act (1991)

In 1991 a Congressional subcommittee held three hearings on the issue of reform of the 1872 Mining Law. The subcommittee heard from both critics and supporters of the current law. In the following excerpts opponents to current mining laws note that mining companies have reaped billions of dollars from the public domain without being required to pay any royalties to the Federal Government. To add insult to injury, abandoned mine sites have created environmental and public health problems throughout the West.*

Members of Congress have tried and failed numerous times to enact hardrock mineral reform. Meanwhile, literally billions of dollars worth of minerals have been extracted from the public domain without any royalties being paid to the Federal Government, while the same companies pay private landowners royalties as high as 25 percent. Thousands of acres of Federal lands have been sold under the Mining Law for $2.50 or $5 an acre, far under their market value. And a significant percentage of the 1.2 million mining claims recorded by BLM are subject to unauthorized uses, used not for mining, but home sites, hunting cabins, and even for drug labs. In California alone, BLM has found 261 illegal occupancies of mining claims.

---

* *Hearing Before the Subcommittee on Mineral Resources Development and Production of the Committee on Energy and Natural Resources,* U.S. Senate, 102 Cong., 1st Session, (Washington: U.S. Government Printing Office, 1991), pp. 53-54; 61; 65-66; 73-77.

Abandoned mine sites across the West have created unbelievable environmental and public health and safety problems. Just to cite a few, according to GAO, approximately 1.2 million claims now cover 44 million acres of Federal land. More than 424,000 acres are unreclaimed, and it will cost about $284 million to repair the damage. Just last month the Park Service reported a fatality on BLM land adjacent to the Joshua Tree National Monument. A rock climber fell 225 feet down an abandoned mine shaft. The National Park Service says there are over 2,000 dangerous abandoned mine openings at Joshua Tree alone. EPA lists 60 mining sites on the national priority list for Superfund cleanup, over half of which are in the West.

For all of these reasons, I believe support for this change is growing.

I read recently in the Washington Times, Mr. Chairman, that the American Mining Congress commissioned a national poll to come up with a strategy for opposing mining law reform, and I quote: "The market research firm surveyed 1,000 registered voters on their attitudes toward the main provisions of the mining law. An overwhelming 82 percent of the respondents thought the mining industry should pay royalties and be forced to restore" lands they mine.

"When the public is presented with the choice, they opt for royalties and reclamation," the survey report concluded. "This question provides the most concrete evidence that the industry should not conduct the mining law battle in public view."

This hearing, Mr. Chairman, is also going to cover S. 785, the Mineral Policy Review Commission Act, and I must respectfully disagree with my colleagues who have cosponsored this legislation to study the Mining Law. It has been studied and studied and studied. In 1977, Scoop Jackson commissioned a study. I would like to insert a copy in the record of the Revision of the Mining Law of 1872, April 1977,* as well as a list of other studies and reports that have been written.

If there are members of this committee or, indeed, of the Congress who are not familiar with how this law works, here's a host of studies for them for their perusal, and we do not need another one.

Finally, Mr. Chairman, I introduced a mining law reform bill 2 years ago. We held three very informative hearings in this subcommittee last Congress. One hearing was a general review of the 1872 law, the second focused on reclamation and bonding issues, and the third on royalties and fees. I learned a great deal from those hearings and tried to incorporate what I learned into S. 433, the bill before us today.

After I introduced it, a number of my colleagues indicated to me they were interested in reform but wanted time to consult with the mining companies in their States to try to achieve a consensus. With the exception of Senator Wirth, who has recently made such a proposal to me, I have not detected any groundswell of mining industry support for amendments to the Mining Law. Rather, I have detected a familiar tactic of delay and stonewalling with a few crumbs of reform thrown out by BLM.

This is disappointing, Mr. Chairman. In any event, I am still interested in working with my colleagues to enact significant reforms of this law.

STATEMENT OF HON. ALAN K. SIMPSON, U.S. SENATOR FROM WYOMING

---

* Retained in subcommittee files.

Senator SIMPSON. You thought I was going to leave too, didn't you?

Senator BINGAMAN. We didn't know.

Senator SIMPSON. I am glad to be here and I thank you, Mr. Chairman and all of you.

I think my colleagues on both sides of the aisle and from the western States have stated themselves very well. I just say to you that it is a very special thing in the West. We have this sharing of ownership, and many of you do not have any concept of what that is who are not from the public land States. Many, not in this chamber today, but in the U.S. Senate have no concept of what it is when you deal with a State with 87 percent ownership by the Federal Government, as in Nevada, and in my State 50 percent of the surface, 63 percent of the minerals. And then try this one for novelty. Along the Union Pacific Railroad for 20 miles on each side, a checkerboard system, some Federal, some private, just on through the entire State of the southern tier of Wyoming. Now, you tell us how to administer that and how to do that sensibly with mining laws and private property rights and things that affect us daily.

And then remember that when the people came west at the direction of their government-that is who sent them that way. It was Grant I think as President who sent Sheridan to the West. He said go out there and find out what they have, and Sheridan wired back and he said all this place needs is good people and water. And Grant wired back. He said that's all hell needs.

[Laughter.]

Senator SIMPSON. So, we have been through all that.

Then we have the terrible problems that after we finished the homesteading, then they carved away parts of the State for parks and forests and wilderness and recreational areas and BLM. We have no problem with that. We host in my State 44 percent of the Nation's wilderness outside of Alaska. Now, that is pretty big stuff for a little old State like Wyoming, and I do not think people have the full concept of what this is. We really literally live off the land.

And I appreciate the concerns of the Chairman of the full committee, Senator Bumpers, and others that we need to pay close attention to the monetary returns of our natural resources. So, this argument, though—and I have heard others state it—about subsidization of the West. Well, I have spent 13 years here and I have subsidized everybody else. I have laid more money on the corn growers in Iowa. I could have rebuilt the road system through Wyoming from what I put into corn and rice in Arkansas. I have been doing that for 13 years. The six commodities of tobacco and cotton and peanuts and wheat and rice and corn—I did not keep a scorecard on that to see who was getting the most subsidy.

I see this great spotlight turned to the West as they try to diddle us on our grazing fees, and they have lots of little thoughts in mind, getting more out of us for the administration of royalties, except they do not know what they are spending to collect the royalties. So, it is difficult to tell why we should be assessed too much. Those are some of the things that are very real in this body of comity and accord in the U.S. Senate.

Frankly, I do not have any desire to sit here and say, well, if you don't do this, I won't do that. I think when you trade bills, you get two rotten bills instead of a good one. So, I am not here to trade or threaten, but I am here to ask you to listen. I think this is a staff-driven projectile, and that is exactly what it has been for years. It is one of those that just sits on the back burner, and they just keep cooking it and stirring it, and up it comes every year for about the last 20 or 30.

So, I hope we will hear each other as fellow U.S. Senators and realize that this is truly peanuts, and I am not talking about the commodity which eats up 50 times what this thing would eat up in the way of expenditures from the Federal Treasury. So, I hope you will listen to us and know that we are not whining or whimpering. We are just asking for fairness.

With the 1872 law, it is easy to get up and say, oh, they sold all the Federal land for $2.50 an acre. Well, that's a bunch of babble. It doesn't have anything to do with reality. These people went on the land. They were told to go on the land and they mined it, they did the assessment work per year, and they paid their taxes. A lot of them are hard scrabble individuals.

I agree totally, and I will help you if you want to do something with some of the abusers of the system. We have abusers of irrigation laws in California. We should do something about that. I am ready to help. We have abusers of the mining laws. I am ready to help. But for heaven's sakes, just to throw out a big net and destroy some of the people who have been involved in this industry honorably so for decades I think is very inappropriate.

And so, I ask you to consider the consequences for our States' economies that we out there, not you, not the Federal Government, will most assuredly have to pay should these changes to the mining laws be made.

I thank you very much for your courtesy and for this opportunity.

Senator BINGAMAN. Thank you very much.

Senator BUMPERS. Mr. Chairman, if I may before Senator Simpson leaves, I would like to make one comment on what he said about helping agricultural States with farm subsidies. I understand that precisely. I would simply issue this small riposte and that is that Arkansas, traditionally one of the very poorest States in the Nation for 35 years, has given well over a billion dollars to assist Wyoming and Montana and Idaho and other donee states to build their interstate highway system, and we never squawked. One of the reasons that the highway bill over on the floor right now is now pretty volatile is because we can no longer justify that with the interstate system virtually finished. But I just want to point out for the 16 years I have been here I have never raised my voice because I understood that that was something we had to do and I was happy to do it.

Senator BINGAMAN. We have one additional witness at the witness table, and that is Representative Vucanovich from Nevada. We are very pleased to have you here. We are glad to see the House of Representatives represented here.

Document 14.11

American Indians Today (1991)

By 1990 the United States Indian population, as enumerated by U.S. censuses and the Bureau of Indian Affairs, had increased to 1,959,234 from a turn of the century nadir of about 250,000. Reasons for the population increase are diverse and complicated. According to the Bureau of Indian Affairs, the increase in population is attributable in part to improved census taking.*

Population

According to U.S. Census Bureau figures, there were 1,959,234 American Indians and Alaska Natives living in the United States in 1990 (1,878,285 American Indians, 57,152 Eskimos, and 23,797 Aleuts). This is a 37.9 percent increase over the 1980 recorded total of 1,420,400. The increase is attributed to improved census taking and more self-identification during the 1990 count. The BIA's 1990 estimate is that almost 950,000 individuals of this total population live on or adjacent to federal Indian reservations...

Reservations

The number of Indian land areas in the U.S. administered as Federal Indian reservations (reservations, pueblos, racherias, communities, etc.) total 278. The largest is the Navajo Reservation of some 16 million acres of land in Arizona, New Mexico, and Utah. Many of the smaller reservations are less than 1,000 acres with the smallest less than 100 acres. On each reservation, the local governing authority is the tribal government. The states in which the reservations are located have limited powers over them, and only as provided by federal law. On some reservations, however, a high percentage of the land is owned and occupied by non-Indians. Some 140 reservations have entirely tribally-owned land.

Trust Lands

A total of 56.2 million acres of land are held in trust by the United States for various Indian tribes and individuals. Much of this is reservation land; however, not all reservation land is trust land. On behalf of the United States, the Secretary of the Interior serves as trustee for such lands with many routine trustee responsibilities delegated to BIA [Bureau of Indian Affairs] officials.

---

* Bureau of Indian Affairs, *American Indians Today* (3rd ed; Washington, D.C.: U.S. Government Printing Office, 1991).

Indian Tribes

There are 510 federally recognized tribes in the United States, including about 200 village groups in Alaska. "Federally-recognized" means these tribes and groups have a special, legal relationship to the U.S. government and its agent, the BIA, depending on the particular situation of each tribe.

Birth Rate—Birth rates were 28.0 births per 1,000 in 1986-88. The U.S. all races rate was 15.7 births per 1,000 in 1987.

Infant Death Rate—The infant death rate was 9.7 per 1,000 live births in 1986-88, while the U.S. all races rate was 10.1 per 1,000 births in 1987.

Life Expectancy—In 1979-81, life expectancy was 71.1 years (males, 67.1 years and females 75.1 years). These figures are based on 1980 census information.

Document 14.12

Grazing and Public Lands (1994)

In 1994 Congressional hearings were held on the Department of the Interior's proposed rule to amend the department's regulations concerning livestock grazing. The Rangeland Reform of 1994 proposed the most sweeping change of land grazing since the Taylor Grazing Act of 1934. Naturally, it faced intense opposition in the Western states. Among the most controversial reforms was the proposal to change the fee formula by which grazing fees were calculated. In the following, testimony witnesses before the committee testify to the detrimental impact of the proposed legislation on their lives. Who would be in favor of this reform? Which westerners would support this legislation, if any?*

STATEMENT OF JODY BRANDAU, MELBA, ID

Ms. BRANDAU. I am Jody Brandau, the daughter of an Owyhee County rancher, and I am the fourth generation on the same land.

The BLM has stated on page 14315 of the Federal Register the purpose of the proposed changes are-and they list six primary purposes for issuing the proposed rule:

1. To make the BLM rangeland management program more consistent with ecosystem management.

---

* *Hearing Before the Committee on Energy and Natural Resources,* U.S. Senate, 103 Cong., 2nd Session, (Washington: U.S. Government Printing Office, 1995), pp. 61-64; 83-5; 284-288.

The BLM has not defined ecosystem management as it relates to the statutory duties and authority granted to the BLM. Any scientific definition of "ecosystem" includes all plant and animal life, but does not recognize land ownership patterns.

The BLM does not own entire ecosystems. Until they can define their participation and relationships with the private, State land, and wildlife components of the ecosystem, they should not proceed with this stated purpose. If the BLM imposes its management decisions on private and State lands, and dictates wildlife management within an ecosystem, the concept should be reviewed by the courts for due process and taking of private property rights.

2. To accelerate restoration and improvement of the public rangelands.

In the past 50 years, the public lands identified as being in good condition have increased by 100 percent, and the lands listed in poor condition have decreased by 50 percent. Much of the credit for improvement must go to the stockmen, whose stewardship has applied new range management knowledge, and stockmen's application of that knowledge is providing for the fastest improvement rate in history, in spite of environmental interests.

The proposed changes in Rangeland Reform 1994 will make improvement efforts much slower, and consequently will result in exactly the opposite of the intended purpose.

3. To obtain for the public fair and reasonable compensation for the grazing of livestock on public land. Grazing fee issues have been debated at great length. If public land grazing costs are increased—

Senator CRAIG. Jody, your time is up.

Ms. BRANDAU [continuing]. To private land rates, private land privileges should also apply.

The fee proposal and Rangeland Reform 1994 would reduce the grazing preference license value to zero and the transfer of rancher equity to the Government without just reimbursement for that equity.

Senator CRAIG. Thank you very much for that testimony.

Credits

Grateful acknowledgement is made for permission to reprint:

CHAPTER 1

Page 20, The West of Walter Prescott Webb: From *The Great Plains* by Walter Prescott Webb. © 1931, © 1959 by Ginn and Company, Simon & Schuster Education Group. Used by permission.

Page 24, The New Western History: From *The Legacy of Conquest: The Unbroken Past of the American West* by Patricia Nelson Limerick. Copyright © 1987 by Patricia Nelson Limerick. Reprinted by permission of W.W. Norton & Company, Inc.

CHAPTER 5

Page 94, Cholera in Missouri: Diary of J.W. Chatham, 1849, The Center for American History, University of Texas at Austin. John Hudgins papers, "California in 1849," Western Historical Manuscript Collection, University of Missouri at Columbia.

Page 102, Slave Women in the West: From *The American Slave*, George P. Rawick, ed., Greenwood Publishing Group, Inc., 1972.

CHAPTER 11

Page 249, Shooting Prairie Dogs: Frank A. Root and William Elsey Connelley, *The Overland Stage to California*, 1901.

CHAPTER 13

Page 296, The Dust Bowl: Reprinted from *Dust Bowl Diary* by Ann Marie Low by permission of the University of Nebraska Press. Copyright © 1984 by the University of Nebraska Press.

Page 297, Down and Out in the Great Depression: From *Down and Out in the Great Depression: Letters from the Forgotten Man* edited by Robert S. McElvaine. Copyright © 1983 by the University of North Carolina Press. Used by permission of the publisher.

Page 300, The Zoot Suit Riots: *Governor's Citizens Committee Report on Los Angeles Riots*, 1943. Carey McWilliams, *North From Mexico*, 1949.

CHAPTER 14

Page 307, The Children of Los Alamos: Reprinted with permission of Twayne Publishers, an imprint of Simon & Schuster Macmillan, from *Children of Los Alamos: An Oral History of the Town Where the Atomic Bomb Began* by Katrina R. Mason. Copyright © 1995 by Katrina R. Mason.

Page 311, Air Conditioning in the Southwest: From "Phoenix in the 1950's: Urban Growth in the Sunbelt" by Michael Konig in *Arizona and the West,* 24:1 (Spring 1982). Used by permission of the Southwest Center, University of Arizona, Tucson.

Page 327, Red Power: From "Red Power: An Eight Point Program," *Akwesasne Notes,* 1 (May 1969), p. 4.

Page 328, Alcatraz: From *Congressional Record*, 91st Congress, 1970.